MODERN MANNERS

The Essential Guide to Living in the '90s

Drusilla Beyfus

HAMLYN

To Milton

ACKNOWLEDGEMENTS

A book such as mine about manners is to some extent bound to be autobiographical. So I would like to thank the many friends, associates, writers and readers who have contributed to these pages, either wittingly or unwittingly. I should also like to thank my family for their patient acceptance of my less than punctilious manners during these days of literary gestation.

Many institutions and authorities have helped me along the way, specifically: The Press Offices of Buckingham Palace, the Church of England General Synod, the Office of the Chief Rabbi respectively. Thanks are also due to representatives of the other leading religious denominations; I am also indebted to the Press Office of the Home Office and to Debrett's.

I am grateful to Mrs William Self for permission to reproduce the wedding invitation on page 78, to Truslove & Hanson for permission to reproduce the letter headings and cards on pages 297 to 304 and to Henry Stokes, Court Stationers, for assistance.

I have been greatly helped by many hands at my publishers, notably, Isabel Moore, Isobel Holland and Julian Brown. My special thanks to Helen Dore for her editing and counsel.

Editor: Julian Brown
Art Director: Bobbie Colgate-Stone
Designer: Sheila Volpe
Additional illustration: Coral Mula
Jacket Designer: John Costello
Production Controller: Michelle Thomas

Published in 1992
by Octopus Illustrated Publishing
part of Reed International Books Limited
Michelin House, 81 Fulham Road, London SW3 6RB

Hamlyn is an imprint of Octopus Illustrated Publishing

Text copyright © 1992 Drusilla Beyfus
Design copyright © 1992 Reed International Books Limited

ISBN 0 600 57523 3

A catalogue record for this book is available from the British Library

Printed in Portugal

CONTENTS

Introduction

This book is about manners in our time. Many-layered and marked by change, the picture is a complex one. Several of the old compass points have gone and new standards have taken their place.

Holding the structure together as winds of change blow hot and cold are the major experiences of marriage, birth and bereavement. The manners and etiquette surrounding these events have held their own as people need recognized methods for managing things well. Manners are in the making in other areas such as divorce, remarriage and the regrouped family.

My task has been twofold. I have attempted to produce guidelines on some of the many uncertainties that beset what is considered polite behaviour. At the same time I have acknowledged where a clear ruling exists.

Underlying my view is that manners are their own defence. Moralists down the centuries have made the point that manners are minor morals, based as they are at core on considerateness and showing respect for the other person. On a less lofty level, I claim that the civilized disciplines are a better technique for achieving objectives than blunt aggression or insensitive conduct.

I cannot pretend, however, that all aspects of my subject are freighted with morality. Much behaviour that is considered acceptable is merely a matter of abiding by what is thought de rigueur, that is, the code of social arbiters of the day.

Taken at its face value, however, knowing the ropes has everything to be said in favour. A knowledge of what to expect is one of the inestimable advantages; feeling at ease is a natural antidote to self-consciousness. Accordingly, I have included in the coverage of the more formal side of things that have a general bearing on the lives of many, accounts of some special occasions which are exceptional dates in the calendar.

Yet overall, many are the situations for which a neat generalisation will not fit. My approach to diversity has been to try to make allowances for special cases and exceptions to the rule.

Complicating the issue is that acts that might pass without notice in one quarter may be thought offhand or even gauche elsewhere. The slippery part of this is that frequently there may be little to distinguish one circle from the other, as far as outward appearances are concerned.

Nowhere is uncertainty more rife than in the field of what is considered acceptable behaviour between the sexes. A definition of gentlemanly behaviour is elusive, to say the very least. We seem to be going through a transitional phase as far as women are concerned in which they are perceived and see themselves in different and often contradictory lights. Much of the etiquette survives that was based originally on womens' role as members of the weaker sex which required a man's formal gestures of protection. At other times, particularly at work, a woman may have the whip hand and distain what she considers to be anachronistic courtesies by men.

In courtship and love affairs, paying attentions is of the essence. There are few romances in which a dash of courtesy is not appreciated. Incidentally, the answer to a much aired speculation as to whether it is acceptable for a woman to invite a man out on a date, is yes, of course. But the style in which the come-on is expressed is significant.

Approaches to sexual encounters in which both parties seek assurances from each other about protection from possible risks, call for a particularly sensitive awareness of mood and timing.

The spoken word resounds with candour in everyday conversation in mixed company which puts a premium on knowing where to draw the line or to risk giving offence. Tact and diplomacy is as useful as ever a means of defusing tense situations or dealing with knobbly characters and allows far more room for manoeuvre on both sides than short or crass ways.

In acknowledging the place of special cases and minority tastes, a form of good manners in itself in my view, I have nevertheless kept my eye on mainstream rulings. Too many concessions to people's special pleadings can lead to fragmentation and further uncertainties about what to do or how to behave – the very opposite of my purpose. Good manners are sometimes said to be only skin deep. Without agreeing with this assumption, I do consider that the complexion looks well on most.

Drusilla Beyfus London.

Author's Note

The personal pronouns 'he' and 'she' are used to connote both genders, in cases where this makes sense. As the masculine pronoun can no longer be read as embracing women, and writing 'he and she' seemed stating the obvious, I have adopted the above shorthand. The choice of 'he' or 'she' is at random.

In order to find all the information given on a subject, please USE THE INDEX. The same subject may be dealt with under different headings.

Some of the ground rules may have changed in courtship but good manners

have held their place. Getting to know the other person remains one

of the principal aims of courtship, and courtesy still has an important

part to play in the process.

Changes in the pattern

It could be argued that in these unmannerly times, a signal sign of a man's interest in a woman is his wish to pay her special attention. Certainly, in the complex and delicate task of establishing a relationship with a member of the opposite sex, knowing how to behave courteously is a measure of protection against awkwardness, a guide in difficult situations and a highly personal means of showing affection.

Young men and women now enjoy an independence unrivalled in the social history of this country. They make up their own minds as to who they will love and marry. The authority of parents has faded as marriage brokers.

When courting offspring are still living at home, all kinds of sensitivities between the generations have to be considered. Such issues as the age at which a young daughter may go off on holiday on her own with a boyfriend, at what stage he – or she – is brought home to be introduced, whether parents acknowledge the fact that their daughter is sleeping with her boyfriend by putting them in the same bedroom, whether the boyfriend or girlfriend is accepted as one of the family when the relationship is clearly a passing fancy, all provoke debate in scores of households. It is noticeable that boys are still accorded much more freedom than their sisters.

A sea-change has affected attitudes towards sex. Few women would feel prudish if they had no wish to go to bed precipitately with a new boyfriend.

The purpose of courtship

The ground rules of courting have become more complex as the timeless roles of pursuer and pursued have a wider number of goals.

What is courtship for? At one stage it could reasonably be assumed that if an eligible male paid court to an eligible female, marriage was on the cards. Nowadays no such thought may dwell in either party's mind. Courtship may lead to live-in affairs in which marriage is not even considered, to passionate friendship without ties on either side, or to the sexual fulfilment of a passing fancy.

This is all very well if both individuals are aware of what is in the other's head and heart. But misunderstandings may easily occur. No general advice holds except to try to avoid self-deception and idle promises.

Male gallantry

An enviable social grace in men is the ability to be polite without seeming stiff or over-formal. Women especially seem to appreciate male gallantry which springs more from spontaneous acts of thoughtfulness than from the dictates of etiquette. Some women are annoyed by observances which they see as the perpetuation of an outdated code treating women as 'the weaker sex'. Others, possibly the majority, are pleasantly surprised when a man opens a door for them or rises to his feet when they come into a room. Many women who prefer to debar gender-based courtesies in the workplace are perfectly happy to accept them in personal relationships.

Paying a woman compliments

A personal compliment should express sincere feeling and focus on some specially cherished attribute, aspect or characteristic. A compliment may be heart-melting or merely affectionate; subtle, simple or clever; but never a flowery platitude. Ideally, a man's compliments should make the girlfriend feel very good about herself, make himself feel as if he has been perceptive, and enhance his reputation in her eyes.

Receiving a compliment

Many women find accepting personal compliments an awkward ordeal. A general interpretation of their gaucheness is that they don't like to seem to concur in any judgment that praises them to the skies, suspecting it is untrue. But a compliment is not a bouquet intended to be deconstructed, analyzed and held up to the piercing light of utter honesty. It is a verbal gesture and should be accepted as such. The recipient may smile enigmatically and say nothing, look unashamedly delighted or parry the remark if it is unworthy, or simply respond with a warm 'thank you'. A flat contradiction is discourteous, even if motivated by modesty.

Refusing attentions

A beau becomes a bore when his attentions are unwanted and he won't take a hint. The situation calls for tact and firmness.

Male reaction to sexual rejection is a potentially explosive area in human relations. Some men may feel that their masculinity is threatened and refuse to take no for an answer. It can be that a woman has exercised her prerogative and changed her mind, but the man may feel that he has been encouraged to believe that an understanding existed, which is being betrayed.

It is rarely sound practice for the woman to resort to provocative acts or insults, tempting as this may be. A man is more likely to be put off by constant discouragement. All invitations should be declined, all presents returned, all attentions given the cold shoulder, all telephone calls deflected and letters unanswered. No explanation need or should be given as such may well provide grounds for possible recriminations and acrimony.

In extreme cases in which the pursuer becomes a pest, the matter may be one on which it is necessary to consult a solicitor on grounds of personal harassment.

Inviting her to go out

Innumerable men on numberless occasions have wondered whether a girl they liked would dream of going out with them if invited to do so. In general, invitations are sprung casually and spontaneity is the rule, though not invariably. When the man is seriously interested in the woman, or he is asking her out on a special occasion for the first time, he will want to take special care to see that things go smoothly.

Women appreciate some details about any formal entertainment that may be mooted, if only in order to know what to wear, and they like to be given an indication of whether a meal is to be included in the hospitality, if only in order to take a decision to eat beforehand or not. Timing and transport are two key factors – especially if the arrangements present difficulties about catching the last bus home or its equivalent.

It is rarely sound practice for the host to put the onus on the guest for choosing the entertainment. It is his responsibility to entertain her, and if the two are not well acquainted she probably won't have the faintest idea about how much money he is willing to spend or what level of hospitality he envisages.

Organizing the occasion

Without suggesting that the host should tackle the invitation as if it were a military manoeuvre, it is a fair warning to say that any diversion involving formal entertainment in a big city requires more effort.

Classic choices are the theatre, a concert or a movie, but there are many even less formal options, such as going off to the country for the day with a picnic. If the theatre or opera is decided upon the host should remember that some managements debar latecomers who arrive after the performance has begun. A host should be aware of times and timing generally and have a clear idea on such niceties as whether a drink can be fitted in before the show begins.

There are no rules implying that a host is obliged to spend more money on the occasion than he can afford nor need he propose any manner of entertainment with which he does not feel comfortable himself. In romantic assignations, people are always more important than places anyway, and investing forethought in arrangements will have a greater appeal than impersonal displays of money.

Eating out
A favourite choice would be lunch or dinner in a restaurant. Breakfast, brunch, or an invitation to tea has its adherents too.

A deciding factor in the host's choice of establishment might be if he is known by the management and can rely on attentive service. Should the host belong to a club to which women may be brought as guests, this neatly sidesteps any discussion about payment. It is a general rule that only club members may settle the account.

Hellos

It was once a routine courtesy for the man to collect his date from her home. To be called for is still very pleasant for a woman. However, distance has lent disenchantment to the custom. Many people meet after work and going home beforehand is usually not a realistic option.

Generally the man proposes a mutually convenient meeting place at a given hour. It would be discourteous to suggest some drab public spot or some location where he might easily miss his companion – railway stations are definitely not good choices!

A considerate escort arrives some five minutes or so before his guest, or earlier if seats have to be found.

Entertaining his companion

Conversation offers boundless opportunities to make a good impression. Unfortunately, nearly all the classic advice tends to discourage the stuff of good talk such as strong opinions on what's in the news, politics, religion, sex and – heartbreaking embargo – gossip about mutual friends. These are safe precepts undoubtedly when people are on thin ice but if followed to the letter would kill any amusing conversation before it started.

Jokes and anecdotes also come in for an official drubbing on the basis that tellers rarely know when to stop and unwittingly become bores. But good humour can bridge uncomfortable silences or gaps which are commonplace when relative strangers converse.

Beguiling talkers often do their homework first, enjoying the idea of collecting impressions, comments, stories which may be judiciously fed into the conversation without any sense of staginess. Monologues are tedious, however. Everyone, or almost everyone, enjoys talking about themselves. That much is self-evident. What is less apparent is the courtesy of expressing genuine interest in the other person's ideas and doings. Absence of curiosity about their life and times is a form of rudeness.

Innuendo is best avoided – unless refreshingly amusing. If a regrettable clanger is dropped inadvertently in the general chat, the best defence is to apologize immediately.

Goodbyes

Romantic goodbyes are not what they were. Saying goodnight at a well-populated bus stop is decidedly lacking in those qualities that make for a memorable finale to a hopefully wonderful evening.

It is often unpractical or downright impossible for the man to see his girlfriend to her home in present-day conditions. She may have a long commute and he has little option but to take her to the nearest bus or rail station and wave her goodbye. But late night transportation plans are worth taking up when the invitation is issued. Women are becoming increasingly apprehensive about travelling late unaccompanied on public transport in cities. If an escort can take steps – even against the odds – which enable him to escort her back to base, it would show great kindness of heart, and be appreciated as such.

If the host has a car and distances are within reason, his companion can expect to be given a lift home. Whether she invites him in for a drink or not is her affair. However it is courteous of him to walk her to the door, and if no invitation is forthcoming he should take the hint and hope for better luck another time.

If the couple are sharing a taxi and all else is equal, the man should ask the driver to stop first at his companion's destination before going on. If distance makes no sense of this courtesy and she is the last passenger to alight it is her responsibility to pay for the shared ride. In this case it would be an act of generosity for the host to arrange to pay the fare in advance with the driver.

When a couple are hailing separate cabs, courtesy points towards allowing the woman to take the first ride that comes along.

Accepting invitations

If you are pleased to be invited out, there is little point in not indicating enthusiasm for the idea. A response to an invitation should be and sound positive, a fact that applies equally to men and women. In the early stages of courtship the way a woman or a man responds to an invitation is one of the few indications of their feelings about the person.

Accepting an invitation to go out presents no problem. But it could be that the invitation has to be declined for bona fide reasons, in which case there is nothing to prevent a person who wishes that they could accept from saying so.

Declining invitations

Some invitations are issued in a way that makes them difficult to turn down politely. Few women wish to cause offence to a man whose company they do not wish to keep, simply because he has invited them to go out. An acceptable get-out is needed.

Among the most problematic invitations are 'When can I call you?' and 'When are you free to go out?' as these gambits are open-ended and leave the recipient little room for manoeuvre. Another is an invitation issued long weeks ahead of the date.

One possible put-off in response to the 'When are you free?' invitation is to name a date at least six weeks ahead without any extenuating circumstance such as holiday leave or previous commitments. The hope is that it might be received in the spirit of the suitor who declared that if a woman couldn't find a moment to see him in five weeks, the lady felt she was wasting her time.

The long-shot invitation may be countered by a transparently clear white lie which only the thick-skinned would miss. Alternatively, regrets may be sent in reply to a formal invitation without any explanation.

If some men continue with their aspirations it may have something to do with the fact that persistence often overcomes resistance.

Preliminaries

Someone who is being invited to go out on a special date needs information in advance about the time, the place, the hour and the occasion itself. It is not at all discourteous to press for a few salient facts.

However, it is rarely sound practice to put leading questions to men about what the others will be wearing and any protocol that might be involved. If he invites her to accompany him to some seemingly grand social function, she will do better to glean some intelligence from the organizers or from an habituée.

Fashions change, but one sartorial precept that remains valid is that people should try to give the impression that they have paid their respects to the occasion and gone to some trouble over their appearance and dress. Being caught 'over-dressing' is a particular dread of some partygoers. It all depends, though. In some circles 'dress up!' is the clarion cry. The best advice is not to stray too far from the proven path of being appropriately dressed, but if anything to err on the side of hopeful anticipation.

Going out together

Being good company on a date is a matter of not trying too hard nor of being so relaxed that the sense of an occasion is lost.

The first attribute of a good companion is to be companionable, to enjoy sharing themselves in some way with present company, to avoid taking every act of hospitality for granted. Praise should not be treated as poison, and genuine appreciation should be expressed.

The person who is being invited out should remember the date, the place and hour and try to arrive on time. More than fifteen minutes behind schedule calls for a convincing excuse and apologies – unless time is of little account. A phone call to warn of a late arrival may be appropriate and appreciated.

Should plans go awry for whatever reason, it is well worth bearing in mind the adage of the classic American etiquette writer, Emily Post: 'Courtesy demands that as a guest you shall show neither annoyance nor disappointment.' At the same time, a perfect guest always resists a passive role – she should offer to help, chip-in or do whatever is required to help avert a crisis.

One individual's idea of a good time can be another's nightmare. In general, the girl who is going out with a man is advised to measure any natural inclinations to wild behaviour against the boyfriend's level of tolerance, trying not to take advantage. And the same goes for himself.

Above all, she should generously suspend the impulse to query motives, always an insidious downer. Should she suspect that he wants something from her that she may be unwilling to give, there doesn't have to be a next time.

On the other hand, if she is enchanted, she may well recall the saying, 'She will never win him whose words showed she feared to lose.'

Thanks

Telephoning thanks the following day gives pleasure because memories are fresh in the mind and the call itself becomes a continuation of the event that is being recalled.

If telephoning is inconvenient, a handwritten letter or postcard shows that the person who was taken out has gone to some reciprocal trouble. Also, writing has the advantage over a telephone call in that the gesture can be for keeps.

Paying the bill

Courtship flies in the face of many egalitarian practices: the male wants to pay the bill. When a courting man asks a woman to go out with him on some special occasion, usually he hopes she will accept his hospitality. Nevertheless, there will probably come a time in the course of a love affair when a 'fair shares' approach falls due, if not overdue. When a couple go out on a regular basis, few women choose to sit back and expect their partner to pay as a matter of course.

However, proposing a 'Dutch treat' should be made advisedly. Splitting the bill tends to interrupt the convivial flow and can end up with both parties grappling simultaneously for cash or credit cards; a good time then becomes a transaction.

A much more civilized approach is for one to pay and the other to accept on the basis that the next time the treat will be on the treated.

As usual, circumstances alter cases. If the man is rich and the girl is much less well off she may with justification allow him a free hand in paying the bills. No man should be used as a private bank however, even when he is in love. And this precept applies equally when genders are reversed.

It is difficult to credit that there was a stage when men did not wish to be seen in public being paid for by a woman, but some members of the old guard do exist. If the woman wishes to repay hospitality to a man whom she suspects would be embarrassed by her paying the bill in public, she may arrange to pick up the tab privately. Theatre and concert tickets can be paid for in advance, and in a restaurant she can make an arrangement with the maître d'hôtel to settle the bill discreetly at the desk. She will probably have to invent some excuse for getting up from the table, but this is easily done.

When the bill is presented

When the bill for a restaurant meal is presented to the host, he is expected to settle the account with good grace. No one would object to a boyfriend voicing protest if he thought he had been overcharged by the management, but he should avoid giving the impression, albeit inadvertently, that his girlfriend's company was not worth the price of the pasta.

Women can choose this moment for saying thank you with conviction and going out of their way to sound appreciative but not cloying.

Going Dutch

If a woman is asked out by a favoured boyfriend on the basis of a 'Dutch treat' and she cannot afford to accept, what should be her response?

All the usual feigned excuses are available but there is no disgrace in admitting to the truth. Running short of funds for fun is unremarkable. The admission may encourage the host generously to offer to stand his guest the treat, but he is under no obligation to change the terms of his original invitation. Similarly, if she doesn't want him to make the gesture, she should decline.

May she propose the first date?

One of the more delightful freedoms accorded to women is that they are no longer obliged to languish awaiting a call from a man to go out. They can and do make the first move, if they feel so inclined.

The canny ones don't go about it like men, however. Tact and discrimination are called for. An invitation issued casually to a boyfriend at a party will seem less premeditated than a telephone call the next day asking him out. An invitation to an occasion at which other friends will be present is softer pedal than asking him out on his own. She could invite him to join a few friends for a drink, or if she has the resources she might organize a small dinner party and include him among the guests. Should she have been invited to a party to which she may bring a guest, she could ask him if he would like to come along with her.

Women have always been adept at dropping a hint. The only difference is that now they may declare their interest more openly without breaching an unwritten code. Exceptions to the rule may apply when the man is one of an older generation or of notably senior rank.

May she invite out a man who has a regular girlfriend?

Much depends on the relationship between the man and his companion which might range from marriage in all but name to a light-hearted affair in which both lead independent lives. If the former fits, it would be considered discourteous to invite the man without his customary partner. If the latter is the case, a new friend may surely chance her arm.

Room for manoeuvre may be found in sending the man an invitation to a party with the option 'and guest' written after his name. This puts the onus on him in deciding whether or not to bring his girlfriend.

Sending flowers

Sending a bouquet to the beloved is a timeless expression of admiration. A man may give a present of flowers to a woman whose interest he wishes to arouse, or in proof of his affection, or as a means of sending love, thanks or apologies. He may send a bunch to someone he scarcely knows but whom he hopes to know better.

It is always best to send flowers promptly. The first requirement is that whatever is chosen, flowers should be in mint condition.

Men are likely to endear themselves through an interesting choice of flowers or an unusual arrangement rather than by sending expensive but unimaginative arrangements. A container planted with growing things that have yet to come into their full beauty is a gesture calculated to give lasting pleasure. The American notion of sending a woman flowers before a party she is giving is thoughtful, avoiding any problem for the hostess in having to arrange them when she is busy receiving guests.

Flowers delivered by a florist should be accompanied by a card bearing the name of the person to whom they are addressed, a personal message and the signature of the sender. The card is placed in an envelope and sealed. It is worthwhile making the effort to write in person as dedications and messages scribbled by an agent are liable to have incorrectly spelled names or words, and inevitably have an impersonal air. Flowers that are sent across counties, countries or continents must of course rely on the services of a local florist to do the honours.

Receiving a bouquet of flowers

A present of flowers that is delivered by anyone other than the giver should be acknowledged by telephone or handwritten card or letter. If someone turns up with a bouquet he will of course be thanked on the spot.

In the doubtful case of whether someone should thank you for thank-you flowers, the answer has to be in the affirmative; the sender will appreciate the knowledge that his gesture has arrived at its destination.

Flowers sent by a man whose attention is unwanted should be acknowledged even so, as the present itself is harmless and demands a courteous response.

A corsage of flowers?

Presenting a girlfriend with a corsage of flowers to wear on a date features in countless vintage American movies. The custom is carefully considered in classic etiquette manuals. Nevertheless, the best advice is to resist this generous impulse, unless absolutely certain it will be welcomed.

Women may understandably object to being put in the double bind of having either to appear churlish by refusing to sport the flowers or of going against their preferences and accepting the idea of wearing an embellishment which in their eyes is unbecoming or doesn't suit their clothes.

If flowers which are given to be worn are passed up some polite excuse will have to be found in order to protect the giver's feelings. Few men, or women for that matter, take lightly the implication that their taste is at fault – one of the few modern heresies.

One approach might be to accept the flowers with thanks, wear them for a short while and then contrive to lose them pretty early in the evening. Feigned apologies would be in order. A compromise might be to carry the corsage like a little bouquet, or to pin the flowers on a coat which is left in a cloakroom.

If the recipient wishes to be accommodating and circumstances permit, she could offer to change her clothes in favour of choosing a more appropriate background for the little bouquet.

A good general rule if giving a corsage is to keep it simple, and to remember that a short, slight or fragile person can easily look overburdened by an opulent spray of flowers affixed to her bosom. A corsage should be presented with several florist's pins so it may be securely anchored in place and, unless delivered by the giver, should be accompanied by a handwritten card.

Who may send flowers?

By tradition men court their fancy with flowers but there seems no good reason why women should not borrow the custom for their own ends on occasions, although at the present time it would be a bold spirit among women who emulated this masculine tactic. The ways of love are incalculable, however, and it could be that a man might be taken by this impetuous approach.

Certainly only a grouch would take exception to the idea of being presented with a delicious flower for a buttonhole as a way of saying hello or thank you, or sending regrets. If a buttonhole is chosen from a florist, it should be accompanied by florist's pins for securing the flower safely, and a card placed in a sealed envelope.

Flowers may certainly be presented as an affectionate cheer-up by a woman to a man who is unwell without any doubts attaching to the act. The flowers may be sent to him at home or at the hospital.

Present giving

It is good news that a woman may now freely accept any present from men, whatever this may be. At one stage and not so long ago a distinction was made between the propriety of accepting a present of the order of a book or a bouquet or a box of chocolates, and personal possessions such as clothes or jewellery. If a suitor wishes to play safe, he can do no wrong in abiding by the old conventions.

Some people might still wish to make an exception in the case of a cash present. But today few women would feel obliged to return a birthday cheque from their boyfriend as a matter of good manners. Even so, offerings of money can easily descend into a mere transaction unless handled with tact.

Similar freedoms exist for women to give their loved one what they wish, like improvements to his person, wardrobe or bank balance.

Choosing a present

Almost too much emphasis can be laid by givers on what the recipient would like as a present and not enough on what they themselves wish to bestow. In courtship it is the 'who' that matters as much if not more than the 'what'.

A present worth the name should always be chosen as an 'extra' and not as some necessity in pretty wrapping paper. Some present-hunters are naturally serendipitous and somehow always manage to chance upon a perfect snap between the offering and the recipient's private longings. Others may rely with confidence on imagination, willingness to keep hunting and a desire to please, all of which attributes are as valuable as money. Probably the only social error that the giver can commit is a lapse of taste, rather than of good manners.

Fortunately no excuse is needed for present giving. Mark Twain, the American author, gave his daughter a handsome musical box 'because it was Monday', and he had the right idea.

Declining a present

It is always embarrassing to have to decline a present, for whatever reason. Few people have a ready-made response. Marilyn Monroe, for example, had a hard time working out how to refuse the present of an elephant from a maharajah until she hit on the obvious. Her place was just too small, she explained.

Where honesty is a get-out and the implication is well on this side of courtesy, there's nothing against keeping to the facts.

A typically awkward situation is when someone whose attentions are unwelcome proffers a serious present. If the gesture is declined, this may give offence. If accepted, the giver may jump to the wrong conclusions. If the decision is taken to return the present, which is probably the least embarrassing course in the end, this should be done gracefully. All personal presents merit acknowledgement and thanks. It is perfectly permissible to take refuge in the formality by which no explanation is required for declining a present (or an invitation).

Where a present of lasting value such as jewellery has been given, and the relationship between the couple has broken up, it is good manners to offer to return the piece. However, some women, and men too no doubt, take the view that whatever is given them remains theirs. Should the bestower be wealthy and have little interest in the return of the token, they may have a point.

Be my Valentine

Valentine's Day marks one of those half-serious, half-humorous, partly ironical customs which gives a special fillip to courtship. On 14 February wooers of all sorts are encouraged to throw inhibitions to the wind and to choose their sweetheart for the coming year. By tradition, Valentine declarations are anonymous, since speculation as to the author is a ritual part of the game. But some unsporting persons twist this edict for their own ends and identify themselves.

Messages are usually conveyed on cards bedecked with heart-shaped motifs and depictions of Cupid and containing cheerfully unambiguous sentiments such as 'I love you' or more sedately, 'Will you be my Valentine?'. The name of the beloved should be written on the missive which, as we said above, should be unsigned.

Latterly, the practice has caught on of publishing Valentine's Day messages in the paid classified columns of national newspapers. *The Times*, the *Daily*

Telegraph, the *Guardian* and the *Independent* all run pages designed for the purpose.

It is accepted form to use nicknames and terms of endearment and, if wished, to compose lines in the coded language of lovers which holds a secret meaning for the person to whom the words are addressed. However, a straightforward declaration of affection will also fit the bill nicely. The lines may be witty or whimsical, amorous or humorous; the only note to avoid is an identifiable public statement that might, for any reason, be a cause of embarrassment to the wooed.

Writing a love letter

Love letters should improve with keeping. The best are even better when read by the recipient after a long lapse of time.

Writing one is a matter of saying what has been said a thousand times before in a manner that conveys the particular traits and temperament of the writer. As the individual to whom the message is addressed reads, an image of the author should spring off the page, their voice should be evoked, their presence recalled like some genie escaping from Aladdin's lamp. Literary skill is not required, though admittedly wordsmiths are at a technical advantage. Against them is the fact that silky-smooth phrases can suggest professionalism rather than sincere rough-hewn passion.

Composing a letter of love is within most people's capacities, can be practised in the head and may be written anywhere there is paper and writing implements. From a recipient's viewpoint, it can be kept discreetly about one's person for continual rereading.

Fortunately there are no rules about what may or may not be said as love has no respect for mere epistolary conventions. Beginnings and signings-off can – and should – be intimate and personal. However, the prospect of illicit eyes scanning the missive may, in some cases, induce a note of caution.

Whether openly or covertly put, love letters generally express an emotional hunger for the loved one and suggest a feeling of incompleteness without their presence. A responsive reader may hear the beating of love's wings between the lines which can give special significance to quite ordinary remarks.

As a message from the heart is essentially personal, quoting examples to be followed runs counter to the spirit of the exercise. Nevertheless, the following letter, written by a man of this century, shows the personal approach of a distinguished writer, and may serve as inspiration to the pen-bound.

From: *Letters of James Joyce*, Vol 1 published by Faber & Faber

James Joyce to Nora Barnacle: 15 August 1904

My dear Nora,

It has just struck me. I came in at half-past eleven. Since then I have been sitting in an easy chair like a fool. I could no nothing. I hear nothing but your voice. I am a fool hearing you call me 'Dear'. I offended two men today by leaving them coolly. I wanted to hear your voice not theirs.

When I am with you I leave aside my contemptuous, suspicious nature. I wish I felt your head on my shoulder...

I have been a half-hour writing this thing. Will you write something to me? I hope you will. How am I to sign myself? I won't sign anything at all, because I don't know what to sign myself.

Public displays of affection

It is not true that the world loves a lover if lovers are oblivious to other people's reactions to public displays of affection.

Many people are embarrassed by couples who indulge in overtly sexy kissing, cuddling and touching and all the other gestures by which lovers show their interest in each other. This level of flirtation does not transgress any formal code of decency, but often does offend a hidden code.

Lovers should make allowances for this deep-rooted response without feeling that the only proper way to conduct a relationship in public is to adopt a marble-cold stance towards their partner. Acceptable gestures of affection are more social than sexual, such as lightly implanted kisses, hand-holding, linking arms and convivial hugs – if specifics are to be spelt out. What is to be avoided are those embraces which suggest that a heavier scene of sexual arousal is under way.

The manners of making love

In sex, there is no accounting for taste but a word may be put in for the art of combining romance and reality. It enables people to choose the right moment for managing practicalities without endangering the mood and allows them to put potentially sensitive questions without causing umbrage.

Where doubt exists, lovers have to come to an understanding about whether the man intends to use a condom, whether the woman has taken (or is willing to take) contraceptive precautions. The shadow of AIDS and other sexually transmitted diseases may not be ignored between new partners who will want to know more about the likelihood of any personal risks involved.

These preliminaries may be routine but they demand tact and prescience. Because trust is all-important in sex, which itself depends on mutual assurances, it cannot be held to be inept or insensitive for a partner to ask to have their mind set at rest. Nor should a lover feel offended if asked to use a contraceptive or give an account of their sexual health. Women carry condoms out of commonsense. It is the moment at which she produces the contraceptive that calls for sensitivity on her part.

When a female wishes to take the sexual initiative with men she may find that a direct approach to seduction is counter-productive. Many men tend to be inhibited rather than stimulated by women who are blatant or brazen about their intentions.

For some people good manners may assist the techniques of love-making, but too much should not be claimed for this approach. It has to be admitted that the art of seduction is a game with as many rules and players and some may find sexual satisfaction in a negation of courtesy.

A *proposal of marriage*

The point at which two singles who are going out together can be said to be a courting couple grows an ever more moot point. Courtship itself may, or may not be with a view to marriage but based purely on motives of love, sex, companionship, or security, alone. 'What are his intentions?' was a dark line in Victorian melodrama, but it remains the litmus test of whether or not he proposes to pop the question – at least as far as most affairs are concerned.

All marriages are based on the question being put and accepted, in one form or another. A proposal of marriage may be spoken in so many words or implied or written, but it must be made at some stage if a love affair is to lead to matrimony.

In romantic literature a proposal is a moment of heartbeat emotion, and in many instances in recorded real life too. Acceptance brings the greatest happiness. It is also a moment which risks embarrassment, discomfiture and possibly rejection, so those who are contemplating the act should tread carefully.

Despite Oscar Wilde's riposte in his play *The Importance of Being Earnest*, when the heroine Gwendolen is asked for her hand in marriage, 'Men often propose for practice', a proposal should not be a playful proposition, but be the real thing. Sincerity is of the essence.

The most propitious timing is obviously the moment that wins an assent, which may be anytime, anywhere when the mood inclines. Many proposals have been stimulated by enchanting surroundings, moonlight, music or even by a particularly good dinner at a table for two in a restaurant. It goes without saying that over-indulgence in drink, perhaps in order to pluck up courage for the proposal, is rarely a good idea and is not conducive to clear thinking.

A proposal may be sparing of words, or be an outpouring of loving sentiments, or come wrapped in some coded remark. The important aspect is that the meaning should be fully understood, so that no misunderstandings can occur.

A suitor can do worse than follow tradition. He may take his girlfriend by the hand, look her steadfastly in the eye, and declaring his love put the proposal, 'Will you marry me?'

The romantically or theatrically inclined may go down on bended knee to put the question, thereby falling in line with generations of suitors. New-fashion old-fashioned girls may appreciate the gesture but some might react like the heroine in Charles Dickens' novel, *Bleak House*, whom readers will recall declared on being proposed to, 'Get up from that ridiculous position immediately', although it must be admitted that in this case the proposal was unwelcome. In any event, some stage-management of the occasion would not go amiss.

In adverse circumstances, when it looks as if facts are against the fulfilment of a proposal, a man may simply declare his faith to his choice that she is the person whom he intends to marry.

The advantage of an articulate, direct approach is that it leaves no doubt in the mind as to the proposer's intentions.

Nobody should follow anyone else's proposal of marriage – personal expression is much more important. Yet something of the spirit of a successful proposal – in contrast to the one quoted from Dickens above – can be gleaned from examples by writers, either in fiction or real life.

Evelyn Waugh, the British novelist, offered his hand in a letter written to 19-year-old Laura Herbert, whom he married in 1937. In it, he attempted to put the pros and cons of the proposition. It is too long to quote in full here, but this is the flavour of it.

'I am restless & moody & misanthropic & have no money except what I earn and if I got ill you would starve. On the other hand . . . there is always a fair chance that there will be a bigger economic crash in which if you had married a nobleman with a great house you might find yourself starving, while I am very clever and could probably earn a living of some sort somewhere. Also . . . you would not find yourself involved in a large family and all their rows . . . All these are very small advantages compared with the awfulness of my character. I have always tried to be nice to you and you may have got it into your head that I am nice really, but that is all rot. It is only to you & for you.'

Receiving a proposal of marriage

A woman to whom a proposal of marriage is put is under no obligation to make up her mind on the spot. She may claim her prerogative of biding her time, and indeed should do so if any doubts lurk as to the wisdom of acceptance.

If on the other hand the offer reflects her heart's desire (and that of her head), she may joyfully accept in an answering breath. If words fail her, she may rely on a simple expression of assent sealed with a kiss.

An unwanted proposal

A situation in which a sincere proposal of marriage is unwanted calls for gentle handling. Few men propose for fun and exposure of a depth of emotion which meets with an insensitive form of rejection can cause real pain. Ridicule is the cruellest means of all.

The fact that a woman doesn't want to accept the proposal should be sufficient without further explanations being called for. But if she wishes to explain herself or is pressed to do so, she could draw on any of the classic defences: that she believes she is incapable of making the other person happy, that she has no intention of getting married, that there is someone else.

Who may propose?

May a woman propose marriage to a man and keep her dignity? Of course she may: many have done so in the past – there are historical royal precedents – and continue to do so in the present. It is only fair to point out, however, that since the weight of tradition is on the side of the male taking the initiative, a woman faces a double uncertainty. She not only risks rejection but may also be doubtful about how the fact of role reversal in the scene will be received.

Note: neither a proposal of marriage nor its acceptance has any legal standing.

Endpiece

The foregoing is intended as guidance only. Human nature is rarely so various, perverse and unpredictable as in affairs of the heart, and lacks the symmetry to fit formula approaches. Qualities such as tact and courtesy help someone to be liked but that is a very different matter from inspiring love.

Betrothal & marriage

Only one question – and answer – matters among the welter of advice that is

offered to those about to marry. Have they chosen each other wisely and well?

The phase of being engaged to marry is essentially a time for planning, yes,

but also of reflection on what the commitment of marriage means.

No prescriptions can guard against the extraordinary vicissitudes of sharing

married life with another human being, but a few elementary precautions

can be taken which may help to get some potential sources of discord

out of the way.

The engagement to marry

Marriage is usually rooted in day-to-day practicalities as well as in love and honour. Shared expectations and assumptions are the bedrock of continuity and need to be aired before a final decision is made.

It is a cliché to say that there are two marriages, the man's and the woman's, without drawing attention to the variety of married lives irrespective of the gender of the individuals. The state of matrimony is flexible in today's climate, and people make of it what they will to suit their needs.

The independence of women has changed so many of the old views of what marriage should be. It is this largely unexplored territory that often turns out to be a minefield.

Is the wife to be head cook and bottle washer as well as contributing to the earned family income? Does the prospective husband hope to come home to find the proverbial hot dinner awaiting? Are children wanted? Who will give up work or put their work second in order to care for the family? Would one partner be prepared to change jobs if the other's work demanded relocation? How will the budget be divided if there is only one income?

Discussion doesn't necessarily help to bridge differences but at least it acts as an early warning system.

'Asking consent'

The formality by which a young man traditionally asked a prospective father-in-law for his daughter's hand in marriage, has lapsed somewhat along with the independence of daughters. Courtesies on the question still exist, nevertheless, even when a proposal has already been made and accepted, and the couple have reached an agreement between themselves.

The suitor could invite his prospective father-in-law to lunch in a restaurant or to drinks. If he happened to belong to an appropriate club, this would preclude any doubt about who was settling the bill as only members may pay.

Fathers are likely to be flattered by the invitation and few would feel justified in playing the heavy parent. Fathers will usually welcome any reassurances to the effect that their beloved daughter's future spouse is a good bet. The younger man can air his hopes and plans and perhaps give an account of his own family and background.

Announcing the engagement

The announcement of betrothal calls for celebrations and congratulations all round. Once the announcement is made public, the nuptial pair are likely to become the centre of attention among family and friends. It is an exciting and testing stage in both their lives.

The custom is for the prospective bride to let her parents in on the decision before informing anybody else – a courtesy which should hold good even in those cases where mother and daughter are not particularly close to each other.

The situation to avoid at all costs is one in which either family picks up the information at second hand. The event seldom comes as a complete surprise but the actuality of the announcement often causes a mild shock all round.

The manner of breaking the news can vary from a telephone call out of the blue to a formal declaration at a family party. It is usually the bridegroom-to-be's responsibility to inform his side of the family.

Upon the announcement, it is customary for the prospective bridegroom's parents to get in touch with the bride's parents in order to express their delight at their son's choice of partner. Naturally, the bride will contact her fiancé's parents if they have not been in touch with her already.

Among separated families

As parents and offspring in these circumstances may be virtual strangers to each other for a number of reasons, it is worth making the point that plans for marriage call for a cessation of hostilities, and the bridging of gaps – if only for the duration. As a matter of courtesy, parents should always be introduced to their son's or daughter's intended spouse, and no announcement should be made public until parents on both sides have been duly informed.

Communication between the families

Once the news is out, congratulations all round are in order. The mother of the prospective bridegroom contacts her future daughter-in-law to send love and congratulations; likewise, the mother of the bride-to-be expresses her delight to her future son-in-law.

The respective mothers arrange a meeting between the two sides, on the strength of the announcement. The bridegroom's family customarily entertain the other side to lunch or dinner, or should they have a country abode, an invitation to stay for a night or two is extended.

However, if it evidently makes more sense for the bride's family to do the entertaining, the meeting is held on their ground. Usually the engaged couple are present as they may represent the one link that the two sides have in common at that stage.

Other members of the family, close friends, god-parents if part of the picture, and benefactors are understandably put out if they are not counted in the privileged circle of those who are the first to be told the news. They will feel excluded, most likely, and the damage done can be difficult to repair.

It is also courteous for the couple to include their respective employers on the priority list. They will probably want to know the key facts such as the date of the wedding and any proposed holiday arrangements.

Doubting friends

By convention, the couple's decision is given the benefit of the doubt, and in public, at any rate, those with private reservations hold their peace. But suppose someone has what they consider to be good reasons for spilling the beans to one member of a couple about the other's character? Should they risk a friendship by turning prosecutor, or hold their peace? Two motives should probably be rejected: that it is for 'their own good', since few of us are able to judge satisfactorily exactly what constitutes someone else's future happiness; that the facts have been withheld deliberately. Love may be blind but if it is as fatally blinkered as all that, the odd shaft of enlightenment isn't likely to make much difference.

One approach is to throw out a strong hint, leaving the individual the chance of following up the scent or to leave well alone.

Formal announcements

Most individuals and families spread the word of the engagement via personal letter or telephone call – customarily the responsibility of the bride's family but now a shared task between the two sides.

Where the bride's family or the engaged couple wish to communicate the information to a wider circle of friends and acquaintances, they usually place an announcement in the Forthcoming Marriages columns of the national press; *The Times*, the *Daily Telegraph*, the *Independent*, the *Yorkshire Post*, *The Scotsman* and the *Jewish Chronicle* are all noted for their personal announcements.

The personal columns of these newspapers and the many leading provincial and local publications also run brief announcements of forthcoming marriages. Newspapers are selected on the basis of those which have the widest circulation among the bride's and her family's acquaintances.

The wording must be submitted to the social or court editor and should be signed by one of the couple or by a parent or guardian.

The bride's family or the couple are usually responsible for the task. It is important for the bridegroom's family to be consulted on the wording and publication date. Divorce, separation, remarriage or bereavement may have to be indicated in the etiquette of the wording.

Fees are payable for the newspaper insertions, usually calculated according to the number of lines of print.

Examples of announcements

All announcements of forthcoming marriages follow an established style but wordings differ according to individual circumstances. The names of both sets of parents are usually given with brief addresses. Sometimes an address is given in full which is a convenience for well-wishers.

If both sets of parents are married:

Mr E.D. Jones
and Miss T.T. Neal

The engagement is announced between
Edward, younger son of
Mr and Mrs K.D. Jones
of Harrogate, Yorkshire,
and Tammy, twin daughter
of Mr and Mrs J.R. Neal
of Weybridge, Surrey

If the bridegroom's father is a widower and the bride's parents are divorced:

The Hon. Jonathan Spragge
and Miss P. MacKenzie

The engagement and forthcoming marriage
is announced between Jonathan,
only son of Lord Spragge
and the late Lady Spragge
of Chesham, Buckinghamshire
and Patricia, elder daughter
of Mr Michael MacKenzie of Brighton and
Mrs Ruth MacKenzie of Pimlico, London

If the bridegroom's mother has remarried and the bride's father is deceased:

Captain P.B. Duncan, R.N.
and Miss S. Royce

The engagement is announced
between Philip,
son of Mr P.H. Duncan of Khartoum, Sudan
and Mrs J.Y. Greenstone of Great Malvern,
Worcestershire, and Susan, daughter of
the late Sir Peter Royce and of
Lady Royce of Dunmow, Essex

If the bridegroom's mother has remarried and the bride's step-mother is a surrogate:

Mr M.J. Booth
and Miss L.S. Jordan

The engagement is announced between
Mark, son of Mr P.H. Booth of Marlborough, Wiltshire and
Mrs Philip Nash of Berkhamsted,
Hertfordshire and Lucy, step-daughter
of Dr and Mrs Eric Sandle of Bridport, Dorset

Letters of congratulation

It is customary for friends and well-wishers to congratulate the happy pair on their engagement to marry. Letters expressing pleasure at the news are addressed to one or both of the couple. More likely, friends will telephone, sending love and congratulations. All letters should be answered promptly; either party can reply.

Long or short engagement?

The length of an engagement is for the couple to decide. Opinion is against protracted engagements on the basis that for a couple to remain under public and family scrutiny for long months or even years is asking a great deal.

Couples often ignore these strictures and go their own way, wishing to make a public avowal of their intention to marry in due course. Often-cited reasons for delaying a wedding are when a course of studies has to be completed; when one or both are working abroad; and most commonly, the need to build up some savings in order to set up home independently. An engagement may be prolonged if there is a bereavement in the family. It is difficult to set time limits, but most would prefer to delay the nuptials by at least a few weeks after the death on compassionate grounds. An alternative would be a very quiet wedding.

It can also happen in families that the bride-to-be's sister has recently married and parents wish to harbour their resources before launching into a new nuptial celebration.

Couples who opt for a long engagement claim that the act of betrothal allows them to plan ahead with confidence, stimulates them to achieve whatever goals they may have set as a pre-condition of marriage, and engenders an extra feeling of certainty in each other's commitment.

How short is a short engagement? Three months is considered a comfortable lapse of time but there are many who prefer the briefest of engagements and arrange the marriage ceremony on the heels of the announcement. If a big wedding is contemplated, the time required to organize the occasion suggests an engagement of not less than six months.

The engagement ring

Women have lost none of their enthusiasm for accepting a ring from their betrothed which symbolizes the pledge to marry. Worn on the fourth finger of the left hand, the engagement ring is treasured for the sake of sentiment as much as anything else.

The tradition is for the woman to choose the engagement ring and for the man to pay for it. However, it is far from unexceptional for the prospective wearer to help share the costs. The couple usually visit a jeweller's together and make a choice from a selection of rings within the price range established by the man. Males on this shopping hunt are asked to display unusual patience as it is probable that the lady will wish to visit more than one jeweller. Here again, much discussion has often taken place about the inroads that a tidy sparkler will make on plans for a posh bathroom. The budget for the ring is likely to be an open secret.

Personal taste is of the essence in choosing a design for a ring that is to be constantly worn. The romantic idea of the giver pre-selecting a style and presenting it to the beloved in a little box can only be recommended to those with a sure understanding of their true love's mind.

If, regrettably, he miscalculates, she is at liberty to ask him to exchange the token for another.

Declining to wear a ring

There is no obligation on a woman who is engaged to be married to accept a ring or wear one, and the same applies to a wedding ring.

Note: the male of the species, said to be the peacock sex, nevertheless does not by custom sport a ring to declare to the community that he is betrothed. There may be scope for reform here.

See page 34 for Engagement presents between the betrothed.

The style of the ring

An engagement ring is by tradition decorative, made of precious metals, and bejewelled. It may also be a piece that appeals to the couple but has no monetary value. The ring may be newly minted or an antique – no superstitions attach to a ring which was once someone else's engagement token. The important point is that the ring is a symbol of betrothal.

Where it comes from is a matter of personal choice. For instance, among the few whose family possesses good jewellery, an inherited piece might be chosen for the purpose. Then again, having a ring made to your own requirements – an option once open only to rich patrons – now has a far wider currency: well-known jewellers are prepared to consider the idea. Also those who value originality and contemporary design might like to commission a freelance jeweller to devise a piece – many different personal associations and preferences can be incorporated in these designs.

Diamonds have been the most popular choice for some five hundred years among the élite. However, modern cutting methods have brought the reality of owning a diamond ring within the means of a wide group of people.

An important aspect to bear in mind when choosing a design is its compatibility with the style of the wedding ring as the two will be worn in tandem. Some women prefer to choose a piece which will serve both purposes.

As an engagement ring is part of the public display of betrothal, wearers need have no hesitation about showing off their treasure.

Engagement celebrations

Celebration parties marking engagements are rarer than once upon a time. The occasion doesn't carry the weight that it did in the past, and the leading participants will probably prefer to save their energies and cash for the wedding.

If a party is to be held, this might take the form of a smallish gathering organized by friends of the couple, or a dinner party might be arranged by one of the families in honour of the event. In second marriages which are arranged and financed by the couple themselves, betrothal sometimes occasions a party given by one set of parents.

People invited to engagement parties are not expected to bring wedding presents, but they might choose to do so as a matter of convenience, especially if the wedding is to be held shortly.

Engagement presents between the betrothed

The bride-to-be usually likes to give the prospective bridegroom a present to mark their betrothal and also as a gesture of thanks for the engagement ring. A memento, some object that he is likely to treasure, is of a personal and lasting nature. Monetary value is of less import than the thought and a happy choice.

Among wealthy families, betrothal may be accompanied by a transfer of property from one partner to the other, or from parents to offspring.

The bridal shower

See page 71 for The Chief bridesmaid and bridal attendants.

The American fondness for holding a bonanza known as a bridal 'shower' has its advocates in this country too. An energetic and close friend, often the chief bridesmaid, invites a number of the prospective bride's closest companions to a party for the express purpose of 'showering' her with presents. Each guest who accepts the invitation is honour-bound to bring a tangible offering.

Company is female, hospitality might be lunch or drinks, and presents are traditionally of a kind to help the newly-weds set up home.

Introduction

It is by no means exceptional for a man and woman who are engaged to marry to jib at introducing the other as 'My fiancé(e)'. It is correct usage, indubitably, but sounds over-formal and possessive.

What is lacking is an acceptable term that broadcasts to the world at large that the person is the betrothed. Sobriquets such as boyfriend, beau, bloke, girlfriend, the person they are said to be 'going out' with, my 'other half', all fail to make evident the prospective marital tie.

In the absence of a better term, people tend to say nothing at all which leaves the uninitiated in the dark about the status of an affair. On formal occasions – such as at other people's weddings, office functions – it is best to use the recognized description of fiancé(e).

How to address and refer to parents-in-law

If instant intimacy has anything to be said in its favour, it must be the diminishment of the timeless embarrassment about how to address your mother-in-law. From a prospective daughter-in-law's standpoint, her future mother-in-law may be a relative stranger yet she is about to become a member of the family.

First names are the general form but not invariably so. It is worth finding out whether the individual in question has strong views on such matters. Some older women object on principle to the conventions of immediate mateyness, and their views should be respected. Where uncertainty exists, the new member of the family would be advised to address her mother-in-law formally, or until the older woman says, 'Do please call me Ruth'.

If the first point of contact is by letter, and a similar dilemma applies, an option is to address her by her Christian name and after writing 'Dear Ruth' to add in brackets the words (may I?). A more thoughtful approach is for the letter to make some mention of the writer's hopes that it is in order to be on first-name terms. Similarly, a father-in-law should be asked at the earliest opportunity if he may be addressed by his first name. It must be admitted that what to call your mother-in-law is a topic for jokes in both music hall comedy and the world outside. Fathers-in-law get off lightly in comparison. Either way, good manners can only improve the situation.

Wives and husbands may refer to their opposite number's parents in conversation or in writing as 'Jack's father' or 'Jessica's mother'.

Parents-in-law are not usually formally introduced by their daughter-in-law with the handle of the family connection, either before or after the marriage. As for the prospective bride, she is by custom introduced before matrimony as their son's fiancée and after marriage as 'my daughter-in-law Mary'.

Welcoming a son-in-law

From a parental standpoint, taking a relative, or maybe complete, stranger into the bosom of the family is a testing ritual. Suddenly, a new member has to be counted in among the flock, and one whom parents-in-law are supposed to love or admire – not always an instant process.

Parents who hope to see much of their daughter after her marriage are advised to be as welcoming to the newcomer as circumstances permit. Certainly, the prospective son-in-law should be regarded as a son of the house, with more privileges than responsibilities.

Efforts should be made on both sides to find some common ground which steers the conversation away from hazardous topics. Parents who can restrain their natural longing to ask probing questions about any future plans the couple may have in mind will be appreciated for their tact.

The offer of friendly hospitality can rarely be misinterpreted, and is likely to confirm the wisdom of Samuel Pepys' observation: 'Strange to see how a good dinner and feasting reconciles everybody.'

Staying with the in-laws

If the prospective son-in-law is invited to stay with his fiancée's parents, his role is to be a good guest, lending a hand where wanted. If it is a rare invitation, he might bring a present of the order of a bottle of wine, or some appropriate indulgence for his hostess such as bath scents or the latest biography. A thank-you letter is a must.

One aspect of courtship that may or may not be sensitive as far as the bride's parents are concerned, and one that may be highlighted during a stay at their home, is overt sexual behaviour between the lovers. Parental attitudes span the spectrum from blithe acceptance of their children's standards to outright disapproval. A middle course is probably best determined by the following accepted limits. Whereas spontaneous gestures of affection such as kissing, fondling and caressing are part of a lover's vocabulary and should not be frowned on, love-making of a more intimate nature can be considered as intended for private delectation only.

The daughter of the house should be able to advise her fiancé on parental susceptibilities in what can be a highly charged area.

Separate or shared bedroom?

Many parents wouldn't think twice about putting their daughter and her fiancé in the same bedroom. Equally, many others might wish to maintain the appearance of propriety and provide separate accommodation, perhaps turning a deaf ear to corridor scurries when the house is quiet. If the parents have an open mind on the matter, their daughter is likely to give a lead.

It is in any case the hosts' prerogative to decide on the manner of hospitality offered under their roof and sleeping arrangements form part of this.

Entertaining the in-laws

It is usual for a prospective daughter-in-law to invite her future parents-in-law to lunch or dinner, either at her parents' house, at her own abode, or if she is living with her prospective spouse, at the place they share.

From the daughter-in-law's standpoint, the occasion is by custom nerve-racking as she is hoping to please her future husband and his parents as well as herself. Also, the probable parental wish for the new member of the family to prove a competent hostess and cook for their son may not necessarily correspond to her own aspirations.

When choosing a menu, the old advice to play it safe and simple is sound but could be a bit dull. If the parents are keen on good food, it might be an idea to include among their known likes a dish that would come as a judicious surprise. On the subject of a drink, a wise hostess will remain at least one glass behind her guests.

If conversation is sticky, the one subject that everyone has in common can be relied on to keep the ball rolling: boy betrothed. Not too many jokes at his expense, however, from his beloved.

Famously dodgy topics in these circumstances are: party politics (unless they are shared); plans to live and therefore work abroad; his/her overdraft at the bank; British cricket.

Death of the dowry

Throughout history, women have entered marriage with a dowry, 'the portion that a woman brings to her husband'. A dowry traditionally consisted of trousseaux – a bride's clothes and a bottom drawer of linen – and, if she was the child of wealthy parents, a nest egg of capital.

Today a woman is more likely to bring her capacity as a nice little earner to marriage than the traditional assets. Nevertheless, marriage remains an occasion upon which parents and relations are prompted to make generous presents if they possess the resources.

Help with a down-payment on a mortgage on a house or flat, jewellery, furniture, works of art, investments in stocks and shares, are all classic examples of gifts to the bride to ease her path as she quits the bosom of her family.

Breaking an engagement to marry

The sooner the word of a broken engagement is made public the better for everyone concerned. It is an upsetting and embarrassing situation but one that has to be lived through philosophically by the couple and their respective families.

It is the woman's prerogative to make the announcement, whether or not she was the one who wished to break up. Usually each member of the couple informs their own side.

Friends are telephoned and relations kept in touch. Except between confidantes, explanations are not called for. The fact of the break-up can be considered sufficient and acquintances of the pair are supposed to contain their curiosity.

If a published announcement of betrothal has appeared in the newspapers it may be prudent to place a notice of cancellation along these lines in the personal announcements columns or in the court and social pages, depending on the placing of the original.

The marriage arranged between Mr Kenneth Brown and Miss
Jacqueline White will not take place.

On the debated issue of whether or not the former fiancée should return her engagement ring, a fair deal seems to be that if she was the author of the broken pledge, she should at least offer to return the token of betrothal. Strict etiquette decrees that the engagement ring should be returned. In any event, all wedding presents should be sent back to the givers with a note of thanks. Presents exchanged between the couple are supposed to be returned but in practice, usage and wear and tear of objects or artefacts make this a fairly pointless procedure. Valuable jewellery or works of art or grand possessions given on the expectation of a marriage taking place should be restored to the senders.

Marriage

Members of the wedding are taking part in one of the oldest ceremonies. The ritual of marriage has an almost mystical hold on society at large as well as on individuals: few people cannot recall their own wedding in extraordinary detail. The quality of a wedding is the combination of formal, familiar procedures which spell nuptial celebrations with the personal and particular. All weddings are the same and all weddings are different.

The ceremony represents interrelated meanings: a couple's desire to assume the responsibilities of matrimony and society's recognition of the institution of marriage. Specifically, it is an official blessing on the union of one man and one woman.

Its sanction is sought, increasingly, and sometimes in ways that might have confounded our forebears. Civil ceremonies are bedecked with social observances that were once considered appropriate only for a religious ceremony. Individuals marrying for the second, third or maybe even more numerous times, may wish to make a public avowal on each occasion.

Whatever the merits of these practices, they show the continuing appeal of the wedding ceremony.

A *background*

Across time, and throughout different countries, creeds and cultures, the ceremonial of marriage displays a surprising number of shared characteristics which seem to correspond to universal needs.

The bride is most often specially adorned or ornamented. Rites of passage mark her departure from her father's house to her husband's or husband's family's territory. Bride and bridegroom are ceremonially paired in public. Presents are bestowed. Beneficent magic may be invoked or Hymen, the god of generation, supplicated, on behalf of the bride's fertility and the blessing of children. A ceremony that combines a solemn and binding pledge with feasting and celebration in the presence of the two sides and their supporters is universal. A wedding is always witnessed.

See page 96 for The Wedding Cake.

A record of continuity binds present-day procedures with many from those of the past. Many of the social customs without which the wedding party would be considered incomplete have their origins in ancient rites. For instance, the father of the bride's speech symbolizes his 'loss' of a daughter while the cake-cutting ceremonies and the casting of confetti alike have their origins in a wish for the bride's fruitfulness.

Marriage ceremonial had a secular origin as a means of solemnizing a social contract. Religion came into the picture at a later stage. Many ceremonies have a religious content which unites the idea of marriage with a particular denomination's articles of faith. Some religions do not practise a special marriage service though all have wedding procedures.

Freedom for people to choose their own spouse on the basis of romantic love came late in the day of marital affairs. It is a Western idea which is still questioned today by Islam's adherence to the custom of arranged marriages.

The ground-rules of marriage

Marriage has been acknowledged as the first bond in society since the days of Ancient Rome and a number of ground-rules applying to it remain constant. Rule One: marriage shall not be entered into lightly.

Law and religion regulate marriage, and those who are embarking on it are expected to mark and inwardly digest its implications.

Legalities

Various restraints apply to certain categories of people wishing to marry which lie outside the jurisdiction of family, religion, race, or caste.

The minimum age for legal marriage in the United Kingdom is 16, but anyone between the ages of 16 and 18 who proposes to get married in England or Wales must first obtain written parental consent (waived in Scotland, hence the romantic tradition of marriage of young runaway lovers at Gretna Green).

Members of the same family tree may not be able to marry. Close blood ties are taboo, but people who are related only through marriage, and where there is no blood connection, may usually now marry legally.

Note: marriage revokes any will that may have been made by a spouse previously. A new will is required.

Taboo marriages

Certain marriages are prohibited on grounds of blood or marital ties. Those wishing to marry who are kinsfolk should consult a member of the clergy or a solicitor in case of doubt about their right to wed legally.

British law prohibits marriage between the following parties: a man may not marry his: mother, daughter, father's mother, mother's mother, son's daughter, sister, father's daughter, mother's daughter, wife's mother, wife's daughter, father's wife, son's wife, father's father's wife, mother's father's wife, wife's father's mother, wife's mother's mother, wife's son's daughter, wife's daughter's daughter, son's son's wife, daughter's son's wife, father's sister, mother's sister, brother's daughter, sister's daughter. The prohibitions apply similarly to the woman and her side.

Changes in the law have enabled marriages previously considered taboo to be contracted. Since Acts passed in the early part of the century a man has been allowed to marry his deceased brother's widow, father's deceased brother's widow, mother's deceased brother's widow, deceased wife's father's sister, deceased wife's mother's sister, brother's deceased son's widow, sister's deceased son's widow.

Further relaxations in the law were introduced in 1960 which enable a man to contract a legal marriage with his former wife's sister, aunt or niece and the former wife of his brother, uncle or nephew. Under previous legislation, these unions were prohibited unless the former spouse was deceased.

The legal revisions apply similarly to a woman and her side's entitlement to marry.

The matter of marriage between individuals of the same lineage remains an issue of controversy among some clergymen. Ministers may not be willing to marry a couple whose kinship ties they consider to be too close for comfort. However, if the couple are legally entitled to marry they may do so in a civil ceremony.

Preliminaries

The different religious denominations and the Superintendent Registrar of Marriages have formal requirements to be complied with by the couple before a marriage can take place. A broad summing up of a complex mass of codes and practices would emphasize: residential qualifications, public announcements of the intention to marry, declarations concerning religious beliefs, the obligation to produce specific paperwork and certificates, and fees.

Marriage rites

The three main authorities for marriage are as follows: you may marry according to the practice of the Church of England; you may marry according to the practice of other religious denominations with a certificate of marriage issued by the Superintendent Registrar of Marriages; you may be married by a Superintendent Registrar of Marriages at a register office in a civil ceremony.

A religious ceremony

The first major decision is where the marriage will take place. Customarily, the bride is married in her parish church or whichever church she has regularly attended, but she may no longer have local connections and may wish to be married outside her home boundaries.

An appointment should be made with the minister of the church where it is hoped that the marriage will take place, ideally with both parties present.

The minister will wish to talk to the couple about the meaning of the marriage vows and the religious basis of matrimony. He will advise on which of the authorized wordings of the marriage service to choose.

All the details of the couple's choices for the service should be discussed, from hymns, psalms and prayers to the placing of flower arrangements. The minister's personal attitudes to any proposed departure from established liturgical or social practice, such as reading poems or favourite passages from literature, or playing pop classics, will determine his willingness to cooperate.

Closer to the day of the wedding the minister will probably wish for a meeting to confirm arrangements. For a big white wedding, he will almost certainly request a full-scale rehearsal with the chief participants or proxies present.

Note: the minister and his wife are always sent an invitation to the wedding.

Baptism and marriage

The Church of England and the Roman Catholic Church expect at least one of the couple to have been baptized into a Christian denomination. If written evidence is required by the minister, this can usually be obtained by applying to the incumbent clergyman at the church where the baptism took place. A small fee is charged.

When one of a couple has not been baptized, the approach adopted by individual ministers varies according to personal conviction. If neither of the couple has been baptized it is unlikely that a minister will be prepared to conduct the service. Adult baptism may be proposed.

Individuals who find themselves faced with this problem are advised to consult a canon lawyer.

Divorce and marriage

The whole question of the remarriage of divorced people is highly controversial within the Churches. The present position is that neither the Church of England nor the Church of Rome may marry a divorced person whose former spouse is living. Whatever the morality of the objection it causes grievous personal unhappiness to those who wish to remarry with the full rites of their faith.

In exceptional cases and where clergy are convinced of a good cause, ministers may possibly be prepared to make concessions – a great deal still depends on individual ministers' personal convictions.

See page 124 for Remarriage.

Religious and civil requirements for marriage

Procedures for most parishioners who marry in the Church of England take the following form: the clergymen of the respective parishes of the bride and bridegroom read out the banns giving the names of the betrothed and their intention to marry. The banns are called during Sunday services in church on three successive occasions in order that anyone in the congregation who knows of any valid objection to the marriage may be heard.

The couple are expected to be in residence in their respective parishes during the period when the banns are called.

As soon as the calling of banns has been completed to the satisfaction of the church officers in both parishes, the marriage may take place on any day between 8 am and 6 pm during the following three months, with certain exceptions in the religious calendar. However, in practice, advance bookings for weddings and the diary of the officiating minister are likely to narrow the options. A summertime Saturday, for example, will be bound to be heavily booked well in advance.

Should the couple not marry during the three-month period stipulated, the banns must be read again.

Fees are payable for the publication of banns and for the certificate of banns.

Marriage by common licence

The three-week wait incurred by the publication of banns may be avoided by applying for a Common Licence. This enables a marriage to take place after one clear day (other than a Sunday, Christmas Day and Good Friday), from the date on which notice was given to the Superintendent Registrar of marriage or his surrogate. The clergyman who is officiating at the marriage will provide information required about obtaining the licence, or may be authorized to grant one himself.

One of the couple is required to be resident in the parish for 15 days before making the application for the licence.

The licence is valid for three months. A fee is payable.

Marriage by Superintendent Registrar's certificate

The Superintendent Registrar of Marriages can issue a certificate that allows a marriage to take place in church without the wait that attends the publication of banns.

One of the couple should apply to the Registrar in whose district they live, seven days immediately before the notice to marry is entered into the notice book. If the couple live in different districts, each should apply to their neighbourhood Registrar.

Twenty-one clear days must pass between the date on which the Registrar records the proposed marriage and the day on which the authorization is granted. From that date onwards for three months the marriage may take place. Fees are payable to the respective registrars.

Note: it does not follow that a clergyman will consent to a marriage without the calling of banns, even if a civil authorization is forthcoming. He may exercise his right to ask the couple to obtain a common licence.

Marriage by special licence

Unusual personal circumstances, such as serious illness, may qualify for a special licence. This authorizes a marriage to take place according to the rites of the Church of England in any building and, in exceptional cases, at any hour. The licence is issued on behalf of the Archbishop of Canterbury through the Faculty Office. No residential qualifications are required, nor need the building in which the ceremony takes place be registered for marriages. Marriage by special licence has been conducted in hospitals, on board ship and in private chapels.

The fees for the licence are higher than those mentioned before.

Marrying outside the parish

When a couple wish to marry at a place of worship outside their own parish or their respective parishes, and should neither of them have previously attended services, it is up to the minister to decide whether he is prepared to conduct the marriage service. If he is agreeable, one of the couple must apply to be put on the electoral roll of the parish, and is usually asked to sign an application form declaring that they have attended church services in the parish for six months.

One of the couple will be required to have lived in the district for 15 days before making the application.

A broad church

The attitude of the mother church towards the marriage service arouses deep and divergent responses among the clergy, which paradoxically can be of great help in special cases.

Suppose a clergyman and the couple fail to see eye to eye on nuptial matters?

There is always the hope that the betrothed may find a more sympathetic response elsewhere and from another priest, but this would in any case depend on the request complying with the proprieties and traditions of the marriage service.

Disclosure of personal information

When individuals do not wish to disclose their full parental origins on the marriage documents, they should apply to the Registrar General's office for guidance, or consult a solicitor.

Note: there is no legal obligation on a person to reveal this information.

Marriage in the Church of England

In the widely accepted wording of the Book of Common Prayer, the Church of England marriage service begins with the Minister's address to the congregation, 'Dearly Beloved, we are gathered together here in the sight of God, and in the face of this congregation, to join together this Man and this Woman in holy Matrimony...' The passage proceeds to explain the purpose of Christian marriage.

The minister now asks the congregation if they know of any 'just impediment' why the couple should not be 'joined together in holy Matrimony'.

If no valid objections are raised, the minister continues the service. He now asks the man, 'Wilt thou have this woman to thy wedded wife?' in a passage which describes a husband's commitment to his partner. The bridegroom then replies audibly, 'I will'. The minister then addresses the bride, 'Wilt thou have this man to thy wedded husband?', and defines her responsibilities to her husband. She replies audibly, 'I will'.

At this point, the minister asks, 'Who giveth this woman to be married to this man?' No formal reply is required by the father (or whoever is giving the bride away); instead, he takes the bride's right hand and passes it to the clergyman who places it in the bridegroom's right hand. The father now returns to his reserved place in the front family pew.

The bridegroom then recites his vows, as instructed by the clergyman. The couple loose hands. The bride takes the bridegroom's right hand in her own and recites her vows. The couple again loose hands.

The best man now passes the wedding ring to the bridegroom who hands it to the minister. The ring is blessed and returned to the bridegroom who places it upon the fourth finger of the bride's left hand. Holding the ring in place, the bridegroom takes his vows as instructed by the priest.

The couple may now be required to kneel in prayer. The service continues with prayers, hymns and readings. An address may be given by the priest: this will have an informal tone, particularly if he knows one or both of the couple personally. The service ends with a blessing.

Alternative wordings for the Church of England marriage service

The wording of the marriage service to be chosen is a matter to take up with the officiating minister. The familiar 17th-century version and the revised version which barely differs from it, can be read in the 1928 Book of Common Prayer in the section now entitled 'Alternative Service, Series I'.

The earlier wording contains the controversial woman's promise 'to obey' her husband which is at variance with the contemporary spirit of equality between the sexes. However, some women prefer to keep the old language and omit the contentious promise, while others stay with the original text in the interests of prose and precedent.

A simply worded modern language service, published as Alternative Service Series III, has found favour with many marrying couples and churchmen.

Marriage in the Church of Scotland

The reading of banns has been abolished in the Church of Scotland and application must be made to the civil authorities.

A Schedule of Marriage is required for the service which is issued by the Registrar following the satisfactory completion of its requirements (see Civil marriage in Scotland, below).

The Schedule is signed by the minister, the bride and bridegroom giving their usual signatures, and two witnesses. The paperwork should be returned promptly to the Registrar.

The Church of Scotland marriage ceremony

There is a usual form of marriage service in the Church of Scotland, though variations are allowed. The liturgy is set down in the Book of Common Order but this is only a guide to ministers and may be interpreted according to the views of individual clergymen and their parishioners.

The order and content of the marriage service may be amended and suggestions accepted for the inclusion of non-scriptural readings, poems or prose passages. However, it is not every minister of the Presbyterian Church that goes along with this liberal attitude.

Civil marriage in Scotland

Procedures are much the same as south of the border. One difference is that the couple's application to marry must be signed in the presence of two householder witnesses. The notice is made public for seven days and if no significant objections are raised the civil authority will issue a Certificate of Publication. The marriage may then take place within the next three months.

See page 52 for Civil marriages.

One of the couple must have an address in Scotland or have lived in the country for 15 days prior to making the application. In certain circumstances, a sheriff's licence is granted allowing a marriage to take place during the ten days following the issue of the licence.

Quaker (the Religious Society of Friends) marriage

A Quaker wedding is unusually simple and informal but the preliminaries have much in common with other religious denominations.

Information for those wishing to be married by Friends is given by the registering officer at the Monthly Meeting. Forms will be supplied requiring written declarations. If these are completed to the satisfaction of members, an announcement of the proposed marriage will be read out at the Meetings. Plans for the wedding may now proceed, assuming no valid objections have been raised.

It is usual to allow about six weeks for preliminaries to take place, considerably longer if individuals are non-members.

A non-member may be married by Friends but they will wish to be satisfied that the newcomer fully understands the nature of Quaker marriage and is in sympathy with Quaker attitudes and beliefs. The non-member will usually meet one or two Friends informally for a talk. They will use their own judgment as to whether he or she shares Quaker values. If assent is forthcoming, the non-member will require two formal recommendations from full members and will be required to sign a certificate.

The Quaker (Religious Society of Friends) marriage ceremony

A Quaker marriage service is simple, open in form and free of pomp and ceremony. No one officiates formally. The couple choose their own readings which may be religious or secular. They decide for themselves during the service when they feel the moment is right for making their declarations (vows).

The wedding takes place during a special Meeting at a Friends' Meeting House. The couple may greet Friends, friends and family as they arrive. A printed sheet giving information about Quaker marriage procedures is sometimes handed out to non-members.

The bride and bridegroom make a declaration to each other in turn, as follows, 'Friend, I take this my Friend (name) to be my husband (wife), promising through divine assistance to be unto him (her) a loving and faithful wife (husband), so long as we both on earth shall live.' There is no provision in the Quaker service for the presentation of a ring but couples may improvise, and select a point after their declarations for one to be given.

During the service a prayer may be said. One or two Friends may express their thoughts, briefly and informally, on love and marriage. The duration of a wedding Meeting is usually about 40 minutes. The end is signified when the elders at the Meeting shake hands with the newly-weds.

The Quaker registrar now arranges for the couple to sign the marriage certificate and reads out from a large scroll the bride and bridegroom's promises to each other. Friends, friends and guests now sign the scroll as witnesses.

Note: if the couple are closely connected to the Quakers, it is likely that their wedding clothes will be quiet and modest.

Marriage in the Church of Rome

See page 43 for Religious and civil requirements for marriage.

When a couple are both Roman Catholic, the banns will be called at the church where the wedding is due to take place, and at their parish church as well, if necessary.

Each of the couple will be asked to fill in a Pre-Nuptial Enquiry Form, giving basic biographical particulars about themselves. The Roman Catholic Church requires formal religious preparation for marriage. Instruction is given by the priest or a recommended married couple. In view of these preliminaries, between six and three months should be allowed for preparation for the marriage.

The priest will wish to see copies of the couple's certificates of baptism and confirmation. Permission to marry at a parish church other than the applicants' own must be obtained from their parish priest.

See page 44 for Marrying outside the parish.

As soon as this dispensation has been given, the couple should apply to the Superintendent Registrar of Marriages for a marriage certificate or licence.

Mixed marriages

Whereas in the past the Roman Catholic Church discouraged marriages between Catholics and non-Catholics, these are now widely accepted. The Roman Catholic partner is required to obtain a special dispensation from the bishop to marry a non-Catholic, agreeing in writing to keep the faith and to try to have any children born of the union baptized and brought up as Roman Catholics. No written statement is required from the other party.

Roman Catholic marriage ceremony

The two most widely used Roman Catholic marriage rites begin with an introduction, scripture readings and the Rite of Marriage. The Rite of Marriage outside Mass, the shorter ceremony without the celebration of the Eucharist, is often used for mixed marriages. The Rite of Marriage during Mass incorporates the nuptial Mass.

When there is no Mass the service concludes with intercessions and a nuptial blessing. Where there is a Mass, the offertory and holy Communion follows as well as the blessing.

A homily by the priest is customary at either rite. The signing of the register marks the end of the ceremony.

Jewish marriage

Under Jewish law the marrying couple must both be of the Jewish faith and free from any previous marital impediment. While commending the ideal of lifelong marriage to the same spouse, Jewish law does not regard the bond as indissoluble. If the marriage breaks up the rabbis may administer a bill of divorce. It is not possible to be remarried in the Jewish faith without this dispensation.

Marriage according to Judaism is said to be the oldest form of religious marriage in the world, going back some 3000 years. Judaism's various branches interpret the ancient scriptures with a different ideological emphasis, which in turn has a strong bearing on attitudes towards the marriage service. A marriage between Orthodox Jews follows precedent with exactitude whereas the Reformed branch allows greater freedom in its observances, both religious and secular.

A Jewish marriage may take place anywhere, in or out of doors, in a synagogue or secular building such as a hotel. Most frequently a Jewish marriage is celebrated in a synagogue, but always takes place under a *huppah* (a canopy).

Marriages are not permitted between sunset on Friday and sunset the following day which is the Sabbath, on the Day of Atonement or on any important festival, High Holy Day or fast day. A Sunday wedding is therefore popular.

The bride and her prospective husband should both attend the office of the Chief Rabbi, to apply for his authorization of marriage. A parent from both sides of the family is usually also present.

Outside London, the local minister or secretary for marriages will usually arrange for the Chief Rabbi's authorization. Couples are advised to apply in good time, certainly not later than three weeks beforehand in the case of a rushed wedding.

When applying for authorization the following information will be required:

the Superintendent Registrar's certificate or licence (see above); the *ketuba*, the Hebrew document showing the marriage lines of the couple's respective parents or, if these are not available, the date and place of their respective marriages; the bride and bridegroom's birth certificates; the Hebrew names of the couple and their respective parents; information as to whether each father is a 'Cohen', a 'Levite' or an 'Israelite'; and a fee.

In case of doubt, query, absence of documents or if one party is coming from abroad, advice should be sought at the earliest opportunity from the Chief Rabbi's office.

Wedding procedures can vary from synagogue to synagogue and may depend on the views of the officiating rabbi or minister. Reform synagogue members are able to interpret religious practice, social observances and marriage etiquette more liberally than those of an Orthodox persuasion.

Judaism does not accept the principle of mixed marriage, although as in all religious denominations, some free-thinking minister belonging to a more liberal branch of the faith will usually be prepared to offer to help in special cases.

Preparation for the Orthodox Jewish wedding

Tradition holds that the bridegroom should attend a religious service on the Sabbath before the wedding – a blessing may be said by the rabbi on behalf of the couple. Orthodox Jewish brides-to-be traditionally visit the *mikvah* (ritual pool) for the first time no more than four days before the wedding and seven clear days after the end of a menstrual period.

The Orthodox Jewish marriage ceremony

A rabbi officiates at the marriage service which is conducted in the presence of a *minyan*, no fewer than ten adult male Jews. A ring is an essential part of the ritual. The bride usually wears white and always a headdress or hat. The men wear hats or skull caps throughout the service.

The bridal party can take the following order on entering: the bride on her father's arm, followed by the bridesmaids, bridegroom's parents and bride's mother on a male relative's arm.

The Jewish marriage service

The service, known as the *kiddushin*, consists of two parts: the act of betrothal (*erusin*) and the marriage rite (*nissuin*).

The bridegroom is formally asked by the minister to approve the two witnesses to the *ketubah*, the marriage contract. He is also asked to accept its terms and conditions.

The bridegroom is led to the *huppah*, the nuptial canopy, by his own and the bride's father. The best man stands a short distance behind him, to his left.

The bride is led to the *huppah* by her own and the bridegroom's mother. The bridal procession consists of the bridesmaids and the bride's closest female

The order of rabbi and bridal party at a Jewish marriage service.

relatives. The bride enters to organ or choral music and takes her place under the canopy at the bridegroom's right. On each side of the couple stand their respective parents.

The betrothal

A brief chant of blessing precedes the rabbi's address, usually a homily upon Jewish marriage. Next comes the blessing of betrothal.

The couple become man and wife in the eyes of Jewish law when the bridegroom places the ring upon the bride's finger, saying, 'Behold, you are consecrated unto me by this ring according to the law of Moses and Israel'. The *ketubah* is then read, and subsequently passed to the bride.

Now follow the seven blessings of marriage. The couple take a sip of wine from the same goblet to symbolize that they must now share the same cup of life.

The attendant beadle then places the glass at the bridegroom's foot and amidst shouts of good wishes he shatters it with his heel. This symbolizes the destruction of the Temple at Jerusalem, and the couple's responsibilities to share the trials of their people.

The bride and bridegroom then proceed to sign the marriage documents. Afterwards they walk towards the door of the synagogue with the bridal attendants and both sets of parents.

An interdenominational marriage

Arranging a mixed marriage service between members of different religious denominations and conducted by the respective ministers calls for informed advice, and, in special cases, the help of a canon lawyer.

Should the service be approved by the religious authorities involved, certain members of the congregation are likely to be unfamiliar with some, or all, of the hymns, prayers and religious procedures. Moreover, some of the ideas expressed or practices followed may be a cause of offence among zealous dissenters. If a shorter observance is admissible, it is probably better to adopt it in preference to the full form.

Civil marriages

A register office wedding is the most popular way of marrying in this country: it is brief, legal and unceremonious. Vows are made before a Superintendent Registrar of Marriages in the presence of a minimum of two witnesses as a legal requirement.

If a person who wishes to be married is under the age of 18, he or she must obtain parental consent or that of a legal guardian, and produce a copy of their birth certificate.

A foreign national will need to supply a passport or identity card.

A register office marriage is the obvious choice of those who are not members of a religious denomination or who are marrying again, and is the only option for those debarred for whatever reason from marrying according to the rites of their religion. Equally, some people who are eligible for marriage at a place of worship elect for civil marriage as the quickest and simplest, and least expensive, means of tying the knot.

Legalities and procedures

The first step is to apply to the Superintendent Registrar's office for an application form. Names, occupations, the office in which the couple wish to be married, and residential qualifications will be required. If a divorce has taken place, a copy of the decree absolute will be asked for, and in the case of a widow or widower, a copy of the death certificate of the spouse. Photostats of documents are not accepted.

Only one of the couple need 'give notice' to the Registrar and will be responsible for signing the declarations.

Marriage by Superintendent Registrar's certificate without licence

The Superintendent Registrar will grant a certificate based on seven days' residence in the district immediately prior to notice of marriage. When both of the couple live in the district of the office where the marriage is to take place, only one person need 'give notice'. If they live in different districts, notice must be given to the Superintendent Registrar in each area.

Marriage by certificate without licence requires a time lapse of 21 days between the day of giving notice and the date of issuing the certificate. A fee is charged.

Marriage by Superintendent Registrar's certificate and licence

Only one 'notice to marry' is required and only one clear day need pass between the date of the notification and the first day on which the marriage may take place (not Sunday, Good Friday or Christmas Day).

If the requirements can be met, this licence helps to hasten procedures. It is obtainable by those who usually live in England or Wales or who have residences within the border on the day of giving notice to the Registrar. One of the couple must be in residence in the registration district for the 15 days immediately preceding the giving of notice. Generally, the marriage takes place at the register office concerned.

Marriage by Registrar General's licence

In extreme cases, most generally that in which a person is dying and wishes to be married, this licence enables the union to take place wherever necessary.

Fees

Fees must be paid for each notice of marriage at the office of the Superintendent Registrar, and for the attendance of the officials at the ceremony. There is a fee for a marriage certificate and an additional fee for a marriage certificate with a licence. Details are available at the Registrar's office.

Civil marriage celebrations

See page 90 for The wedding reception.

Celebrations after civil marriage may range from the full traditional wedding reception to an impromptu round of drinks. A popular choice is a lunch party for close family followed by a celebration later to which numbers of friends are invited.

Sometimes the bride's parents, but more often the newly-weds, are hosts at the big party. On the other hand, if simplicity, economy and lack of ceremonial are the order of the day, a civil marriage can appropriately be followed by a completely informal celebration – a picnic, for example.

Who pays for what

The division of costs at a civil marriage follows the lines of a denominational wedding. The bride's side is customarily responsible for meeting most of the costs, with the Superintendent Registrar's fees being settled by the bridegroom.

See page 57 for The division of costs.

Some do – but more do not – obey the established pattern on the division of responsibilities between the families for funding the marriage.

Clothes for a civil marriage

Marriage calls for best dress, out of respect for the occasion.

The bride's choice for herself, and the nature of the celebrations after the marriage, will set the general level of formality expected of the men and the women in the wedding party.

The bride's dress

There are no set conventions about the bride's dress at a civil marriage but the custom is to wear smart day clothes. She will usually carry flowers but again, this is at her discretion.

Her preferences are likely to be determined by such factors as whether this is her first marriage, and whether she wishes to introduce the atmosphere and social observances that are traditional at a denominational marriage. If her fiancé has not been married before, his side might prefer the men to wear morning dress, and the wedding dress should have a comparable air of formality, but some sense of moderation has to be shown here.

The purity of white and the veiled visage of the bride have their origins in the rites of religion. If carried to extremes, such emblems can only appear anachronistic in the secular surroundings of a municipal office.

Most women have an image of how they wish to look on their wedding day. Those whose minds are a blank, or who are at any rate uncertain, may use as a criterion of choice the way in which they would like to remember themselves on this day in the future.

The bridegroom's clothes

No rules for him, either, but conventions. The usual form for the man who is marrying at a register office is to wear a lounge suit and sport a buttonhole. Like the bride, he will dress in a manner that is appropriate for the celebrations to follow the marriage. If a formal wedding reception is planned, he has the option of wearing morning dress.

Timing on the day

On the day of civil marriage the bride and bridegroom, the witnesses and the wedding party assemble at the register office. If the traditions of a formal wedding are being observed, the bride and bridegroom travel separately, the bride accompanied by her parents and/or witnesses, the bridegroom likewise.

It is not advisable to arrive more than ten minutes ahead of the allotted hour as the party will almost certainly overlap with the preceding group. The party awaits the Superintendent Registrar's call in the waiting room.

The ceremony, supervised by the Superintendent Registrar and the Registrar, takes about 15 minutes. The couple will be reminded that the vows they are about to take are binding and solemn, and asked to declare that there is no lawful impediment to the marriage.

A ring may be given by the man to the woman during the ceremony and vice versa, but this is at their discretion.

The couple then call on their witnesses, and the signing of the register follows. Both parties give their usual signatures. The witnesses add their signatures as do the Superintendent Registrar and the Registrar. A marriage certificate is now handed over.

Planning a civil marriage

The time it takes to organize a civil marriage depends on the requirements of the civil authority and on the character of the celebrations following the ceremony.

If a wedding reception is planned along traditional lines, about two to three months is a realistic provision.

When a couple wish to arrange a Service of Blessing in church after a civil marriage, followed by a formal wedding reception, sufficient time must be set aside for organization. Synchronizing the various bookings and reservations could take up to six months. At the same time, it should be borne in mind that notice to the Registrar may not be given more than three months in advance of the marriage.

Register office marriages take place between 8 am and 6 pm, usually on a weekday. Unfortunately, the majority of offices do not remain open all day on Saturday, and those hoping for a popular Saturday morning booking may find themselves disappointed. It is advisable to start making arrangements in good time.

See page 54 for Clothes for a civil marriage.

On the whole, Registrar's premises deserve their reputation as atmospherically uncongenial places in which to be married, so the wish to introduce festive notes such as a bridal dress, witnesses wearing traditional bridal attendants' attire, and flowers, into functional arrangements, and to make the civil contract into a memorable occasion, is very understandable. Credit must be given to those local authorities who have tried to improve surroundings.

All social arrangements must be discussed with the Superintendent Registrar, who will also advise on procedures, rules and regulations. It is important to establish in advance the number that can be seated in the room where the marriage takes place.

Most register offices provide flowers (for an additional fee). Couples who wish to make arrangements with an outside florist, or to provide their own display, should raise the point with the Superintendent Registrar.

Usually, photographs may be taken in the waiting room before and after the marriage but not during the ceremony. A fashion has developed in recent years for photographs to be taken of the bride and bridegroom during a simulated signing of the register after they have concluded.

Planning a wedding

Weddings don't just happen. The organization of a wedding in the family is a major undertaking if more than the minimum of celebration is contemplated. A white wedding can be compared to planning a military manoeuvre, particularly if it is to be memorable.

Whatever the scale of the wedding, sharing the workload is the only way in which the majority of families manage to plough through the tasks and bring the day to fruition. The mother of the bride, the betrothed couple, siblings, bridegroom's parents and friends and supporters on all sides may well be involved to lend support.

By custom it is the bride's day and her ideas, hopes and vision should always be given priority. The style and personal emphasis of the wedding are in her hands, and its celebration will reflect her personality and family background.

The date and the time

Spring and summer are the most popular seasons for marriage but weddings take place throughout the year. However, certain dates in the religious calendar place restraints on marriage services. The Church of England and the Roman Catholic Church do not encourage weddings to take place during Lent, for example.

Sunday is rarely a good day to choose as the officiating minister is likely to be busy with regular services and his parishioners. Easter, Whitsun and June are much in demand and are usually reserved months in advance.

Sunday is the favoured day for Jewish marriages. Register office marriages may take place on any day except for Sunday, Christmas Day and Good Friday.

See page 49 for Jewish marriage.

There are also family circumstances which may affect decisions, or the unavailability of one or more of the chief members of the bridal party. Personal factors such as the bride's menstrual cycle may play a part too.

Whether religious or civil, marriages may be conducted at any hour between 8 am and 6 pm. Points to bear in mind when deciding on the exact hour include the couple's honeymoon departure arrangements, the convenience of guests who are travelling long distances and the level of hospitality that will be suggested by the time. A late morning wedding invitation indicates that a midday meal will be provided, while an afternoon timing suggests lighter refreshments, but on this point much depends on the customs of the bride's community and circle of friends.

See page 103 for Goodbyes.

A widely favoured formula is as follows: a Saturday wedding, held at 3 pm, with a service of under one hour, followed by a wedding reception of about two hours' duration with the couple leaving before 6 pm and guests following suit shortly afterwards.

Jewish marriages are frequently held in the evening, with the service beginning at 6 pm as a favoured hour.

The division of responsibilities

With so many different individuals involved, there is nothing like a family wedding to bring out all kinds of buried sensitivities about personal rights.

There is the voice of the bride's papa who may have decided views, as he will probably be footing the bill. The bride herself, whose day it is, may feel that *she* should have the last word. It seems as if there are two sides to every question.

Consultation and collaboration may seem soft options to throw into the teeth of this timeless domestic drama, but they do work. Keeping both sides in touch with developments is conducive to an atmosphere of trust which in itself has a soothing effect.

The division of costs

A pattern has become established over the years of each side's responsibilities and financial obligations. A summary is given below.

The bride and bridegroom in consultation with both sets of parents usually decide on the nature of the marriage ceremony and the date and time it will take place.

The bride's side undertake most of the arrangements for the wedding. It is a fact that despite changes in family relationships, the wish to celebrate the nuptials in a traditional way maintains its hold as strongly as ever on parents and prospective brides alike.

The bride's side

The bride's family organizes and pays for the following: the bride's clothes for the wedding and honeymoon; the bridal attendants' clothes; flower arrangements at the place of worship and choir and organists' fees; transport for the bridal party; fees for the wedding photographer; all published announcements of engagement to marry, marriage or cancellations; the wedding invitations; Order of Service sheets; the wedding reception.

The bridegroom's side

The bridegroom's side undertakes to arrange and pay for the following: the bridegroom's clothes; fees in connection with the place of worship (see above for exceptions); the wedding ring; the bride's bouquet; flowers (if liked) for the bride's mother and the bridegroom's own mother; flowers for the bridesmaids; buttonholes for the bridegroom, the best man and the ushers; presents for the bridesmaids; the honeymoon.

Note: sometimes convenience dictates that one family picks up the tab for costs that are supposed to be shared. Transport expenses are a case in point. Where one car hire firm is supplying vehicles for the bridal party and for the bridegroom's trip from church to wedding reception, there may be a case for putting all the charges on one invoice.

However, if costs are not going to be shared in the usual way, the matter must be sorted out between the two sides before instructions are issued to firms about invoicing.

Changes in the pattern

Exceptions to the way in which weddings are financed have probably become the norm. It has become unremarkable for the two sides to share expenses in a more equal fashion.

In addition, the mother of the bride or the prospective bride herself may well be in a healthier financial state than the father and consider it only fair to pay the larger share of costs.

Daughters who are earning good salaries and have led independent lives since leaving home may be reluctant to accept the parental authority that can be the price paid for financial support on this occasion. They may prefer to pay their own way, at least in part. An accepted compromise in an otherwise traditional division of costs is for the bridegroom's side to be recruited to make a contribution to the reception, either in cash or kind, largely as a means of making it a better and more hospitable party. Some help with the drinks bill or flowers for the place of worship or reception would be a thoughtful gesture.

Whereas at one time the bridegroom was expected to pay for the honeymoon, it is highly likely that costs will be shared between the couple today.

Perhaps the most significant switch is that changes to the so-called 'correct' way of dividing costs can now be contemplated without causing embarrassment to either side.

Not every family will agree with the above. It must be remembered that the wedding is a ceremony which above all others engenders a respect for custom and tradition. No one, by repute, is more sensitive to these implications than the father of the bride. The manner in which his daughter is married represents to the majority of fathers a barometer of his family's status in society as well as a gesture of love and generosity. Many fathers will still grit their teeth and pay full whack, whatever it may cost, and woe betide anyone (especially someone from the bridegroom's side) who suggests otherwise.

Second marriage

Sometimes a second marriage is accompanied by more ceremony and celebration than the first. It may be that one party has not previously been married, or any previous wedding was a quiet affair at a register office and a mutual wish exists between the couple to make a public avowal of their commitment.

How far the bride's family are obliged to support their daughter's inclinations is a moot point here. Where will and wherewithal combine, the idea is a generous one. But most considerate daughters would take the view that if the family have pushed the boat out on their behalf once before, they should be exempted from the obligation of funding a similar exercise.

Friends who accept an invitation to the wedding usually produce a present, irrespective of the fact of having given one for the previous alliance.

Members of the wedding and their roles

Aspects of a wedding can be compared to a production of a play in which each member of the cast plays a defined part. Some are stars, some play character roles, others have a walk-on status only, but each and all are essential to the success of the drama.

The bride

Almost since primitive times, the bride has been compared to all things good, beautiful and fruitful. Poets and storytellers have sung her praises in all languages, and rites and rituals involving the bride bear a remarkable similarity from one religious denomination to another.

The unfamiliar status of being a bride, together with all the undoubted challenges involved – the commitment, the formalities and the celebrations – make exceptional demands. It shouldn't be a pious hope that the family circle do their best to keep calm themselves, try to absolve the bride from as many organizational tasks as is practicable, and find time to instil confidence and reassurance.

See page 89 for Church procedures.

Many of the special effects which make a wedding may echo the personal tastes of the bride: for example, the style of the flower arrangements, and the programme of music both during the ceremony and at the reception. The bride is also responsible for making any bookings in connection with her personal appearance, which will probably include a hairdresser and manicurist.

See page 76 for The wedding guest list.

Note: friends who perform these services on an honorary basis should be included in the wedding guest list.

Wedding dress

The style of dress is entirely the personal choice of the bride. However, beyond a few loners who elect to go off at a tangent, women have remained loyal to the custom of dressing in a manner that unmistakably proclaims them as bride.

For very many years now, this has involved a long white, cream or ivory gown worn with a headdress and personal adornments, bouquet in hand. Threads of gold and silver, and gentle flower petal shades also have a traditional place in bridal apparel. Rich materials have always been favoured by those who could afford them. In this century, silk, satin, tulle, taffeta, chiffon and especially lace constantly recur in wedding dress, either in their original form or as synthetic versions. Hemlines go up and down, the silhouette changes: the bride's dress has always reflected the influences of fashion.

Choosing a wedding dress

A wedding dress is the one dress about which the wearer should have no doubts. Surprisingly, many women profess a sixth sense about the attire in which they will be married and are prepared to go to great lengths to realize their vision.

Whatever style is decided upon, it is worth remembering: a back view is as important as the front in a wedding dress to be worn at a place of worship; fabric should be resistant to crushing and creasing; style should be appropriate to the scale and character of the building where the marriage is taking place. No bride need feel constrained by the current emphasis on bridal white, the symbol of purity which first caught on in the 18th century and became firmly established by Queen Victoria's own choice of a white wedding dress. If white seems anachronistic or doesn't suit either her complexion or tastes, a bride can wear a best dress in a favourite colour. The idea of wearing a scarlet robe, symbol of happiness, has its fans.

In cases of doubt or disagreement

A wedding dress worn at a place of worship is expected to conform to standards of decorum and decency. If any doubts exist as to the appropriateness of a particular design, the officiating clergyman should be consulted before any decisions are taken. A few members of the clergy are prepared to go along with innovation but most are likely to take a more conservative view.

It is by no means exceptional for the bride to favour a dress which may fail to appeal to the parent who is expected to pick up the bill. No easy solution presents itself and if the bride insists on her choice, she may have to be prepared to pay for the privilege herself.

Generally, parents are expected to go along with their offspring's wishes, recognizing that a pre-condition of a confident state of mind is a feeling of satisfaction with the dress.

Wedding-dress customs

All manner of fancies rooted in folklore continue to fascinate brides. It is good luck, according to the ancient ditty, to wear 'Something old, something new, something borrowed, something blue' for marriage. This is often translated in terms of antique jewellery, new clothes, borrowed finery and a blue garter. Some women like to stitch a small piece of a family wedding-dress or family veil into the new one. Carrying lucky charms such as silver horseshoes holds undying appeal.

A long-standing tradition is for the bride to wear her mother's or grandmother's dress or a family veil. Among well-to-do families who possess valuable jewellery the custom is to lend a piece, most often a tiara, to the bride. The bridegroom's family also lend adornments such as jewellery or lace, but if strict etiquette is to be observed, this is all they may contribute to the bride's effects, except for her bouquet, and of course the rings on her fingers.

Among families whose children will be baptized, the custom is to save some material from the mother's wedding dress which is usually taken from the train. It provides the fabric and a family link for the christening robe to be worn by the baby.

An order of dressing

There are as many attitudes towards how the hours immediately before marriage should be spent as there are brides. Some like to pre-plan to the point of calculating the length of time taken for the final coat of nail varnish to dry. Others set store by spontaneity and prefer to work speedily at the eleventh hour.

An order of dressing is helpful, however. A comfortable time to allow for preparations and getting dressed is about three hours. If a visit to an outside hairdresser is envisaged, more time should be allowed for arrangements.

One suggested sequence is as follows: take a bath; have a manicure; apply base make-up, reserving the use of paintbox cosmetics until later; hairstyle to be arranged; complete any make-up effects requiring blusher, mascara, eyeshadow or lipstick (placing a tissue over glossed lips if the dress goes on over the head); don the wedding dress; put on any personal adornments; arrange headdress and veil.

The processional order: the officiating minister leads the bride, her father and bridesmaids to the altar.

Departure for the marriage ceremony

The father of the bride escorts his daughter to the place of worship. The question of how long the bride may keep the congregation waiting for her arrival is a matter on which the bride and the assembly are unlikely to agree. As the demands on photographers and video cameramen increase, so the time taken to do good work makes inroads on the timetable.

Desirable as this may be, the main priority is to get to the church on time out of respect for the priest, assembly and the commitment of marriage. About ten to fifteen minutes behind schedule is acceptable; a much longer delay without good reason will appear inconsiderate and casual.

At the place of worship

The bride's dress and veil are given a final adjustment at the entrance to the place of worship. At a given signal, the bride steps out on the right arm of her father (or whoever is giving her away) and proceeds up the aisle. Bridesmaids and pages follow, walking in pairs. If the bridal dress has a train, it is held by the attendants.

The officiating minister awaits her at the chancel steps. The bride takes up her place, facing the altar. Father and daughter disengage their arms.

The order in which the participants stand, from left to right, facing the altar, is as follows: the father of the bride, the bride, the bridegroom, the best man.

The order of priest and bridal party during the marriage service. The bride's friends and relatives are in the pews on the left and the bridegroom's on the right.

If the bride is wearing a full veil, she usually puts it back at this point, assisted by the chief bridesmaid who also takes charge of her bouquet. If no adult bridesmaid is appointed, she manages the veil on her own and hands her flowers to her father, who slips them to the bride's mother. The bouquet is restored to the bride later, in the vestry, after the register has been signed – something which all couples in all marriage formalities, whether religious or civil, are required to do; the bride signs in her maiden name.

The moment at which the bride's veil is lifted is at her discretion. But she greets the congregation as a married woman with her veil lifted.

The recessional order

At a given signal, the organist strikes up a triumphant piece of music, and the bride, on the left arm of her husband, proceeds down the aisle, smiling at the congregation. After the married couple walk the bridal attendants in orderly pairs, followed by the chief bridesmaid and best man. After, in the following order come: the mother of the bride escorted by the father of the bridegroom, the mother of the bridegroom escorted by the father of the bride, pairings which symbolize the unity of the two sides.

The recessional order: bride and bridegroom, bridal attendants, mother of the bride and father of the bridegroom, and mother of the bridegroom and father of the bride.

The bride at the wedding reception

On her arrival at the reception, the bride usually poses for further formal wedding photographs. In group pictures, if convention is to be followed, she stands at the left of her husband. On her left stand her parents.

At the party she greets guests as they arrive. If there is a full receiving line with both sets of parents, the order in which they welcome everyone is as follows: the mother of the bride, the father of the bride, the mother of the bridegroom, the father of the bridegroom, the bride, the bridegroom.

However, there are many good reasons, such as divorce and the presence of step-parents, why a parental line-up may be inappropriate or inconvenient. In addition, many people feel that the custom is time-consuming and slows up the proceedings, especially the natural progress of a guest towards the first drink which usually reposes on a table or tray tantalizingly just beyond the row of handshakes.

However, a point in favour of the formal way is that everyone gets a chance to meet the bridal party, and vice versa, and this is particularly relevant at large weddings.

Speeches and toasts

There is no good reason why the bride herself should not say a few words in response to a toast. Some among the gathering might think it an unconventional gesture, but she would be given the benefit of the doubt by the majority.

If the bride is looking for an opportunity to speak she might take on the task of adding her own thanks to her husband's two parents, family and friends, which would be appropriate and timely.

See page 71 for At the wedding reception; page 69 for The bride's father; page 66 for The bridegroom; and page 74 for The best man.

'Going away'

The bride changes into her honeymoon travelling clothes, attended by the chief bridesmaid and any other close women friends of her choice.

Parents usually say their goodbyes privately at this point.

The couple rejoin the party for a traditional send-off. It was once customary for the throng to throw confetti for luck after the departing pair, or flower petals (real or fake) or rice. But objections are likely to be raised by the authorities responsible for cleaning up the debris, unless permission has been given.

The bride's final gesture, amidst goodbyes and parting kisses, is to toss her bouquet into the assembly. Superstition holds that whoever catches it will be the next to become a bride.

Going-away clothes

The custom of the bride changing into smart day clothes for going away has survived the knocks of reality. Even if she usually lives in jeans and a t-shirt, or if she is departing for a spot of d-i-y-ing at home, there is usually little evidence to suggest a humdrum destination in her choice of clothes to enter the outside world as a married woman.

At an urban wedding, going-away clothes tend to have a citified air. At a country affair dress tends to be more relaxed all round, which is reflected in the clothes in which the bride departs on honeymoon. An exception is the grand country wedding from which the bride customarily makes her exit as if to spend the first night at the Ritz. A hat, gloves and jewellery are likely to be worn.

The bridegroom

In most wedding planning the bridegroom is a surprisingly undefined figure, overshadowed by the bride and parental forces. The contemporary prospective husband, though, may well have distinct ideas of his own.

See page 90 for Order of Service sheet. See page 77 for Wedding invitations. See page 57 for The division of costs.

The bridegroom has always come into his own in conversations with the officiating minister during which decisions are taken on the order of marriage service.

He provides his side's guest list for the wedding and, if asked to do so, handles the sending out of these wedding invitations. In expressing his views to the bride's side, he is obliged to bear in mind that they are shouldering the costs of the occasion and are the formal hosts.

If the potentially embarrassing issue of sharing costs is to be mooted to the bride's side, it is often the bridegroom who broaches the matter, suggesting perhaps that his family could produce the drink for the party, or provide a location at which the party could be held. Traditionally, he chooses the honeymoon destination and pays all costs.

The bridegroom's clothes

It is the bride's prerogative to choose whether the men in the bridal party will wear morning dress or lounge suits. Obviously the bridegroom may express his own opinions, but he is generally expected to comply with the bride's wishes.

Sartorial convention does not seem to allow much scope for originality of thought in male formal dress but items that are subject to personal tastes include the style and design of necktie or stock, tie pin, waistcoat and buttonhole. The last is often a carnation or rose but could be any sprig of the wearer's fancy, perhaps a flower which also features in the bride's bouquet. A grey topper is a traditional accessory but some men prefer to go to marriage bare-headed.

Social procedures on the day

Secrecy still plays a part in the traditional conduct of the bride on her wedding day. It is considered taboo for the bridegroom to set eyes on the bride until the beginning of the marriage ceremony. Likewise, details of the bride's dress are supposed to be concealed from him in advance of the wedding.

Departure for the place of worship

The bridegroom places the wedding ring in the safe custody of the best man.

The best man drives him to the place of worship. Procedures from this stage onward vary somewhat according to custom and religious practice.

At the church

The bridegroom and the best man await the arrival of the bride in the vestry or, most often, the choir stalls. At a given signal, the bridegroom takes his place at the chancel steps before the altar, with the best man standing at his right. The vicar leads the procession preceding the choristers and the bride. If the choristers do not form part of the procession he welcomes the bride at the chancel steps as she takes her place at the bridegroom's left.

The clergyman then addresses the congregation.

Signing the register

The bridegroom, with the bride on his left arm, proceeds to the vestry for the signing of the register. After receiving congratulations and greetings from both sides, and when the bride is all set and ready, he gives her his left arm, and together they lead the bridal procession down the aisle.

At the wedding reception

After receiving guests as they arrive at the reception, the bridegroom mingles with the gathering. On a reminder by the best man he and his bride forgather beside the wedding cake, for the cake-cutting ceremony.

See page 96 for The wedding cake.

It is the bridegroom who replies to the toast of 'the bride and bridegroom'. It is invariably said that the best speeches are short, and so they are, but it is a great compliment to the gathering if the bridegroom's few words are well considered. His speech may provide many among the assembly with their first opportunity to sample a measure of the man who has won the bride, and he is much more likely to arouse admiration if he puts his heart into the task.

The primary purpose of his speech is to say thank you. Whatever else he may choose to utter, he should thank the parents of the bride for their daughter and the wedding, likewise the guests for their support and presents. Absent friends may be remembered. He ends by thanking the bridesmaids whose health he proposes.

Following the speeches, his remaining formality is to assist the bride in the cake-cutting ceremony.

'Going away'

If tradition is to be adhered to, bridegroom and bride change separately. If the bridegroom is wearing morning dress or uniform he changes into a lounge suit and leaves his wedding clothes in the hands of the best man who is responsible for them until he returns.

Together with the bride's, the bridegroom's departure is announced and the pair reappear before the gathering for their 'going away'.

Amidst good wishes and goodbyes, the bridegroom makes his exit holding the hand of his wife as often as not.

Note: sometimes guests like to keep up the old custom of forming two parallel columns and joining hands held aloft to form an archway, through which the bridegroom and his bride gallop before saying farewell.

The bride's mother

In theory, the mother of the bride acts as director-in-chief of the wedding proceedings. In practice, mother and daughter put their heads together and share the tasks and the decisions. Collaboration and consultation between the two generations is probably the only way in which frictions can be contained and arrangements concluded to everyone's satisfaction.

Among the bride's mother's traditional responsibilities are the following: deciding in consultation with her husband and daughter on numbers and names to be invited to the marriage and reception; liaising with the bridegroom's family; talking over with the mother of the bridegroom the question of what each proposes to wear in order to avoid any incompatibilities of colour or style, particularly the hat; informing the males in the wedding party that the bride would prefer morning dress to be worn; sending out the wedding invitations including those to the bridegroom's parents; arranging – if wished – for the bridegroom to manage the invitations on his side's list; keeping a record of acceptances and refusals; deciding in consultation with the bride on plans for the flower arrangements; passing round the word on the wedding present list; taking in any presents for the couple; borrowing possessions for the wedding, if need be, such as cooking equipment, vases, china and cutlery, caring for them and arranging for their safe return; making all the arrangements for the wedding reception (in consultation with the bride's father and bride); acting as hostess at the reception.

On the day

The bride's mother is in charge of events at home on the day of the wedding. She attempts to persuade the bride to eat a morsel of breakfast, briefs the participants along job demarcation lines, and keeps an overall eye on the timing of the various stages of preparation and helps the bride get ready. Ideally, she remains an oasis of calm, wisdom and common sense in the face of comedy and chaos. However, it is important that she be allowed time to dress and collect her thoughts.

The timing of her departure to the place of worship is ahead of the bride. She travels in the car with the chief bridesmaid and any child attendants; if there are no attendants, she is usually accompanied by a male relative or friend. When the marriage takes place at a register office, the bride's mother either follows the above arrangement or accompanies the bride.

She usually arrives at the place of worship about ten minutes before the bride – her presence signals the impending arrival of her daughter. She receives an Order of Service sheet and is escorted by an usher to her seat in the front family pew on the left-hand side of the nave.

It is the mother's task as the bride takes up her place at the chancel steps to take charge of the bouquet – unless there is a chief bridesmaid or bridesmaid of an age to be relied upon to hold the flowers safely.

After the vows have been taken, the bride's mother is accompanied by the bridegroom's father to the vestry to witness the signing of the register. If she has the bouquet in her care, she returns it to the bride for the procession down the aisle. Her place in the recessional order is after the bridal attendants and on the left-hand side of the bridegroom's father.

Outside the church, she will be photographed for the wedding album. Her traditional place in the group is between the bridegroom (on her right), and the bridegroom's father. As hostess, she then hastens to the wedding reception, accompanied by the bridegroom's father.

At the wedding reception

The mother of the bride is by custom a proud and supportive presence at the wedding reception but her general stance is discreet as a way of publicly acknowledging that this is her daughter's day. How free she is to act as hostess depends on the level of help available with the catering arrangements. If professional caterers are employed, she will hand over to them though keeping a watchful brief on the service.

Her place is at the head of the family line-up receiving guests one by one as they arrive. The families stand in this order: bride's mother, bride's father, bridegroom's mother, bridegroom's father, bride and bridegroom. In a formal receiving line with a large number of people to greet it is easier to accept kisses than to bestow them. Sometimes, if a formal line-up presents family difficulties or for reasons of preference, this formality is dispensed with and the newly-weds alone greet the guests. In this case the bride's mother circulates among well-wishers, receiving congratulations and kisses.

As hostess she makes introductions between the two sides of the wedding party and, in a perfect world, ensures that anyone who is feeling out of things is looked after and included. Her primary responsibility is to free the bride and bridegroom from any concern about the smooth running of the occasion – if plans should go awry she and the bride's father try to deal with the situation.

Naturally the bride's mother is a visible presence at all the nuptial ceremonies such as the cake-cutting, the toasts and speeches. The bride's mother does not customarily make a speech but the time cannot be far away when she will do so without, as at present, running the risk of flouting convention.

Goodbyes and thank-yous

The bride's mother waves off the newly-weds along with the throng of guests. She may wish to say goodbye privately to her daughter as she embarks on married life and for some mothers this is an emotional moment. On occasion, goodbyes and thank-yous are said in public – much depends on the excitement of the moment and also perhaps on the relationship between mother and daughter.

The bride's father

The father of the bride gets short shrift in most advice about weddings, which is all the sadder because customarily it is he who pays.

Some fathers choose to stand aside and allow the womenfolk to make all the preparations but equally, many like to participate and make their voice heard.

The bride's father's role is to support his daughter in every way, emotionally, socially and financially.

The bride's father's clothes

The bride usually expresses strong preferences on whether she wishes the men in the wedding party to wear morning dress or a lounge suit. The bride's father will expect to be consulted on the level of formality of dress and may have views of his own; however, he will probably accede to his daughter's wishes in the end.

If the bridegroom wears morning dress, the bride's father will be similarly attired. Otherwise he will put on his best lounge suit, a carefully chosen necktie and sport a buttonhole of a rose or carnation, or perhaps a sprig from the garden.

A wedding is an occasion when the father of the bride may want to don any ceremonial attire to which he is entitled. Scotsmen rush into kilts, men in the armed services into dress uniform. The Anglican clergy lay aside the surplice (which also applies to a bridegroom in Holy Orders).

At a Jewish marriage which traditionally takes place in the evening, the father puts on a dinner jacket and black tie and wears a hat.

Departure for the ceremony

The father of the bride is usually called upon to sustain his daughter's morale at this stage by escorting her to the place of worship. It is his responsibility, as far as human nature allows, to get her to the church on time.

If the marriage is taking place at a register office the bride may decide on whether she wants to be accompanied by her father as there is no etiquette involved. But he is the usual choice.

At the place of worship

Marriage services vary according to religious practice and with them, the part played by the father of the bride. In most ceremonies he escorts his daughter up the aisle on his right arm.

In the Church of England marriage service he takes up his position before the chancel steps with his daughter standing to his right. During the liturgy, when the clergyman asks, 'Who giveth this woman to be married to this man?' he takes the bride's right hand which he gives palm downwards to the clergyman who then passes it to the bridegroom. He is not required to reply formally but some fathers make a voiceless response.

At this point in the ceremony, the father returns to his reserved place in the front pew on the left-hand side of the aisle. An Order of Service sheet should await him. When the priest has declared the couple man and wife, the father escorts the bridegroom's mother to the vestry for the signing of the register, and congratulates everyone present.

His place in the procession down the aisle is after the bride's mother and the bridegroom's father, escorting the mother of the bridegroom at his right hand. The parents do not usually link arms.

Outside the place of worship he will probably have his photograph taken, after which he leaves for the wedding reception, accompanied by the mother of the bridegroom.

At the wedding reception

The father of the bride is host but he underplays his leading role in acknowledgement of the star casting of the bride and bridegroom.

He may welcome guests in a formal receiving line, in which case he shakes hands standing beside the mother of the bride or, if the couple welcome everyone unaided, he may simply join the throng and hope to enjoy himself. He may be involved in making introductions between the two sides of the wedding party and being introduced to new acquaintances himself.

Together with the bride's mother and the best man he keeps an eye on the general conduct of the party, stepping in if behaviour gets out of hand. He is responsible for the supply of drink and will probably need to keep an eye on the limits of his generosity. He is also responsible for paying any gratuities to any staff involved in connection with the wedding reception.

After the cake-cutting ceremony, the bride's father proposes a toast 'to the bride and bridegroom', whom he may address as such, or he may name the couple, e.g. 'Laura and Fred'. The speech that follows is renownedly light-hearted and draws on family recollections and humorous asides – libidinous jokes should be made with caution, if at all.

Novice speakers may be reassured by the certain knowledge that wedding audiences are almost by definition the kindest and least demanding of any. Sincerity and brevity can always be relied upon to good effect. However, if the bride's father prefers not to speak, he delegates the honour to a male friend of the family.

Once the newly-weds have departed, he usually calls a halt to the flow of liquor as the send-off concludes the party. Besides, he has his depleted stock of credit at the bank to consider.

The evening of a daytime wedding tends to be something of an anticlimax for the hosts, especially for many a bride's mother. The aware bride's father responds to the occasion and opens a bottle of something especially good.

The chief bridesmaid and bridal attendants

The bride makes up her own mind on whether she wishes to be attended by helpers and if so, who will be appointed to the role.

She may prefer to dispense with the bride's court of assistants but the majority vote remains in favour of at least one attendant. Bridesmaids are by definition unmarried. They are usually members of the bride's family, a sister,

step-sister, or half-sister, or a favourite niece, or are chosen from among the friends closest to her. If a married woman is chosen, she is known as a matron of honour. If the letter of the book is to be followed, however, bridal attendants are unmarried. Pages (young boys) are likely to be family, or sons of the bride's good friends.

If the marriage takes place in a register office, it has become accepted for bridesmaids (often doubling as witnesses) to be among the bridal party.

Who is chosen to attend the bride is a subject that can arouse considerable animosity and jealousy among likely contenders for the honour. A member of the family who perhaps considers she has a prior claim to the post, and is passed over in favour of another (possibly prettier, younger, thinner, perkier) candidate may leave no one in any doubt as to her feelings.

The quicker decisions are taken and announced, the better for all concerned: the bride may have to exercise the greatest tact in some cases, perhaps relying on the irrefutable explanation that for some reason her chosen ally helps to give her special confidence.

Child bridesmaids and pages contribute special charm to the wedding procession as they trot solemnly along in their costumes, clinging to the bride's train as if their life depended on it.

It is as well to remember though that infants under three years of age may find the demands of the ceremony overwhelming. However, a wedding is an occasion at which sentiment wins, and if a young relation or child is to be recruited, it is a sound idea for their parent or an adult whom they know and trust to be parked at the aisle end of a pew.

Who pays the costs

The bride chooses the clothes to be worn by her attendants and they (or their families) pay for the privilege.

That is the custom. However, the bride should exercise her discretion in the matter of style and responsibility for the costs involved. If her chosen designs are unlikely to have a post-wedding use for the owner, or are exceptionally expensive or the helper is known to be broke, the bride should offer to stand the costs.

Refusing the invitation

It is always embarrassing to refuse an invitation which is considered an honour – assuming that acceptance is a viable option. Dislike of dressing up and formality, the need to keep an open diary for professional reasons, a belief that others should be given precedence, financial stringency, are possible grounds for regrets.

The chief bridesmaid's duties

The chief bridesmaid helps to dress the bride on the day of the wedding. She is in charge of the other bridal attendants. Together with the mother of the bride, she accompanies the bridesmaids and pages to the place of worship. If the marriage takes place in a register office, it is up to the bride to decide whether she wishes to be escorted by a bridesmaid or whether the attendants will travel independently.

At the place of worship

She keeps an eye on the young attendants as they await the arrival of the bride at the entrance of the place of worship. She ensures that the bride's wedding dress and veil are in good order. As the bridal procession sets off, her place is after the other bridesmaids and pages.

When the bride takes up her position at the chancel steps, the chief bridesmaid may help to lift the veil from her face, and takes charge of the bouquet. Alternatively, she may perform this service in the vestry after the marriage service. During the marriage ceremony she stands behind the bride, facing the altar.

After the marriage service, she follows the bride and bridegroom to the vestry for the signing of the register, escorted by the best man.

She now restores the bouquet to the bride. Her place in the recessional order is after the bridesmaids and pages, escorted by the best man at her right.

At the reception

At the wedding reception a dutiful chief bridesmaid continues her supervisory role. If young bridal attendants are without their parents she attends to their welfare. Towards the end of the party, she punctiliously reminds the bride when it is time to change and if she is changing on her own, helps her to dress. Unless the bride is leaving from home, she is expected to take charge of the wedding dress and any other personal effects, until the owner returns.

During the speeches, she should look particularly pleased and appreciative during the toast of 'the bridesmaids'. She will receive a small present for her pains from the bridegroom, usually presented before the wedding. He should be thanked for the thank-you.

The best man

The bridegroom appoints his best man. In theory, the best man is supposed to be a good organizer, sober timekeeper, and trusty morale booster. In practice he is likely to be the bridegroom's brother or lifelong friend, regardless of his suitability for the role.

The best man's responsibilities include: helping to choose the ushers with the bridegroom, liaising with the bride's family to update himself on arrangements for the wedding, taking advance delivery of the printed Order of Service sheets, arranging the stag night (the all-male spree traditionally held for the bridegroom before his nuptials) but preferably not on the eve of the wedding and makes certain that his man gets home safely. He makes sure that the bridegroom's honeymoon luggage and going-away clothes are safely deposited at the hotel, hall or house where the reception is to be held. He is also responsible for ensuring that the bridegroom's luggage is on board the honeymoon vehicle.

On the day

His role is a combination of helpmate, paymaster, toastmaster and sheepdog. He makes certain that the bridegroom's clothes and his own are in order, which may be no small task, and also takes charge of the wedding ring, and drives the bridegroom to the place of worship. On behalf of the bridegroom he pays any fees due to the minister, organist, bellringers. He makes sure that the ushers know what their responsibilities consist of at the place of worship. He hands them the seating plans for the family pews and the Order of Service sheets. He and the bridegroom find a quiet spot, usually in the vestry or choir stalls, to await the signal of the arrival of the bride. A few minutes before the bride begins her procession up the aisle, the best man and the bridegroom take up their appointed places, the best man standing to the right of the groom. He remains at his station during the service, producing the wedding ring for the bridegroom on cue. He escorts the chief bridesmaid to the vestry for the signing of the register by the bride and bridegroom and witnesses. His place in the bridal procession down the aisle is after the bridal attendants, at the right of the chief bridesmaid.

After the ceremony

After a pause for wedding photography, the best man sees the newly-weds into the car destined for the wedding reception.

He accompanies the chief bridesmaid and the bridal attendants to the party.

At the wedding reception

At a big wedding he liaises with the toastmaster on the right moment for the cake-cutting ceremony and the order of speeches. Agreement should be reached on whether the order is to be cake before speeches as is the general choice, or the other way about which is an accepted option too.

When there is no toastmaster, he acts as master of ceremonies. Having established that the newly-weds are stationed beside the wedding cake, he announces the ceremony of the cutting of the cake. He requests silence for the toast of the bride and bridegroom by the bride's father and the bridegroom's reply. He replies to the bridegroom's toast of the bridesmaids. If there is time, he reads out messages from absentee well-wishers, using his tact on which bits to skip.

He reminds the bridegroom of the hour when he is due to change and generally keeps him aware of the timetable of departure. He sees that the honeymoon car is brought to the door from which the couple will make their departure, remembering to make sure that the bridegroom's luggage is on board!

When the bride and bridegroom are ready to leave, he makes the fact known to the gathering so everyone may witness the traditional 'going-away' send-off .

Note: one time-honoured extra-curricular activity is to decorate the newly-weds' car with announcements or good luck tokens designed to proclaim to the world that the travellers are just married. Although this prank invariably causes a certain amount of embarrassment to the couple, it provides a fillip to proceedings as the party draws to a close.

The ushers

The ushers are chosen by the bridegroom and best man – ideally, well ahead of the day. They are usually recruited from members of the families involved in the wedding, or are longstanding friends of the couple. The task often devolves upon younger brothers, cousins and nephews, as it is an honour which strengthens the involvement of the whole family.

Except at a big wedding where greater numbers are required, three ushers are sufficient. One is delegated to stand at the door of the place of worship, to hand Order of Service sheets to guests as they arrive. One takes up a position inside the entrance in order to be able to show arrivals to their appointed seat or to find them a good place. The third does likewise and may have a special brief as well, such as escorting the mother of the bride to her seat.

Ushers are given a seating plan for the family front pews or their equivalent, and should be kept in touch with potential family frictions or sensitivities. They are also expected to keep a solicitous eye on any guest who may be elderly, frail, feeling under the weather, or have physical disabilities.

On the day, the ushers foregather at some quiet spot at the church about an hour ahead of time in order to be prepared for the likely eventuality of early arrivals. After the ceremony the ushers help to see guests off to the reception or may escort a lost soul who has a claim to be looked after.

Flexible family formalities

It often happens that wedding etiquette has to adjust to the impact of death, divorce or separation in the family. Remarriage and the presence of step-parents may also change the picture, for better or worse.

If the day is to go well, sympathetic consideration has to be given to social protocol that takes into account family frosts and feuds and potential sources of embarrassment.

A far from uncommon situation is when a parent has remarried or has a new romantic attachment and the former spouse objects to the presence of the unofficial member of the wedding.

If discord on this issue appears to be irreversible the only course of action is to relax social formalities as far as possible. For instance, the newly-weds can greet wedding guests on their own without the parental line-up. A buffet-style wedding breakfast allows guests to choose their own company and eliminates the need for a top table seating plan.

When the bride's parents are divorced

The prevailing custom is for divorced parents to fulfil their formal parental obligations at the wedding of their daughter. The invitation cards are sent out in both their names, the father 'gives away' his daughter, the mother of the bride plays her part at the place of worship and, if they so wish, they stand side by side in the receiving line, take their place in the wedding photographs, and at the top table. They appear in their roles as the mother and the father of the bride in which their divorced status is immaterial.

The question of the presence of step-parents may best be managed by according them the role of distinguished guest. They have a reserved seat at the place of worship and their needs are taken care of but they do not participate in any of the parental formalities.

A not uncommon occurrence is for the divorced mother of the bride to be on her own. Family and friends are called on to rally round and where an escort is required one should be to hand.

When the bride's father is absent

In the event of the death or absence of the bride's father, the usual procedure is for a close male relation such as a brother, cousin or uncle on her side to assume the paternal role.

A mother or widow may 'give away' her daughter at a church service. She is not expected to escort her daughter up the aisle – this is undertaken by a male relation – but she steps out from her place in the family pew and stands by her at the chancel steps in the position usually occupied by the father.

The wedding guest list

The bride's family decide on numbers, which are divided equally between the two sides. A consultation between the families to discuss the matter is customary, although it is important for the groom's family to recognize that the bride's side have the last word.

Parity of numbers can be a tricky point. As the bride's side are hosts, they can increase the number of guests they invite without too much embarrassment. On the other hand, if the bride has a small family and her prospective in-laws' side is numerous, some tactful adjustment has to be made to the equal numbers rule.

Who is invited is a timeless source of family debate, feuds and frosts: the subject of whether batty cousin Billy will object if he is dropped from the list, whether the bride's previous boyfriend should be invited, or whether influential work colleagues will be offended if ignored have provoked discussion in one form or another since weddings began. Compromises, adoption of the 'win some lose some' philosophy on both sides is the way of peace.

Once numbers are agreed, it is the bridegroom's responsibility to produce his side's guest list, with names and full addresses.

Wedding invitations

Except in the instance of a very quiet wedding to which guests can be invited by telephone or letter, it is a considerable convenience all round to have printed cards. They are useful reminders and can also act as keepsakes. Cards bearing the wedding invitation can be printed in trad, pop and designer style.

Established, classic style is a dignified missive, without graphic decoration, ideally engraved on good-quality white or cream paper. Flat print is less expensive than engraving, but the latter process has a relief form which stands out distinctively on the card. The format is an upright, folded card measuring 14 × 18 cm (5½ × 7 inches). The wording appears on one side only. Black lettering is usual, although silver is a traditional option.

Plain or decorated ready-printed cards are popular and convenient. The lay-out designates spaces for information which can be filled in by hand.

Creative spirits may prefer to design cards with their own format and wording which can be hand-made or specially printed. One word of warning: it is important that the design is not allowed to obscure the essential information about who, what, when and where.

Some senders take the opportunity to enclose a personal note written on a card or sheet of writing paper, slipped into the fold of the invitation. Should a separate party be held to celebrate the marriage at which the couple are hosts for example, this invitation too might be included in the envelope along with the wedding invitation.

The wording

Whatever the format, the invitation should state the following: names of the bride's parents or other hosts; forename of the bride; forename and surname of the bridegroom and the style by which he is correctly addressed (e.g. Mr Michael Hills or Captain George Hills or Sir Justin Hills); place of worship; date, month and year of the wedding; time denoting am or pm with 'Noon' as a midday reminder; wedding reception location; and an address to which guests can reply, if different from the venue of the reception.

D 736

Countess of Bedington
requests the pleasure of
your company at the marriage
of her daughter
Pamela
to
Mr Charles Rayne,
at St George's, Hanover Square,
on Saturday, August 3.rd
at 2.30 p.m.
and afterwards at
Claridge's.

R.S.V.P
Molton Lodge,
Hamble,
Hampshire.

Mr. John Chancellor &
Mrs. Richard Windsor Clive
request the pleasure of your company
at the marriage of their daughter
Katharine
to
Mr. William Self
at the church of St. Mary-the-Virgin
Nettlecombe, Somerset
on Saturday 10th June 1989
at 1.30 pm
& afterwards at Combe
— RSVP —
Combe, Nettlecombe, Taunton
Somerset TA4 4HS

There is a set wording and lay-out in traditional cards (see illustrations). The text runs: 'Mr and Mrs John Budd request the pleasure of your company/request the honour of your presence at the marriage of their daughter Elizabeth to Mr James Edward Cave at St Michael's Church, Mexforth on (date month year) at (time) and afterwards at (reception location), RSVP (parental address).

The announcement should make clear how the hosts and the bride are related to each other. Death, divorce and remarriage on the bride's side can be accommodated within the arms of tradition as the following examples show.

The bride's mother is a widow: 'Mrs John Brown requests the pleasure of your company at the marriage of her daughter…'

The bride's parents are divorced: 'Mr John Brown and Mrs Veronica Brown request the pleasure of your company at the marriage of their daughter…'

The bride's mother has remarried: 'Mr John Brown and Mrs Lesley Hutt request the pleasure of your company at the marriage of their daughter…'

The bride's mother and step-father are hosts: 'Mr and Mrs Sean Lawley request the pleasure of your company at the marriage of her daughter Elizabeth.' It may be advisable to add the clarification of the bride's surname in this instance.

The bride's single mother is host: 'Helen Todd requests the pleasure...'

The bride or the bride and bridegroom are hosts: 'Miss Polly Datchett... at her marriage to...' or 'Mr Peter Whipple and Miss Polly Datchett request the pleasure of your company at their marriage...'

The bride's proxy parents are hosts: 'Mr and Mrs Kevin Hope request the pleasure of your company at the marriage of Georgia, daughter of the late Dr Robert Cross and Mrs Edina Cross of New York, to...' Alternatively, 'Mr and Mrs Jason Clark request the pleasure of your company at the marriage of his... (niece, ward, god-daughter, cousin) Alice, to...'

Note: Continental Europeans and members of the practising Jewish community send cards in the names of both sets of parents, e.g. 'Dr and Mrs Laurence Starr request the pleasure of your company at the marriage of their daughter Deborah to David, son of Mr and Mrs Sydney Rosen...'

The format and wording of invitations to a wedding reception only or to a Service of Blessing followed by a reception may resemble that of a traditional wedding card.

Respectively, 'Mr and Mrs John Brown request the pleasure of your company at a reception following the marriage of their daughter Vicky to Mr Christopher Clark . . .' 'Mr and Mrs John Brown request the pleasure of your company at a Service of Blessing at St Mary's Church, Bloomgrove, on (date) at (hour) following the marriage of their daughter Patricia to Mr Trevor Green. Afterwards a reception will be held at (address).'

Invitations to wedding receptions only can take any of the forms that apply to parties in general. 'At home' cards, informal wordings, specially printed or ready-printed cards are all suitable.

Addressing invitations and envelopes

The bride's side issue invitations to the wedding six weeks in advance. Plenty of time should be allowed for the delivery of specially ordered cards. Any proof copy should be minutely scrutinized for error before being approved for printing.

In cases where guests are likely to be involved in complicated or distant travel arrangements, it makes sense for notice to be given as soon as possible.

Invitations are dispatched to: the bridegroom's parents (but not to the bridegroom); the best man and ushers; the bridesmaids and bridal attendants; the officiating minister and his wife; and to any friend or acquaintance who has lent a hand with proceedings. The bride's siblings receive cards whether or not they live at home, and of course, all the guests.

Generally, each guest should receive a card. Married couples may share, as do siblings living at the same address.

Guests' names

In the case of a traditional, specially printed or engraved card, the guest's name is handwritten at the top left-hand side of the page. Sometimes, though, the wording requires the name to be included in the announcement. Ready-printed cards are filled in by hand.

Family and close friends are usually addressed informally, e.g. 'Richard and Sandra'. Otherwise guests are given their usual prefixes, e.g. 'Mr and Mrs Paul Picton' or 'Sir Gerald and Lady Shipton' or 'Canon Anthony and Mrs Caswell'. Young children have their names written after those of their parents, e.g. 'Mr and Mrs Paul Picton and Jake and Tabby'.

Note: parents should assume that the invitation is for them alone if their children's names are not specified.

Cards are fitted into their envelopes and sealed. Guests' names and addresses are handwritten.

Wedding presents

A marriage inspires presents from family, friends and supporters. Offerings both given and exchanged are an historic aspect of the wedding celebrations. Traditionally, presents to a marrying couple are chosen to help them over the hurdle of setting up home. Today, although the bride's list may cover numerous special indulgences, the presents usually centre on the time-honoured trinity of linen, china and glass.

The bridegroom's side

The bridegroom customarily produces an engagement ring for his betrothed, and her wedding ring. He also chooses thank-you keepsakes for the bridesmaids, which he delivers before the wedding.

The bridegroom's mother, if she so wishes, presents her prospective daughter-in-law with a memento – traditionally a piece of jewellery such as a brooch or pair of earrings.

The bride's side

The bride may wish to exchange presents with her fiancé and give him a commemorative token. Her parents also may like the idea of paying their future son-in-law the compliment of giving him a memento. They customarily produce, in addition, a present for the couple.

Exceptional family presents

The responsibilities that are incurred by marriage have long persuaded well-to-do and generous parents to make a significant bequest to their offspring. If given by father to daughter it is the equivalent of a dowry, even if the word is never mentioned. The gesture can take many different forms, from the leasehold of a house, or a down payment on a house, or a weekend cottage, to stocks and shares, or the transfer of valuable family assets such as pictures or furniture. Among families with good jewellery, the tradition is to bestow some personal pieces on the bride for use at the wedding and after.

The bride's list

A sound lead on the selection of artefacts and equipment for the household was given by William Morris: 'Have nothing in your houses that you do not know to be useful or believe to be beautiful.'

Approaches to organizing a wedding list have become a good deal more professional than formerly. When a couple are asked by wedding guests what they would like, a list offers dispensation from the usual code of politeness that demands a suitably vague response; a list may quote item, size, brand number and any other specifications.

Whereas the method may cramp the style of perceptive present givers, or annoy some others, the procedure has in its favour that it minimizes the likelihood of duplication of offerings.

The form is for the marrying couple to place a list of choices for presents at one or more department stores offering a service to brides. Sometimes couples like to make one of the suppliers a specialist, such as a craft or kitchen shop or a wine merchant. Also, in the case where the prospective bride or groom is based abroad, it could be convenient for a list to be placed at a store in their city or locality.

A bride's list should contain a wide range of options as far as purpose, design and price are concerned in order to accommodate those who wish to give grandly or modestly. If a major investment such as a dinner service is requested, the couple may suggest that friends choose individual components as presents. In this way the whole service can be collected piece by piece.

When an item is ordered from the shop, the sales assistant deletes it from the list. Brides' lists are usually made available shortly before the wedding invitations are posted, and kept open for several weeks after the wedding for the sake of belated benefactors. The service usually includes the provision of a card for givers' messages, and packing and mailing and delivery.

Givers and abstainers

As a general rule, every guest who accepts an invitation to the wedding gives a present. If regrets are sent there is no obligation to produce an offering, though many will wish to do so for reasons of personal ties.

Presents dispatched before the wedding are addressed to the bride and often sent for convenience's sake to the bride's parents. Those sent after the wedding are addressed to husband and wife and sent to their address.

The habit of bringing a present to the wedding reception is not to be recommended. Small objects in particular can easily be mislaid or identification tags lost amidst the celebrations and the giver is left wondering why they never received an acknowledgement.

Presents are accompanied by cards addressed to the bride and bridegroom, bearing messages of goodwill and congratulation, written by hand, and signed by the giver, e.g. 'To Posy and Jim, with our love and fond wishes for your lasting happiness, from Kim and Jerry'.

The bride's mother

The mother of the bride usually acts as a clearing house for presents, spreads the word on the whereabouts of the bride's list, advises friends on appropriate choices and takes charge of any deliveries.

Thank-yous

One way in which the couple can show their appreciation of a present is to send a prompt, thoughtful thank-you letter. An immediate acknowledgement also enables recipients to keep an orderly record. In the usual pre-nuptial rush, it is all too easy to lose track of who sent the duvet cover and who the pillow cases.

Letters or cards of thanks should be handwritten. Cards with ready-printed wordings may save time but they are impersonal.

Letters should be personal and in conveying thanks contain some convincing remarks on the usefulness/charm/beauty of the offering. They may be written by either the bride or bridegroom, the tendency being for the partner closest to the giver to be responsible for writing.

A timeless dilemma requiring great tact is when a present fails to please or duplicates another. Can one suggest an exchange to the giver? As a general rule it is rash to assume that givers won't take offence if asked to swop their offering, however politely the point is put. Duplication offers a more reasonable excuse however, and it would be a thoughtful gesture for the couple to offer to undertake any chores in connection with the transaction.

Note: a receipt or proof of purchase will probably be required by the shop if goods are to be exchanged.

Unless there is sound reason to suppose that the friend or relation will take the request in good part, it is probably safer to stay mum and pass the white elephant on to a good home at the earliest opportunity.

A *display of presents*

A custom that seems to be losing its hold is for the bride's family to display all the wedding presents for guests' viewing at the wedding reception.

Offering many levels of satisfaction to family and guest alike, the display propitiated guests' curiosity about what old Uncle Sam sent, and, no doubt, the prospect of your few humble teaspoons being surrounded by grander offerings tended to encourage generous giving.

Few bother with the idea now, and fewer still in the present climate of opinion which denigrates such shows of conspicuous wealth. But some families like to keep up the tradition which may have local roots.

Caution: owners should take out insurance as items on display do have a habit of walking. Whilst we are on the subject, insurance should be taken out on any substantial cache of wedding presents. This applies even if a parent or friend has offered to caretake during the honeymoon.

A *cancelled wedding*

In the event of a cancelled wedding, wedding presents sent by guests are returned by the bride with letters of thanks. Detailed explanations are not necessary.

See page 100 for Announcement of a cancelled wedding.

Among the first to be notified of a cancellation should be the management of those shops where the bride's list is placed.

Wedding photography

A balance has to be struck between the marrying couple's eagerness to acquire a memorable set of wedding photographs and the dignity of the marriage ceremony. It is important for the bride and bridegroom to discuss their ideas on the subject fully with the officiating minister or the Registrar. The authorities' views may not coincide with the couple's. If a place of worship is small in scale, the minister may consider that a professional photographer would be intrusive. Similarly, no photographs may be taken during the actual marriage ceremony at a register office. These restraints also apply to video cameramen.

As a general rule, reasonable requests for permission for professional photographers to be given access to a building or event are granted with the proviso that their presence will not compromise the solemnity or privacy of the occasion. Guests who bring cameras are advised to use them with discretion or risk turning the nuptials into a fashion shoot.

Choosing a photographer

Wedding photography has come to mean much more than a formal portrait or a few snapshots. Beyond any other memento, photographs evoke the reality of the occasion. For one thing, they often enable people to see the event in close-up for the first time. Charming, humorous, odd, peculiar, romantic and truthful details emerge which the participants may have barely noticed on the day.

Therefore the choice of a wedding photographer calls for discriminating forethought. It is not bad manners in the least for a potential customer to ask a photographer to produce a portfolio of their latest prints and colour transparencies. This will give an idea of their usual range of work and preferred styles. A photographer does not have to specialize in weddings in order to take interesting pictures of the occasion. However, a local professional specialist will offer the advantage of contacts with the various religious authorities or the Superintendent Registrar, and should be familiar with all the wedding reception places.

Nationally known photographers whose work is published or exhibited may be approached by clients wishing to commission wedding photography. Like any other professionals, they will consider a promising assignment, but the wedding would have to catch their interest for some particular reason. In any case, fees are likely to be considerable.

Should a personal friend who is a professional be asked to take pictures, it is unwise to assume that they will be happy to work for love. Fees should be offered and paid, and waived only if the photographer shows a genuine desire to offer the pictures as a wedding present.

Another factor to be borne in mind is that a congenial personality stands a better chance of being able to control his subjects without upsetting anyone, and of coaxing natural attitudes out of people in somewhat contrived situations.

Once decided upon, the photographer should be given a clear brief on the pictures he is expected to shoot, with names of the chief participants, and notice given of any prevailing awkwardness within the family.

Briefing the photographer

All professional photographers will have their own ideas on subjects for good pictures but if they specialize in weddings they will be able to advise on possibilities and any problems.

At a big wedding it is usual to employ two photographers, one for the formal group shots and the other for reportage shots of the whole occasion.

Certain pictures have an honoured place in formal portraiture: the group in which the bride and bridegroom, both sets of parents, the best man and the bridal attendants appear; the bride and bridegroom as a double portrait; the bride alone.

There are significant moments during the ceremony and reception which provide opportunities for evocative pictures. These might include: the bride leaving home; the bride arriving at and leaving the place of worship; the signing of the register in the vestry or (in a simulated scene) at the register office. At the reception further situations to be covered are: the speeches and toasts, the cake-cutting ceremony, the 'going away'.

It must be remembered that photographers are not magicians. Prevailing light conditions both in and out of doors, the state of the weather for all outdoor shots, and especially the leading participants' willingness to give the photographer sufficient time and co-operation to do a good job, will all have a crucial effect on the outcome. Reportage pictures often catch the spirit of the occasion much more neatly than the posed shots. Asides, and quirks of human behaviour, can be caught by an observant photographer. Among the set-piece situations that might be covered are the following: guests arriving at the church and leaving after the ceremony; the receiving line; the bride and bridegroom circulating among the gathering; there is no shortage of subjects.

Black and white film is the medium of reportage photography and many memorable portraits of well known public figures by recognized photographers are in black and white.

A video of the nuptials

Recording the wedding on video is becoming increasingly popular and many commercial firms are prepared to undertake the commission. The subjects for coverage are similar to those of still photography, namely the highlights of the day. But obviously a movie comes into its own in recording action.

A qualification is that some participants may take the view that a video camera is an unwarranted intrusion at the wedding ceremony. Among them may well be the vicar, especially if his church is small and offers few private vantage points from which the cameraman can work discreetly.

Who pays for photography

The bride's side customarily pays for wedding photography, but the question may arise of who among the bridal party should be given prints? There are no fixed rules on this. It would be thoughtful to make a present of a set of prints to the bride, asking her to make her own choices from the contacts. A similar gesture would go down well with the parents of the bridegroom, taking care to include one flattering likeness of their son!

If members of the wedding wish to order in large numbers they should most certainly offer and expect to pay for the prints. Among the leading participants who would no doubt appreciate a present of a print are the bridal attendants, the best man, the ushers and anyone who has made a special contribution towards the success of the occasion. The gesture is a time-honoured way of saying thank you.

Also, absent friends or relations who may have sent wedding presents are often rewarded with a photograph as a memento. Photographers sometimes take orders for prints at the reception, which can be an embarrassment for guests. They may find it hard to say they are not interested in a shot of one of the grown-up bridesmaids when raising a convivial glass with her mother. There is certainly no obligation on a guest to order photographs.

The wedding ring

The wedding ring is the symbol of the marriage contract, a pledge given by the man affirming his commitment. The Romans are said to have introduced the custom to Britain: early records tell of rings made of iron (liked by the Romans), steel, copper, brass, leather and rush. As a significant piece of jewellery the wedding ring has aroused the ire of both Church and State. Cromwellian puritans frowned on the symbol as popish and the Church of Scotland marriage service ignored the wedding ring in earlier times. The custom came out of hiding with the return of the Royalists in 1660 and has been with us ever since.

Ring traditions

Wedding rings today are usually of gold or platinum and are worn on the fourth finger of the left hand. This custom has numerous legends attached to its origin, of which the most piquant is the belief that an emblematic nerve runs from that finger to the heart.

The wedding ring is rarely removed, even on death. On the occasion of divorce, opinion varies on whether the ring stays but the tendency is to remove it. When a woman marries again, in any case, she discards the symbol of a former commitment in order to make way for a newly received token.

Whether a man receives a wedding ring depends on his country of origin, the customs of his family and friends, and, perhaps, on his own preference and that of his wife. It is customary for men from the Continent and elsewhere overseas to wear a wedding ring but no corresponding tradition exists in this country.

Ring design

A wedding ring, usually spoken of as a band of gold, takes innumerable forms. It can be of any width or weight to suit the tastes of the recipient, be a remarkable object or in the plainest design.

The custom of giving a personal meaning to the token remains popular. The inner surface can be engraved with the couple's initials, a monogram or names, or sometimes an inscription of lasting sentiment is chosen.

Ring refusal

There is nothing untoward about a married woman preferring not to wear a wedding ring, but the general approach is to take pride in wearing the token of marriage. However, should the marriage service require her to receive a ring from the bridegroom, she will be expected to comply with the rite.

Wedding flowers

Flowers enhance any occasion, and in particular a wedding, with their beauty, freshness and scent. They also offer skilled flower arrangers, whether amateur or professional, a first-class chance to make the most of their talents. Ideally, flowers should be part of the vista wherever the bride goes.

The bride's bouquet

The flowers worn and carried by the bride are chosen by her with a view to complementing her overall effects. Naturally, she will consider the flowers she likes best if they are in season or are available within the budget but matters such as the style of the wedding dress and any colours she is wearing will influence decisions. There are many different types of bridal bouquet, and fashion itself plays a part. A bouquet may be a countrified posy, a sheaf of blooms, a careful arrangement, a basket of flowers, a single stunning stem or be made without flowers, of foliage, berries, grasses and ferns. Dried flowers too can make a lasting memento. The bride's veil may be held in place by a crown of flowers which according to folklore includes orange blossom.

Flowers for members of the wedding

Whereas it is traditional for the men in the wedding party to sport a buttonhole (the bridegroom, the fathers, the best man and ushers) it is a matter of personal preference only for the mothers.

For the men, a white or red carnation or a rose is popular, but there are many possibilities. The flower chosen should have some strength to its life or it may wilt before the day is out. A pleasing option is for the bridegroom to choose a flower that also appears in the bride's bouquet, or a sprig of heather for luck, or a sprig from his or her parents' garden.

The bride sets the mood for the bridesmaids' choice of flowers. Bridesmaids usually include flowers in their personal adornment but much depends on the total picture that is being created by the bridal procession.

Flowers at the place of worship

It is important to discuss the question of the position of the flower arrangements at the place of worship with the minister. Some clergymen will allow the altar to be decorated, others are strongly opposed on grounds of sacrilege.

The usual positions for flower arrangements are the chancel steps, the window sills, the pew-ends. During popular months for weddings, it is possible that another marriage service may be held in the place of worship on the same day. In this case the two brides should contact each other in order to discuss the flowers and perhaps arrange to share costs.

After the ceremony and following the forthcoming Sunday Service, the flowers should be distributed to a deserving cause such as a hospital, an old people's home or wherever they may be appreciated.

Flowers at the reception

Flower arrangements depend on the venue and the programme. It is pleasant for guests waiting in line to be able to admire an arrangement of flowers set out in an entrance hall, and arrangements may suit a top table and vantage-points in the room where the reception is held. Marquees present a problem, but this can be overcome with hanging baskets of flowers and arrangements on individual tables.

Flowers are frequently used to bestow an air of festivity and charm upon halls, rooms and spaces which without them might look rather bleak and inhospitable.

Choosing a florist

Word of mouth or direct personal experience is by far the best method of choosing a florist as standards of service in a given district may vary considerably. Choosing flowers for the wedding depends on seasonal availability and costs – bought flowers can be alarmingly expensive.

A professional florist will be able to give much better service if fully briefed by the bride's side: as much information as possible should be provided on colours, choices, preferences and prejudices. Fabric samples are useful, too.

If the order is considerable, the florist may wish to visit or revisit the place of worship or register office and the reception venue.

If a hall or rooms are being hired for the reception, flowers are often included in a total package. The service of the florist concerned should be looked into by anyone who hopes that the flowers will be especially attractive. There is also the possibility of sharing costs with a bride who is holding a reception in the same place on the day before or the following day.

A far from unusual predicament is when the florist delivers flowers that do not exactly correspond to the bride's order, for example with the pink of the rose petals far deeper than suits her complexion or the dress.

If sufficient time is allowed a reputable firm will try to supply acceptable alternatives, but this may depend on the luck of availability.

Church procedures

It is important for the bride and bridegroom to discuss their ideas for the marriage service fully with the officiating minister. Their suggestions for the order of service, flower display and programme of music, among many other points, must meet with his approval.

Giving time and thought to choosing the pieces of music to be played is worth every second as the composition should express all the emotions conjured up by marriage. Music can change the mood from solemnity to celebration, which is the order of the day. In a small parish the standards may not match the bride's aspirations. In this case, the question should be discreetly raised with the clergyman as to using outside talent without offending local feelings.

The placing of flower arrangements should be talked over as the majority of ministers hold strong views here. It is a pleasing idea for a small vase of flowers to be placed in the vestry where the register is signed, but the minister's approval must be gained.

See page 87 for Wedding flowers.

Whether or not photography and recording equipment will be permitted during the service should be discussed before any bookings are made. In a small church or chapel, either may justifiably be regarded as intrusive.

The couple may have a relative or a close friend who is a member of the clergy or a college or school chaplain whom they would like to conduct the marriage service. Obviously, the incumbent clergyman should be consulted on the matter before any such invitations are issued.

Church fees

Fees are paid by the bridegroom to the minister. It is customary for these to be paid in advance, usually by the best man on behalf of the bridegroom shortly before the ceremony begins. Fees are not paid to visiting clergy but a thoughtful present would be in order.

Fees are usually paid to the organist of the parish. Sometimes his fee is combined in a 'package' with those of the minister, choirmaster and choir and bellringers. If a video camera is recording during the service, the fees of the organist and choir are usually doubled.

Order of Service sheet

An Order of Service sheet offers guidance to the congregation in several ways. It sets out the hymns, psalms, readings and prayers with attributions, which have been chosen by the couple to celebrate their marriage. It contains reminders about when to remain standing, when to be seated and when to kneel in prayer. The programme of music is given, with titles of the compositions and the composers. The names of the principal participants are listed – the officiating clergyman, those who give readings and any soloist musician or singer.

The format is an upright white or cream card, folded in half like a booklet. The front is printed with the name of the place of worship, the date and year of the wedding and the initials or Christian names of the marrying pair. The Order of Service is printed on the inside only.

The wedding reception

The marriage ceremony is traditionally followed by a wedding reception. The bride's family provide hospitality and entertainment to the wedding guests as a send-off to the newly-weds. The party enables the two families and their allies to meet on friendly ground, thanks to be expressed and hospitality to be offered as some recompense for the support and generosity of the assembly. It introduces the bride and bridegroom respectively to each other's family circle and hopefully ensures that the first few hours of married life are filled with congratulations and gestures of affection.

Despite the undoubted challenges involved in entertaining a group of people who probably do not have much in common apart from their association with the newly-weds, a happy reception knits together many disparate elements. Friendships between individuals who might not otherwise have come across each other are founded, old rivalries tempered, romances born, generation gaps leapt over, long-lost friends reunited, and relations restored to the family circle.

Variations on a theme

A party celebrating a marriage ceremony takes many different forms, custom more and more frequently bowing to circumstance. Many couples celebrate with a small family gathering following the marriage ceremony, such as a lunch or drinks party. A party to which numbers are invited may be held at a later date, perhaps with the newly-weds themselves as hosts. Or the bride and bridegroom may elect to follow a formal wedding reception held during the day with a party which they give themselves in the evening. There are innumerable variations to enable newly-weds to celebrate their marriage in a style which is appropriate and which suits their circumstances.

Who is invited

Everyone who is invited to the marriage ceremony is also asked to the party that follows. The converse does not necessarily apply. Sometimes only a small gathering can attend the ceremony for one reason or another and further numbers are invited to a reception.

The officiating minister should receive an invitation to the reception, and also his wife if he has one. The same applies to family, friends or acquaintances who have made a special contribution to the wedding.

The question of whether professionals who have been employed to give their services should be included in the guest list depends on the relationship between them and the bride and bridegroom and their families. Few florists or caterers would expect to be on the guest list, unless they have a personal link. However, the kind neighbour who supplies flowers from her garden or whose offer of accommodation for wedding guests is accepted might with justification feel piqued if excluded from the festivities.

Planning the reception

Important points to check in connection with the place at which the reception will be held include adequate cloakroom and lavatory provision, facilities for guests with disabilities and those in a wheelchair, clear instructions about car parking arrangements, and the provision of seating for guests who may be tired or elderly or frail when the reception does not include a sit-down meal.

An economy note is that it is sometimes possible to share the costs of the flower display if they are being used for some other function.

The bride's side as hosts

The bride's family is formally responsible for making all the arrangements and paying the costs of the wedding reception including: the food and drink and the wedding cake; the caterers; any staff on duty; the toastmaster; the photographer; the flower arrangements; any musicians or entertainers; the disco; any security arrangements or insurance premiums.

It is also the task of the bride's side to arrange and pay the costs of transport in conveying everyone who travelled to the church from the bride's house, to the reception. Correctly, the bridegroom's side is supposed to settle the costs of transport for himself and the bride from the church to the reception.

How far hosts are responsible for the comfort and convenience of their guests takes on special significance at a wedding.

By the nature of the occasion some guests will be required to travel long distances in order to witness the marriage. The location of the wedding may be in some remote part of the country or be inconveniently located for accessible public transport services.

A good host goes to a great deal of trouble to ensure contented guests, but he is not responsible for paying their fares or hotel accommodation. That's not to say that if his pocket permits he will not provide private transport such as a hired coach or minibus for the transportation of guests for all or part of the journey.

If people are expected from far afield they should be sent local travel information such as the locations of the nearest/most reliable rail or underground station, coach station or airport, and the names and telephone numbers of local minicab and taxi services and hire car firms. A considerate host will provide a check list of local hotels and pubs able to offer accommodation, taking care to include a range of price levels. Motorists will be thankful for a map giving directions to the place of worship and the reception locality with details of parking arrangements, if any.

Entertaining the bridegroom's side

The bride's side do their best to ensure that the bridegroom's side are well looked after over the nuptials. In cases where the wedding is to take place far from their home base, the bride's family usually try to arrange accommodation and hospitality on their behalf in the neighbourhood.

Entertaining the chief bridesmaid

See page 71 for The chief bridesmaid and bridal attendants.

If space and all else permits, it is customary to invite the chief bridesmaid to stay at the bride's home for the wedding.

The country house wedding

See page 95 for A grand country dance.

At a big country wedding, the bride's side may ask wedding guests whether they would like to be included in a houseparty. Friends of the bride's family who live locally may be willing to put up unknowns as well as old friends. A judicious bride's mother will take care in matching guest to houseparty hostess.

The entertainment

For those who wish to push the boat out, wedding parties offer unrivalled opportunities for flights of inspired extravagance and fancy. The occasion may be a sequence of celebrations such as a wedding reception followed by a dinner and dance for all the wedding guests.

Many a wedding reception has been immeasurably enlivened by music. It may be classical or pop, but it should be light enough to appeal to a varied age group, and never loud enough to offend. The musicians may be members of a string quartet or a jazz band, but whatever musical programme is chosen the pieces should reflect the taste of the bride and bridegroom, bearing in mind the nature of the occasion.

As far as most hosts are concerned, there is at any rate an obligation to provide wedding guests with food and drink. The scope varies from a sit-down wedding breakfast consisting of three or four courses accompanied by several good wines to canapés and champagne (or a champagne substitute).

At an afternoon reception it is always a good idea to offer a cup of tea as well, and a supply of non-alcoholic drinks is essential at whatever hour the party is held.

Where to hold the reception

Wedding receptions take place in any accommodation that is suitable for a good party. Ideally, the party and going away ceremony takes place in the bride's home of childhood but few parents can measure up to these expectations. It is more likely that the reception will be held at a hotel, at banqueting rooms, a restaurant, or hired premises that range from village hall to stately home. Members of clubs with appropriate clubhouses or accommodation may be able to hire rooms and engage staff for the occasion. The club secretary will advise.

A party at home

Several hard questions have to be answered before giving a wedding reception at home, other than a very small affair. Are distances from place of worship or register office a realistic proposition for guests? Is there sufficient space to accommodate comfortably the number of people expected? Are lavatory and cloakroom arrangements adequate? If a wedding breakfast is to be provided, could either caterers or whoever else may be doing the work function effectively in the kitchen? Is there space for a bar? Can cars be parked in the vicinity? Are taxi services available?

On the credit side, there is tradition. It is a symbolic gesture for the daughter of the house to leave home as a married woman. Also, if there is a pretty garden and lawn, what more could either bride or guest desire on a fine summer's day? However, uninvited neighbours may not necessarily take the same view. They should be notified of the event in advance, as a matter of courtesy.

Choosing a caterer

Sufficient time in which to compare catering services and estimates is important, as caterers with a good reputation tend to get booked up months in advance. Customers should obtain at least three estimates before making a final decision. All orders should be confirmed in writing.

In the absence of any previous knowledge of the firm, references should be asked for and taken up. If the caterer runs a restaurant or hotel, try to order a meal on the premises. One guideline is to take note of the general punctiliousness and care in the management of your order and of your enquiries.

A caterer will need to know the date and time of the reception, numbers of guests, the level of hospitality to be provided, and limits on charges per head. As these are usually on a per capita basis the numbers of guests confirmed will be charged for, whether they appear or not.

Drink supplies

Wine and spirits are usually provided on a sale or return basis; a more important consideration is the amount of drink per head that the caterers are authorized by the host to provide. A parsimonious approach is ill-advised as it runs counter to the spirit of the occasion but some compromise will have to be reached between total liberality and the soaring costs of providing it.

An average of half a bottle of wine per head is a usual calculation, but serious drinkers will disparage this limit and abstainers may perceive Bacchanalian dissipation in the measure. In general, drinking at parties is decreasing because guests who are driving home sensibly don't want to take any risks.

The wedding reception has no great reputation for providing especially good or interesting tipple. Any host who is knowledgeable about wine and has guests likely to appreciate vintage or producer would do the occasion a great service.

Choosing the menu

Caterers are likely to have standard menus at fixed prices but it is always worth asking about special orders. One of the problems inherent in the catering is the need to satisfy so many disparate palates: dieters, vegetarians, gourmets, children, are among the incompatibles as well as the bride's own preferences. The safe answers tend to be stereotyped which is no doubt why wedding reception food has little reputation for imagination.

A few guidelines: fresh food in season is always the best value. Ideally an alternative to a main course should be provided for meat eaters or non-meat eaters as the case may be. Hot food is likely to give greater pleasure than chilled food, if well chosen. If buffet service is decided upon, a number of dishes is preferable to offering one main item such as a York ham, or roast turkey or salmon with limited accompaniments.

A dance at the nuptials

As a celebration a dance offers an unrivalled opportunity to extend festivities. Dances are held in the ballroom of a big hotel, or can take place in village hall or green. The few who have houses with a ballroom, or space where a dance floor could be laid, or grounds where a marquee for the dance could be set up, rarely have a better excuse to put their good fortune to excellent use.

The usual form, however, is to hold a dance at a big hotel and to provide dinner for all the guests. Sometimes only the members of the wedding are invited to dinner and guests are invited for 9.30 or 10 pm.

Invitations to the dance are often separate from the wedding card. They stipulate whether black tie is to be worn or indicate by the word 'Informal' that formal evening attire is optional.

A grand country dance

Invitations to a grand nuptial dance at a big country house may or may not include dinner for all the guests. Invitations may be timed for 10 pm and guests may be expected to find their own accommodation and make their own transport arrangements to and from the house. Sometimes guests are asked if they would like to be included in a houseparty in the neighbourhood where the host will be going on to the dance.

As many more people are likely to be invited to the dance than attended the wedding, a separate invitation may be sent. Sometimes the dance is given by the couple themselves and invitations are issued in their single names.

Hospitality offered depends as elsewhere on the generosity of the hosts. A dance in a private house is likely to go on until dawn and a late (or very early) cooked breakfast is on the list of attractions. The couple may dance until the small hours, stay the night at the house where the party is held or depart with a formal 'going away' ceremony shortly after midnight.

Once again, decisions on music should appeal across the generations if the dance is to go with a swing. One way is to have more than one band but no one is suggesting this as an economy measure.

Wedding breakfast seating plans

The seating plan for the bridal party at the wedding breakfast is based on the principle of the unity of the two families and their chief supporters. The leading males on one side appear in public partnering the leading females from the other camp.

Whichever family members are involved, this practice holds good. Divorce, remarriage and the presence of step-parents may necessitate changes in the old order, but tact and partners found for unaccompanied members can usually gloss over any problems.

The lay-out of the tables is a matter of personal preference. Some like the idea of an elongated top table at which the bridal party and chief guests are seated (if the officiating minister is present he is always seated at the top table).

A unifying idea is to try to seat all the guests at one table. An arrangement which provides a surprising amount of seating is to have the usual long top table with an extension added at either end, set at right angles to the main table and parallel with each other. Guests can be seated on either side of the table space.

Others may prefer to have a top table together with several smaller tables. These could have place-cards or guests could sit where they please.

Note: however informally arranged the party may be, it is as well to have place-cards at the top table so there is no dithering among the honoured guests.

Top table plan involving both sets of parents: (left to right) chief bridesmaid, bridegroom's father, bride's mother, bridegroom, bride, bride's father, groom's father, and best man.

Table plan to include step-parents for both bride and bridegroom.

A top table plan including both sets of parents

The bride and bridegroom occupy centre stage in the tableau. The bride's place is at the right of the bridegroom. On her right side is seated her father, on his right is seated the mother of the bridegroom. On her right sits the best man. On the bridegroom's left sits the mother of the bride, on her left sits the bridegroom's father and on his left sits the chief bridesmaid.

In the event of a double wedding, the elder bride takes precedence and sits between her bridegroom and her father.

The wedding cake

The cutting of the wedding cake usually takes place before the toasts and speeches, but some prefer the ceremony to conclude proceedings. Whichever order is chosen, the ceremony is announced by the best man or toastmaster.

The wedding cake is given pride of place on a table at the reception, and usually reposes on a silver stand on a white tablecloth. As a symbolic gesture of fruitfulness, the bride cuts the first side of the first slice of wedding cake. Taking up a silver knife (or, as some traditionalists prefer, a sword), she cuts through the

crust of white icing which is usually resistant to pressure. Aided by the bridegroom who places his hand over hers, together they lever the implement through the cake.

Afterwards the cake is cut up into small pieces and handed round to the guests. People who don't particularly enjoy cake in the usual way make an effort to consume a crumb or two in the interests of goodwill.

Note: among families whose newborn will be baptized there is a tradition of keeping the top layer of a tiered plum cake to offer at the christening party.

Souvenir cake

Little pieces of wedding cake are sometimes dispatched as a memento for absent friends. Diminutive cake boxes for the purpose are available which protect the contents in the mail. The custom is to send a small slice of the whole cake (cut to fit the box) with icing, marzipan and all, and to include a card with a message of love and the names of the senders.

A break with tradition

The traditional rich fruit wedding cake mixture has rivals in the favours of many brides. Some prefer a big iced chocolate confection which, in addition to a popular flavour, has the aesthetic bonus of contrasting white icing and silver decorations with a chocolate brown mixture. Plenty of table napkins to hand, please, should the cake be rich and sticky.

A wedding cake can represent the interests, hobbies and associations of the couple. The design can take the form of a monogram, or be made in the shape of a boat for keen sailors, or be decorated in any way that echoes the couple's interests.

Children at the wedding reception

Children are a welcome element in the guest list at a wedding reception, as marriage is about founding a new family unit. Older children are expected to form part of the line of guests that are greeted by the bridal party and to shake hands. School-age youngsters mingle on adult terms with the guests and are offered a glass of champagne if they enjoy it.

Children tend to form their own party if given half a chance, and rush about making adult guests feel overly sedate. A bridesmaid who is known to some of the younger members might usefully be detailed to help to keep them amused. As far as young children especially are concerned, arrangements should be made for them to be able to play and let off steam, especially if they have sat through the service in church. Their interests should also be borne in mind when planning a menu or offering refreshments at the party.

At a wedding breakfast, children are expected to sit at the table and share the menu – though here again their food tastes might be considered when planning the menu. If there is dancing, they will take to the floor solo or in twos or hop, skip and dance wherever they may.

Parents are likely to be involved in a delicate balance of considerations: if their child becomes unhappy or restive, at what point do they do the decent thing in the interests of the party and whisk him (or her) away, when this means they will have to take their leave as well? Guests should make every allowance for excitable small fry whether they are their own or not, but draw the line when their behaviour begins to disrupt the harmony of the occasion.

Parents may find themselves having to invent some plausible explanation for why their offspring was not chosen as a bridal attendant – a love of playing star roles seems to start young. Truth is always a defence; try with reassurances that wedding guests are exceedingly important, which they are too and that there will be other opportunities.

Wedding announcements

Formal announcements of a wedding spread the word and are part of the record. Officially, the mother of the bride places the announcements of marriage in the local and/or national press, but in practice members of either side of the family do so. The wording usually follows a set form with variations depending on the amount of information to be given and personal preference.

Published announcements appear in the Births, Marriages and Deaths columns of national and local newspapers, and in the court and social page of national newspapers. In the latter instance, the text must be submitted to the social editor. *The Times*, the *Daily Telegraph*, the *Independent*, *The Scotsman* and *Yorkshire Post* all have a widely read social gazette.

It is courteous for the bride's side (responsible for placing the wedding announcement) to liaise with the bridegroom's family about the wording and date of publication. Opposite are various examples of wedding announcements:

A short announcement in the personal columns

> *Jones:Brown.* On 21 May, Robert Jones of Runcorn, to Katy Brown of Bayswater, London, at St Anselm's Church, Middington.

An announcement as above giving fuller details

> *Prichard:Morgan.* The marriage took place in Reigate on 5 August of John Prichard, elder son of the late Dr M.B. Prichard of Basingstoke and Mrs Alice Prichard of Eastbourne, and Anne Catherine, younger daughter of Mr and Mrs Stephen Morgan of Bromsgrove.

A standard wording for an announcement for the Court columns of a national newspaper

> *Mr G.E. Timmus*
> *Miss J.B. Rendle*
> The marriage took place at Pulborough, Sussex, on 14 June, of Gordon, only son of Mr and Mrs Richard Timmus of Stoke-on-Trent, and Jane, daughter of Mr and Mrs Alan Rendle of East Grinstead, Sussex.

A detailed announcement for publication in the Court columns

> *Mr I.B. Fenston*
> *and Miss A. Munster*
> The marriage took place at St Michael's Church, New Muxton on 6 April of Mr Ian Bernard Fenston, younger son of Mr and Mrs Ivor Fenston of Edinburgh, and Miss Alexandra Munster, daughter of Mr and Mrs T.H. Munster of Bath. The Rev. Brian Fielding officiated. The bride, who was given in marriage by her father, wore a gown of cream chiffon and a veil held in place by a chaplet of pearls. Tracy Munster, Rosemary Letts and Paul Barker attended her. Mr Pierre Ronsard was best man. A reception was held at Wyck Hall and the honeymoon will be spent abroad.

Note: it is customary to give the style of address of the bride and bridegroom.

An announcement of a register office marriage followed by a Service of Blessing for publication in either the Court and personal columns:

> *Mr T. Katz*
> *and Mrs Alison Payne*
> The marriage took place in Glasgow of Mr Tom Katz and Mrs Alison Payne, followed by a Service of Blessing at St Anselm's Church. The Rev. Colin Burrows officiated.
> *Note:* it is not necessary to give the name of the register office.

An announcement of a Service of Blessing as above
Mr S.O. Winter
and Miss K.B. Lomax
A Service of Blessing was held on 21 May at Christ's Church, Chelston,
of the marriage of Mr Scott Winter, elder son of Mr and Mrs Ian Winter
of Chelston, Wessex, and Miss Katia Lomax, only daughter of the late
Mr Neville Lomax and of Mrs Lesley Lomax of Potters Bar,
Hertfordshire. The Rev. Miles Bright officiated.

Private wedding announcements

When the couple have a wide circle of friends and colleagues, a convenient way of
notifying people is to have a wedding announcement specially printed on a card
combined with an address notice.

An example:

Michael Miller and Georgia Smith have much pleasure in announcing that
they were married in London and are living at 15 Glanville Grove, Manchester.

The cancelled or postponed wedding

Weddings are postponed or called off for endless reasons, all of them causing
dismay and upset. It is the bride's side's responsibility to make the necessary
announcements, and either to cancel or postpone orders for any goods or services
connected with the nuptials.

Decisiveness and speed are of the essence. The officiating minister should
be taken into the confidence of the bride's family. Guests should be notified by
telephone or letter, and wedding presents returned if the wedding is cancelled
rather than postponed. Outside the circle of family and close friends, there is no
need for explanations.

If the wedding is cancelled the shops at which the bride's list is placed
should be notified as soon as possible.

Announcements of a cancelled wedding

It is usual, if an announcement of the couple's engagement to marry has been
published in a newspaper, to place notice of the cancellation in that publication.

A *short notice*

The marriage arranged between Miss Lisa Phillips and Mr Francis
Byford will not take place.

or

Mr and Mrs A.D. Phillips regret to announce that the marriage arranged
between their daughter, Lisa, and Mr Francis Byford will not take place.

How to be a wedding guest

Weddings need to be witnessed, hence the importance of the wedding guest. Being a guest at the nuptials is to take part in a ceremony which time has touched but lightly. It is an invitation to be both solemn and joyful, to give and to receive, and to help make the day memorable.

The wedding invitation

An invitation to a wedding should be answered promptly as advance knowledge of numbers is of more than usual importance to the hosts. A wedding is one of the ace invitations in the social pack which friends worth the name do their utmost to honour. Regrets need to sound convincing, especially if coming from intimates.

See page 77 for Wedding invitations.

Replies should be written by hand, put in a sealed envelope and, by custom, addressed to the mother of the bride as hostess. Some people have relaxed this convention and reply to both hosts. Replies are written in the third person or written informally, depending on what has to be said.

Acceptance implies attendance: last-minute cancellations should be relayed to the hosts, where possible.

The often-asked question of whether it is acceptable to bring an uninvited friend has to be that it is unwise to chance your luck in this direction. However, in special circumstances, the request can be put to the hosts, but offence should not be taken if the answer is a negative.

Wedding presents

The old rule holds good. Everyone who accepts an invitation to the wedding produces a present. If regrets are sent, there is no obligation to send a present, but many will wish to do so for reasons of personal ties.

See page 80 for Wedding presents.

What to wear

A surprisingly wide range of clothes is apparent among wedding guests. In general, people put on their Sunday best out of respect for the occasion and the customs of the church. Those, and there are many today, with an aversion to the formalities of dressing-up put on their usual clothes without compunction. A useful indication of the expected level of dress is the chosen attire of the bridegroom: a morning suit suggests that guests are expected to rise to the occasion sartorially.

Female guests

The clothes chosen by a female guest are likely to be determined by what she has in her wardrobe and the scope of the celebrations that follow the religious service. Dancing at the nuptials, a drinks party or a country picnic might each have a different bearing on her choice. Also, questions of decorum need to be borne in mind if the marriage is held at a place of worship.

Whether to wear a hat or be hatless is a matter of personal preference only, and the requirements of the outfit.

If a woman's companion is wearing morning dress, her own clothes should have an air of comparable formality.

An invitation to a grand society wedding is a signal to put on fashionable glad-rags. Most will wear smart day dress, a celebratory hat, gloves and jewellery. If the occasion takes place in the evening best party dress is called for, worn with or without a hat according to taste.

Note: the one-time social error of wearing black or white at the nuptials has gone the way of many another sartorial edict: it is now a question of personal choice.

Male guests

At a grand wedding, men generally wear morning dress which consists of a tailcoat, striped trousers and a waistcoat, worn with a stock or collar and tie, and a topper, of black or dove-grey. The strictness of the sartorial code is perhaps one reason why men often break out into remarkable neck-ties or stocks on this occasion. At any rate, this is an option in which personal judgment can come into play. A buttonhole is *de rigueur*. However, there are few weddings today at which a lounge suit is out of place.

Even if the men in the bridal party are wearing morning dress, it does not follow that the other male guests are expected to conform.

At an Anglican wedding held late in the afternoon, men may prefer to wear dinner jackets. This is a point to take up with the bride or the hosts. At a Jewish marriage traditionally held late in the day and followed by a formal reception, the custom is for men to wear dinner jackets and a hat at the marriage service.

At the place of worship

Guests who are invited to the marriage service are expected to attend. Those who give it a miss are advised to have a good excuse ready.

A comfortable hour at which to arrive at the place of worship is about ten to fifteen minutes in advance of the time stated. Those who cut it fine run the risk of coinciding with the bride's arrival, or of being given a back seat.

Guests are handed an Order of Service sheet as they enter the place of worship. They may be asked by an usher whether they belong to the bride or bridegroom's party. The former are shown to a pew on the left-hand side of the aisle, the latter to a pew on the right-hand side.

Subdued conversation and smiles of acknowledgement fill the pause until the arrival of the bride.

Religious observances

A marriage service frequently brings together under one roof people of differing religious denominations. It is likely that some of the hymns, prayers and procedures will be unfamiliar to several members of the congregation. The usual approach of such dissenters is to adopt an ecumenical view in the interests of the marriage, and to take part in those aspects of worship which are acceptable to them. However, those whose faith does not permit this latitude or who are zealous in their dissent should try to avoid causing embarrassment to the minister or the congregation. It would be better, perhaps, for them as well as for others if they did not attend the service.

After the bridal procession has made its progress down the aisle at the end of the ceremony, during which the assembly remains standing, the occupants of the family pews are given precedence on leaving. Once they have passed down the aisle the rest of the throng file out slowly, greeting friends as they go.

At the wedding reception

Guests are expected to make their own way from the place of worship to the wedding reception. Where distance is involved the host may think to provide transport, either cars or a coach or a minibus. If in doubt, try to check with the bride's side, or organize a lift with friends. It is an occasion when it would be unlikely to be regarded as an imposition if a request for a lift was made.

There is usually a pause on arriving at the reception while the bridal party is photographed. If tradition is to be adhered to, guests wait patiently in line to be received by the bride and bridegroom's parents, the bride and bridegroom. Sometimes, the newly-weds receive their guests unaided. In any event, handshakes or a social kiss and a brief remark or two is all that time allows for at this stage. Guests who have not met one or other member of the families are introduced as they pass by.

Following the welcome, guests usually make a beeline for the nearest tray of refreshments and proceed to circulate. As there is rarely anyone responsible for making introductions, newcomers have a choice of treading a lonesome trail or doing the honours themselves.

The wedding breakfast

Unless there is a seating plan at the wedding breakfast, guests help themselves to food and drink and sit where they please as at any buffet party. If there are place-cards guests are expected to accept whom they are given as neighbours at table with good grace: husbands and wives are usually separated.

Toasts and speeches

When the master of ceremonies or best man announces the toast of the bride and bridegroom conversation ceases, the party spring to their feet, and, raising a collective glass to the couple, drink their health. The gesture is enacted whether the tipple in the glass is champagne, mineral water or just a few last drops.

Goodbyes

Guests should try to stay until the couple have departed on honeymoon. When their departure is imminent, the best man (or toastmaster) announces that the couple are 'going away' and everyone rallies round for a rousing send-off. If confetti or rice or flower petals are to hand, guests throw the lucky emblems after the retreating figures of the couple.

See page 65 for 'Going away'.

Now celebrations are over and guests take their leave. Unless the party is very small and it would seem discourteous to conspicuously avoid saying goodbye to the hosts, guests don't usually seek them out. For some brides' mothers, but by no means all, this is a low moment.

Thank-yous

Letters of thanks or telephone calls of congratulation are not expected by the bride's family in the usual way, but everyone appreciates a guest who takes the trouble to say thank-you. Some write to the bride's mother, others to the bride.

Photography

Happy snapping by camera-carrying guests has become part of the entertainment at wedding receptions. Even though this practice is now commonplace, it is always a good idea to check with the hosts as to whether they have any objection before pressing the button. It could be that some members of the gathering would prefer not to be snapped off guard.

The use of cameras by members of the congregation at a place of worship is not to be encouraged. Popping flashbulbs or whirring photographic equipment can only detract from the solemnity of a religious service.

The honeymoon

Most just-married couples like to take time out in each other's company after the nuptials. The custom survives equally among those whose courtship may have taken place across distances and those who have been sharing each other's life and bedroom for a good while.

Honeymoons have a contradictory mythology, of romance and disappointment. The word itself originally referred to the first month that newly-weds spent together. One cannot escape the implication that succeeding 'moons' were likely to be less honeyed.

If strict convention is to be followed, the bridegroom undertakes all the necessary travel arrangements and pays for these as his major contribution to the wedding. In practice, this convention has become considerably more relaxed, though not invariably so, it must be stressed. Some men like to abide by the old ways but the general practice is for responsibility for making the arrangements to be shared, likewise the costs. Even when the man prefers to adopt a gallant stance and settles all the bills himself, the drain on the family income could mean that his partner would have to compensate financially in some way at a later stage.

It would certainly be misleading to suggest that practicalities have curbed the bridegroom's prerogative to keep the honeymoon destination secret until the moment of embarking on the journey. Brides and their partners collude in the joys of secrecy and suspense.

The break tends to be fitted into work and personal priorities rather than the other way about, and consists of varying durations and timing too.

Some couples choose a one-night or weekend stay away and make a swift return to their work place. Others may defer their holiday until a more convenient date. It is by no means remarkable for those who have been going out together for some time to take a pre-nuptial vacation with the wedding itself as a grand finale. Mostly, though, couples look upon a honeymoon as a specially good holiday in which to recover from the demands of a family wedding. Those with the leisure, the will and the means regard the occasion as meriting an extended spree across continents and oceans.

Married good manners

Couples who have not lived together in close physical intimacy before marriage are called upon to be particularly understanding of each other. What may add to general puzzlement is the difference between short-lived periods of being together and making love in snatches and the exposed sharing which is marriage.

At best, a honeymoon is a chance to establish a pattern of civility and good manners for everyday usage, as well as of showing respect for a spouse's sensitivities and perhaps inhibitions.

Small gestures of consideration make an enormous difference to the atmosphere of a marriage. It does no harm to greet each other with a friendly 'good morning' (especially if it is anything but) and to kiss goodnight as a nightly benediction. If these become formalities in later years the gestures are never less than small ways of signalling that a person is not taken for granted.

Physical intimacy can perplex and even alarm very private people, even in today's climate of rude awareness. They may be embarrassed about their own nudity, or their partner's, have fears about making love in a revealing light, have anxieties about bodily functions. They may expect to claim total privacy in situations which the other considers should be shared naturally with no closed doors between each other. Besides, it is by no means everyone who wishes to be an open book, even before their nearest and dearest, or indeed especially with them.

A couple could find they have different levels of tolerance towards caressing in public. For instance, some men just don't enjoy having the back of their neck stroked in a public bar and, equally, women can bridle at any proprietorially motivated fondling in front of strangers. Others are happy to merge whenever.

A honeymoon can be a voyage of discovery or a shipwreck. Displaying some tact and attempting to understand the other person's vulnerabilities, no matter how peculiar they may seem, is the least that is required for the first steps of a happy marriage. The blessing of good humour is a balm.

Contraceptive methods

Contraception is not only concerned with manners, of course, but it would be thoughtless, to say the very least, not to consider the issue before getting married.

Few couples come to marriage without some knowledge of birth control methods, whether or not they have had sexual intercourse with each other, or indeed with anyone else. The manners involved are concerned with trust and truthfulness. Whatever views individuals may hold on this sensitive topic, and whatever the proposed approach may be, the other partner should be made fully aware of the facts.

A virgin female will probably consult a doctor or perhaps a trusted ally with a view to considering various forms of birth control unless, of course, there are plans to start a family as soon as possible. Getting married is in any event an opportunity for a health check-up for both partners at which sexual or gynaecological concerns could be raised, including that of virginity and in rare cases genetic abnormalities. Tests for the HIV virus associated with AIDS and other sexually transmitted diseases should be considered too. Also women who suffer from pre-menstrual tension, for instance, might seek advice on their case. As is well known, there are several widely used forms of birth control, each having its advantages and disadvantages. Choices may depend on considered health risks, the importance of avoiding pregnancy, the reaction of a woman's body to a particular drug or device, and moral considerations. Science and technology have not yet discovered a fail-safe, reversible, convenient and cheap contraceptive, and abstinence has never been a popular method. Therefore, the choices should be considered carefully.

Male doubts

Not every man is as sexually experienced as public opinion is led to believe. Many may think that their limited contact with women may place them at a disadvantage as a husband. Unless these doubts have a serious origin, it could be best to turn first to their prospective partner in the hopes of gaining her understanding.

Male contraception

A man is under an obligation to go with his partner's preferences and wishes as a general rule. If she wishes him to wear a condom, this should be given the greatest consideration as it is she who will bear the consequences of any mistake.

A free and open exploration of the subject is a precautionary measure in itself.

Newly-weds

Couples who are publicly recognizable as newly-weds can find that although the world smiles upon them, the world also nudges and winks. Since it is fairly pointless to voice displeasure at such a deeply embedded response in human nature, the best reaction is to bear the innuendoes with fortitude.

Those who suspect that they or their other half would be seriously discomfited by such exposure are advised to select their hotel and its clientele with special care. An elementary precaution, in any event, is for the couple to brush off every trace of confetti before setting foot in the foyer.

For women especially, the first few weeks of married life can induce a self-consciousness about ordinary social behaviour which makes even sophisticates feel silly. Whatever form the awkwardness may take in public, be it forgetting to sign in a married name or not responding to being known as someone's wife, no apologies are called for.

Family, friends and colleagues

The custom is to leave honeymooners on their own, undisturbed by claims from the outside world, whether they wish this or not. Usual contact by telephone, telex or fax is suspended for the duration, emergencies excepted. It is the prerogative of the couple to decide whether they wish to make contact with family, friends and colleagues, or lie low.

Changing a name

Women are usually proud of their married name and use it as a matter of course. Family, friends and colleagues of a newly wedded woman now address, introduce and refer to her by her married style.

The outside world awaits notification, however. Among official or professional bodies who should be informed of a person's change of name are the following: the bank (if an account is to be opened in the woman's married name), the Inland Revenue, the solicitor, the doctor, credit card companies and insurance companies. If the newly-wed wishes to be known by her married name at work, she should inform her boss (likewise if she wishes to keep her single status) and the personnel department. If a passport is to be issued in her married name, application must be made to the nearest Passport Office. If the prospective bride wishes to have the name on her passport changed in time for honeymoon travel abroad, sufficient time must be allowed for the application to be processed.

There is no legal obligation on a woman to change her name on marriage, but her marriage certificate is a legal proof of identity.

The idea of women keeping their single-status names after marriage is widespread among those who are known professionally in their field. A very general compromise is for people to continue to use their professional name at work and to be known by their married style in private life.

Some women think differently and opt for a change in their professional name on marriage – perhaps preferring it to their own or wishing to be known henceforth by their married name for reasons of logistical simplicity. A variant is the old practice of amalgamating surnames between the couple. It was once fashionable, for instance, for an heiress to ally her name to that of her spouse's if he was due to inherit the estate, hence the rise of the 'double-barrelled' surname. These days, this custom is more likely to be a means whereby a woman can retain her professional identity yet declare her married status. The result may prove a bit of a mouthful, however.

Divorce, separation & remarriage

Divorce has two faces, one public one private. As far as the outside world is concerned, divorce is increasingly condoned as a necessary escape clause from human fallibility. The following suggests ways in which a more personal spirit of tolerance and courtesy could prevail between the couple and their family and friends.

Untying the knot

Certainly times have changed since someone who was involved in a difficult divorce was automatically excluded from holding senior office and ran the risk of being ostracized by society. Despite official voices being raised in concern about the break-up of the family from time to time, the widely prevailing view is that marital divorce is a private affair.

Yet against this backdrop of detached, liberal opinion, those caught up themselves in the actuality of divorce are likely to experience hostility, antagonisms and emotional upsets which are far from cool and impersonal.

The radical nature of the dissolution of a marriage may seem to relegate the role of good manners to an irrelevance. Showing courtesy could even be dismissed as a sign of weakness. This has to be false reckoning, however. Marital break-up can so easily lead to situations in which the participants lose their self-control, and to behaviour which in retrospect both sides regret. An effort to be polite even under extreme provocation has one precious advantage: it engenders self-respect which may have a special currency in the context of divorce.

Church and state

Divorce procedures have been with us for over 1,000 years. Moses allowed 'a bill of divorcement', though Jesus spoke against 'whoever divorces his wife' and remarriage. Confronted with the facts of marital breakdown, religious leaders have found the issue of divorce and remarriage one of the most sensitive with which they have to deal. A compassionate attitude is urged by some churchmen whereas a firm line is adopted by the majority who stress the obvious inconsistencies in taking vows twice.

Legalities

One of the few encouragements to behave well under the stress of a marital split is to try to contain the fears of uncertainty. Knowing where you stand formally as far as your rights are concerned and understanding the legal side can only help to promote rational thinking, and with it, the opportunity to maintain your dignity.

This book does not attempt to deal with the legal side of divorce beyond counselling against hasty action. It is well known that wrong-footed decisions taken in the heat of the moment can adversely affect the final settlement terms.

In the usual course of events, a couple must be married for a minimum of one year before divorce proceedings can start. The sole grounds for divorce today are that a marriage has run into terminal trouble, has reached 'irretrievable breakdown', to use the formal term. As a rule, the court is prepared to accept as grounds for the dissolution of marriage, evidence of adultery or separation.

The majority of divorces are uncontested, but whether they are or not the question of moral blame has lost its legal sting since the 1969 Divorce Reform Act removed the 'guilty party' clause.

When both agree on divorce, the minimum period of living apart before divorce proceedings can be started is two years. When a divorce is contested (that is to say one party objects) the minimum period of living separately is five years after which the court is usually prepared to dissolve the marriage.

Other evidence which may be considered as grounds for divorce includes behaviour which the court considers 'intolerable' such as refusal to consummate a marriage, desertion, and mental cruelty. Grounds such as these may be used to hasten a divorce but these are the exception.

In general, marriages are dissolved by the courts in a shorter space of time than in previous generations and 'quickie' divorces are a byword. Nonetheless, the battle grounds of maintenance, custody of children, access to children, and the division of property are fought over as protractedly as ever. In fact, the post-divorce stage by general consent, makes greater demands on the tolerance of former partners than the divorce proceeding itself.

Endings

A marriage is dissolved by the courts in two stages: a decree nisi is granted after which the decree absolute can be applied for and is usually issued. A time lapse of six weeks between the two is customary and may have a particular significance for the person who is planning on a second marriage as soon as permissible. Divorced couples should obtain certificates as proof of the court's decision.

Legal separation

Significantly, lawyers use the term 'separation agreement' in place of the layman's terms 'trial separation' or 'legal separation'. What marks the move from a personal decision to live apart is that the arrangement is underpinned by a legal contract which is enforceable. It may cover many of the issues which would be decided by a court covering maintenance, custody and suchlike.

In some instances where a person's religious faith does not recognize divorce among its members, the believer may obtain a judicial separation. This procedure precludes any need to admit that a marriage has ended. An important condition in all legal separation agreements is that matrimonial sexual rights are suspended.

Legal separations have been criticized on grounds of inflexibility and failure to acknowledge the changing circumstances of one of the couple. And also because terms agreed to may be enforceable in any subsequent divorce action to the detriment of one party. Still, there is always the hope of reconciliation. The couple remain legally wed. Outsiders are expected to respond to couples who have split in this way as if the nuptial bond was loosened but not completely untied.

Annulment

An annulment publicly declares that a marriage did not exist. In dictionary terms it is 'the act of reducing to nothing'. Grounds for annulment might be that sexual intercourse did not take place between the couple after marriage, or that one person did not conform to the rules of eligibility for matrimony.

In the instance of Roman Catholics, seeking an annulment can be a long, complex and usually costly procedure involving specialist advice of a canon lawyer. It is reassuring to know that any children of an annulled marriage have all their rights of inheritance and are not considered illegitimate.

Practicalities

Once separation is embarked upon various authorities will need to be informed: the bank, building society, taxman, accountant, doctor, and any stores with whom the couple had a joint account. Contacting a solicitor will be a first move, and it should be taken as read that each side has its own lawyers. The wills of both husband and wife will be revoked on divorce. If children of the marriage are to be beneficaries in a future will their interest may have to be safeguarded.

Division of money and possessions

To be able to come to amicable terms over the division of money and assets in a divorce settlement is a supreme test of courtesy. Hostilities may flare up over the rights to possession of even humdrum objects. Material goods tend to assume a symbolic as well as monetary meaning and attachment to property is rarely more strongly felt than during the upheaval of divorce. The thought that the other may plunder shared possessions worked for by both only heightens the bitterness.

It is certainly true that some free spirits count the world well lost for the sake of freedom, and quit the marital home with their clothes and the cat. But a parent with dependants and an empty piggy bank is in no position to make grand gestures; the weak do go to the wall. Efforts are currently being made to make fathers more accountable for paying maintenance for wives and children, but it is difficult not to believe that much of an all too common sorry mess could be averted if more allowances were made for human frailty, and if the education system helped to prepare young people for the realities of marriage.

Overshadowing the need to make decisions is the knowledge that where agreement is not reached, the case will come within the jurisdiction of the courts. A few grace notes exist which if managed amicably might help to create a more harmonious atmosphere and in any event reassure the couple and their families that they have shown consideration. For example, it would set a civilized standard if enough room for sentiment were allowed in the carve-up to enable each side to keep a few of their personal treasures and especially cherished belongings.

It is usual for personal belongings, works of art and furniture to remain with the side that brought them to the marriage. Presents given jointly to the couple by their respective friends tend to remain with the side to whom the donor was closest. Gifts exchanged between husband and wife are supposed to be returned but few people aspire to this level of correctitude.

Nuptial rings

Divorced women rarely offer to give back their engagement ring, whatever its monetary worth. Many either sell the piece or keep it on behalf of a daughter of the house. On the question of whether a divorced woman (or man) continues to wear the wedding ring of the former marriage, personal attitudes are all and manners have little to do with it.

Family jewels

Families with valuable jewellery may give some pieces to a wife for her pleasure on marriage. As a general rule these are restored to the donors when the marriage is dissolved, but the law courts testify to many exceptions. Much depends on the character of the wife and on her divorce settlement.

Collector's luck

Collections, whether of art or porcelain or pop memorabilia or found objects formed during marriage are liable to be broken up as the result of separation. Many are the wives and husbands who in the good days, gave prized pieces to their opposite number as presents. It is famously difficult to reclaim personal gifts, and as a result gaps exist in the collection.

A plea may be put in for collector's luck in which individuals are allowed to retain items for which they have a special affection, or which represented to the discoverer a coup in its way. This, assuming that any imbalance in the total reckoning that might result, is rectified.

Briefing a solicitor

A solicitor's role is to remind his (or her) client of their position under the law, and to give an opinion on how best they may proceed. It is up to the client to decide how far to go in petitioning for whatever they can get. Much of the mystique that surrounds the law may intimidate even a normally self-confident person who is not accustomed to dealing with family lawyers.

The important points to remember are to keep a cool head, to be as matter-of-fact and precise as possible and to put all thoughts of embarrassment out of mind. One of the advantages of seeking professional legal advice is the absence of any emotional overtones in the lawyer–client dealings. The business-like atmosphere of the consultation room may help facts to be seen more clearly and dispassionately. In the normal course of things, a solicitor is not a counsellor who is qualified to advise on the wisdom of proceeding with a marriage break-up. He is under a strict obligation to remind a client of any aspects of a course of action which they may be contemplating, which he considers detrimental to them.

A sound practice is to prepare questions to raise at the meeting, and to try to make a note of the replies. For one thing this may minimize the need to make telephone calls to the solicitor's office to double-check points. A solicitor's time is money, and could be your money – the extra work involved may increase costs.

When private fees are to be paid, clients owe it to themselves to abandon any hint of reluctance about enquiring directly about cost. The question can be put to the solicitor's office on the telephone when making an initial appointment, or a letter stating fees can be requested (this is supposed to be sent to clients in any case), or the point can be raised face to face.

A client is under no obligation to remain with a solicitor and as with all professionals, a second opinion can always be sought without giving offence.

On the matter of the division of legal costs, this is often a subject for negotiation between the parties concerned. Factors having a bearing on who pays for what might include whether the divorce is contested, the comparative financial standing of each person and the involvement of dependent children. Personal reasons are all important. Someone who is in a hurry to be free of wedlock might well be more amenable all round to accepting proposals for the divorce settlement and shouldering legal costs.

Two axioms on legal fees apply: divorce is cheap but the costs of working out the divorce settlement is where the money goes; always hire the best legal opinion that can be afforded.

Alimony's heirs

Dividing the spoils in a marriage in which both parties are healthy earners or equally well set up in life, presents a very different tale from that of the dependent ex-wife with mouths to feed. Yet now that so many marriages break up after only short duration and women's earnings compare favourably with men's, it seems worth pointing out that nothing reveals character like an approach to alimony.

A quiet word may be put in in favour of guarding against greed and the urge to go for every penny as well as Aunt Kate's non-stick saucepan. A fair attitude may enable those involved in divorce to stay at peace with themselves, to settle an argument that may have been active within their own bosom, and to retain the poise that follows the knowledge that they at least have not been seduced by the dirty tricks department. Adopting an ungrasping view is not synonymous with weakness. People have to secure their own interests but there are ways and ways in which this can be achieved.

Extended family ties

Divorce sometimes brings about a break with all links with the past, but equally, may also lead to a continuance of a whole network of family connections. Relationships between the separated spouses and their former in-laws, step-children, the elders of the other family and their friends need not die upon the parting. Also, the separated couple may themselves remain in the same orbit and be obliged to greet one another in public. In a few instances, the new partners on each side may get along quite well.

Nevertheless, even in these favourable circumstances it would be wiser for the two sides to keep a distance between themselves and close members of the other side during divorce procedures. Blood is thicker than whatever runs in the veins of friendship and fraternization with the in-laws' camp might be construed as disloyalty. After a cooling off period, hopefully, a new chapter can begin.

Save the children

Everyone knows that the real problem of divorce is sharing children of the marriage, or trying to.

Whatever happens, young children are more likely to need reassurance than explanation and will almost certainly wish to hear that their parents love them very much. Little children may appear accepting but it is common knowledge that they are prone to emotions of guilt, supposing themselves to be bad or unworthy and the cause of their parents' troubles.

Divorced parents are urged to try to keep their grievances and reproaches to themselves when they are in the company of their children. Usually, coming to terms with their parents' separation is difficult enough for children to handle without having to cope with a character demolition of one of their nearest and dearest by the other.

Visits and treats

Growing children appear to need both parents and except in cases where the child is likely to come to some harm, close contact is to be encouraged between son or daughter and the parent who is living apart.

These visits, so familiar to the divorced, are more beneficial all round if the following points are borne in mind.

Visiting parents should try to be punctual and only cancel if they absolutely have to. Arrangements that have been made in advance for an outing should be kept, like all good promises.

While few would raise objections to generous gestures, some balance has to be kept if one parent is able to bestow treats and presents beyond the resources of the other. If parents are sufficiently open-handed, the money could be more equitably shared to enable them both to indulge their offspring. Frequently, absented parents try to compensate for their feelings of guilt about failing to spend enough time with their children by attempting to buy their way out. Although children are just as greedy for rewards as adults, ultimately they tend to recognize this deal for what it is.

Parents who manage to bridge the distances best are those who take a genuine interest in their children's doings and hobbies and sports. They telephone, or write and stay in touch so the lines of contact are kept humming. Many fathers separated from young children try to take them on holiday – with or without a new partner. On this last point, a holiday is often chosen as the means whereby children are introduced to a prospective stepmother or stepfather.

Intelligent parents try to resist the temptation to ask leading questions of their children, after a visit or holiday. In any case, it is unlikely that the children will be very forthcoming.

A *mannerly separation*

People involved in the break-up of a marriage need, above all, non-judgmental support and kindness. In the interests of a peaceful solution, friends, family and familiars should desist from fanning the flames of antipathy between the couple.

Such may be a counsel of perfection, particularly for loyalists of one member of the couple, but this is not to confuse courtesy with cowardice. Allies' opinions can be valuable but the best (and the rarest) attempt to steer proceedings into the clarity of calmer waters.

It has to be remembered that few outsiders know the true nature of a marriage, and if they are under the impression that they do, there is a good chance their perspective is biased. The old precept about not taking sides in public has a special relevance. Those who are splitting up are often in a highly vulnerable state and prone to feelings of being discriminated against, or being done down by other factions in a close circle, whether this is a reality or not.

Perhaps the most sensitive key to approaching people who are getting divorced is to be found in the experiences of those who have gone through the hoops themselves. They tend to stress the sense of personal failure that follows rage, the familiarity with anxiety, guilt and loneliness. To all who have experienced such emotions during divorce the following consolation is offered by one divorced male: 'A bad marriage gets worse. A bad divorce gets better.'

Friendly relations with an estranged couple

A separating couple are in a twilit area of being attached by bonds that have worn thin but have not yet been 'put asunder'.

From an outsider's point of view, much of the uncertainty of the situation hinges on whether the pair should continue to be considered as a couple, or be regarded as born-again singles. A further possible hazard is that the couple themselves may be ambivalent on this point, depending on the state of their relations.

Beyond the question of manners are legal niceties such as if they are citing separation as grounds for divorce, the fact of being together under the same roof may have implications that affect the timing of the case.

As far as all formal purposes are concerned, a married couple are considered to be living together as husband and wife – until there is some public announcement that is intended to change their state. Until that point they should be invited to social events in the usual way as a couple. Except for intimates, it is probably premature to mention an anticipated break-up in conversation with either side. Good friends wait to be told.

A change of partners

Many situations can arouse divided loyalties, between friends and the couple themselves, and between friends of a new emotional attachment of one of the married pair. It is not unusual for the same friends to have links with each member of the eternal triangle.

At what stage can a married man who is breaking up with his wife ask his acquaintances to include his girlfriend to the party, or expect them to extend the courtesies that are due to a recognized couple?

There are no set answers to questions such as this and many allied considerations. So much depends on the circumstances and the attitudes of the people involved. A safe rule which everyone knows is to avoid inviting antagonists to the feast, especially if a new beloved is sitting across the table. In addition, there are the customs of the circle in which the protagonists move – what may be unremarkable among the chattering classes in the big cities could cause some surprise elsewhere.

See page 167 for Old loves.

Discretion is called for in any case, and the ground should be tested before any similar proposition is put or invitation issued. It may be that the host has loyal feelings towards the other partner, and would resent being asked to be seen to encourage an illicit liaison at the expense of a close ally. If the request is made, the proposer should be prepared to swallow a polite refusal on grounds of disloyalty. What might make a difference is the known acceptance of the affair by the wife and an apparent unconcern about appearing on the same stage; or perhaps the occasion of a big party at which it is easy for guests to escape each other's notice without appearing discourteous.

Keeping a distance

It is tempting to take people at their face value and to assume that they are as impervious to hurt as their pride dictates. A safe general rule is to keep a distance between married people and their unfaithful acts, until a new chapter begins formally.

Similarly, the sort of merry, heartless gossip that goes on between friends of the couple has to be filtered for relay to parents and siblings of the estranged partner. They are unlikely to take a liberal view of the erstwhile married spouse's gallivanting.

The point has been made that friends and relations most likely to survive the crossfire of a dissolving marriage, are those who for one reason or another manage to stay out of a partisan involvement in procedures. However, partisans or not, the main contribution of friends and confidants is to offer whatever help they can – a cash loan, offers of accommodation, help with the children or moral support being at the top of the list. Tact is golden throughout – both outsiders and insiders would do well to consider the value of keeping inflammatory and hitherto unknown information detrimental to one partner, to themselves for the duration, especially if they hope to remain friends with both of the pair.

Announcing the break-up

Frequently the announcement that a couple are to split comes as little surprise to friends and associates of their immediate circle. The declaration is often regarded as a confirmation rather than news.

Among the first to be told are any children of the marriage especially if they are young and liable to pick up a distorted account at second-hand.

The couple's parents should be told as soon as possible, each side informing their own. Parental attitudes vary widely on the subject of divorce and no hard-and-fast rules apply, but one eventuality to bear in mind is that what may have been general knowledge to siblings and familiars may be only half-suspected by a divorcing couple's parents.

In the case of frail or vulnerable parents, the announcement should be made with special tact and as good a complexion as possible put on events.

As far as friends and associates are concerned, the first intimation of the split may be the arrival of a change of address card from the spouse who has moved on. Otherwise, the information tends to seep into the consciousness of interested parties as the word gets round. If a letter is written announcing a divorce or separation the usual convention holds good that no explanations are necessary.

We don't seem to have taken to the idea in this country of formally announcing a divorce or separation by printed card or in the paid announcement columns of the daily press. Newsworthy persons, however, may be chased by the press for a statement or they may choose to make an announcement for publication. This may apply not only to the married. One prominent British sportsman placed an announcement in *The Times* to the effect that he and his long-standing girlfriend had decided with regret, to part.

Parents will in all probability need reassurance, and an address and telephone number if their offspring has moved. It may well be that basic assistance is needed in the form of ready cash or an offer of temporary accommodation, or if young grandchildren are involved, effort made to share the responsibility of caring for them over the crisis.

When love affairs or serious liaisons outside marriage break up, the consequences pose many of the problems associated with marital break up. Gender seems to have little distinguishing effect on the emotional traumas of a split between couples, whether these be heterosexual or homosexual. The usual rules of courtesy hold good. Expressions of sympathy and support are likely to be appreciated in all cases.

Parental roles

Thoughtful parents try to curb their curiosity and avoid asking too many leading questions. It is certainly not the moment for a reminder that they had been right in the first place about that man or woman.

Changing a name

Up until the time her divorce is made absolute, a woman may continue to use her married style, e.g. Mrs Robert Smith. Afterwards, she discards her former husband's first name and is known by his surname, her own first name, and the prefix of her married style, e.g. Mrs Lucy Smith. Some women prefer to revert to their maiden name (unless they are contemplating remarriage), particularly in instances where the first marriage was of short duration, or if they are known professionally under their single name.

Etiquette related to the styles of former wives of men of title is not so simple, and those who are unsure of their protocol in this field can refer to the chapter, 'Modes of Address', on pages 314-333 in this book, or consult a fuller account in Debrett's Correct Form. A useful general ruling is that the former wives of noblemen continue to use their married styles prefixed by their Christian name, for example, Mary, Countess of Steadford. Similarly, the wife of a life peer would be known as Anne, Lady Foxleigh. Signatures remain unaltered unless the lady marries again.

See page 314 for Modes of address.

New loves, old loves

An important figure to be considered in the family equation is a separated couple's new attachment – a live-in lover perhaps or a steady companion who may or may not be a prospective step-parent.

Step-parents, most notably stepmothers, have had a bad press ever since Snow White's ordeal, but their increasing numbers seem to be accompanied by a gradual revision of image. Certainly, numerous stepchildren speak with affection of the person who has brought happiness to their parent as well as being an ally to them.

However, the process of integrating a new member into the family group calls for a recognition of possible danger areas such as sensitivities about rights threatened, territory annexed and loyalties supplanted.

Parent – child – step-parent triangle

There seems to be certain classically ill-timed approaches towards this lesser-known eternal triangle. In the eyes of a concerned parent living apart from the family, any attempt by the former spouse's new partner to undermine his or her parental role is contentious. Experience suggests that divorced fathers and mothers more than appreciate it if the surrogate parent tries to support their authority: for instance, when a child has to be reprimanded, to take the line that their father or mother would not like them to do that. By all accounts, a supreme irritation is when the step-parents resident boyfriend (or girlfriend) behaves in a proprietorial manner towards the children in the presence of their real parent.

Usually, the visiting parent takes the children off for the day or the weekend but those experienced in this situation say that family meals are much relished by young offspring. If all goes well, however, there may be hard questions to be answered afterwards about why anyone has to leave.

Children's courtesies

As in so-called 'normal' families, remembering birthdays, anniversaries and feast days is a way of showing consideration. It would be thoughtful if the parent with whom the children lived encouraged the idea and produced the wherewithal for the gesture in favour of the away parent. Separated parents have been known to increase their infants' pocket money on the spot so as to enable them to produce a birthday present. One who did said the event 'made him feel better'.

Step-parents are often in an invidious position here. Are they responsible for maintaining these links between their 'steps' and the absented parent? Strictly speaking, this should come within the province of the real father or mother, but such distinctions often no longer hold water; a gesture of kindness never goes amiss.

The bedroom door

It is improper for a young son or daughter to find their parent in bed with a lover, without any advance preparation for the encounter. Circumspect parents do their best to avoid the occurrence but many admit that the problem is high on the agenda of separation.

First of all, the new member has to come to be accepted within the family circle and to count as something more than a bird of passage. The stage of liking or at least not objecting to the person in question may lead to a preparedness on the part of children to accept the idea of the intimacy of a shared bedroom. Public displays of affection are probably best introduced in tactful stages.

At some point, privacy is going to be essential for the adults. Children will probably accept that their parent and lover require some uninterrupted time on their own, and this stage is a cue for firmly closing the bedroom door.

Parents who find themselves being interrogated by their young after being taken unawares may take refuge in the recommendation of Judith Martin, the American etiquette authority: there are some things in life about which one does not wish to give an explanation. A pro tem strategem which will probably require further thought.

Steps for step-parents

A very general complaint by new or prospective step-parents concerns the initial hostility and rudeness of stepchildren. Stepmothers in particular often have a difficult time.

Those who manage best seem to be able to carve out a special role for themselves which is a hybrid between a surrogate parent and an elder sibling. Of course, not everyone is prepared to accept the diminution of authority that this presupposes. Much depends on the approach of the biological parent: it is down to them to lay the ground-rules, and a firm hand may have to be taken with offspring who are unable to accept their choice of mate.

In this sensitive situation, good manners can be a balm and the foundation of a way of containing friction.

The insolence of children is probably best left uncorrected in the early stages as the new parent is probably being tested for reactions. Genuine displays of interest in their welfare, and an attempt to approach them as individuals in their own right rather than as inherited relations, are likely to help nip incipient jealousies in the bud.

Children are the original Me generation and effort expended on nurturing their talents and abilities will probably awaken an appreciative response. Playing with aspiring tennis players, encouraging novice cooks to cook, helping with revision before an exam, assisting a toddler to make the better sand-pie are all paths to mutual respect so long as they are carried out in a spontaneous, unpreachy manner.

Certain actions between step-parents and older children are known to cause resentment but are difficult to avoid. Annexing a resident stepdaughter or stepson's favourite den is one. A frequent justification is the arrival of a new baby and a lack of suitable space elsewhere. The move should be mooted well ahead of time and some recompense found to make the transfer of territory seem more acceptable to the dispossessed: making the room more attractive to the occupant perhaps.

A difference of attitude towards punctuality at mealtimes, table manners and food tastes can be a source of conflict especially when the new parent is more punctilious in this regard than the separated parent. A battleground, indeed. There may be a case in favour of establishing a few ground-rules which are to be adhered to and turning a blind eye to all the other potential sources of irritation. Certainly in cases where two sets of children from different marriages converge on one household, it is unlikely that they will have been brought up with the same approach to the question of good manners.

The point must be made here that someone in the family circle has to think that the effort and compromises involved to make a success of the rewelded group are worthwhile and that a conciliatory approach is more likely to succeed than heavy-handed discipline. Good food is usually an attraction, and, dare it be said, a light hand on the principle of equal shares as far as domestic chores are concerned. The vaunted ideal of collective cooking, serving and clearing away usually contrives to make hard work for everybody and relaxation for no one. But if family togetherness is to continue, men must be capable of playing mother too.

Making allowances for snobbery and the undeniable fact that uncongenial manners grate like a nail on steel in a class-conscious society, true courtesy consists in self-control and in preparedness to see the other person's point of view. Perhaps the best hope for the mannerly parent is that their standards will prove themselves under the scrutiny of the unconverted.

Introducing steps

Step-parents and their ready-made progeny are usually on first-name terms from the start. Introducing step-parents and stepsons and stepdaughters, and referring to them, can give rise to uncertainty, particularly where different family names are involved. Family links may have a byzantine complexity and spelling them out would need exceptional tact. Thankfully there is a tendency to ignore the exact biological provenance of each member of an extended group and to introduce them in the simplest way.

Usually, parents put the matter straight, when the point needs to be made and will say something like, 'This is Lucy's son, Ben', or 'My stepdaughter would like to meet you'. Stepchildren tend to introduce or refer to their step without bringing in the connection, and will say 'That is my father and Ann over there'.

When formal introductions have to be made, a stepson may say, 'Can I introduce my father, Arthur Bond and my stepmother, Patricia Bond?'

If children are wrongly referred to they have a way of correcting people in a way that has often become easy through use. 'I'm not Tracy Brown', they will say, 'I'm Tracy White'. Similarly, step-parents usually put friends right in private if stepchildren are mistaken for their own. Step-parents who acquire older children tend to be punctilious about this. In any case the atmosphere surrounding the topic is one of no offence meant or taken.

One upshot of multi-faceted, loosely connected family grouping is the number of grandparents per grandchild in evidence. When young children grow up with their step-parents, or their parent's chosen companion's mother and father, they may adopt them as fully fledged grandparents. Indeed, it is a sad reflection on the state of matrimony that many grandparental ties with children – whether steps or natural – long outlast the parental marriage that created them.

Post-marriage

A characteristic of the post-marital stage is the former couple's awareness of it as a watershed. Both have acquired single status once more and are free to remarry. Many people find that the aftermath of separation and divorce is concerned with tidying the loose ends of the untied knot.

Social sense

Many females, especially those who are no longer young, find social life problematic without a partner. Former girlfriends and wives of friends and acquaintances are known to regard the typical divorcée as a predator and invitations tend to be limited to hen parties, coffee mornings and heart-to-hearts with women; invitations to mixed occasions become strangely thin on the ground.

Good friends of both sexes should try to rally round the new-born single. It would be considerate to make a point of inviting him or her to any jollies to which they would have been invited as a married couple. Admittedly, this begs the question of sides taken by friends in the split-up. A tactful approach, at any rate in the early stages, is to attempt to share gestures of friendship with both of the couple, taking them in turns, almost literally. Regrettably, it is in the nature of separation and of friendship too, that many of the original circle float off, or members drift more towards one side than the other.

The party that suspects they are being dropped could always make a determined effort to knit the defecting ally into their new life through invitations of their own. Often, friends of friends who have been through a rocky divorce are uncertain about where they stand in the affections of each member of the former couple. The woman, for it is often she who is the most vulnerable, can signal a desire for continuing friendship.

Escorts

Escorts are essential for women who don't wish to be in purdah. Friends and allies and relations who can offer an arm make more than a social gesture and can help guard against the isolation that may follow separation.

Many women rely on the companionship of males who have nothing else in mind other than a convivial date. Gay men too play a role that reflects the epithet in its light-hearted sense; numerous are the friendships that spring up between older women especially and gay companions.

Opportunities to meet marriageable males are renownedly scarce. As a motive it seems self-defeating. New liaisons seem more likely to come about through involvement in personal interests and pursuits in which participation in the activity or sport is the thing and introductions to eligible individuals are incidental.

Walking out again

Divorced males with responsibilities for maintenance and child care are in a special position as far as any future romantic entanglements are concerned. It would certainly show consideration to any girlfriend – who is more than a passing fancy – to put her in the picture sooner rather than later. Quite often, the fact of divorce and the surrounding circumstances reveal themselves almost unconsciously in conversation when the divorced give an account of themselves. Few women who are in love with a man who is divorced would wish this to be otherwise.

Remarriage

See page 39 for Marriage.

Marrying again involves all the legal and administrative requirements of changing single status. Persons who may remarry are widows and widowers, the divorced whose decree absolute has been granted, those whose marriage has been annulled. Couples who have been previously married to each other and divorced may remarry.

Remarriage and religion

A point was made earlier in this chapter about the approach of the leading religious denominations in Britain towards divorced members with a living spouse who wish to remarry with the full rites of their faith.

The Church of England's official position is shared by the majority of the clergy but not by all. For example, some ministers may be prepared to cast a kindly eye on those whose marriage took place in a register office and who therefore have not taken their vows. There is also the consideration of one of the pair who may be a loyal parishioner and who has not been married before but whose prospective partner is divorced. Determined, informed and time-consuming research is the only valid approach to finding an opening in this enclosure, with the help of a sympathetic clergyman. In some instances, though, difficulties may prove insurmountable.

The Church of England Service of Blessing

The difficulties encountered by many divorced people who are debarred from a full marriage service in church have led to the widespread acceptance of the

Service of Blessing. The marriage is blessed by the minister in a service of hymns and prayers but vows are not taken.

How far social observances may follow the pattern of a full solemnization of marriage and take on the air of a white wedding, is for the individual minister to authorize. For example, his view will determine whether a formal wedding dress, bridal attendants, special flower arrangements, a choir and a peal of bells will be appropriate. As a general rule, ministers prefer a low-key and discreet approach.

The service is usually held on the day of the couple's marriage at the register office but sometimes it is more convenient for the church ceremony to take place at a later stage.

Remarriage in the Church of Rome

A Roman Catholic who is divorced has some hope of remarriage with the full rites of their faith. The Church of Rome has traditionally dissolved marriages on grounds of nullity, which means that the marriage did not exist in the eyes of the Church, despite outward appearances to the contrary. The subject of grounds on which nullity is granted is too specialized to enter into here usefully, and the advice of a canon lawyer is recommended.

One point may be of particular interest to Roman Catholics whose previous marriage took place in a register office. The religious authorities may agree to have the marriage declared null and void on the basis that it does not exist in the eyes of the Church.

The path will not be easy but procedures are said to be more flexible – and less costly – than in the past.

Remarriage of widowers and widows

As far as the major religious denominations are concerned, the status of a widow or widower is comparable to that of a person who is marrying for the first time. Whether a woman whose previous spouse has died wishes to re-create some of the social observances of a traditional white wedding at her remarriage in church will probably depend on her inclinations and those of her husband-to-be and on the style of her first wedding. The Church would be unlikely to have any objections.

Social observances in remarriage

The way the wedding goes will probably be determined as much as anything by whether one of the couple had remained single previously. There is understand-able feeling that a person in such a position should not be deprived of his or her opportunity to make a public avowal with all the celebration and witnessing that this involves.

Nevertheless, if the bride has been married before, some restraint has to be exercised in her choice of bridal attire. It does not make sense to adopt all the paraphernalia and outward array that is associated with religious tradition based on the concept of marriage as 'till death us do part'. Choice is a matter of taste and cannot be categorized into what is appropriate and inappropriate. Of course, if the prospective bride has not been married before, and it is her fiancé who has been, her options are open.

If the bride so wishes, men wear morning dress. A factor here is that if it is the bridegroom who is marrying for the first time, both he and his family may prefer formal dress to be worn.

The wedding party

Second marriage may be quick and simple but is no longer by definition a cue for a quiet wedding. Friends may forgather, glasses raised, speeches made, wedding cake cut and the inescapable tin can tied to the boot of the departing honeymoon couple's car.

Financing the wedding

The usual custom of the bride's parents paying may or may not apply in the case of her second marriage.

Much depends on individual circumstances, the financial standing of the bride and her prospective husband, and parental willingness to foot the bill once again. Many parents who perhaps splashed out on the occasion of a daughter's previous marriage may take the view that second-time round calls for a release from their financial involvement. It would be considerate, in any case and regardless of financial issues, for the bride at least to offer to shoulder some of the costs.

Many compromises are worked out with propriety, ranging from the couple running their own show, issuing the wedding invitations in their name and picking up the bill, to parents giving a pre-nuptial celebration as their gesture in the knowledge that the couple will be the hosts on their day.

Parents of a remarrying bride

Parents of the bride who is marrying again are given full courtesies at the wedding whether they have paid for any part of the occasion or not. It would be polite for them to be shown to a seat in the front pew or its equivalent at the place of worship. At the register office, the bride might like to ask her parents to sign the register as witnesses.

There is no reason why the father should not propose the traditional toast. He can play as much a part in the proceedings as he and the bride wish him to.

Family frictions

Weddings can bring out the worst in family relationships, especially where there is bitterness in the aftermath of divorce or separation. The appearance of new partners on such a public occasion may well provoke resentment and uncover old wounds. The ideal, which is to forgive and forget at least for the day, is no doubt much easier said than done.

One stratagem is for the step-parent to be present as a distinguished guest but to forgo playing a part in the formalities or ceremony. She or he should be shown to a good seat wherever the crowd gathers.

In the event of the mother of the bride being on her own, an escort should be provided to accompany her at all stages of the ceremony. The rare tactful relation should be rallied to the cause, or a grown-up son or, if there is an available boyfriend, he should be sent an invitation.

Divorced or separated parents may stand side by side in a receiving line, or be placed next door to each other in the formal wedding photographs. If this causes embarrassment, the bridal couple can welcome guests on their own, and the shots be confined to the happy pair. In circumstances in which the father of the bride is unavailable or deceased, a stepfather who is close to his stepdaughter may be asked to give her away. In any event, he may also be asked to make one of the speeches.

More important than any of these formalities is a sympathetic approach towards the bride, who, in the situation under discussion, may be all too aware of the hazards of marriage. Every effort on the part of divorced or separated parents should be made to set aside their differences and put their daughter's happiness first on this of all days.

Children of a previous marriage

Opinion holds that any children of the bride or bridegroom's previous marriage should be present at the remarriage of a parent if at all possible. The occasion symbolizes the foundation of a new family unit. As the children are likely to be a permanent part of the regrouping, it is important for all concerned that they are in at the start. If young bridal attendants are to feature at the nuptials, it is a friendly gesture to invite any prospective stepchildren to play the role. In some cases the marrying pair may have produced an offspring of their liaison who is of an age to manage the honours.

At a register office ceremony, steps should always be invited to join the few who witness the marriage. Usually, stepchildren of the pair appear in the family wedding photographs as would, naturally, any child of the union.

Wedding presents

It can be difficult to get married without being given wedding presents, the automatic reaction on the part of family friends and associates being, 'What do you want as a present?'

Clearly, much depends on the personal circumstances of the couple and whether they have need of things for setting up in a new home. The general custom among younger people who are marrying again is to provide a wedding list in the usual manner. A less formal way is to put the word round among people who ask, to the effect that wine or plants for the garden, for example, would be very much appreciated.

However, supporters who have produced a generous offering on the occasion of a previous marriage may take the view that a token offering is acceptable.

Announcements

*See page 30 for
Examples of
announcements.*

Obviously no announcement of engagement to marry shold be initiated by the couple until both are free to tie the knot.

It is common courtesy for a former spouse to ring or to write to inform their previous partner of their intention to marry again, before the word is announced in public.

The style and wording of the betrothal and marriage announcements follows the usual pattern, with the exception that in the case of a bride who has been married previously, her married prefix and name are given as shown.

An example of an announcement in the Court columns of an engagement to marry in which the prospective bride has been married previously:

Mr J.M. Nicholls
and Mrs S. Kemble

The engagement is announced between Michael, elder son of Mr and
Mrs K. B. Nicholls of Bloxton, Essex,
and Suzanna, elder daughter of Mr and Mrs Samuel of Hoxley,
Buckingham.

An announcement of marriage in the Court columns when the bride has remarried:

Mr C. Phillips
and Mrs P. Hoshino

The marriage took place on Saturday in Loughborough of Mr
Christopher Phillips, son of Dr A. Phillips and the late Mrs Sally
Phillips, and Patricia, daughter of Mr and Mrs D. Brice.

An announcement of marriage in the Court columns when the bride-to-be is a widow and she wishes to mention her late husband in the wording:

Commander F.G. Harpole
and Mrs V. Macrae

The marriage took place on Thursday in Sussex of Commander F. G.
Harpole, son of Dr A. Phillips and Mrs Eileen Phillips, and Veronica,
widow of Captain T. E. Macrae.

An example of a briefer wording of a second marriage announcement to appear in the personal columns:

Jessop-Olumba – On Saturday (month, date) at Priory Methodist
Church, Bedford, Nigel, son of the late Mr and Mrs D. Jessop to
Deanne, daughter of Mr and Mrs Z. Olumba, of Johannesburg.

Wedding invitations for second marriages

When the prospective bridegroom is marrying again and the bride is a spinster, the wording and style of the wedding invitations follows the usual form. There is considerable latitude in the design of invitations to the wedding but the traditional style of black engraving on a white card remains a favourite.

See page 77 for Wedding invitations.

When the bride is marrying again, and her parents are the hosts at the wedding, there is no need for her married name to appear on the invitation. It may follow the usual wording.

When the bride and bridegroom are sending the invitations in their own names, the wording may be informal, i.e. 'Michael Smith and Juliet Blakemore request the pleasure of your company at . . . on . . . at . . . and afterwards at . . .' If the bride is issuing the invitations the wording might be 'Mrs Sarah Cullins request the pleasure . . .', or simply, 'Sarah Cullins requests . . .' When the couple are issuing invitations for a party the wording might be, 'Richard Shaw and Joan Watkins at home following their marriage at (address) on (date) at (time)'.

When the bride and bridegroom are hosts at their own wedding reception, it may be that one or both sets of parents choose to give a pre or post-nuptial celebration. 'At home' cards may be sent, if wished, or a specially worded invitation. One form of words for a pre-wedding party given by the bride's side might be 'Mr and Mrs Robert Foxton request the pleasure of your company at (address) . . . on (month and date) . . . at (the hour) to celebrate the forthcoming marriage of their daughter Janey to Mr Bam Dowling'.

Another wording (if appropriate) and if the party was to be given by the bridegroom's divorced parents could run, 'Mr George Elliot and Mrs Maureen Elliot request the pleasure of your company at a reception immediately preceding the marriage of their son (name and style) to (name and style).' As social life grows increasingly less formal, some couples who are giving their own wedding party might drop styles on the invitation, and use forenames and surnames only, i.e. 'Michael Green and Kathy Black request the pleasure . . .'

First & last rites

Entrances and exits on the human stage are commemorated with a strange

mixture of the solemn and the sociable. Birth and death alike are harbingers

of ceremonial, offerings and many rituals designed to pay special respects.

If there is a contemporary way of managing these rites of passage it is to

try and do justice to both the serious witnessing and the softer sides. Also

there is a tendency to delve for fresh meanings in the old forms in the

light of today's needs.

The following section deals with ways of handling the welcomes and partings of existence, covering some of the human situations that arise, as well as setting out the leading procedures both religious and secular. Firstly, the birth of a baby and the initiation of a new member of the family into society, without which there would be shortly no manners at all.

Prospective motherhood

The contemporary stance of a woman who is expecting a baby is to carry on as normal without seeking any special consideration. She is unlikely to wish to disguise the appearance of pregnancy as far as dress is concerned. Nor, in the usual way of things, does she enjoy being made to feel incompetent as the result of her state, through an excessive show of attention.

However, it is polite for men to make a point of opening doors, offering to carry heavy baggage and giving up a seat in a crowded bus or train, as soon as it becomes apparent that she might appreciate these courtesies. In a perfect world these gestures would be made as a matter of course between the strong and the dependent irrespective of gender, but in an imperfect world, they should at least be observed when a woman's pregnancy is evident. If a pregnant woman decides to stay on in her job and work up to the last moment, she should bear in mind the reactions of colleagues and associates. If her type of work demands physical stamina or calls for long and tiring hours, it can be inconsiderate to go to the limits as associates and colleagues will almost certainly have to shoulder part of the work-load.

Working mothers-to-be should take care to establish the exact terms of maternity leave at their place of work and how these might apply in their case. When a prospective parent's post is being kept open for them, it is courteous to keep an employer in touch with developments. Inevitably in a lifechanging situation such as this one, an element of uncertainty hovers over plans made before the event. Health factors, or simply a change of heart, may alter previous commitments. The person who is deputizing for the absent parent-to-be, his or her future has also to be considered.

This whole matter calls for understanding on all sides and a preparedness on the part of the parent to communicate intentions sooner rather than later.

Now that paternity leave is established in many sectors of employment, the above remarks may have a bearing on the father and his employer, too.

Present at the birth

Prince Charles set the royal imprimatur on father being present at the birth of the baby. The idea of fathers playing a supportive instead of a passive role has proved rewarding for both parents.

In acknowledging the trend, some thought has to be spared for dissenters who for one reason or another, prefer to let others take on this responsibility. Some men may have doubts about their competence in the role of quasi-midwife and prefer to take the old path of worrying in absentia until after the baby is delivered.

It would be intrusive to cast aspersions on the father's motives or to tease him about his decision. It is certainly in order to ask a father-in-waiting if he intends to be present at the birth, but in the event of a negative reply, he should be allowed to go his way in peace. It should be said that in general, husbands stand to gain more from helping their wife through labour if they have attended an ante-natal class for fathers.

Whom, among members of the family, the mother-to-be wishes to have by her side during childbirth is obviously a personal matter influenced by medics and arrangements for the birth. Many like to have their own mother on hand whether they are attended by the husband or not, or at least to have on their side a close member of family who has had a child herself. Where facilities permit, fathers, mother's mother and closest siblings are all within call.

First announcements

It usually falls to the father of the baby to spread the first word of the new arrival. As soon as the mother feels herself again, she continues the communication process.

Often, the father will have been present at the birth of his baby and so will be familiar with all the clinical aspects of the confinement. How far he discusses these depends on the listener. Some are thirsty for details, others – often including male members of the older generation – prefer a more reserved account. There is also the predilection of the mother. She may prefer a more romantic approach to the announcement.

First to be told will be the mother's own mother, if she wasn't present at the time – and the other grandparents, together with the newborn's aunts, uncles and cousins. Prospective godparents and anyone specially close to either mother or father, should be informed as soon as possible. Probably, this will include a call to the mother's workmates and her boss. In the usual way of things, the other women who have worked alongside the prospective mother during her pregnancy have a natural curiosity about the baby and the welfare of their associate. Details are likely to be appreciated.

Usually, the news is telephoned or conveyed in person. What is generally announced is the gender of the baby, his or her weight at birth, any forenames that may have already been decided upon, and any reassurances that can be given about the well-being of mother and babe, not forgetting papa.

The wider circle is kept in touch by letter, or more probably by cards announcing the birth, by telephone, or by published announcements in the papers. Cards will be celebratory in style, wording and illustration.

One proud father had the notion of mailing family and friends with a first snapshot of mother and child, with the announcement of birth written on the reverse.

Published announcements

Notices are published in the Births columns of national and local newspapers. *The Times*, the *Daily Telegraph, Independent, Yorkshire Post* and *Jewish Chronicle* have widely scanned personal announcements which are placed at advertised rates. The Court columns of national newspapers publish announcements of birth, at the discretion of the Social Editor. In the case of prominent figures, these may be inserted free of charge, otherwise they are paid for at the usual rates.

Standard announcements give the family name, the date of birth, the gender of the child and the first names of both parents. Additional information sometimes includes the name of the hospital where the baby was delivered, and details: 'a brother for Millie' or 'a sister for Sally'.

An example of a brief announcement:
> *Lane* On 28 July, to Meg, (née Fitch) and Dean, a daughter.

An example of a more detailed announcement:
> *Abuhoul* On 3 December at Tenby Maternity Hospital, to Anna (née Lister) and Abdul, a daughter, Ayesha Lara, a sister for Ahmad.

Adoption

Announcements of the adoption of a child are placed in the Births columns and personal columns of the above-mentioned newspapers, by the adoptive parents.

An example:

> *Green* to Paula (née Black) and Martin, an adopted son, Richard Jonathan.

Single and unmarried parents

Announcements of the birth of a child to a single mother or to parents who are not married to each other, are no longer an oddity in the Births columns.

An example of an announcement of a birth to a single parent:

> *Gedding* On 11 May, at Kingsbury District Hospital, to Sara, a son, Richard Peter.

Legalities

In England and Wales, births must be registered within 42 days with the Registrar of Births in the district where the baby was born. Either parent can sign the register.

Unmarried parents in dispute over registration are advised to consult the Registrar or a solicitor.

In Scotland, where everything is always done a bit differently from south of the border, the grace period is 21 days and the registration may take place as above or in the mother's district.

Naming the newborn

Naming the child is a bundle of considerations. First must be the likely response of the growing child to the choice of the name, or parental guesses as to what this might be. The second is what is fitting with the style of the surname and whether the two sound good together when pronounced. The third might be considerations within the family.

Endowing a child with the name of a grandparent or close relative maintains a most attractive link between the generations. If there is competition between the two sides of the family, the child might be given more than one name which would allow for a choice of one from each branch. If this proves impractical, there may be the hope of a future sibling who could be the recipient of the name from the neglected side – at any rate the point could be made in amelioration of any ruffled feelings.

Other factors to bear in mind are the importance of weighing up the style of the diminutive of the chosen name – the shortened version is much more likely to be used these days than the full name. Meanings as a basis of selection are selective. Whereas few parents seem to reject Mary because it means bitterness, or Paul on grounds of meaning small, for example, a name with a pleasing meaning may be selected for that very reason, such as liking Stella meaning star, or Richard, meaning powerful.

Giving a child more than one name at least guards against the eventuality of their disliking their first name when they grow older.

The poet T.S. Eliot, surely had humans in mind when he wrote his famous verses about the nomenclature of cats:

'The Naming of Cats is a difficult matter
It isn't one of your holiday games:
At first you may think I'm as mad as a hatter
When I tell you a cat must have THREE DIFFERENT
NAMES.

Presents for mother and child

After the birth proud fathers are traditionally in a mood to produce a present for the mother to commemorate the occasion. Jewellery is a time-honoured choice – whatever is given usually has the character of a keepsake.

From earliest times it has been customary to welcome a new member of the family with offerings. Close relations, friends and supporters send or bring a present, often of a practical nature such as a contribution to the layette or an item for the nursery.

Grandparents and, those all too rare figments of novels, benefactors might choose to bestow a more substantial gift which helps to secure the financial security of the child. A transfer of shares, opening a savings account or a trust fund in the child's name, are established acts of generosity. Putting down wine and port for future delectation is a gesture in the grand manner. As so much attention is bound to focus on the newborn, thoughtful friends and family remember the mother too. It would be kind to produce a present just for her such as a bottle of favourite scent, a book, a clutch of the latest magazines, or a video recording. Offerings that are sent should be acknowledged either by telephone or note.

Flowers and cards

Friends and relations wishing to send flowers and congratulations to the mother in a maternity ward are advised to check on the duration of her stay before sending. The turn-over in many busy wards is such that patients are out almost as soon as they are in. It may be best to send to the home address a few days after the birth.

Flowers should be addressed to the mother with a signed card bearing a message of love and congratulation. A handwritten message by the donor is always preferable to a ready-printed one. But sometimes, when distances separate sender and recipient, this is an impractical aim.

An example of a message might be, 'Welcome to Rosie and congratulations to you and Peter'. Printed greetings cards tend to run to pictures of storks and blue-for-a-boy sentiments which may be stereotypical but do convey the essential message. Aesthetes may search for more satisfying graphics or compose a letter.

When the new parents are non-white members of an ethnic group, the problem can arise of finding an illustrated card that chimes with their culture. Gooseberry bushes have little connection with birth outside these islands. It is probably best to eschew the more markedly pale-face images and legends, and opt for a card with universal appeal. In any case, the sender is probably more sensitive on this point than the recipient.

All flowers should be thanked for, either in person or in writing. Greetings cards, unless these contain a long personal message, seem low on the thank-you list. The notion of giving young siblings a present in order to stave off pangs of jealousy is unsurprisingly effective. Whereas others cannot be expected to rise to this occasion, parents and godparents might take note.

Baby showers

The idea has caught on in Britain from the United States of giving a baby shower for an expected infant. This is usually in the form of a tea-party and is given by a close friend of the prospective mother, often a godparent-to-be of the child. It is understood that everyone who accepts the invitation will bring a present for the baby. Friends, most likely female, and their offspring attend. As in the case of bridal showers, the host should not be the parents or close member of the family that stands to gain.

Some consider that the celebration is premature. The majority view, though, holds that the occasion is a cheer-up for the mother during the final weeks of waiting and the offerings may feather the baby's nest most propitiously.

Those who prefer to play safe or to wait for the gender of the newborn before choosing a present are perfectly entitled to do so.

Visiting the baby

Admiring the baby is an essential part of any visit. Patience should be shown by those who are not among nature's baby worshippers, when parents find in their ewe lamb qualities utterly remarkable.

Conversely, delighted parents should show understanding of friends and family if their tolerance of the baby topic has distinct limits. When visiting a new baby, it is a good idea to pay attentions to any siblings as they may feel left out.

Single parent predicaments

Few need reminding that the considerate approach of others towards the single mother who is expecting a baby is to include her in, like any other prospective parent. Courtesy suggests that friends and allies do their best to help equalize the chances of mother and baby with those more conventionally placed. Most of the advice in this section applies.

The surrounding circumstances of single parenthood need to be borne in mind by others when considering their actions. The category includes those in very different situations. Some who are pregnant may be waiting on a divorce before marrying the father, or may have a settled relationship with the father akin to a marriage, but many may be on their own.

If the father shares the joys of prospective paternity, naturally he is congratulated and friends make an effort to do what is normally done. On the other hand, it can happen that the desire to have the baby is the woman's alone and in this case, any probing on the identity of the father or trying to involve him in procedures, would be extremely discourteous and intrusive.

Complications

When complications occur involving either mother or child, friends should desist from pressing for a fuller report on developments than is issued by the hospital or the family.

In the case of a home confinement where friends suspect that extra help would be appreciated, offers should not be delayed.

In general, the interested outside world has to wait to be informed about the health and well-being of the two.

A miscarriage

The approach to someone who has had a miscarriage is usually determined by the person who has lost her baby. Probably, it is wisest to wait for the topic to be raised, and if silence on the subject is maintained to confine any expressions of sympathy to a passing remark. If the matter is to be aired, it is thoughtful to adopt a positive and optimistic view of future prospects for maternity – assuming all else is equal.

Women tend to feel physically low after a miscarriage and morale-raising gestures are likely to be appreciated.

Termination

Much of the advice above also applies to the woman who decides to terminate her pregnancy with the difference that the conscious act to have an abortion makes emotional demands of a different order. Usually, confidentiality surrounds abortion which though crucial in cases often denies the parent the support she needs.

Friends who are in the know should offer assistance immediately following the operation which is likely to be the sufferer's low point.

In the event of a baby's death

See page 160 for Letters of sympathy.

When a newborn baby dies suddenly, the custom is to honour the infant with the rites and formalities that accompany the dead.

First rites

Many families of a particular religious persuasion wish their child to be initiated into that faith. The first rite of babyhood is usually followed by ceremonies marking stages of spiritual progress and growing acceptance of adult responsibilities. Baptism, Bar mitzvah and Khatme Koran are among the widely known rites of passage for Christians, Jews and Moslems, respectively.

Even if parents are not practising members of their faith, they may nevertheless retain the conviction that a child should be integrated into the family's religious beliefs. Some parents feel that they should not pre-empt a child's views, others may be members of a branch of religion, such as the Quakers, which does not hold with ceremonial. In general, though, religious initiation rites have become a mixture of piety, custom and tradition. In most instances the religious ceremonies are accompanied by a social celebration of some kind.

The whole subject of initiation rites is far too diverse and multi-faceted to be usefully summarized here. The following guidelines are therefore related to the most familiar religious denominations in Britain – Anglican, Roman Catholic, Jewish and Moslem.

In the Church of England

Arranging a christening

The church now officially discourages the old practice of private baptism in a separate service. Stress is laid on baptism which takes place during a normal Sunday service in front of a congregation. Nevertheless, the idea of a private service attended only by parents, godparents and friends is cherished by many, and when it happens, is an occasion to remember.

If a private baptism, sometimes known as a social baptism, is to be held, attended primarily by family, godparents and friends, the order of service, hymns, anthems and prayers to be included may be discussed with the minister. The question of whether special flower arrangements will be placed at the font should also be raised, if these are wished.

Parents may wish to discuss their own religious background and that of the godparents. It should be noted that many ministers hold absolutely fast to the Church law that parents and godparents must be baptized and confirmed Christians. Any deviations should be aired with the minister and it is unwise to announce a christening date until his agreement is given.

Some ministers are prepared to cast a kindly eye on parents who are not themselves Christians but who wish their child to be baptized. In fact, most clergymen are pleased to welcome a new member of the flock but will want assurances that the child will be given a Christian upbringing.

Choosing the officiating minister

Some families have a member of the cloth among their number or a friend in holy orders whom they would like to officiate at the baptism. The procedure is to put his request to the incumbent vicar.

Note: the Roman Catholic Church accept the practice of private baptism. Arrangements should be made with the parish priest. Public baptism is performed during Mass, also.

Baptism

The baptism of babies and young children is central to Christian belief. In addition, the christening ceremony can be said to be the first public occasion at which the newborn's Christian names are declared before a congregation.

The baptismal act takes place at the font in church, often one and the same church where the parents were married.

During the ceremony, parents and godparents gather round the font. The priest asks them to affirm their Christian beliefs on behalf of themselves and the child. They are called upon to repent their sins and renounce evil.

Water is then poured into the font and blessed. The mother gives the baby to the chief godmother who hands it to the priest. The priest asks the godparents to 'name this child'. This they do, giving the baby's Christian names. The priest then names the baby after them, and sprinkles the water on the baby's forehead. He baptizes the baby 'in the name of the Father and of the Son and of the Holy Ghost.'

The priest then makes the sign of the cross on the baby's forehead. The babe is returned to the mother.

The godparents are reminded of their responsibilities towards the spiritual development of the child. If fully implemented, this would mean ensuring that their charge was confirmed in later years.

A further ceremony may follow in which the minister gives a lighted candle to one of the parents to symbolize the passing of darkness into light.

Alternatives in service wordings

The traditional wording of the baptismal service is set out in the Book of Common Prayer (1662 version). Those having a baby baptized should read the service as the best guide to meaning.

However, there are other wordings written in more everyday language published in the Alternative Service Series.

Practicalities

During proceedings at church, it is usual for the father to go into the vestry and enter the baby's Christian names and data in the church register together with the names of the godparents.

A fee is required for a copy of the certificate of baptism. At a private baptism a contribution to church funds would be acceptable.

Service of Thanksgiving

Parents whose consciences do not allow them to make the full baptismal pledges may take advantage of a Service of Thanksgiving for the Birth of a Child (a similar service may be used in the case of an adopted child). The wording appears in The Alternative Service Book.

Church of Scotland

At a baby's baptism in the Church of Scotland, it is usual for the father to hand the child to the minister. Afterwards, the minister hands the child to the mother.

Godparents do not play a formal part in the ceremony and have no responses. Their secular equivalents, however, may be present at the font during the baptism.

True to its reputation as a broad church, Church of Scotland ministers may be prepared to baptize an infant whose parents, or one of whose parents, are not members. The tendency is to judge each case on its merits.

The Church of Rome

The Roman Catholic ceremony is longer and more elaborate than its Anglican counterpart. Another difference is that the mother holds the baby throughout the baptismal rite.

The priest makes the sign of the cross on the baby's head which is repeated by the parents and godparents. The priest anoints the child with catechumens (signifying salvation) and then follows the laying-on of hands. The parents and godparents renounce the devil and affirm their beliefs before baptism is administered. The child is then anointed with the chrism, sacred oil, and wrapped in a white garment. The father or godfather lights a candle from the priest's candle, representing the light of salvation.

The service may include a homily, and concludes with a blessing.

Berit Milah

The first rite for an infant male Jew is circumcision at the age of eight days. Judith Martin, the American etiquette writer, has commented. 'The Berit Milah, like all great ceremonies in life, is designed to be enjoyed by everyone except the guest of honour.'

The religious ceremony is attended by parents, godparents, grandparents and invited friends. Prayers and a blessing over a goblet of wine take place and the baby is given a Hebrew name, signifying initiation into the faith.

The baby is held for circumcision by a male member of the family. The operation in which the foreskin is removed is performed by a *mohel*, a professional.

A small reception follows to which those who attended the ceremony bring presents for mother and child.

Many non-practising Jews and non-Jews have their infant sons circumcised on grounds of health.

When a daughter is born to Jewish parents, they take her to the synagogue on the first Sabbath after her birth. The father reads the Torah and the baby is given a Hebrew name.

Members of the Reform and Liberal branches have pruned the ceremonial aspects of Berit Milah. At these temples, both boy and girl infants are taken to be blessed during usual Sabbath worship.

Moslem rites

Newcomers attend the ceremonies and parties that are part of a young Moslem's religious upbringing. First rites take place in boyhood, and are followed in the way of many other religions, by feasting and a family gathering. As soon as the child is of an age to take part in a watershed rite, the attainment is marked by a family gathering of family and friends.

Kahtme Koran is a ceremony at which a twelve- to thirteen-year-old reads from the Koran. Afterwards, a party is usually given to which the young friends of the child are invited. It is not usual for guests to bring a present.

Godparents

The institution of godparents has everything to recommend it. The pity, in many people's minds, is that the practice has not been adapted for the children of non-believers.

A godparent is expected to fulfil a dual role, to sustain their godchild's religious beliefs and to be a special ally and trusted friend. A traditional part of godparenting is to produce a present to commemorate the child's first religious rites and to keep up the good work at birthdays and feast days throughout their upbringing.

A close bond between godparent and godchild is mutually rewarding; each taking a pleasure in the other's company because of the special relationship. Popular godparents take out their godchildren on their own when they are of an age to enjoy treats and occasions, and always remember birthdays and feast days.

Sometimes, as godchildren grow up they may confide in godparents if the bond is close in a way they may find difficult with parents.

Godparental presents

It is customary for godparents to produce a keepsake to commemorate the ceremonies that mark a godchild's religious education. The first offering might be a silver mug engraved with the recipient's name or initials, silver eating implements, a necklet of coral or pearls. A longstanding tradition is to begin a collection for the child, such as the first volume of a set of children's books, or the first pearl which can be added to over the years to form a complete necklace. Sometimes a decorative object for the child's room is produced such as a picture.

This is an occasion on which it is perfectly acceptable to give cash as a present. If bank notes are to be handed though, they should be placed in an envelope.

Choosing godparents

Parents usually choose godparents from their closest friends or favourite members of the family. In theory, godparents should share the religious beliefs to which they will commit the godchild, but in practice, some latitude exists on this point. It is a matter for the individual conscience of the godparent if he or she is a non-believer or a member of a different faith. Another factor is the approach of the minister who will be officiating at the service or rite. If it is thought that his views are highly orthodox, this may affect the choice of godparent.

In general, parents invite those to whom they can entrust the honour, bearing in mind that a variety of talent is desirable. A well-to-do benefactor is often a consideration but wealth can disappear with the Dow Jones index. Rich and kind is something else.

The invitation to be a godparent should be made in good time in case others have to be found.

Accepting and declining godparenthood

It is a great compliment to be asked to be a godparent and it is almost too easy to accept without considering the commitment involved. Although godparents who give their name to the role, produce the occasional present and are never heard of again by the child are far from uncommon, a sense of let-down does exist in later years. Even, especially perhaps, by the godchild who makes a joke of it.

It is better for an equivocal potential godparent to decline. Acceptable explanations are an oversubscribed number of godchildren and a decision to close the lists, a genuine unwillingness to take part in the religious side, not wishing to take on social responsibilities which you are unlikely to fulfil, absence. Unacceptable are a dislike of the child, disapproval of the parents or unavailability at the ceremony, as proxies can stand instead.

Declining should be prompt, as replacements will probably have to be found. No apologies are required.

Accepting requires only joyous assent.

Christian godparents

In the Church of England, a male child has two godfathers to one godmother, a female child has two godmothers and one godfather. According to Roman Catholic practice, boys and girls alike have one male and one female godparent. For reasons given, these numbers are often exceeded. Four godparents for a child is not unusual.

Godparents are expected to attend the christening ceremony. Should they be unable to be present, Proxies may stand. Proxies are chosen by parents or godparents. Again, it is thoughtful for godparents to keep everyone in touch with their intentions.

It is usual to ask members of the family to stand proxy as inviting a friend who might have been chosen as a godparent could seem insensitive.

An age for christening

A child may be christened at any age (mature baptism is far from unusual) but the rite usually takes place some time between the age of six weeks and four months. Some children are not baptized until they are toddlers, for one reason or another. Various factors which might delay baptism include the health of the child or the availability of both parents for the ceremony.

Preliminaries

The minister of the place of worship where the parents wish the baptism to take place should be contacted by telephone or letter, or the matter raised informally after a church service.

Some parishes provide preparation for baptism which may range from a private conversation to classes over several weeks.

Christening clothes

A christening followed by a celebration suggests best dress for the leading participants.

Parents, godparents and proxies are expected to put on smart day clothes. Women usually wear a hat. Men don a lounge suit and necktie. Other members of the congregation appear in whatever they feel comfortable in that is consonant with the religious nature of the occasion and the party afterwards.

The baby traditionally wears a white or cream robe which may be long or short. Some families can produce christening robes which have been handed down for succeeding generations to wear. An old tradition is to have a robe made up from a piece of silk or lace taken from the train of the baby's mother's wedding dress, or perhaps from special fabric kept for the event.

Some parents invest in ready-made dress equivalents of these elaborate designs but everyone may rest assured that the simplest little dress is more than acceptable today.

Young children are christened in short clothes of the kind they might wear to a party, not necessarily in white.

Christening parties

The party following the baby's baptism is usually a family affair, with grandparents and other relatives, godparents, friends and related children in evidence. Timing depends on the hour of the church service. If the baptism is private this will probably take place in the afternoon and a tea party follows.

The officiating minister should be asked to attend and, if appropriate, his wife.

See page 96 for The wedding cake.

Celebrations call for a christening cake, iced in white. Sometimes this is the top tier of the parents' wedding cake which has been reserved for the purpose.

Usually the baby's health is proposed by a friend of the family, often a godfather, and celebratory glasses are raised. No set speeches occur as a rule.

The star of the day is the baby and compliments are in order.

Guests are not expected to produce a present but those who have not given anything so far might like to take advantage of the opportunity.

Announcing a christening

Christenings may be announced in the Court columns of national newspapers. It is customary to give the following information: the names of the parents, the baby, the officiating clergyman, the place of worship and the location, and the date. The names of all godparents (whether present at the ceremony or not) are given, and those of any proxies.

The announcement is submitted in writing to the Social Editor. The usual advertising rates apply.

Rites for older children

Many of the world's leading religions perform rites of passage for young members. Generally, ceremonies mark stages of progress in a child's understanding of their faith and their ability to participate. A period of religious instruction preparing them for the ritual is common to all. Usually, the ceremony is a family occasion.

Confirmation

Confirmation in the Church of England usually takes place when the child is between the ages of twelve and fourteen. At a special service, at which the bishop usually officiates, ordained for the 'laying-on of hands', the child is asked to take for himself the vows that were made on his behalf at his or her baptism. A first communion may be incorporated in the service.

Parents, godparents and close friends attend and their number should include one baptized and confirmed Christian.

Dress is Sunday best for both boys and girls. Occasionally, commemorative presents of a religious nature are given.

Confirmation for Roman Catholics usually takes place when a child is between the ages of eight and nine. The rite may be part of a Mass or be performed at a special service. Parents participate in the ceremony.

In the Jewish faith, Reform and Liberal branches like their young to be confirmed at the age of sixteen plus. The ceremony is for both sexes. The feasting and present-giving associated with Bar and Bat-mitzvahs does not apply here.

First Communion

First communion is an important rite and social event in the life of a young Roman Catholic, which usually takes place when the child is between the ages of seven and eight.

The priest administers the sacrament at a special Mass. Girls don a white dress and veil (also the attire for first communion), boys dress in their best. Frequently, a party rounds off the day.

Bar-mitzavh

At a bar-mitzvah, a young Jew is called up in the synagogue on the first Sabbath after his thirteenth birthday, to read from the Torah. It is an occasion of great moment to the Jewish community and especially to the boy's parents and supporters.

The celebratory ceremony marks the boy's passage from childhood to manhood. He is reminded of his responsibilities towards his family, the Jewish community and his faith.

Non-practising Jews and non-Jews frequently attend the ceremonies of bar-mitzvah and bat-mitzvah, and join in the celebrations that follow.

After the service, a *kiddush* is given by the parents at the synagogue. Light refreshments and wine are offered to the whole congregation.

Visitors should remember that congratulations to the bar-mitzvah boy and his proud parents are very much in order.

Bat-mitzvah

A girl of the Jewish faith may read from the Torah in the synagogue, when she has attained her twelfth birthday. This takes place at a separate service on the Sabbath. Approaches to procedures depend on the branch of Judaism. Some Reform and Liberal members are bringing the age of the girls into line with the boys' initiation at thirteen years.

A *kiddush* follows.

L(a)st rites

Formalities are determined by the authorities but attitudes towards

mourning are looked upon as a private matter. Nowadays there are no

formal codes of mourning with the exception of royal protocol and certain

religious practice.

As a general rule, a period of seclusion is allowed to the bereaved immediately following the death. Bereavement is grounds for cancelling previous engagements, and employers usually grant compassionate leave to those with funerals to attend or duties to be performed.

The preferred stance of keeping grieving as a personal concern should not deter friends and allies of the bereaved from openly expressing sympathy and support. It is usually better to make some mention of the death in conversation even if this is only some brief sentiment along the lines of 'I am sorry to hear about your mother'. At least the thought shows regard.

Certifying a death

The two officials who can certify a death are either a doctor or a coroner (a coroner will be a qualified doctor, or solicitor or barrister).

When someone dies in hospital, the doctor who attended them during their last illness, usually establishes the 'cause of death' and completes the certificate which enables the next of kin to register the death.

If the deceased is to be cremated, signatures by two doctors are required. A qualification of the doctors who sign is that they should have attended the person who has died within fourteen days of the death or twenty-eight in Northern Ireland.

The coroner

If the doctors have reasons for not showing the death certificate, or the Registrar of Births and Deaths is dissatisfied with the case, the death will be referred to the coroner.

Deaths are reported to the coroner by the doctor in the following cases: no medical practitioner attended the person during the fourteen days immediately preceding the death (twenty-eight days in Northern Ireland); death occurred during an operation or its immediate aftermath; the demise was violent, sudden, unexplained or accompanied by suspicious circumstances.

Deaths may be reported to the coroner by the police, and also by relatives who are concerned about the surrounding circumstances of the death of a member of the family.

The coroner's main task is to establish the cause of death through the evidence. Should he decide (as he does in the majority of instances) that this was due to 'natural causes', there will be no need for a post-mortem or inquest. He will then be able to grant a certificate of death to the registrar and if required, a certificate of cremation.

The coroner is obliged to hold an inquest if death occurred as the result of industrial injury, a car crash or a rail or air accident.

Note: The procurator fiscal undertakes these responsibilities in Scotland.

Post-mortems

When a post-mortem is held, the coroner decides who will conduct proceedings. These are usually handled by a hospital pathologist. In the majority of cases the pathologist's report confirms 'natural causes' and there is no need for an inquest. In the event of suspicions continuing an inquest will be held.

Registering a death

This is a bureaucratic procedure not to be undertaken lightly. The information given to the Registrar of Births and Deaths must be correct, and the person who informs him or her must be entitled to perform the task.

Form-filling at this stage is usually an onerous business for the bereaved for whom it can be reassuring to be accompanied by a morale-raiser.

In England and Wales a death should be reported within five days, but two weeks' grace is given before formal registration is required. The death must be registered at the registration sub-district office in the area where it occurred. The address of the Registrar is listed in the telephone directory under Registration of Births, Deaths and Marriages.

People who are legally entitled to inform the Registrar are as follows: a relative of the deceased; a person who was present during the last illness or at the death; someone who lived in the same house as the deceased; the person in charge of the institution where the death took place; the person who is making the funeral arrangements.

The Registrar will need to be satisfied that the 'informant' meets the legal requirements to act as such. Assuming all is in order, the informant will be asked for his or her full name and address and, when the form is completed, to sign it with the Registrar's pen and special ink.

The information that will be required by the Registrar is as follows: the name, sex and home address of the deceased; the date of death and where this occurred; the date and place of birth of the person who has died; the occupation of the deceased and whether he or she was retired at the time of death. In the case of a married woman: her maiden name; the name of her spouse and his occupation and whether he is retired. In the case of a widow: her maiden name; the name of her late spouse, his occupation and whether he was retired at the time of death. The medical cause of death of the deceased will be given to the Registrar via the services of the doctor or coroner. In the case of the death of a young person under the age of fifteen, the names of both biological parents will be required and their occupations.

Note: It may assist in settling the affairs of the deceased if the names in which the death is registered correspond with those on the birth or marriage certificate. In the case of people who are known by professional names it is recommended that these are given as well, in the interests of establishing identity.

Special points

If a person dies in hospital, the relevant department or ward sister may provide a medical certificate and if necessary a certificate of cremation with the required signatures by medical practitioners.

The certificate signed by the doctor need not specify the cause of death as the doctor will give this information to the Registrar. If the registrar is satisfied with the reasons given for the cause of death, he will register the death accordingly.

A death that has been reported to a coroner cannot be registered until the Registrar receives an authorization from the coroner. It is helpful if whoever visits the Registrar has available the deceased's National Health Service number.

Registering a death in Scotland

Procedures are similar to those in England, but in the usual way, not identical. In Scotland, eight days' grace is given in which to register a death. The death can be registered in the area in which the deceased lived irrespective of whether the death took place in that district.

Burial

The notion of being buried in a country parish churchyard beneath the yew tree where one's ancestors are interred is very appealing to members of the Church of England. Yet it has only ever applied to a few, and today land for graves is running short. Other solutions have to be found.

Nevertheless, everyone, whether pagan or pious and wherever their death took place, has a right, in theory, to be buried in their parish churchyard. If there is no churchyard in your parish you may ask if your relative may be buried in that of a neighbouring parish. Permission in this case has to be obtained from the minister concerned and his parochial church council.

Unless the deceased had previously arranged for a grave space in a churchyard or cemetery, fees must be paid for one. A document known as a 'faculty' is needed for a churchyard, and a 'deed of grant' for a cemetery (Scotland's document is called a 'lair certificate').

Burial in a cemetery

Many cemeteries are now open to all, irrespective of religion. However, in some cases, areas of the land are set aside for different denominations. There is usually a chapel in which services are conducted and clergymen who will officiate.

Church fees

Fees at a funeral service are due for the choir, the organist and the soloist(s), and also for burial in the churchyard, for putting up a headstone, for removing and replacing a family headstone. A contribution to Church funds is usual.

Fees for burial in a cemetery

Charges vary according to district and parts of the country. A scale of charges is obtainable either from the local authority that administers the cemetery or the company that does. There are different charges for different types and orders of grave according to position, maintenance and preparation.

Special cases

If a person wishes to be buried on their own land they must obtain planning permission. Sometimes the deeds of the land prohibit the burial.

Burial at sea

It is possible for a landlubber to be buried at sea but a number of somewhat quirky procedures have to be negotiated as a pre-condition. The act is regarded by officialdom in the same light as if a body was being taken out of the country; permission has to be obtained from the local inspector of fisheries who may not be able to allow committal at the chosen point of the compass, and a private boat may have to be chartered with a specially weighted coffin. However, a simpler course awaits the cremated. Ashes may be cast into the sea, at will.

When someone dies abroad

When the family wish to bring home the body of someone who has died abroad, they should consult the consular official in the area or the Foreign Office consular section in London.

If death occurred on a holiday organized by a tour operator, the local representative should be able to assist in the repatriation of the body.

Dealing with all the paperwork and documentation required from the two countries – home and abroad – is a major project. Seeking the advice of a funeral director should be a priority.

Arranging the funeral service

A funeral service may take place as soon as the necessary documentation has been obtained for burial or cremation.

Timing should take into account those whom the family especially wish to be among the congregation, as well as the views of the minister and undertaker. If people are having to bridge distances, an afternoon ceremony would probably be best, allowing them the morning for travel. If the chief participants are locals, however, a morning ceremony may suit just as well.

It is worth mentioning that seating arrangements at a funeral and public involvement in formalities in general is a subject which calls for particular tact from all parties concerned.

Former spouses of the dead person, extra-marital partners of consequence, children from the deceased's previous marriage, step-sisters and step-brothers may or may not wish to play a part in proceedings and these desires may be in conflict with the family's idea of propriety.

It would be courteous for the widow or widower to show tolerance of an ex-spouse's wish to pay their respects on this occasion. It would be considerate if the living spouse invited a child of a first marriage to undertake one of the readings. As to etiquette in relation to a lover when there is a living spouse, personal attitudes determine actions in the absence of any recognized guidelines.

Emotional support is of crucial importance to the bereaved during the funeral. Those who have had to undergo long journeys possibly in a state of shock may need a firm shoulder to lean on, or at least a hand held. If a funeral is being held in the country and family and friends are travelling distances, it is only courteous for the family to offer hospitality to a greater number than might otherwise be the case.

The usual custom is to offer friends and family some refreshment before and after the ceremony. It would be considerate for guests to offer to help as funerals are a time of great strain in the usual way of things.

Customs about death vary according to nationality and creed. The Irish, for instance, are for the riotous wake that marks the vigil beside the dead. Merry-making, music and lamentation are mixed in equal measure and solace is offered in the form of a funeral feast.

Procedures for the family

Details of the order of service will have been discussed with the minister. Prayers, hymns and readings should be carefully chosen. It is usual to ask a son or daughter of the person who has died or their close relation to read a lesson or a passage from the scriptures. Some ministers will allow secular literature to be read but this is not usual. The spouse or parent of the deceased is excused from participating in the readings.

An important decision is the person invited to give the address. This may be the officiating minister or a friend in Holy Orders, but is more likely to be a close friend or colleague or teacher who will speak informally and for the most part admiringly about the character and life of the dead person.

The chief mourners leave together for the ceremony. The coffin is transported in a hearse to the place of worship, accompanied by the undertaker's bearers. The family occupy the front pews or equivalent at the place of worship.

A verger may be available to help show people to their seats and ensure that space is kept for the family, or someone else could be deputed to do the job.

At this point procedures depend on whether the coffin is set in place at the chancel steps before the family arrive at the church, or whether the coffin precedes them as it is carried up the aisle by the undertakers' bearers. In the latter case, the family follow behind in an orderly procession.

After the last prayers and blessing the coffin is removed by the bearers in a slow procession down the aisle, followed by the chief mourners. The next step depends on the destination of the coffin, to an adjacent churchyard, to a graveyard in another district, or to a cemetery for burial, which will probably be some distance from the church.

Burial after a church service

When burial takes place in a cemetery or graveyard some considerable distance from the church where the funeral service is held, the chief mourners usually take their leave promptly and follow the hearse in an orderly procession of cars.

Sometimes there is a pause and the chief mourners receive friends and family outside the church for a few minutes. So much depends on the circumstances of the death and the state of mind of the bereaved.

Cremation

Many of the ancient fears that persisted about cremation have faded through a growing acceptance of its practicality. It has considerable advantages in a land-hungry country and in addition is economical in terms of labour, aftercare and ritual. Most crematoria chapels are non-denominational and the family may follow their own religious practice or arrange a secular farewell.

The secular origins of cremation have unfortunately produced some decidedly uninspiring architecture and surroundings. Also, the very brief, standardized denominational services are thought, by some, to be impersonal.

Arranging a cremation

Since evidence of any malpractice disappears when a body is cremated, safeguards mean that the number of forms involved are more complex than in burial.

Cremation cannot take place until the exact cause of death is known.

A disposal certificate from the Registrar is required in addition to the following paperwork:

- An application for cremation signed by a close relative or executor, counter-signed by someone who knows the signatory.
- A form signed by two doctors, one the medical officer who saw the deceased during their last illness, the other a medical practitioner who is unconnected either with the co-signatory or the dead person. A fee is payable.
- A form signed by the medical referee of the crematorium (a doctor). If he is dissatisfied with the case, he has the authority to call for a post-mortem or to refer it to the coroner.

Note: the form that is required to be signed by two doctors referred to above is not necessary where the coroner has provided a certificate for cremation.

Disposal of the ashes

There may be little formal ceremony but much sentiment connected with the disposal of the cremated remains. Approaches depend on personal belief and on predilection. The ashes can be disposed of by the crematorium, or collected and retained by the family.

Usually, the ashes are given to the family the day after the cremation has taken place. Sometimes mourners return to witness the interment of the ashes at the cemetery, or they are removed for burial elsewhere, or they are removed and placed in an urn for safe keeping. Ashes are scattered ceremonially to the four winds, strewn on a favourite patch of earth or cast into the deep. A spouse or grown offspring or a good friend usually undertakes the act.

In remembrance

At the gardens of remembrance at crematoria, various means exist whereby the dead are commemorated. It may be a rose tree or a wall plaque or an entry in a memorial book.

Funeral services

In the Church of England

The liturgy of the Church of England affirms the Christian belief in life after death. The form of the funeral service can be read in the revised Prayer Book of 1928 in which there is a separate one for the death of a child.

The traditional form and wording are included in Alternative Services Series 1 and are available in print. Those who are drawn to religious services written in a modern idiom might like to study the Alternative Service Book of 1980.

The exact order of service will be discussed between the officiating minister and the family. The minister's views are likely to be forthright. However, the personal character of a funeral service finds a sympathetic response in many cases.

Usually there are hymns, prayers, psalms and readings. The minister gives a short homily on the life of the dead person. The Lord's Prayer is said, followed by a blessing. Pall bearers with the coffin and the mourners then proceed to the graveside. The priest says, 'We commit her (his) body to the ground; earth to earth, ashes to ashes, dust to dust; in sure and certain hope of the resurrection through eternal life through our Lord Jesus Christ.'

An ancient rite is for the mourners to strew some earth on the coffin at a burial after it has been lowered into the grave. Customs vary according to different parts of the country. Pall-bearers play a part in some districts. They accompany the coffin but do not bear its weight which is the task of the undertaker's men.

In the Church of Scotland

The Scots are quite open-minded about the form of their burial service. The service may be held at home or in a chapel or at the crematorium. In some rural areas, the body is placed in an open coffin and the service takes place in a domestic atmosphere, with hospitality provided afterwards. A more general approach is for the service to be held in the undertaker's chapel. The minister may use a form of service in the Book of Common Order but there is no special burial liturgy. A formal homily is not said though the minister will mention the deceased in his remarks. Sometimes, special readings and music are included in the observances.

In Judaism

The Jewish community, family and friends keep up traditions rooted in the Old Testament. The degree to which religious practice is followed by individuals depends a great deal on the branch of Judaism and, too, on their personal wishes. Rites and rituals allow for sorrow to be expressed openly.

Funerals

Funerals take place as soon as they can be arranged – not later than three days after the death and not on the Sabbath, the Day of Atonement (Yom Kippur) and other festivals. Orthodox Jews order burial; Reform and Liberal Jews may be cremated and able to have their ashes interred in the Jewish burial ground.

The body, by custom, is wrapped in a plain shroud and not cosmeticized in any way. In the case of a man, he is given his prayer scarf or shawl, the Tallit. An unadorned wood coffin is usual. The extreme simplicity of these last rites is based on Judaism's belief that you should leave the world as you came into it.

The service

The service of prayers may take place at a synagogue, cemetery or crematorium. The coffin is placed in the chapel, and when the service has ended, is taken to the grave or removed to the crematorium. Mourners at the graveside strew a spadeful of earth on the coffin. During the burial the custom is for mourners to visit other relations' and friends' graves as a mark of respect. Mourners return to the chapel for a ritual washing of hands. More prayers are then said.

Mourning

At the service male Jews wear skull caps and the dress of mourners tends to be sober and dark but formal black is not a requirement. Orthodox Jews observe the ancient rite of the cutting or tearing of clothes to symbolize the wearer's grief.

Non-Jews of either sex wear hats or a head-covering during the service. Again, the point has to be made that social observances are shaped by the branch of the faith.

The ceremony of Shivah follows the funeral. By tradition this consists of seven days of mourning but depending on the religious practice of the family may take place on one day only. Mourners and family friends assemble in the house of one of their number and sit on low stools, which is known as 'sitting Shivah'. Prayers are said. During the formal mourning period, the bereaved may not perform any practical or household tasks, go to work or leave the house. Friends and other family members attend to the household, and the custom is for them to bring food, or prepare the food. Sometimes the men do not shave and looking glasses are covered. Visitors are important – they come and go and offer sympathy and help. It is usual to greet each mourner with the words 'I wish you long life'.

Non-Jews unfamiliar with these traditions who are invited to take part will be certain of a courteous response from a rabbi, minister or their Jewish friends.

In the Church of Rome

In the Christian tradition, the Roman Catholic Funeral Mass for the Dead stresses life hereafter. The Mass may be held on any day except a Holy Day of Obligation, a Sunday in Advent and Lent or Eastertide.

As in other denominations, certain aspects of the service are at the discretion of the priest and the family of the deceased, but in general the Roman Catholic Funeral Mass follows a set form. Mass is followed immediately by burial, and the final rites take place after the Postcommunion or at the cemetery.

Traditionalists who wish a Requiem Mass with the old Latin liturgy may obtain permission from the local Ordinary.

Flowers for remembrance

Sending flowers on the occasion of death is a way of paying respects to the dead person and their family. Flowers can convey affection, love, sympathy and remembrance, and make the ordeal of many mourners less grey and grim.

However, not everyone desires their family and friends to say it with flowers. Moreover, many religious faiths have embargoes on the convention.

Generally speaking, people who attend a funeral do send flowers, as well as those who would like to but are unable to attend. Usually, flowers are sent to the undertakers or to the place of worship or to the house of the chief mourners on the day before or the morning of the service.

Flowers are not part of tradition at a Jewish funeral. Quaker belief frowns on floral display except from close family.

Flowers are addressed to the deceased in the usual way without the prefix 'the late'. Similarly, the cards accompanying the gesture carry a handwritten personal message of affection for the dead, with the sender's full signature. For example, at the actor Lord Olivier's funeral in Sussex, Elizabeth Taylor's flowers carried a card sending her love and a message of one word, 'Adieu'; Sir John Gielgud's card read 'With loving memories'. Frequently, the wreaths and bouquets are displayed outside the place of worship. Cards are collected after the service by the family or undertakers depending on arrangements. All flowers received should be acknowledged and thanked for.

The request 'no flowers' should be respected but does not apply to close family whose tokens are placed on the coffin. Friends and family may always send flowers in sympathy to those who are bereaved.

Choosing flowers

Flower lovers will wish their gesture to reflect their own predilections or those of the deceased's. Season and availability will obviously influence options. Sometimes funeral directors will supply sample illustrations of flowers for funerals for people seeking ideas. Similarly, good florists will have their experience to put at the disposal of the customer. People who can cut flowers and foliage from their garden may well wish to make up their own bouquet.

Wreaths tend to be the choice of close family and also of business associates and clubs. Increasingly the mood is for informally arranged bouquets or posies.

The flowers should be delivered on the day before the funeral or the morning of it. Timing is important if the flowers are to appear fresh yet arrive on schedule.

When sending flowers to a faraway funeral, arrangements may have to be made by telephone or fax via the sender's florist to a florist in the district where the funeral is being held. The firm should arrange for a message to be written on a card and the flowers delivered. An alternative choice of flowers is a sensible precaution in case the delivering establishment has run out of the preferred variety.

Attending a funeral service

Information about the date, the place and the time of a funeral is given in announcements in the Births, Marriages and Deaths columns of the local and national press. The request 'no flowers' should be respected except by members of the close family. If donations to a charity are suggested in the notice, these are usually made in lieu of a bouquet.

Family and close friends are likely to be kept in touch with details of the funeral arrangements ahead of publication. Anyone outside the family circle wanting information without getting in touch with the chief mourners should contact the undertakers.

It is not necessary to be invited to attend a funeral at a place of worship, but if the notice states 'private funeral', people should check with the family, who may prefer to confine the congregation to a chosen few. There are other considerations – the chapel or hall may have limited seating; a memorial service or service of thanksgiving may be held at a later date to which all would be welcome.

Generally speaking, if a notice of a funeral is public, without any suggestion to the contrary, acquaintances can feel free to attend without further ado.

Behaviour at funerals is subdued and every allowance should be made for those who are making an effort to control their feelings but may not yet have regained their composure. Reactions to emotional stress vary with individuals. For example, no precipitate conclusions should be drawn if the bereaved appear to adopt a robust approach to the occasion.

An opportunity for friends to express sympathy, shake hands and kiss members of the family may occur after the service. Sometimes, if the circumstances are appropriate, the chief mourners forgather outside the church or chapel and exchange a few words with their supporters. Flowers that have been sent are sometimes set out on display with their cards.

Only those invited attend any hospitality offered by the family.

Strict rules about dress for funerals very rarely apply. The tendency is to wear sober colours and men may wish to put on a black neck-tie. Black is sometimes the choice of close family and best friends. It is not an occasion for frivolous or conspicuous personal adornment but people like to look their best out of deference to the dead and the bereaved. Hats are worn by women as a matter of personal choice only except in denominations where it is obligatory to cover the head.

It is good to know that an attempt to make the outward trappings of funerals less impersonal is being attempted in some quarters. Artists and craftsmen are making caskets which are intended to be objects of beauty, a revival of an old custom. The work embellishes the casket with personal emblems and symbols of the man or woman's life, interests and devotions.

Choosing an undertaker

For a number of reasons, people often rely on the services of an undertaker to help them through, and increasing responsibilities laid at the undertaker's door led to the formation, in the late 1970s, of the National Association of Funeral Directors. A Code of Practice was set up for all members. One of its most important provisions is that firms should give a written estimate of all costs incurred to their prospective clients.

An undertaker will advise on every aspect of funeral arrangements and will carry out the wishes of the family. It is usual for them to care for the body, seeing to the laying out if the person dies at home. They will place the body in a coffin or casket, and advise on where the body might rest. Some families wish to retain the dead, so that members of the family may say a last goodbye in familiar surroundings. In some cases, an open casket is preferred, with the body prepared for viewing. But in either instance, the custom is fading in favour of the coffin being removed by the undertakers and retained on their premises. Arrangements can be made for family and friends to visit to pay their respects. If religious practice requires this, the coffin rests in chapel or church.

When someone dies in hospital, as is increasingly the case, the nursing staff attend to the body. In some hospitals and hospices there is a chapel of rest to which the dead are taken at the request of the family, before being removed for the funeral. Next of kin and close family may wish to be the first to visit the chapel.

Last goodbyes

Whether a person dies at home, in hospital or elsewhere, it is very likely that those close to them will wish to say goodbye privately. There is a long-standing custom in which spouses, sons and daughters and those closest kiss the deceased. A note to the unwary is that the body may be cold.

Some people prefer to gaze upon the body only. Others who perhaps have little experience of death, may understandably lack the courage.

On such a profoundly personal and private matter, however, etiquette has little to offer.

Special funerary points

After death, the body is usually wrapped in simple, clean linen for the last rites. An ancient custom which still survives though is for the dead to be specially attired. The chosen garments are representations of the individual; men often wish to be buried in uniforms or robes of office, whereas in the past women have preferred their bridal robes.

In practical terms, such wishes may be put in a will or told to the next of kin. Usually, the family tries to abide by the request.

Clothes in which the dead are buried or cremated should appear always to lend comfort and add decorum.

Formal remembrance

A memorial service is usually held some time after the funeral rites in order to give sufficient notice to relations, friends and associates who might wish to be present. If a small 'family only' funeral service took place, as is frequently the case, the memorial observance that follows tends to be a more public occasion attended by a wider circle.

Occasionally, a memorial service is held for someone who died away from home or perhaps in another land. Every member of a denominational religion may be remembered in this way.

Members of the congregation will be drawn from the profession or work and associations and interests of the person who is being commemorated, as well as from family and friends and private life.

The different denominations have their own approach to this form of remembrance. The Church of England's Service of Thanksgiving or Service in Memory salutes the achievements and worldly contribution of the deceased, the church of Rome's Memorial Requiem Mass includes prayers which stress the spiritual support for the dead, some branches of Judaism believe in consecrating the physical memorial of the person being remembered in a ceremony at the graveside.

Secular remembrances are many and varied, and are frequently held in a building or rooms that can be hired for the occasion marked by some special connection with the person's work or endeavours.

Announcements

The announcement of a memorial service or memorial requiem mass is made through the family and also in the columns of the local and/or national press. Family and close friends usually hear through personal contact but as far as the wider world is concerned the first intimation of a service is likely to be through a published announcement.

A family arranging a service of thanksgiving is advised to give friends and associates fair notice in order that those who might wish to attend can make the necessary arrangements. A usual timing is to announce the occasion about four weeks or so after the funeral giving about a month's grace. Often the lapse of time between the announcement and the date is far longer – up to two months in some cases.

Fees at a memorial service are payable for the choir, the soloist(s), and perhaps for heating the church. A donation to Church funds is usual.

Forms of announcements

Hurst: a Service of Thanksgiving for the life of Canon Peter Hurst will be held at St Clement Dane's, on Friday 29 June at midday.

Thomas: a memorial service for Alf Thomas, for fifty years Oxford University Boatman, will be held at Great St Mary's Church, Oxford on Saturday 16 June at 11 am. Blazers encouraged.

Hope-Martin: a Requiem Mass for Mrs Jane Hope-Martin will be held at All Saints Church, Axminster, on Wednesday 5 October at noon.

Arranging the service

No residential qualifications are required for a memorial service. The arrangements are made between the clergyman and the family.

At an Anglican Service of Thanksgiving for someone's life, or at a Service in Memory of a deceased person, there are prayers, hymns, readings and an address. The music and singing by the choir are usually uplifting. In some ways, the programme has become a form of animated biography, focusing on the best of the person being remembered and drawing a courteous veil over any serious lapses. The lessons are generally read by friends or members of the family and the address is given by a notable who is particularly well placed to speak of the achievements and efforts of the departed.

Readings may be scriptural or taken from secular literature. Poems and favourite passages of prose are frequently chosen. It is not unusual for the programme of music to include sacred and secular compositions and classical and popular pieces. Jazz players, steel band performers and opera singers and soloists can all make a contribution to proceedings. The occasion represents the interests, likings and beliefs of the remembered.

Order of service sheets

It is usual for printed order of service sheets to be handed to people as they enter the place of worship. The cover gives the names of the person being commemorated, the dates of their birth and death, the name of the church and the date and hour of the service.

An order of service sheet can be a token of remembrance in itself.

Letters of sympathy

When someone dies a letter of sympathy should be dispatched to their nearest and dearest as soon as possible. Letters are generally sent to the closest member of family such as a spouse, or a parent or a grandparent or a sibling, but others outside the family circle may qualify. Those living in unconventional coupledom are thought of conventionally and sympathies are expressed to the surviving friend or companion.

The art of writing a letter in these circumstances is to keep the tone light and direct, reminiscent of private conversation. The task is far from easy because the awesome absolutes of death and bereavement are hard to express in a way that does not sound hackneyed and routine. Still, if all else fails, many of the tried and trusted phrases can be relied upon, such as 'We send our heartfelt sympathies' or 'Please let me know if there is anything I can do' or 'We send our fondest love and thoughts to you at this time'. These at least say what they mean.

It is best to skip any euphemisms about the dead such as 'passed on' or 'passed over' in favour of plain speaking. Subjects to draw on are any special memories of the dead person that the reader would like to hear about, any tribute that can be paid to their work, character or efforts, any aspect of the relationship between the reader and the person who has died, that redounds to the credit of both of them.

It should be remembered that a sense of guilt often follows a death. Any word about the care and attention given to the loved one by the recipient of the letter will strike a warm note.

Writing to a former spouse or lover or mistress

Whether to send a letter of condolence to a former spouse or ex-lover on the death of their onetime partner is a debatable point. It largely depends on the recipient's likely response to a reminder of a previous commitment. A general rule would be negative, especially if the former partner has formed a new attachment. However, where lives have been intertwined between correspondent and reader, writing can be a way of validating shared experience. However, perhaps a more promising alternative could be to write to any offspring of the former union.

A show of tact

Suppose a person is known to have behaved appallingly towards the partner or other relative whose death has occurred and you are faced with writing a letter of condolence? Set aside human frailty for the duration and concentrate on the good times. This is not a moment for moral judgments.

When a famous person dies

The volume of letters in the above circumstance may amount to an avalanche which is beyond the means of one family to answer individually. Sometimes, an announcement is placed in the Court pages or Personal columns of national newspapers to the following effect:

'Lady X wishes to thank all those who have kindly sent messages of appreciation on the death of her husband, Sir Mark X. She hopes to be able to reply personally in due course.'

On occasions, the notice merely expresses thanks without a mention of an individual reply. However, this would not apply to letters from close family and friends.

Writing to a widow

Widows are addressed in the usual way, using their husband's first name or initials, i.e. Mrs B. E. Farley or Mrs George Ross. The style, Mrs Michelle Robbins, would indicate that the addressee was divorced. Despite the widespread loosening up of conventions in correspondence, some women take umbrage if they are incorrectly addressed in this manner.

In the case of a titled heir

Custom has it that except in the case of the Monarch ('The king is dead, long live the king'), titles that pass on to an heir upon death of the holder, are not used until after the funeral.

Writing to the deceased

Convention does not allow you to address the dead except in memorials.

Note: When a public announcement of a death in the local or national press states 'no letters' this should be observed by all except family and close friends.

Replying to letters of condolence

Approaches vary on the matter of answering letters of sympathy and condolence. There is no doubt that correspondents do appreciate an acknowledgment, if only to ensure that their kind words arrived safely. Some people do not reply, however, and no discourtesy is intended.

Writers of letters should be thanked for their pains. If ideas for replies are wanting, mention can always be made of the comfort and consolation derived from messages of sympathy. Also, if the comments made in a letter were particularly gratifying, the point need not be overlooked.

Then again, if the correspondent is someone who helped the dead person in their work or sport or hobbies or interests, any high value set on their contribution would be a nice point to make. Similarly, had the writer the magic gift of making the person laugh during difficult days, that would surely merit a mention.

Theoretically, acknowledgments should be sent immediately, but most correspondents make allowances for a lapse of some time.

Handling a big post

The aftermath of the death of someone with a wide circle of friends, acquaintances and colleagues may well produce a volume of tributes which is beyond the scope of a single hand to manage within a realistic time-span. If possible, other members of the family should be recruited to help.

One expedient which is acceptable is for the bereaved to compose a formula letter of acknowledgment to which they add a personal postscript. It has become usual for these standard letters to be typewritten.

An example of such a letter:

'Thank you very much for your kind letter of sympathy. We are greatly comforted by the many messages of appreciation from my mother's friends and admirers all over the country.

As a family we are immensely proud of her many achievements. She will be missed beyond words.'

Explaining to children

Death is a mystery yet children need explanations. Exactly what is said to a child faced with bereavement is probably of less import than that they have been brought into the confidence of the family and not excluded.

Children need reassurance in this situation as they can easily imagine that they have been responsible in some way for bringing about the death and the resulting family unhappiness.

Depending on the age of the child, some attempt should be made to explain the meaning of death. There is no easy way, but as so much of their lives is inexplicable to them children do have a remarkable capacity to accept the mysterious ways of existence.

The corporeal disappearance of a loved figure can be explained in terms of the fact that every creature on earth has a beginning and an end, and the point could be made that the person who has died will not be forgotten but will live on in memory, in their achievements and in the family.

Parents who have faith in the religious afterlife have their own answer.

Children at the funeral

Some parents, understandably, wish to spare their young offspring from the rigours of attending a family funeral. They may feel that the procedures are too much of an ordeal and that it would be better to pack them off on a cheerful outing.

The current view is such stratagems, however well-meaning, may be misguided; children should be encouraged to be participants on this occasion and share in the family grieving process.

When a child attends the funeral service of someone dear to them they should stay beside someone they trust for reassurance. Although children tend to throw off the burden of mourning spontaneously, they can also be surprisingly sensitive to their parents' emotional needs.

Bequests

There is nothing morbid about asking a friend or a member of the family if they would like to choose a personal memento to be left to them in a will. Nor is there any good reason why someone who wishes to accept should not name their piece, be it a trinket, picture or object. However, it would seem graceless to select a possession of considerable monetary value unless the donors themselves proposed an item of comparable worth.

A point worth considering is the propriety of asking if a person who has died has left you anything in a will. This would seem highly premature. A solicitor or executor will be in touch with all the beneficiaries of a will in due course.

Blood feuds and squabbles are endemic in the contents of wills. Sometimes confusion reigns through chance and not intention. When a person dies intestate (without making a will) possessions are divided between the next of kin. It can happen therefore that a friend or someone outside the immediate family finds that their token or remembrance has passed to spouse or an offspring. Would it be courteous to ask for the item? Only if the request was for a memento without serious cash value.

Entertaining &
weekending

Since the first invitation, certain conventions have had to be observed by host

and guest alike if the gathering is to go well – as true for a do as a weekend

away. Nevertheless, rules never made a good party: imagination,

spontaneity and a commitment to doing things well is far nearer the mark.

Party procedures

Generally speaking, any date is good for a party, which needs no other excuse than itself – witness the young host who, on being asked if there was a reason for the jamboree, replied, 'Because it is Tuesday'.

Although sociable 'do's have never been so popular at almost every point of the social compass, a universal common code remains elusive. Much is determined by who, when and where. Age group within the same circle can make a big difference, and what is acceptable in the capital may be anathema to country folk.

Differences there may be but certain principles are unshakeable wherever a party is held or whoever gives it. One is that the success of the occasion is made or lost in the guest list.

Choosing the guests

Much has been written on the ideal number of guests at a seated dinner party. Disraeli thought that a dozen, 'no more than the Muses', was perfect, but parties of twelve, ten and eight tend to divide in two during the meal unless the party-giver can keep the conversation general. A dinner party for six is cosy but some hold that if they are going to go to a deal of trouble on behalf of four or five guests they might just as well extend their hospitality to a few more friends. Obviously, decisions are likely to be influenced by the space, table size and equipment available, as well as the appropriate people, not to mention the budget.

The priority is to devise an entertaining mix of guests, rather in the manner of inventing a cocktail. Every host has to consider the impact of guests on the others. It is usually sound practice to combine some familiar faces with new ones. Certainly, from a guest's point of view, it can be a daunting experience to walk into a room full of strangers. The main criterion is to consider whether people will actually like and stimulate each other. Choosing guests with shared interests is an often-quoted formula unless they prove to be antagonists, or have said their say already to each other. Another point to watch is that they may turn the party over to shop talk which may exclude fellow guests. When everyone is included in, there is no talk like shop talk, it has to be said. An element of competition does no harm and one would be foolish to deny that attractive women enhance the scene.

A party has a psyche and doesn't come together solely on the strength of people and food and drink chosen. If only few numbers are involved it becomes a proportionately greater responsibility to make sure that everyone present is likely to hit it off.

This brings us, unhappily, to the question of 'musts' and 'obligations'. It may well be misguided to invite too many guests just because they are owed hospitality rather than for the pleasure of their company.

Then again, the balance of talkers to quiet people has to be considered carefully. One host works on the formula of three shouters to five listeners. She finds that a gathering of all chatterers makes for pandemonium, with some guests left feeling affronted because of competition, whereas a preponderance of strong silent types produces a sticky evening with each uncommunicative guest waiting for someone else to take a lead.

Compiling a guest list for a big party is a breeze, relatively speaking, because numbers can encompass all sorts. A mix which might be uncomfortable in a more intimate gathering poses no problem in a crowd.

Inviting the guests

The length of notice for a party depends on the nature of the occasion and on the availability of the guests themselves.

Invitations for a formally arranged dinner party are usually issued about three weeks ahead – longer if the host is endeavouring to bring together people who, for one reason or the other, are hard to pin down. Very formal occasions may require up to six weeks' notice. Invitations for a drinks party are usually issued two to three weeks ahead.

Generally, invitations are telephoned, but may be handwritten in a letter or on a postcard. For a big party, it is a great convenience to mail invitations (see 'Forms of Social Correspondence'). Some meticulous partygivers who have already contacted the guests in person like to send an invitation card reading 'To remind' with 'RSVP' crossed out. It is important to keep a note of acceptances and regrets.

Except between close friends, hosts are advised against pressing guests to accept an invitation that for some reason they seem reluctant to accept. If, however, a guest says they would be delighted to accept, it is cheering to hear that the host is pleased. Any verbal invitation should be totally clear as to the date, time and place.

On the debatable point of equal numbers, the nature and style of the gathering is the best guide. At most formal seated dinner parties equal numbers remain the norm. At buffet and large parties where any disparity in the distribution of the sexes will not be noticed, few people bother to tot up six of one and half dozen of the other, although a fair mix of the sexes does generally make for the better party. Continuing the generations adds variety, too.

May you invite spouses without their other half? This is a sensitive issue and the answer depends on the individuals concerned. As a general rule, married couples are invited as a couple. However, work, travel and other commitments mean that pairs do get separated and people on their own may particularly welcome a party.

If one of a couple is unable to accept, the hostess can rely on the convention that allows her to withdraw the invitation to both in order to ensure equal numbers. She should apologize and say something along the lines that she hopes they will both be able to come next time. The guests may make things easier for the inviter by indicating that they will have to decline because one of them is unable to accept. This leaves the way open for the hostess to accept the regrets without further ado, or to extend the invitation to the person who is available.

If no invitation to the free member is forthcoming, he or she is expected to swallow any irritation and to imply that the reason is understood.

From a host's viewpoint, whether to take an extra male or female on board depends on the type of party and on the person concerned. Increasingly, however, the equal numbers convention applies to formally structured parties only.

Calculating risks

One of the pleasures of parties is meeting the unexpected. But whether it is worth the gamble to mix people whose views are known to be bitterly opposed is a very moot point.

Everyone will agree that differences of opinion add spice to conversation. There can come a stage, however, in which divergence becomes incendiary and the party goes up in flames.

The sensitive issues may be purely personal or related to the broader considerations of racism, religion, political and sexual orientation. It is distinctly unwise to assume that the characteristics of our so-called 'plural society' in which colour, creed and class rub shoulders can necessarily be contained within the small world of private entertaining. There will always be a risk of causing real offence. That said, one of the genuine rewards of giving parties is providing an opportunity for people who usually occupy different camps to meet on friendly ground.

Hosts probably need to weigh up the fine odds of the likelihood of any confrontation leading to the disruption of the occasion. It's not a bad idea to have someone on hand who could cool the situation if unpleasant rows threaten.

Old loves?

Since people tend to move among small circles, the question may arise of the advisability of inviting a guest's marital ex, or their former emotional attachment. An allied consideration is the likely response of the third member of the triangle, the guest's current favourite.

A very broad guideline in a situation which is fraught with exceptions is that any potential embarrassments are more easily contained within a big party; people can keep their distance if wished. At a small dinner escape may be more difficult.

Accepting invitations

Good guests reply promptly. Turning up or not as last-minute circumstances or whim dictate plays havoc with the host's forward planning. Not the least of the problems is knowing how much drink to order.

Dinner party invitations are obligatory exceptions to the general casualness about replying to invitations. Hosts can expect, and generally receive, answers to their invitations within a week. Replies should be hand-written and sent off in a sealed envelope. If telephoned, friends are expected to return the call with an answer as soon as possible. A verbal acceptance is as binding as a written one.

See page 295 for Saying thank you.

In the event of a guest being unable to take an immediate decision, it would be courteous to let the host know.

A written invitation requires a written reply – unless a telephone number is given. If the card is formally worded, guests usually reply in the third person. An acceptance might read: 'Mr and Mrs Tim Cottlestone (or 'Anne and Tim Cottlestone') have much pleasure in accepting Lady Blank's kind invitation to her daughter Catherine's twenty-first birthday party on Saturday 15 October at Fairways, Sunbury'. The date is written at the foot of the letter which does not require a signature.

An informally worded acceptance might read: 'Dear Lady Blank, Tim and I will be delighted to accept your invitation to Catherine's twenty-first birthday party on Saturday 15 October at Fairways, Yours sincerely'. The letter can include personal comments, if wished. It is signed in the usual way with a first name only or with a first name and a surname, depending on the writer's standing with the correspondent.

If the invitation is addressed to a guest 'and partner' the former replies on behalf of both. Thus, 'Alexandra Smith and friend have much pleasure in accepting Stephen Brown's kind invitation to drinks . . .' The acceptance should mention the name of the person who will be brought, where possible: the important point is for the guest to indicate whether they will be bringing a friend.

When a number of people give a party – perhaps a family or a group of friends – it is courteous to mention all the names given on the card in any written reply, unless this becomes too cumbersome.

Style varies considerably in the approach to wording replies to invitations. A useful guideline is to echo the form of the invitation itself. If this is formally designed and worded, a formal reply is appropriate, written in the third person. If guests' prefixes are written on the invitation, they may reply in like vein, 'Mr and Mrs Alan Stanbrook have much pleasure. . .'. If invitations read with guests' forenames only, replies could be in the informal, first person, and begin 'Dear Hugh and Kate', and if the third person form is used the reply could begin without prefixes, 'Alan and Josie Stanbrook have much pleasure. . .'.

Should the party include grandees and VIPs, friends who are invited should not be surprised to receive a call from the host on the day of the party or the previous day to confirm acceptance.

Declining invitations

Should you not wish to accept an invitation and lack a valid excuse, etiquette provides perfect protection in the cool formality of the third person form of sending regrets: 'Miss Otis regrets she is unable to lunch today . . .' without further explanation.

A straightforward note of regrets can read: 'Mr and Mrs Paul Palmer thanks Mrs Anne Shaw for her kind invitation to a dinner dance in honour of her daughter Gayle's marriage to Mr Jim Berry, but regret they are unable to accept'. A shorter version reads: 'Mr and Mrs Paul Palmer regret they are unable to accept Mrs Anne Shaw's invitation to a dinner dance on Saturday, 15 July'. The date is written beneath the letter (see above).

The formal style sounds rather ridiculous if the stated reasons for sending regrets are of an acutely domestic nature. In these circumstances, skip the third person and write an informally worded letter in the first person or telephone.

A strategy always open to those who do not wish to risk giving offence is to take refuge in a white lie. Stock excuses concern a feigned previous engagement, work, holiday arrangements, babysitters, transport problems. It is as well to realize that most standard get-outs are recognizable for what they are but they at least indicate a willingness to be considerate. The most convincing excuses are those which contain a grain of honesty but are economical with the truth.

An uninvited friend?

Oddly enough, despite general free-and-easiness about social conventions, there seems to be no let-up in the embargo on bringing an uninvited friend to the feast. A distinction must be made here between formally structured entertaining where numbers matter such as seated lunch or dinner parties and the more flexible arrangements at drinks or cocktail parties or a dance. Few hosts who have carefully worked out a guest list will warm to the request.

Hosts may decline without compunction but with apologies. Guests should size up the possibilities of acceptance before chancing their arm, and phrase the request in a way which allows the host a polite get-out.

Possibly this reticence is peculiarly British. In the United States, for example, hosts are much more open-handed and there is a tradition of welcoming strangers to the feast.

Gatecrashers

Uninvited guests who gatecrash have become a feature of many parties but they are rarely remembered with pleasure. Hosts feel affronted by the intrusion, and only extremely youthful sparks are able to get away with it. Hosts may need to resort to employing bouncers on the door if gatecrashers are anticipated. Also at a formal party, the device of including the line on the card, 'Please bring this invitation with you' has obvious uses in this connection.

Hosts and guests

Most people are called upon at some time or other to be a host and to be a guest. Indeed, the British writer Max Beerbohm declared that mankind is divisible into two great classes, hosts and guests, which leaves most of us wondering where our talents lie. Good hosts are people who enjoy people and by definition are rarer birds than good guests. They enjoy taking the lead and gain satisfaction from giving their friends a good time. An interesting fact is how few parties people have to give in order to earn a reputation as a notable host, although it is doubtful if any memorable party ever was given by a reluctant host. Guests, on the other hand, tend to prefer enjoying the ride and showing their appreciation of being appreciated.

Host's responsibilities

The host is king which ever the gender. It is his or her responsibility to choose and invite the guests and to decide on the logistical points such as when and where and at what hour. Hosts decide on the level of hospitality to be offered, and on any entertainment to be provided. They choose the food and drink and, most distinctively, pick up the bill for all the costs involved.

It is the host's prerogative to signal the style of dress for the occasion and he or she may indicate that the men are expected to put on dinner jackets, or appear in fancy dress or come as they please.

Being a guest

The art of being a guest is to enjoy the party and to look at ease without behaving presumptuously. The chief dilemma is that hosts hold all the cards: guests may neither know what to expect nor what is expected of them. When in doubt it is usually best to check with the host, but this can sound naive. A better strategy is to take soundings from other guests in advance, if possible. Otherwise, taking a cue on the spot from those who know the house or the hosts is the best line.

Good guests make an effort to show their appreciation. At a tedious gathering, keeping observable signs of boredom at bay is a social grace. In general, warmth is preferable to reserve but no one would wish a guest to behave artificially. In any case, gushing enthusiasm is rarely welcomed.

Parties are outlets for exuberant behaviour. How far wilder excesses will be tolerated depends on the host and his friends. Boisterous carryings on that will pass unremarked in some quarters may arouse disapproval or disdain elsewhere. The threshold of tolerance differs not only between different social groups, circles, classes and cults but also between people of similar background, education and habit: reactions are peculiarly unpredictable, and this is one of the main factors complicating etiquette and manners generally. Perhaps the state of the party itself is as good a test as any. The merrier it is the more acceptably may barriers be breached.

Grounds for cancelling

Last minute cancellations by guests are annoying and discourteous, especially on a well-organized occasion. The myth that absent guests will hardly be noticed by busy hosts at a big party is rarely borne out by experience. The absent guest is nearly always noted.

Sometimes sending late apologies is unavoidable. Generally acceptable excuses are connected with unanticipated work loads, sudden illness, babysitting problems, children's ailments and emergencies of all kinds. When the party-giver is obliged to find a replacement, candour rather than a cover-up is in order. Tact has to be deployed. One of the golden rules in entertaining is that not being invited to a party can cause great offence, even among close friends.

Party prescriptions

The secret of a successful party is elusive. No one has come upon a fail-safe method – luckily, perhaps, or else all parties would have a deadening similarity. As mentioned earlier, choosing guests who have a genuine interest in being in each other's company is one guideline. Also, there needs to be a sense of generosity about the hospitality provided. This is not an argument in favour of inappropriately lavish expenditure, but a feeling of giving is all-important at a party. Any sense of meanness quickly communicates itself and cramps the fun. However, this definitely does not rule out parties on a shoestring budget: sharing the little you have has nothing in common with tight-fistedness.

Hospitality should respond to guests' likes and dislikes. At table, offers of second helpings will probably go down well. In order to accommodate the uncertainties of appetite, more food may have to be produced than is consumed. Some waste is almost unavoidable.

Drink should flow hospitably. The measure of the 'right' amount of drink to be offered has always been a debatable topic. Between half a bottle to three-quarters of a bottle of wine per head for receptions is generous, but small parties tend to drink more per head than large parties. Leisurely lunch or dinner parties at which people linger at the table are famously heavy on wine. Guests needing to drive have to watch their intake or have their intake watched.

In general, for a number of reasons, many people seem to be reducing their consumption of alcohol at parties, which suggests that hosts may be able to reduce supplies. Certainly, providing low-alcohol and soft drinks as well as hard liquor is very much in order. Nevertheless, responses to drinking are highly personal – some are happy to while away an evening on a glass or so of wine and others put away a bottle or two. Those who like to imbibe should not sense that the host is counting every glass. Not everyone is obliged to drive themselves home, and to be caught short of drink is a classic embarrassment for a host.

Anniversaries

Certain milestones in a person's lifespan and experience are celebrated with special attention. Star birthdays are, respectively, an Eighteenth, a Twenty-first, a Fiftieth and a Sixtieth; a day of birth marking a new decade often calls for extra celebration. Children's birthdays should always be commemorated joyfully.

Wedding anniversaries of note are a Twenty-fifth, known as a Silver Wedding, a Fiftieth Golden Wedding and a Sixtieth Diamond Wedding. The names denote the gifts deemed appropriate for each in folklore.

Anniversaries generate memorabilia such as books of signatures of people present at the party, special greetings cards, albums of snapshots.

Festivals and feast days, or a house warming – these are just some further causes for celebration.

Timing

Although today there is more give and take all round on the timing of private social occasions and the need for punctuality, basic etiquette on this point has remained pretty constant, except that dinner parties seem to take place later and later.

The following is a summary of usual timings and the latitude allowed to guests within the bounds of politeness.

Working breakfasts: invitations are usually for 8 am to 9.30 am. Punctuality is of the essence at this get up and go occasion.

Brunch: like its name, the meal is a combination of breakfast and lunch. Guests are usually invited for about 11 am onwards. Tardy folk who arrive as for lunchtime run the risk of finding the hot coffee past its best and supplies of food and laced drinks running low.

Pre-lunch drinks parties: invitations are for 12 pm to 1 or 1.30 pm depending on whether guests are expected to lunch elsewhere. If token food is provided, the party may go on until 2 pm. Because these parties are relatively short, guests should arrive a few minutes after the appointed hour and not later than 12.20 pm.

Lunch invitations: are usually for 12.30 pm or 12.45 pm for 1 pm. Guests should arrive before 1 pm.

Tea party invitations: usually for 3.45 pm, 4 pm or 4.30 pm, the earlier hour often suiting country-based hosts or children. Children's tea parties usually end at between 5.30 and 6.00 pm Guests of all ages are expected to arrive punctually for tea.

Cocktail party invitations are for 6 pm to 6.30 pm, although some urban hosts are delaying the hour to 7.00 pm. Unless numbers are very small, a certain flexibility surrounds drinks parties at all hours, which is one of the reasons for their popularity. A typical drinks party in town might start around 6.30 pm and run until 9 or 10 pm – or until the drinks run out. Guests may arrive at any hour except ahead of the appointed time or very late, though punctual guests are always very welcome.

Dinner party invitations are for any time between 7.45 and 9 pm, the most usual being 8 pm Some party-givers write on the invitation '8 for 8.30 pm' which is a signal that they expect to serve dinner shortly after 8.30.

Attitudes as to what constitutes unacceptable lateness on the part of a dinner party guest vary with the host and the occasion. The more formal the event, the greater the embarrassment of unpunctuality. Very broad guidelines might be as follows: it is embarrassing to arrive ahead of the hour for which you are invited. If you have reservations about not wishing to be first on the scene, time your entrance for about ten minutes after the stated hour of the invitation.

Being up to fifteen minutes late calls for an apology. Being half an hour late calls for a graceful apology and a good excuse.

Late drinks parties are usually timed for 10 pm Guests are expected to arrive before 11 pm unless a dance is being given or the party is expected to swing until the small hours.

Timings convey information about the hospitality offered whether or not a specific meal is mentioned. An invitation for around 1 pm or 8 pm suggests that a meal will be served. A grey area exists around 9 pm which might mean supper or not, might mean a seated dinner or a buffet, might mean drinks only. Hosts please take note and make the invitation clear.

Parties in servanted country houses are more structured than their counterparts in a big city and punctuality is essential. Pre-lunch drinks on Sunday, teatime, swimming, tennis or croquet parties, lunch and dinner and drinks parties are held, as they have always been, with a sense of everyone knowing what (and what not) to do, and that includes knowing when to arrive (and depart).

Goodbyes

Taking your leave presents a classic conundrum. Some hosts try to make life easier for themselves and their guests by writing on the invitation beneath the word 'Drinks' the hour at which the party is supposed to end, e.g. '6 to 8.30 pm' This has the added advantage of indicating that dinner is not offered.

The approach of the host makes all the difference. Some, including the most hospitable, make no bones about their preference for guests' prompt departure before midnight. Others judge the success of the occasion by the number of stayers who want to keep the party bubbling into the small hours. Whether hosts are owls or larks by temperament comes into it – but for a host there are few more signal indications of failure than premature departure from the party. Early leave-takers should bear this in mind.

It is probably wisest for a guest aiming at an early getaway to make a quiet exit without saying 'goodbye' formally to the company, leaving the host to explain their absence. Otherwise, early leavers can wreck the mood of a party. Suddenly, everyone is reminded of the hour and the onset of tomorrow. Furthermore, some may mistakenly assume that the prompt departure was an inspired hint from the host. The host's first yawn or reference to a heavy day ahead is as good a sign as any of the moment to go. Another hint – perhaps the most telling – is hostly reluctance to offer another round of drinks.

Opinions vary as to whether one of a couple may retire before the other without seeming impolite when they are playing hosts. Good manners would deem this improper. Then again, may one of a couple who are guests leave before the other? It happens often enough but there will always be those who hold this to be inconsiderate, to both the remaining partner and the host.

Shaking hands on it?

As every actor knows, exits are more difficult than entrances, and real life bears this out. Choosing an appropriate moment to break off a conversation, knowing exactly what expression – if any – to use as a parting salutation, and whether to shake hands on it or kiss or whether to amble off amiably without any gestures at all remain perennially uncertain areas.

Sensitive timing and decisiveness are all-important. But suppose your companion has just embarked on a long story and it seems as if there is a long, long way to go before the punchline? Leave-takers will have a friend for life if they hold on until the storyteller has finished. Should the last bus be imminent, they should try to stem the flow before he or she gets into their stride.

It is not the exact form of farewell that matters but the manner of it. Once thank-yous have been said on the spot the idea is to depart promptly without seeming abrupt. At a big party it may not be easy to locate the host or hostess and you will be forgiven for taking your leave without formalities.

Famously awkward moments for leave-takers occur when the host is engaged in making a heavy play for another member of the party, or – more difficult to gauge – when he seems about to hear something to his advantage. It is almost invariably tactless to attempt to bid farewell to a party-giver seeing off the guest of honour. Guests of honour, by definition, take priority.

Thank-yous

Unquestionably the nicest guests ring up the day after to say thank-you. What a host most wishes to hear is that you had a good time. If thanking a relative stranger, compliments concerning the food or drink or table decoration or members of the party are in order, as well as the hostess's appearance. It is also a form of compliment to ask about the cooking of a delicious dish or the region of a wine served.

Written thank-yous should be sent for lunch or dinner parties. Drinks parties, by convention, are thanked for on the spot. If a guest was unable to thank at the time, a written or telephoned thank-you would be polite. Messages of thanks may be left on answering machines but inevitably these lack heart.

Organizing a dinner party

The way individuals approach giving a dinner party is a clue to character. Perfectionists are divided from pragmatists. Romantics separate from realists.

A successful dinner party is an accomplishment. It combines the skills of good cooking, choice of wine, conversation, table setting, and above all the art of making people feel cherished. The special charm of a dinner party is the way it allows people enough time to get to know one another or to renew a friendship.

No wonder that dinner parties take place on so many different levels, from the grandly formal to the very casual. Distinctions between 'dinner' and 'supper' have become increasingly blurred. Supper once meant a late meal served without ceremony which could equally well describe dinner today. However, if an invitation makes the point specifically that the meal is 'only supper', guests should not expect too elaborate a repast.

Dinner party procedures

The mood of a party is often set in its opening stages. Ideally, the host should welcome guests personally at the front door, exchanging kisses or shaking hands as appropriate. At a party where larger numbers are expected, this may not be practical. If help is to hand the task is usually delegated.

Guests should be relieved of their outdoor clothes and any belongings they wish to park, or shown where they may put their things. An entrance hall or bedroom is the usual choice. Making a bedroom available has the added advantage of providing some privacy for those who wish to tidy up.

Introductions

Good hosts don't delay pouring drinks or making introductions. Generally, everyone is introduced to everyone else at the party. At a large dinner party, some hosts prefer to take each new arrival round the room making introductions. Others introduce people to a small group to begin with, stay with them for a while in order to knit newcomers into a conversation, and make the remainder of the introductions a little later. Strangers or shy people will especially appreciate a host who takes the trouble to stay by their side for a while.

See page 314 for Modes of address.

If a host is in doubt as to whether two guests know each other, which would make introductions spurious, it is probably better to err on the side of formality. The open-ended remark, 'Have you met . . .?' is invaluable here.

Guests at a dinner party

Guests are expected to make themselves at home, but only up to a point. Rulings on this are difficult because so much depends on the relationship between host and guest. Making telephone calls without the host's permission, having calls put through to the house, asking what's for dinner?, complaining about the temperature of the room where the party is standing, putting another log on the open fire, opening (or closing) a window, begging a cigarette, adjusting the television set, are unexceptional acts between friends. But when guests feel unsure of their ground or wish to make a particularly good impression, the urge to treat the host's place like home should be monitored carefully.

Few hosts will raise objections to their guests using the telephone but if the call is expensive, an offer should be made to pay, if not at the time, then later. When calling a number abroad reverse charges have an attraction for hosts.

No one need have any qualms about asking for a soft drink if none is offered. It is in order to help yourself to the cigarettes if they are put out for general consumption. If no other person is smoking tobacco and there is a conspicuous absence of ashtrays in the room, courtesy demands that those who wish to light a cigarette should ask if there are any objections to their doing so.

See page 346 for Unholy smoke.

Spills, breakages and mishaps

If a guest inadvertently breaks an object or causes some damage, he or she should apologize immediately and offer to clear up any mess. However, this is not the moment to dwell on the mishap.

Apologies should follow: sending flowers or offering to replace what was broken (if possible), is a way of making amends.

Conversation

Recommendations for opening remarks inevitably sound artificial verging on the banal. However, a word may be put in for the much despised art of small talk which aims to bridge silence or awkwardness. Would-be conversationalists can snatch at any current news item, or another well-known gambit is to cast some light on your connection with the host or their partner or family. Asking questions is a standard approach which may now have fewer adherents than previously: a new form of rudeness is an utter lack of curiosity or interest in the doings of other members of the party.

Announcing dinner

At one time, the announcement that dinner was served caused a sonorous interruption in proceedings as a manservant delivered word from the cook. Today, since the host or hostess is likely to be doing the cooking, the announcement may be a shout from the kitchen.

Timing the announcement obviously depends on the state of the cooking, and on whether all the guests have arrived; also on whether the host prefers extended pre-dinner drinks – if canapés and appetizers are served, the hostess may feel more relaxed about getting the meal on the table.

See page 172 for Timing.

As a general rule, dinner is served about half an hour after the time for which guests are invited, but the time lapse can be considerably longer. (Where the last bus home is important or babysitters have to be relieved of their charges, there is more pressure on a hostess to keep to a timetable.)

The hostess announces that dinner is ready and attempts to shepherd the party toward the dinner table.

Going in to dinner

At one time strict rules of precedence governed going in to dinner such as who went before whom and with whom, an indication of minute gradations of social rank.

Nowadays people make their way as they will to table. If the party is moving to a dining room, the usual rules of courtesy should hold good: women before men, with the male host last. If a senior female is present, she takes precedence over the other women, as a senior male does over the other men. However, self-conscious manoeuvres by younger or junior members of the party are unlikely to gratify their elders. If the gesture can be done naturally, well and good, but not otherwise.

Notable exceptions to the mood of informality include state banquets, official dinners, diplomatic and embassy parties, receptions held by City guilds, receptions for foreign dignitaries – all are official occasions at which rules of precedence and protocol may be strictly observed.

Seating the guests

Among a host of considerations concerning who to seat next to whom, custom favours separating the sexes. Married couples are separated on the basis that if they have anything to say to each other they have already said it. Engaged couples and pairs who are going out together are usually seated beside each other. However, it generally makes for a more sociable evening if couples are separated. Host and hostess usually sit at each end of the table. If the sexes are to be divided equally and depending on numbers (a party of eight, for example) it will be necessary for a male guest to sit at an end. In this case, the hostess is seated on his right.

The principle underlying a seating plan is that every guest should feel they have done well by the arrangements. If bigwigs are present it is sound practice to avoid an obvious 'top table' or senior cluster. Scatter stars liberally.

A minor ploy which helps to distribute honours is to consider a couple collectively. Thus, only one of a pair will be seated beside the host or hostess and the other takes their place in the body of the party. Such details may sound pedantic or over-formal but there are occasions when people's sensitivities to what is due to them need special attention. The gesture of greatest respect to a couple is to seat her on the host's right and him on the hostess's right.

Place-cards

At a party with several tables or a fully occupied big table, it may simplify seating arrangements if a place-card bearing the name of the guest is put at each setting. Sometimes these repose in purpose-made holders.

A certain amount of etiquette is involved in the styles of address used. Depending on the degree of formality of the occasion, the card may give a person's prefix, first name and surname, e.g. Mr Charles Box or Sir Charles Box, or state a first name and surname without a prefix, e.g. Charles Box, or simply bear a first name or nickname as in 'Charles' or 'Charlie'. In addition to signifying a place, the information on the card indicates to nearby dining companions their neighbour's name and handle, if any.

It is not considered polite, even in the interests of communication, to style a married woman as 'Mrs Jane Box' as this applies to divorcees. Her married name is Mrs Charles Box. However, writing 'Jane Box' avoids that problem, even if it leaves her married status a matter of conjecture.

One advantage of giving a married woman her professional name is that if her work is known to members of the party, identifying her in this way may help to touch off a conversation or two.

Guests of title are given their informal styles on place-cards at a private occasion. E.g. Viscount Darcy's style is Lord Darcy, Viscountess Darcy's style is Lady Darcy.

Order of seating

The hostess is the first to be seated, followed by the women followed by the men. Men are supposed to pull out a lady's chair and to refrain from seating themselves until their female companions are comfortably seated. Polite males manage a gesture along these lines without necessarily following the exact prescription.

Dinner party diary

Some hostesses like to keep a record of the seating plans and menus for each party as a means of avoiding repetition – which also forms an interesting diary.

Traditional hostmanship

The custom is for the head of the family to sit at the head of the table, to carve any meat or game on the menu and to see to the serving of wines as well as choosing the bottle. He tries to ensure that no one is neglected or passed over. He remembers it is improper to turn his back on a woman and to devote himself to only one of the people seated next to him.

Traditional hostessing

A hostess plays the star part. She is on home ground and her capacity to care for friends, produce good food and create a sense of originality and comfort in her own environment are given fresh rein. Humour, generosity and conviviality are characteristics of a successful hostess, and good looks and charm have never been a disadvantage.

She supervises the food and drink, the table setting and the arrangement of the rooms where the party is to take place. She shows the guests to their places at the table. The roles of the host and hostess have come much closer, and therefore, if wished, the man may do the flowers, lay the table and be cook, and his lady may see to the wine, serve the food and pick up the tab for the party.

Hostess on her own

When a woman gives a party she has to juggle single-handed with what is usually a double role. It can make for a smoother service if she enlists the support of a friend to help her with some of the tasks such as pouring drinks. Probably of greater value than practical support is someone who can be depended on to keep the party spirit alive during her enforced absences in the kitchen. Offers to help clear the table of plates and so forth are kindly, but it is doubtful whether the party-giver should encourage them. She can all too easily find herself sitting at an empty table while guests mill around attempting to be helpful.

It is also best for the party as a whole if guests feel free of domestic involvement while being sensitive to the need to lend an occasional hand. Offers to help with the washing up should be politely turned down.

Bachelor hosts find themselves in much the same position as women and the same guidelines apply.

The good table companion

Good guests show their appreciation of the hospitality and generally make an effort without being gushing to contribute to the success of the occasion.

Turning one's back on a neighbour at table for a long time, conducting a rowdy conversation across the table to the detriment of other talkers, neglecting to pass the sauce boat as it languishes at one's hand are all considered signs of bad manners.

It is polite for diners at least to attempt to talk to both their neighbours at the table and to avoid giving one person the feeling that they are way down in their neighbour's favours. It is certainly very pleasing for a guest to get the impression that the person who is seated beside them is delighted with their luck.

A point may arise in which general conversation takes off. If someone happens not to have anything to say on the topic it is tactless for them to start a tête-à-tête which always runs the risk of fragmenting the round table discussion.

Dinner party style

It is important to pitch arrangements at a level that can be sustained by the facilities, space and resources of the house. As numerous playwrights and novelists have discovered, nothing is more comic than pretension because it is so easily punctured. The menu, the table setting, all the arrangements and the service should be of a kind, and within the energies, finances and capacities of the giver.

Giving a dinner party involves effort, the degree of which can only be determined by the host. An unfashionable plea may be made for taking trouble, as one of the pleasures of the party is the opportunity for guests to enjoy the taste and imagination of their hosts.

Order of service

One of the greatest compliments a hostess can be paid is to be told that she seems as carefree as her guests. If professional help can be called in, and the party-givers are able to brief freelance cook, waiter and tidier-upper to carry out their personal instructions, they have it made. But such service is costly and if dinner parties depended on it, precious few would be held.

The form of the service at table also makes a tremendous difference to the smooth running of the meal and the best method is the one that suits you. There are a number of variations. Factors determining the manner of service include: whether the guests are to remain seated throughout the meal and pass food among themselves: whether they will get up and help themselves buffet-style for one or two courses; whether guests will be waited on for one course and left to help themselves buffet-style to the rest of the meal.

When guests are waited upon at a seated dinner party, dishes are served on the left. This allows the diner to get an easy grip of any serving implements in the dish with their right hand.

If formality is to be observed, the woman on the host's right is served first, the male host is the next to be served, and service continues round the table in a clockwise direction. An alternative, more formal method is for all women to be served before all the men, with the woman on the host's right being the first to be served; the man on the hostess's right is the first of his sex to be served.

When a woman is host she may appoint a male as co-host, in which case procedures are as usual. Otherwise, methods of serving are whatever suits.

When dishes are handed round between guests at table the convention follows waiter service, to pass right so the dish is held at the neighbour's left.

If only one person is waiting, care must be taken to keep the service moving smoothly. If there are too many separate hot dishes to be handed round in turn, there is a risk that the people who are served first will face congealing food as they wait until the others are served. It is best to wait on the guests with the main dish and have the party pass the other dishes and accompaniment among themselves. A short delaying tactic is in order here for guests who are among the first to be served. Even if the host declares, 'Please begin', it is tactful to wait a short while in order to avoid finishing before the others have barely begun. Eating implements can be put into pretend service, if the host is insistent on the point.

If a hot first course is to be offered, warm plates are put round as soon as the guests are seated. Many hostesses take the simpler option of setting out a first course that will not spoil on individual plates at each place to await the arrival of the guests.

No plates should be removed from the table until everyone has finished each course, including second helpings. If waiters are at work, they collect plates in twos. If the hostess is doing the work, guests usually pass the plates down the table to her. Stacking is convenient but a pile of greasy plates is not a pretty sight and where possible should be avoided.

Fresh plates are put round the table for the course to follow and accompaniments that will not be needed again removed.

Side plates remain throughout the meal and serve for bread and butter, salad or cheese. Perfect service would produce or previously have set a fresh side plate for the salad whenever it was to be served, whether with the main course or with cheese.

When guests help themselves buffet-style, a relaxed way of arranging things is to set out the first course in advance at each place-setting and to invite the guests to help themselves to the main course and accompanying dishes from a sideboard. Plates are provided for collection near the food. Sauce and extras to which people can help themselves are placed on the table. People may also return to the sideboard for seconds and pudding. It is thoughtful for host or hostess to stand by and supervise the self-service, helping guests to food as necessary. This buffet-style works well enough for a small party but if guests are asked frequently to get up and serve themselves it disrupts conversation and the table tends to have permanent gaps.

At an intimate party, the hostess can serve each guest from a sideboard or kitchen work top and pass the plate along the table. She can check on everyone's likes and dislikes as she goes along. She serves herself last.

If the hostess is handing dishes round in waiter style, she takes a helping for herself as she passes her place – better still, some kind guest undertakes the task as her hands will be full.

Serving coffee

If the party is going well many hosts prefer to serve coffee at table. Usually the hostess pours the coffee herself and guests help themselves to cream and sugar. If staff are employed they hand the coffee and accompaniments. If coffee is served elsewhere, the same applies.

Wines, wine-based aperitifs, port and liqueurs

Wine is as important as the food at a dinner party. The grape is one of the oldest of beverages and comes in many different forms, flavours and strengths appropriate to every stage of a meal. All the drink on offer matters, but the wine that is produced at dinner reflects the host's taste and level of hospitality. A well-chosen bottle immeasurably enhances the dishes with which it is served.

A good knowledge of wine is not beyond the reach of ordinary, relatively inexperienced mortals. The renowned wine authority André Simon maintained that connoisseurship is a question of 'being able to use your senses and your common sense'. One of the unsung advantages of acquiring an acceptable palate for the grape is that friends and family who are asked to dinner are likely to share the benefits.

The following is a very general guide to serving wine.

Wines served before a meal

Dry sherry is offered most usually before or at the beginning of a meal. Sherry is best served cool and is poured into small, stemmed glasses. The wine may be decanted. Dry sherry should be sipped appreciatively and never tossed back like a nip of vodka.

Wine-based aperitifs sharpen the appetite and are usually served chilled. Vermouth, made with white wine, is served straight or with ice and perhaps a measure of Cassis, in a long glass. It is the making of many classic aperitifs such as a dry martini and long drinks such as Pimms.

Wines served at table

Red, white and rosé bottles from vineyards great and small find their way to the dinner party.

Red wines are served at room temperature as a rule. A good red wine deserves to have the cork drawn a while before serving which allows the contents to 'breathe' and the flavour and bouquet to bloom. Reds of bottle-age are often decanted as the wine throws sediment which is unpleasant to taste. The art of decanting is said to be to pour the wine very slowly and carefully from the bottle into the decanter so as not to disturb the sediment at the base. In this way, the drinker is spared the dregs. Decanting is reserved for specially good wine and it might be thought pretentious to decant anything less. White and rosé wines are served chilled.

Wines served at the end of the meal

Sweet white wines accompany the dessert course, Sauternes, Beaume de Venise and Monbazillac are known choices. The wine is usually served well chilled and is poured into wine glasses. The sweetness of the drink is best appreciated by being imbibed slowly.

Port accompanies cheese and/or dessert. A certain amount of etiquette attaches to passing the port on formal occasions. Port is usually decanted and passed round the table clockwise among the guests who help themselves as the decanter arrives at their hand. It is considered bad manners to arrest the progress of the port on its journey by neglecting to pass it. The decanter is usually placed in front of the host, who helps the lady on his right and then passes the port to the person at his left. Port is poured into small stemmed glasses.

Liqueurs such as sloe gin or elderberry wine can be offered with cheese and dessert. The wines are poured from the bottle into small liqueur glasses.

Brandy makes its appearance with coffee at the end of the meal usually but may also be offered as an aperitif. It is poured from the bottle into liqueur glasses or brandy balloons. Brandy drinkers often like to mull over their tipple by gently circulating the liqueur in its big glass held in the palm of the hand, with the stem slipped between index finger and third finger. The warmth of human contact against the glass helps to release the bouquet gently.

Serving champagne

Champagne is regarded by many as the prince of wines. It may be served before and after a meal, and throughout, providing the dishes go well with it. It should be served cool but never ice-cold.

Opening a bottle requires care and a certain adroitness if the cork is not to fly out dangerously nor precious bubbles be wasted. The instructions are as follows: the gold foil on the head of the bottle is peeled off and the wire securing the cork is loosened and removed. The neck of the bottle should be pointed in a direction away from any danger zones. The bottle is held firmly in one hand and the cork is gripped by the other. Using a slow, measured action which simultaneously unscrews the cork and draws it out, the bottle is opened. The cork should never be jerked from base and should remain in the hand when drawn. As the 'pop' is sounded, the champagne gushes forth and is poured immediately but steadily into the glass. Too hasty a pour and the effervescence will rise above the brim. If this occurs, the bubbles can be caused to subside by placing a hand lightly across the mouth of the glass. Care should be taken not to shake the bottle.

Pouring wine

It is the host's job to ensure that guests' glasses are filled as soon as they are seated. Whether one wine is served throughout or whether the food commands two or more wines is a matter of personal judgment and the nature of the dishes served. No one need apologize for offering one wine but it would be unusual to do so at a grand dinner party.

Wine is poured from the right. The pourer first fills the glass of the person on the host's right and continues on the round in a clockwise direction. The male party-giver's glass is the last to be filled. It is the host's responsibility to keep the wine flowing. If the bottle is placed on the table, diners will most likely help themselves without being invited to do so. If the wine is placed on a sideboard it is easier to keep control of the intake.

Wine should be poured liberally but with respect. When a good wine is being served, it is best to fill the glass to about three-quarters of its capacity as this will allow the bouquet to be savoured. When a pleasant but ordinary thirst-quencher is on offer, a fuller measure is in order. An exception to the above is champagne, which may be poured generously.

Thoughtful hosts provide capacious wine glasses. It is a sign of a mean heart to put out glasses with undersize bowls.

Guests may decline a wine – a hand held over the glass will do the trick without words – or ask politely for more of a wine that was served with a previous course in preference to the one being poured. It would be impolite to ask for a wine that had not yet been served.

May a diner ask for his or her glass to be replenished? In circumstances in which someone is trying to make a good impression, probably not. But with friends, by all means.

Planning a menu

Guests are always delighted by good food. Whatever the scale of the gathering, homely or lavish, the menu is important.

Planning what is to be served is usually shaped by the resources of the host, time available and degree of confidence.

The only bad manners would be to produce a meal which gave the impression that the guests were scarcely worth bothering about. Another point to remember is that guests like to be in the company of the host, especially at the beginning when the party is finding its feet. Choosing dishes which mean that the cook has to be incarcerated in the kitchen for the better part of pre-dinner drinks is a renowned downer; guests may feel neglected or guilty about not offering to help. Every good meal requires some last-minute attention but the aim at all but servanted parties is to rely on advance preparation and the minimum of culinary attention just before the serving stage.

Keen cooks usually seize the opportunity to try out a new dish on the party, and assuming a sporting chance of success, should be encouraged to enlarge their repertoire. Obviously, cooks have to pick their friends carefully if a serious experiment is on the burner. This is no place to attempt to describe the art of menu planning but a few basic principles do apply. Courses shoudl be nicely balanced for flavour, content and appearance. Variety is a positive spice and main ingredients should not be repeated. Good food should stimulate the taste buds through combinations of flavours that enhance one another.

Number of courses

While simplicity and an emphasis on good cooking are keynotes at the modern dinner party, customs vary on the number of courses that are the party's due.

Generally, at least three courses are served, not counting coffee. A fourth course may be added or, for those who hold that enough is by no means as good as a feast, a fifth.

What is of much greater weight than such questions as the number of dishes produced is that the whole occasion should give the impression that the host has gone to some trouble to please the guests – how much toil and trouble is a debatable point. Some cooks set a limit of an hour on preparation time as a criterion for choosing a menu. Others gain pleasure from the act of cooking and are prepared to lavish as much time as they can spare, and more, on the task. Good cooks who wish to economize on effort might like to produce two prepared dishes and rely on well chosen cheese as the third.

At grand occasions, at which four or five courses are being served, the order of a classic menu might be: soup, fish, meat, pudding, cheese. At banquet-level meals, the custom of offering a sorbet (a water ice) in between rich courses has its rare adherents, as a means of cleansing the palate.

A nice point concerns the order of serving pudding and cheese. Either way is acceptable and is a matter of taste.

Ethnic cuisines

Many keen cooks are attempting to produce authentic dishes from ethnic cuisines such as those from Japan, China, India and Thailand among others. The order and methods of serving at table are often quite different from Western traditions, and deserve to be followed if the food is to be done justice.

Likes and dislikes

Choosing a dish that everyone round the table will enjoy can be a problem, although fortunately more people than ever before are now prepared to try interesting, unfamiliar dishes. However, there may be certain occasions when it is wise to play safe, for example by proscribing offal. If in doubt about serving a dish, it is always possible to check out the matter beforehand. Few guests object to giving a straight answer about whether they like devilled kidneys.

Food taboos

The proliferation of food taboos has given rise to a complex situation in which it is difficult to distinguish bona fide objection from crankiness. Round the table may be seated members of the Orthodox Jewish faith (no pork or shellfish among other forbidden foods), strict Roman Catholics (no meat on Friday), vegetarians (no meat at all), vegans (no dairy produce or meat or fish), those on a cosmetic weight-loss diet – you name it. If all these proscriptions were obeyed, dinner parties would surely come to an end, which would be a great pity. Some sense of proportion has to be re-established.

Special requirements

If a non-vegetarian, for example, invites known vegetarians as guests it would be discourteous to offer a meal largely consisting of meats. If the party includes catholic tastes, one idea is to offer plentiful helpings of a dish (or dishes) that are acceptable to the cultists and which also go well with the mainstream dishes. Obviously it is considerate to offer an acceptable alternative to those to whom a certain dish is taboo, and it is tactful to make these arrangements with the minimum of public display. If in doubt as how best to cater to a friend's special culinary requirements, by far the best counsel will come from the person in question.

Laying the table

A well-laid table is a promising prelude to a party. Above all the effect should be inviting and suggest that a good meal is on its way.

Laying a table successfully can be accomplished by anyone with a mind to do it, though some people have a magic knack of arranging a table that is a pleasure in its own right. All the facets of a creative composition such as colour, texture, decoration, pattern and lighting are brought into play. Those who own good china, silver and glass will share them to good effect, while others can get by with even the simplest arrangements.

There is no complete answer as to how much equipment is needed to give a dinner party. China, glass and linen are akin to props in a play and depend on the occasion, the food and drink to be served and what the party-givers have in mind.

China Standard and useful equipment includes soup plates or soup cups and saucers; main-course and first-course plates; side plates for bread, salad, cheese or dessert, and separate dessert-course plates. The dinner service is usually of a matched or co-ordinated design although the desset plates are sometimes of a different make. The illustrations show relative sizes. A dinner service will also include serving dishes, a soup tureen, vegetable dishes and covers, sauce-boats, salt and pepper shakers and mustard pots. A coffee service comprises the pot, coffee cups and saucers, cream jug, sugar bowl.

Silver . Classic equipment includes: soup spoons, smaller-size knives and forks for the first course, large-size knives and forks for main courses; spoons and forks for pudding; fruit knives and forks as an elegant extra and serving spoons and forks. Silver is also used for salt, pepper and mustard pots, sugar bowls or sifters, coffee pot, coffee spoons and also for candlesticks and candelabra. 'The silver' is a flexible description which may refer to hallmarked artefacts for the dining-table but equally may apply to several alternatives such as silver plate, Sheffield plate or stainless steel.

Owners of beautiful silver for the table use as much of it as they have call for at parties but those without can manage very well. A good sense of design and a personal touch when creating a table arrangement can more than compensate for the absence of a traditional show of silver.

Table linen should be as fresh as the day and add to the general effect of care and attention. Requirements depend on whether the table is to be spread with a cloth or set with place-mats. A fine polished table is shown to advantage with place-mats but a tablecloth always looks crisp and welcoming. Linen is often of white or cream but colour offers decorative options. Lace, damask and linen are fabrics particularly associated with the table but as these are extremely expensive many alternatives have won acceptance.

Napkins should always be provided. Paper napkins are adequate, especially if large and absorbent, but anyone who has tried these and the fabric type knows how much more efficient are the latter.

Napkin lore Table napkins can be laid in the centre of a place setting or put on the side-plate. They can be folded simply in four or made into shapes of origami-like complexity. Whatever its design, a napkin should always look and feel freshly laundered.

Napkins are shaken out as soon as the diner is seated and the linen spread over the lap. Unhappily, any sensible method such as securing it to your belt is considered uncool. Some brave spirits emulate the Gallic style and tuck a corner into their neckline or waistcoat so the napkin becomes a bib. But the principle hasn't made much progress so far on this side of the Channel.

Hands are wiped on napkins, lips are dabbed but serious ablutions are taking the matter too far.

At the end of the meal, the napkin is left on the table in a rumpled state. To refold would suggest that it was to be reused by another person without being laundered.

Drinking glasses A supply of standard wine glasses and tumblers will suffice for the majority of parties but there is much more to the subject. Glasses are designed to enhance their contents. For example, long-stemmed glasses are appropriate for chilled white wine as they enable the warm-blooded hand of the drinker to keep its distance from the drink. A balloon-shaped brandy glass is designed to fit snugly into the palm of the hand as the warmth of contact releases its aromatic bouquet.

Especially useful glasses include those for red and white wine: flutes for champagne; small glasses for sherry, port and liqueurs, and large brandy balloons; tumblers for gin and tonic, whisky and soda, water, non- or low-alcoholic beverages; large glasses for lager and beer. Goblets are a handsome alternative. Cocktail glasses are a must for those who have a keen cocktail shaker in the house.

On the table

Almost everyone knows how to set a table for an ordinary meal but arranging an array of silver for a dinner party calls on wider knowledge. The general principle is that knives are placed to the right and forks to the left; spoons can be set to the right or across the top of the place-setting with a fork.

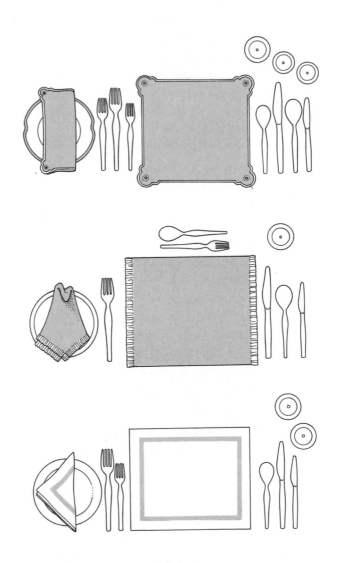

An example of a formal place setting with the dessert spoon and fork set upright on either side.

An example of an informally arranged place setting with the dessert spoon and fork set horizontally across the top.

An example of a place setting for a three course lunch or dinner.

A setting for a three-course meal consisting of a first course, main course and a dessert takes the following order, working from the outside right inwards: a knife for a first course, a knife for a main course and a dessert spoon. If a separate knife for the side-plate is to be provided this can be placed on the plate – or set as the first implement on the right hand side. On working from the outside left inwards: a first course fork, a main-course fork and a dessert fork.

A setting which includes soup as a first course follows the above order, substituting a large spoon for the first-course knife and omitting the first-course fork on the left.

A setting for a four-course meal comprising a first course, main course, pudding and cheese takes the following order, working from the outside right inwards: a first course knife or big spoon, a large knife, a pudding spoon, a smaller knife for cheese; on the left, working from the outside inwards, a smaller fork for the first course (unless soup is served) a large fork, a smaller fork for dessert.

Knives are placed with the blades facing towards the place setting except for those put on a side-plate, in which case the blade faces outwards. Spoons are set with the declivity of the bowl resting on its back. Forks are set with the prongs curving upwards. A combination of spoon and fork placed across the top of the place-setting are set spoon above fork. The handle of the spoon points to the right hand and the handle of the fork points towards the left hand (see illustrations).

On the subject of place-setting design, some prefer an absolutely symmetrical layout with each implement having its companion whether or not the eater is likely to find a good use for it.

When dealing with a small or crowded dinner table, one strategy is to lay the silver for the first and main courses and to bring in reinforcements for pudding and cheese later. This is a boon when equipment is running short.

Fish knives and forks

Opinion is divided on whether to use separate, purpose-made knives and forks for a fish course. There seems little point unless the blade or prongs of the implements are made of silver, which is said to be compatible with fish. However, people who possess fish knives and forks tend to use them if only as an indicator of the dishes to be served.

A setting for a three-course meal with fish as a main course takes the following order; working from the outside right inwards, a first-course knife (or soup spoon), a fish knife, a pudding spoon; working from the outside left inwards, a small fork to accompany the first-course knife, a fish fork, a dessert fork.

A setting for a four-course meal with fish served as a course after the beginning dish and before the main course takes the following order, working from the outside right inwards: a first-course knife or spoon, a fish knife, main-course knife, a dessert spoon; working from the outside left inwards, a fork to accompany the first-course knife, a fish fork, a main-course fork, a dessert fork.

If fish is served as a starter, obviously the implements replace those given for that course in the examples above.

Arranging the glasses

Wine glasses and their companions are usually placed in a group at the right of each person's table setting, arranged just above or around the point of the blade of the largest knife. As to exact placings of the different sizes and functions of the glasses, no firm rules exist. The setting depends on what looks good, on the number of wines to be served and on the size of the table. The style of the arrangement should be consistent at each place-setting. With the exception of pot luck repasts, it is usual to provide a separate glass for each wine to be served. Also, it has become standard to place a tumbler or goblet for water or soft drinks alongside the wine glasses.

Some people choose to arrange the glasses according to shape and size, others use the criterion of the order in which the wines will be served, the glass for the first being placed nearest to the reach of the diner, and the others being ranged accordingly.

Table extras

Appearance and accessibility are the twin principles involved in completing a table setting. It is obviously more comfortable to have whatever you may need in the way of spices or accompaniments within easy reach, rather than to have to wait for them to be passed.

Sauces with well-known brand names such as Worcester are served in the bottle and French and German mustards can be offered in the shop-bought container. Whether to turn out ready-prepared sauces into a pretty dish which disguises the fact that they are not home-made may trouble the conscience of serious cooks. Others will do so cheerfully.

Cream is brought with the dish it accompanies. Bread is cut and handed at the beginning of the meal and offered from time to time. Fresh water should always be to hand.

Serving dishes are usually returned to the sideboard and the salad bowl likewise. Ashtrays are set out with the coffee except in households with a 'No Smoking' embargo.

See page 346 for Unholy smoke.

Finger bowls

Finger bowls provide a pleasant refresher. Small glass bowls filled with fresh water are set before each guest after a course such as asparagus which has involved eating with fingers. Some hosts like to add a slice of lemon or rose petals to the water for extra value. The required gesture is to dip the tips of sticky fingers into the water and to dry them off on a table napkin. Anything suggesting serious ablutions would be taking things too far. Finger bowls are removed before the next course is served.

Table decoration

The centre of the table should be worth a second glance. Centrepieces may be purely ornamental or fulfil a practical function as well, such as holding candles, flowers or fruit.

Candlelight creates a romantic atmosphere but it is important to remember, nevertheless, that people do like to have a clear view of what they are eating. It may be advisable to combine lit candles with discreet, back-up electric light.

Flowers

An arrangement of fresh flowers gives every dinner table a lift and if seasonable stems are used marks the time of year attractively.

Points to avoid are to be found in the high-rise floristry that the great British flower arranger, Constance Spry, and her present-day disciples have done so much to reform. The massively tall blooms and their containers that were popular at one time have mercifully given way to smaller schemes that can be admired without screening eye contact across the table. Part of Constance Spry's legacy is she has made flower lovers aware of a whole range of stems – flowers, foliage, grasses and branches – which have creative decorative potential.

Clearing away

At servanted parties, the dishes, accompaniments, spices and silver which related to previous courses and for which there will be no further use are cleared away in preparation for the pudding and/or cheese. When the hostess is managing the work largely on her own, a more relaxed view of proceedings would remove used plates, used eating implements and any redundant serving dishes whilst leaving the smaller objects on the table, whether they were useful of not. Butter dishes may remain on the table until the end of the meal as some people like a bit of butter with their last cheese biscuit or piece of bread.

Table manners

The purpose of table manners is to help make eating a more graceful spectator sport. It has to be said that watching people eat with naked gusto can put more sensitive souls off their oats.

Historically, the British are considered to have led the field in table manners with their emphasis on order, restraint and grace at table. Some customs are class-based and others derive from common sense, but all are conscious of the mannerly approach to eating. Critics may detect an underlying puritanism in British ways here as politeness tends to be inhibiting and seldom encourages an unabashed display of delight in the sensuality of food. Yet there is skill to be found in the accepted methods which have withstood the test of time.

Comment by people round the table on the cooking is now general except perhaps on official occasions, and will probably be expected and certainly appreciated by the host. Expressing likes and dislikes, asking how a dish has been prepared, exchanging cooking tips and recipes has become accepted conversation for both sexes.

Knife and forkery

King Charles I is said to have put it about that 'It is decent to use a fork'. Since then the fork has become the most indispensable of the trio of feeding implements, it is perfectly acceptable to manage any dish with a fork alone when it can be done comfortably.

This is done by transferring the fork to the right hand and normally using it as either a spoon or a cradle for food with the prongs (properly described as 'tines') facing upwards. The upper part of the handle is held between the index and middle fingers, with the thumb used to hold the fork steady. The fourth and little fingers are closed together in support of the fingers gripping the handle (see illustration). Cakes and pastries can be eaten with a fork alone.

Holding a knife and fork

When a fork is used in conjunction with a knife, it is held in the manner of a knife (see below and illustrations) with the prongs facing downwards. The handle of a table knife is held with the end covered by the palm of the hand and the index finger resting on the length. The handle is supported by the thumb on one side and the remaining fingers on the other. This method ensures a good grip, helps to prevent the sharp edge of the blade from slipping dangerously backward against the hand and also enables the eater to keep his elbows to his sides instead of digging into the ribs of any neighbour.

It is not considered good manners to hold a knife as if it were a pencil with the handle sticking up (see illustration).

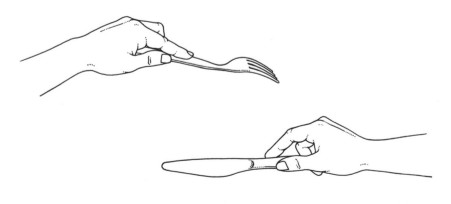

Cutting up food on a plate is a more finicky business according to British manners than in other countries. The method is to cut one piece at a time from the whole portion, and to eat it before repeating the process. Chopping up your slice of beef into pieces before beginning to eat is considered incorrect, for instance.

A knife is also a pusher – the width of the blade helps to push food on to the back of a fork. Sadly, it is not considered the best of manners to take the easy way out and heap food on to the cradle of a fork (see illustration).

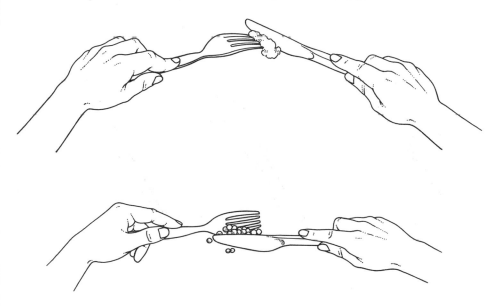

Holding a spoon and fork

A soup or dessert spoon is held in the manner of a fork when used alone (see illustration above) with the bowl facing upwards. When used in conjunction with a fork, the spoon digs into a dish and the fork acts as a pusher (see illustration).

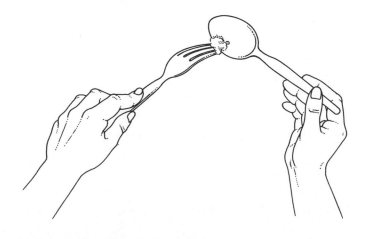

Chopsticks

The popularity of Chinese and Japanese dishes has led to the adoption of chopsticks in private houses as well as in restaurants. Knowing how to manage chopsticks is a technique that should be acquired by everyone who enjoys Far Eastern cooking (see illustrations). Novices will quickly learn through practice. At a private party, however, it would be considerate to offer a knife and fork to any guest who admits his chopsticks technique is elementary. Guests may ask to be rescued.

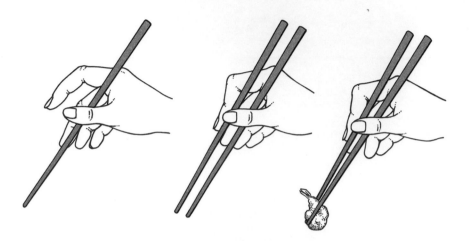

Eating etiquette

Bread: French bread and bread rolls are eaten from a side-plate, or from the table at the left-hand side of a setting if butter is not served. The method is to break off a small piece of bread, to butter the surface if wished, and to eat it before repeating the process. It is not considered correct to spread butter over the whole of the helping of bread as in making a sandwich (see illustration). Toast is eaten in a similar way at lunch or dinner, but at breakfast or teatime, spreading the butter all over is fine.

Salad: A salad is eaten with a knife and fork or with a fork alone if the ingredients are manageable without using a knife. Whether to place your helping of salad on the main-course plate or on a side-plate is largely a question of flavour combination. Some like to eat salad mixed with the main course, others prefer to keep it separate. If a special salad plate is set out, use it.

Soup: Techniques for drinking soup depend on both the type of broth and the shape of the dish in which it is served. Slurping soup is a temptation to be overcome.

Soup may be served in a tureen with a big ladle for helpings. Soup is always sipped from the side of the spoon, never from the tip. When the broth is served in a soup plate, dip the spoon into the dish and draw it gently to the far side of the plate. Lift out a spoonful of soup and raise to the lips. In this way any surplus plops into the plate and not on you. As the soup goes down, tilt the plate away from you in order to accumulate the remainder and spoon up. Leave the spoon in the plate, set a little to the right to show you have finished.

When the soup comes in a cup with handles on a saucer, pick up the cup by both hands and drink. Set down the cup in its saucer in-between mouthfuls. If the soup is thick, use a spoon. Should a soup with a drinkable consistency contain solids, use a spoon for the morsels and drink the liquid from the cup. Leave the spoon in the saucer.

When soup is served in a cup set in an empty soup dish pour the contents into the dish then proceed as described above for drinking soup from a soup-plate. The empty cup is put to one side. Leave the spoon in the soup-plate.

Snails come hot in their shells bathed in melted butter, parsley and garlic, arranged on your plate.

Restaurants like to serve this dish with special equipment such as a plate designed to hold the shells steady and pairs of tongs to grip them by which makes eating easier. Hold a single shell in the tongs and detach the snails with a fork. Dip the snail in the savoury sauce and eat whole.

Perhaps because of the Gallic origin of this method of cooking snails, it is considered perfectly polite in this country to mop up the sauce with bread.

Leave the empty snail shells on the plate.

Fish on the bone

Fish served on the bone presents the dilemma of whether to skin and fillet the fish before tucking in or to leave the fish on the bone and strip as you eat. Filleters should opt for the former as once accomplished the dish is easier to manage: use a knife and fork (taking up any purpose-made cutlery) and lift off the fillets from one side of the spine. Turn the fish over carefully and repeat the process. The stripped bones are left tidily on the side of the plate. Use a knife and fork for fish on the bone, and these or a fork alone for filleted fish.

Note: if the standard hazard should occur and a fishbone be lodged in your mouth, have no misgivings about removing it with your fingers. Put the debris discreetly on the side of the plate.

Whitebait comes hot as a pile of little fishes fried with their heads on, accompanied by a wedge of lemon and bread and butter. Squeeze the lemon juice over the golden heap, add seasoning if wished, and eat them whole with a knife and fork or fork alone.

Grilled sardines are served whole in small numbers. Some people like to bother with filleting sardines, others eat them whole, save for the head and tail. Beware of bones.

Shellfish

Scallops come hot or cold, in or out of the half shell, with or without a sauce. Use a knife and fork, or fork alone.

Fresh oysters come in half shell set out on your plate as a dozen or half dozen. Sometimes the plate rests on a bed of ice. Oysters are customarily served with a wedge of lemon and black pepper. Squeeze the lemon over each oyster and add seasoning, if desired. Hold the shell steady in one hand and use a fork – a special oyster fork may be provided – to lift out the oyster. Oysters are swallowed whole if wished. Then drink the liquid from the oyster shell.

Note: The seemingly innocent act of squeezing a segment of lemon over a dish can have unfortunate consequences for a neighbour as the juice is liable to squirt waywardly. Preventive measures are to keep the hand holding the lemon well hooded over the operation, to squeeze low rather than high and to press gently to begin with when the lemon is juiciest.

Cooked mussels often come as a pile of black-brown shells containing the little molluscs, in a thin soup, as in the French dish *moules marinières*. Detach the mussels with a fork, holding the shell in the fingers, and spoon up the broth. Put the empty shells on a fresh plate if one is to hand, otherwise return the shells to base. *Note:* The French have a simplified way of managing this dish which is to use a half shell as a spoon.

Lobster in the shell comes as a half or as a whole divided into halves on your plate, complete with claws. Traditionally, mayonnaise is served with cold lobster and melted butter or Hollandaise sauce when it comes hot.

Ladle out some sauce on the side of your plate. Cut off a piece of lobster meat with a knife and fork, dip it into the sauce. As usual, eat the separated piece before digging in for another. You may prefer to hold the big shell steady with one hand and use a fork only. Novices should remember that the coral of the lobster is edible.

The big claws are usually cracked in readiness. Pull the shell apart in the fingers and use a fork to remove the meat. A lobster's attachments contain many delicacies but it requires application to reach them. Sometimes a special fork is provided, designed to prise out meat held in the crevices of the shells. Otherwise the meat is sucked out discreetly.

Leave the lobster shells on the plate.

The same rules apply to eating crab.

Prawns and shrimps are served in or out of the shell. They are peeled in the fingers, the technique being to remove the head and the tail shell and then to unwrap the body. The debris is put at the side of the plate. If the prawns are of manageable size they may be eaten in the fingers. If large, they should be cut with a knife and fork and eaten piece by piece. These crustaceans are usually accompanied by a

segment of lemon, black pepper and perhaps a sauce. If a sauce is served, it may
be advisable to use a fork.

*See page 190 for
Finger bowls.*

    Note: At a formal dinner finger bowls may be provided when shellfish in the
shell is on the menu.

First courses

Pâtés and terrines come as a slice on your plate or whole in the dish in which they
were cooked. If the latter, cut an even slice and put it on your plate.

    Pâtés are usually served with hot toast or French bread. Spread a little pâté
on the toast or bread and take a bite. It is not considered polite to spread it all over
as for a sandwich.

Pasta comes in a large dish or as an individual helping. A sauce and/or grated
cheese may be handed separately. Help yourself to the accompaniments and mix
all the ingredients on your plate. Experienced pasta eaters plunge a fork into the
middle of the plate of noodles and twirl it round so a few lengths are secured on
the prongs. Raise the laden fork to the lips, nonchalantly ignoring any stray strands
that may dangle over the lips. An alternative method is to use a spoon and fork,
turning the noodles round the fork as before but using the spoon to 'lean' against.

Smoked salmon comes in thin slices covering your plate or on a large dish from
which you take a helping. Classic accompaniments are brown bread and butter and
a wedge of lemon and seasoning. Squeeze the lemon all over the fish. Use a knife
and fork or fork alone to cut off a piece and eat before taking another helping.
Help yourself to the bread and butter in between whiles.

Quails' eggs come hardboiled in their shells (or sometimes ready-peeled), arranged
in a dish from which you help yourself, or set out on your plate. They are usually
offered with celery salt or ground pepper.

    If the eggs are in the shell, pick them up one at a time and peel in your
fingers. Dip the egg into the seasoning and eat in a bite or two.

Caviar comes in a round stone jar, sometimes on a bed of ice with a serving spoon.
Accompaniments vary but classics are hot toast and butter and a wedge of lemon.
Help yourself to a spoonful or two. Squeeze the lemon juice over the mound of
caviar. Heap a little of the mixture on the buttered toast and take a bite. Repeat.
Your luck is in.

Vegetables

Asparagus comes set out on a big dish or on your plate, with the stalks pointing in
the same direction. It is served hot with melted butter or Hollandaise sauce, or
cold with a vinaigrette dressing. The sauces are handed separately. When ladling
out the sauce take care not to cover the base of the stalks. Pick up the thick white
end in your fingers, dip the soft green head into the sauce or dressing and lower

some asparagus into your mouth. Continue with the procedure until the part of the stalk is reached which is tough. Lay the remains tidily at the edge of the plate. Note: some young or thin asparagus is sufficiently tender to be eaten from tip to base.

Corn-on-the-cob comes whole on the plate. It may be spiked at either end with special holders, to provide a handle. Melted butter is handed separately.

This is a messy business and cannot be recommended to diners who wish to remain pristine. A buttery chin or nose is almost inevitable but corn-on-the-cob lovers consider this well worthwhile. The cob is eaten in the fingers and held in either hand. Roll the cob in the buttery sauce and raise to the lips. Bite off the rows of ripe corn. The bare cob is left on the plate.

Globe artichokes come as a small cabbage shape on the plate or in a dish from which you help yourself. When hot they are served with melted butter or Hollandaise sauce, when cold, with a vinaigrette dressing. Sauces are handed separately.

Eating artichokes satisfactorily requires application. The method is to pull off a green leaf with your fingers, starting on the outside, and to dip the fleshy base into the sauce. Extract the artichoke flesh by a combination well known to artichoke addicts of sucking the vegetable through the skin held in the teeth. Continue removing the leaves in this way until the heart is approached. Before the reward is reached you must first remove, using a knife and fork, a layer of small flat leaves which are not interesting to eat and then the thistle-like covering known as the choke. Cut the cushion-like artichoke heart with a knife and fork, taking one piece at a time and dipping it in the sauce. Pile up the discarded green leaves neatly on a fresh plate, if provided, or on the side of the plate.

Potatoes baked in their jackets come halved or whole on the plate, or in a big dish from which you lift one or two. You may eat every morsel of both skin and flesh, or scoop out the white potato inside, leaving the jacket – it is a matter of personal taste. Use a knife and fork or fork alone.

Peas are the very devil to eat elegantly. You may spear a few on the prongs of the fork, or press some on to the back of a fork using a knife as a pusher. Using the fork as a cradle for the vegetable is considered unmannerly (see illustration).

Game birds

Small game birds such as roast quail are served whole on your plate. The most convenient method is to eat what is readily accessible such as the breast and outer leg and to say goodbye to the rest. But those with time and inclination will find many other succulent morsels for the picking. Whether you may pick up the bones in your fingers is a matter of circumstance. At a formal affair desist.

In the case of inexpertly shot game, it is by no means unknown for the unwary to find themselves biting on lead shot. Remove the metal and meat from the mouth with your fingers at once and put the debris on the side of the plate as unobtrusively as possible.

Fruit

To peel the skin or to eat whole? To use fingers or a fork? To remove the stone first or pit in the mouth?. These are a few of the uncertainties that surround the polite eating of fruit at table. At a formal table, it may be more convenient to eat fruit that is usually managed in the fingers with a knife and fork.

See page 207 for Coping with canapés.

Peaches, nectarines, apricots, cherries and plums present the problem of how to remove the stone from the mouth gracefully (the same is true of olives). Hold up a cupped hand to the lips and shoot the stone into it. Put the stone on the side of the plate. When a knife is used, the stones can be cut out on the plate. When unpitted fruit is served in a pudding such as cherry pie, a spoon held up to the mouth acts as a useful receptacle for stones. Put the stones on the side of the plate.

Fresh fruit with pips such as grapes, oranges, tangerines and clementines are eaten in the fingers. Large grapes can be pitted in the fingers, the smaller kind are eaten whole. See above for disposing of the pips.

The most enjoyable ways of eating an orange tend to turn the eater into an orange and cannot be recommended when appearances count. A more fastidious method is to remove the peel and pith and then to separate the fruit into segments when it can be depipped and eaten piece by piece in the hand, or with a fork.

Grapes are served on the branch in a big cluster from which the eater helps himself to a smallish bunch, with grape scissors if provided. It is not considered good manners to pick off the grapes one by one from the main bunch.

Lychees consist of a thin, pinkish-brown shell and juicy white flesh with a large shiny brown stone. Peel in the fingers and eat the fruit whole or, if the flesh parts easily from the stone, remove the stone and leave on the plate. See above.

Avocados are green and pear-shaped with a large stone. They come as a half with the stone removed on the plate, with a filling or plain. If the latter, a vinaigrette dressing is usually handed separately. Ladle some of the dressing into the hollow left by the stone. Use a spoon to scoop out the avocado flesh and any filling which may be served. Leave the empty skin on the plate.

Fresh figs can be eaten in the fingers or with a knife and fork. They may be skinned or eaten as they come, according to taste.

Pineapple may be presented as a whole fruit from which the diners are expected to help themselves. The technique is to lay the fruit on its side and to use a sharp knife to cut off a juicy round. The base may be sliced off first and the fruit cut across its circumference. The eater should remove the outer skin from the slice and perhaps cut out the core if it is tough. The fruit is eaten piece by piece with a knife and fork or a spoon (for ladling up the juice) and fork.

Mangoes may be cut in half along the length of the fruit, the large stone prised out and the fruit eaten in the skin with a spoon or knife and fork.

Paw-paws are treated similarly but are depipped.

Kumquats may be served cooked or raw but are always eaten whole.

Guests' dilemmas

- May guests ask for their place at the table to be changed so as to be seated next to someone else? Not if they hope to be invited to the house again.

- May guests bring their own rations if they are on a strict diet, for whatever reason? If you are able to convince your hosts that your diet is important and you do not wish to put them to the extra trouble of preparing something especially for you there may be a case for it. But the practice is anti-social and undermines the whole spirit of hospitality which is to do with sharing. A safe approach is to decline dinner and ask if you may come in afterwards.

- What is to be done on an occasion when you are served a dish that gives you an allergy? Nobody should feel obliged to eat food that is a health hazard to them. It is best to mention the fact when declining a dish and to avoid dwelling upon details.

- May guests help themselves to wine if the bottle is placed on the table? Opinion is divided on this. Strictly speaking, the act is impolite as the host may be pouring carefully. However, if a guest does decide to help himself he should always offer to replenish his companion's glass before pouring his own.

- How to indicate that you have finished a course? Put the knife and fork together a little to the right-hand side of the plate, and the same applies to a spoon and fork or fork alone. The fork should have the prongs facing upwards, the knife have its blade facing the fork and the spoon should rest on its back.
    When you pause in between mouthfuls, set the eating implements down in the apart position in which it is comfortable to take them in hand again.

- If you are seized by a choking fit, ask for a glass of water quickly. Try not to panic. Don't allow a next-door neighbour to thump you between the shoulder blades, which adds shock to discomfort. If the offending morsel comes to light, take it out of your mouth with your fingers and discreetly put it on the side of the plate. In extremes, leave the room with a helpmate. When you return, try to stay quiet for a short while to recover your composure.

- Suppose you covet an invitation to a party to which you do not appear to have been invited. One or two chinks within the proprieties can be explored, possibly to good effect. You may sound out mutual acquaintances who have received an invitation which allows them to bring an unnamed guest. You might even stoop to the stratagem of asking the giver of the party to drinks or to a meal in hopes that this might produce an invitation. Those who ask the host directly for an invitation or why they are not on the guest list lay themselves open to a rebuff.

Hosts' dilemmas

- Can you invite known antagonists to share a jar? This depends on the characters of the individuals and the state of the feud. It is a risk, clearly, but one of the functions of a party is to provide a neutral ground on which all sorts can meet and converse. Many conflicts have been resolved in this way and opinions modified or revised, but the greater probability is that the party will be turned into an extension of the rivalry. If feelings run high, it is an idea to test the waters by consulting with at least one side to see how they would react.

- Is it good practice to ask guests to switch places during the course of a meal? In favour of the idea is that it may revive flagging conversation and give guests a chance to spend some time with another member of the party. Against is that separation may occur not from a bore but a favourite and the move may disrupt burgeoning personal links. The state of the party is the best criterion. If it is buzzing, leave well alone.

- If fish is being served, are special fish knives and forks necessary? They are not necessities but people who possess them put them on the table.

- Suppose gate crashers are anticipated? At a big party it is worth hiring a bouncer to keep watch at the door.

- What to do about the friend who is decidedly the worse for alcohol and who proposes to drive himself home? The initiative should be taken by the host, as tactfully as possible. He should raise the offer of a lift or arrange a cab. If necessary he might offer a bed for the night as the penalties for being caught by the law are unpleasant.

- How long should the dinner party wait for an unpunctual guest? It is up to the host to decide when to call it a day and go in to dinner. Some people believe in putting the matter to the vote, but few good cooks can contemplate with equanimity the prospect of their efforts being compromised. Therefore the moment at which a dish is likely to deteriorate noticeably is as good a signal as any for going in to dinner. Otherwise a general guideline is to wait for about fifteen to twenty minutes after the meal was due to be served. At table, leave the absent friend's place setting for a while as it is a greater bother to have to restore it if he turns up. If he or she does put in an appearance, introductions take place at table, apologies should be accepted and the episode buried for the duration unless a really gripping story caused the delay. It is hospitable to offer the latecomer any course that he may have missed but it is polite for him to decline at least one if this means serving a complete meal when people are well into their dessert. On the other hand, if the chair remains empty, it is best to remove it with the place-setting as nobody likes to sit next to nobody for long.

Washing-up

A large view has to be taken of the washing-up situation. Helpful as it may be to have a loyal supporter on hand at the end of the party, hosts should stiffen their resolve and say 'No, thank you' as if they meant it. To expose the party to the drab mechanics of the sink and tea-cloth is to destroy the ease and comfort of the occasion. Besides, hosts may be counting on feeling morally free to sit back and relax when it is their turn to be guest.

To some extent the advent of dishwashers has dispelled the feeling of obligation to offer to help. Somewhat unfairly, this applies whether the household has a machine or not.

Bringing a bottle

Many are the guests who would not dream of going empty-hand to a dinner party and numerous are the hosts who happily accept the offering. But not every host views the gesture warmly. Considerations of generation, age and wealth have to be taken into account.

It is safe to say that anyone who is young, or a student, or otherwise starting out in life, or saddled with a heavy mortgage, will be appreciative of a bottle. So will close friends of all ages and stages and anyone who has arranged a sociable gathering at short notice. An invitation to pot luck suggests that an extra bottle would not come amiss.

On the other hand, if the host is someone with whom you feel obliged to mind your Ps and Qs, think carefully. It is probably better to abandon the notion. They might privately think your gesture a shade impertinent, or worse, a reflection on their standards of hospitality.

One way round in these circumstances is to produce a bottle of the calibre that qualifies as a personal present, thus making its purpose as a contribution to the evening's hospitality secondary. It should be wrapped and given with a word to the effect that the hosts might like to keep it for some quiet evening. If it is a big party it is advisable to make sure that the present bears your name as otherwise your gesture may lose its identity in the general scrum and be drunk.

Bringing a bottle is basically a way of saying thank you and is not intended primarily for your own delectation. It is improbable that you will set eyes on your tipple again. In any event, one bottle is likely to be insufficient for the table and the hosts may not wish arbitrarily to mix their wines.

On the question of what to choose, wine is a favourite in all its colours. But at the risk of sounding snobbish the point has to be made that few people are likely to thank you for a bottle of plonk or even superplonk. Wine brought to parties should be well chosen, not the first bottle off the supermarket shelf. It is worth remembering that champagne is always especially welcome for its own sake and because it can be drunk before, during and after a meal. Another advantage – the giver can drop a hint about opening it by bringing a chilled bottle.

Hosts are expected to thank givers warmly but at the same time avoid giving the impression to those who came empty-handed that they have done the wrong thing.

Guests with disabilities

Guests with disabilities should be considered as guests, first and foremost. They will want to have a good time, just like anyone else.

If the person is confined to a wheelchair for example, the main priority is to ensure ease of access to any spot they need to get to. Any special arrangements should be as natural as possible. Extra hands may be necessary to help lift the wheelchair and occupant over obstacles. At the party, people should come up to the person with the disability rather than the other way about. If numbers are expected, it might be a good idea to extend hostly attentions by detailing one or two allies to bring people over for a chat and to make the introductions.

At table, should the guest's disability require him or her to be fed, it should be recalled that this will be an everyday occurrence and does not call for comment. It might be a good idea to arrange for the disabled guest to be placed between a feeder on one side who can attend to their charge's needs and a convivial talker on the other.

If in doubt as to whether a proposed act of assistance is a help or a hindrance, the best source of advice is always the person on the receiving end.

One factor hosts may have to prepare themselves for is that some people become acutely embarrassed in the presence of severe human disability. No doubt the reaction at least partly disguises sympathy but it has the unfortunate effect of cutting off easy communication, a predicament that calls on a host's diplomacy .

Children at the party

Older children and adolescents get a raw deal from parents as sociable animals. Grown-ups mistakenly tend to exclude the young on the dubious grounds that they would be 'bored' or would 'prefer to be with their own generation'.

The fact that so many parents find their children's response to participating in any formal occasion uncivilized is most likely a reflection on their having been excluded from the fun during their formative years. The result is that when they do turn up at a dinner party given by their parents, they are ill at ease and apprehensive. Children who have helped cook and prepare for a party and have shared family meals at which visitors are present are more likely to be able to manage their own social life in later years than those who have been neglected in this way.

Obviously some occasions are more suitable than others for a mixed generation guest list. Some parents compromise by having the children look in for pre-dinner or post-dinner drinks in order to meet everybody. But there seems no good reason why the children of the house should not join the table as soon as they can sit and converse amiably.

At drinks parties young boys and girls make diligent waiters, solemnly handing round crisps and canapés. It may be the devil's own job to get them to bed later on, however.

May I bring the baby?

Babies go everywhere, meet everyone. Papoose-like, they tend to be taken wherever their parents happen to go.

Nevertheless it is not always convenient for a baby to come to the party and parents should give notice in advance.

Parents should bring whatever an infant is likely to need for the duration of the party and not count on the host providing special arrangements.

Baby and bassinet are best parked in a quiet spot within earshot, ideally a bedroom. It is up to the host to suggest a comfortable place where any cries would be audible.

Feeding and changing the baby

Babies are bottle-fed anywhere in public and usually changed where there is a degree of privacy. Breast-feeding in mixed company, on the other hand, often calls for a sense of decorum. Much depends on the company and on the nursing mother's ability to manage the feed discreetly. But it has to be said that not every male guest is liberal on the issue. Some are genuinely discomfited by being a spectator. If a private corner can be found, well and good. If the men present are friends of the mother, no doubt greater latitude exists. At a formal dinner table or a structured do, however, it is doubtful is breast-feeding in the public eye is yet acceptable.

Young visitors

The same provisions apply as to a younger child. It is the parent's responsibility to ensure that their ewe lamb arrives with whatever will keep them happy and contented. A favourite plate and mug, playthings or a comforter are obvious appendages.

Drinks parties

People tend to be superior about drinks parties, claiming they are overcrowded, noisy, you can't hear yourself speak, and so forth. But they are by far the most popular form of entertaining among all age groups.

For guests, a big drinks party is a lottery, hence its attractions. You can never be quite sure who you will bump into. For hosts, inviting a crowd to drinks is a convenient way of seeing numbers of friends, repaying hospitality and of introducing people to each other. It also avoids the demands of providing a meal.

Timing

Drinks parties are held before lunch and before and after dinner. Usually, the occasion lasts for a couple of hours or until the host's own dinner arrangements become apparent.

The extended mid-evening drinks party has become a favourite in the capital, beginning at 7 p.m. and continuing until 9.30 or 10 p.m. Its advantage lies in greater flexibility: people can make the party in time to go out to dinner afterwards or look in after an early dinner. It is sound practice to write the time when the party is expected to end on the invitation.

See page 208 for Late drinks parties.

Invitations

An 'At Home' card is fine, with the word 'Drinks' written on the bottom right-hand side and, as mentioned on page 205, the time when the party begins and ends.

It is probably too optimistic to assume that guests will RSVP, which is not to condone failure to do so but to reassure hosts that if they don't receive any replies it doesn't necessarily mean a wave of regrets. The few hosts with answering machines may have better luck in this regard.

Invitations are often telephoned or spread by word of mouth. Due notice should be given for a big drinks party, about three to four weeks is usual. But many gatherings take place on the spur of the moment.

Guest list and room arrangements

An acknowledged advantage of drinks parties is their elastic nature as far as the guest list is concerned. Young and elderly, old friends and new friends, strangers and family can all be invited. However, too indiscriminate an approach can lead to a featureless occasion which never coalesces as a party. The old advice applies: invite people who like you and want to be in your company; include some sociable characters who are known to enjoy parties; try to bring in individuals from different worlds who are likely to hit it off; and mix in some outgoing singles – a preponderance of happy young marrieds may be good for the social fabric but rarely makes a party buzz.

Like a good restaurant, cocktail parties should be full of people, so hosts should err on the side of higher rather than lower numbers.

Obviously, the size of the room has to be taken into consideration, and the amount of furniture and whether a big serving table or bar is to feature. A 5×7 metre (15×20 foot) room can hold about 50 standing guests comfortably; a 7×10.5 metre (20×30 foot) room will accommodate about 100 standing (maximum). Since few hosts have large spaces available for entertaining at home, it is becoming popular to hire indoor and out-of-doors accommodation for big 'do's'. Garden locations with accessible shelter in case of bad weather are highly appealing.

The room in which the party is held should look inviting, with bowls of flowers and an array of sparkling glasses and promising bottles. Good carpets should be protected if possible with old rugs.

An axiom on these occasions is: you cannot have too many ashtrays on these occasions. Dainty small ones are useless and should be replaced by capacious bowls or deep ashtrays. Containers filled with sand are handy as a tip for ash, cigarette butts and rubbish and help to absorb the smoky smell – but they should be placed at various points with discretion.

Ventilation is important at a big party. If the hosts are otherwise engaged someone else should be delegated to take notice of whether the room has become too stuffy or is becoming unpleasantly chilly, and adjust the ventilation and heating accordingly.

Chairs are a comfort at drinks parties as not everyone will wish to remain standing and in any case they are more appropriate for a *tête a tête*.

Hard-back dining chairs may be hired, with or without cushions.

What to serve

Drinks parties were known as cocktail parties before the demise of the art of cocktail mixing. Ironically, now that cocktails have come into their own once again, their identity has become lost in an invitation to 'drinks'. At smaller gatherings, mixing cocktails is a practical notion but few would contemplate such a time-consuming method of serving drinks when numbers are involved.

In general, wine is widely served, with champagne or champagne cocktails as a generous option. If drinks are to be circulated on trays among the guests, glasses might be filled with a choice of red or white wine, or champagne, as well as soft drinks and fruit juices. Coca-cola and mineral waters also go down well with non-drinkers. In chilly weather a hot punch can be heart-warming.

On the vexed question of how much drink to allow per head, it may be useful to remember that a bottle of wine contains about six medium-sized glassfuls. If white wine or champagne is served, large quantities of ice for keeping the bottles chilled is important. A bath or plastic dustbin can make a giant ice bucket when packed with ice.

See page 171 for Party prescriptions.

Coping with canapés

The party will appreciate a bite or two to eat with drinks. It is always a good idea to offer at least a nibble of nourishment, as food helps to prevent alcohol from going to the head too quickly. Food on this occasion should be of a kind that can be eaten easily in the fingers, without plate or fork. It is worth saying that canapés have grown up in culinary terms since the days of the ubiquitous salted peanut and potato crisp and now qualify as a branch of delicious delicatessen which can be served hot or cool.

Canapés are usually served on trays and circulated among the guests. People help themselves. If the little savouries are served with a cocktail stick, and there is a separate sauce, the form is to dip the laden stick into the sauce and eat the ingredients in a bite or two. Disposing of the little stick discreetly remains one of life's unsolved social problems, along with the stones of unpitted olives. A hiding place may have to be found if no receptacle for the purpose is provided for the purpose (hosts please note). Ashtrays, empty glasses, empty vases are familiar if imperfect solutions.

Closing time

Ending a large successful drinks party is problematic. People may simply hang about in the hope of another round of drinks or, more likely, because they can't summon the energy to depart.

It is not impolite to ask people to leave, assuming the hour is late. Hosts can try the one about suggesting guests help to tidy the place up and collect the glasses, which usually prompts an exodus. Switching lights off is another signal. Asking people if you can call a cab for them is a broad hint. Perhaps the best approach is to enlist the support of the most sober among the remaining guests and get him or her to pass the word round that the party is over.

Late drinks parties

An invitation to drinks for 10 p.m. has a number of attractions, especially for city dwellers. It leaves the early part of the evening free and extends the day late into the night. Sometimes the host gives a dinner party which is followed by a fresh influx of guests, or the occasion can kick off under its own steam supposedly after the guests have eaten elsewhere. In practice, at late drinks parties good hosts provide a bite or two of delicatessen.

Verbal invitations are along the lines of 'Please look in after dinner' or 'We are giving a party'. Printed invitations can be 'At Home' cards with the word 'Drinks' and the time written bottom right.

Arrival times are sensitive. Too early may mean that dinner has not yet finished. Too late and the party may be beginning to break up. A general rule is to give the hosts not less than fifteen minutes' grace.

Night-owl party-givers testify to the importance of ensuring that a proportion of the guest list is young and unattached. They are often late birds by choice, and, in contrast to their pair-bonded seniors, have little compulsion to go home early.

As a form of hospitality intended to repay more elaborate entertainment, however, an invitation to this type of party won't do. The prospect of having to turn out late, perhaps having to travel some distance to the party destination, without the prospect of a decent meal, may strike some older people as more of an imposition than anything.

Late drinks

The basis of choosing the drink is what is suitable for serving after a meal. Wine is always popular, champagne being the celebratory favourite. Hard drink need not necessarily be offered but if it is, whisky-and-something invariably finds takers. Mineral water and soft drinks should be included.

Attending a drinks party

Most people experience a sense of apprehension at having to plunge into a room filled with party-goers absorbed in chatter. However, in the usual course of events, doubt is a passing shadow as each newcomer becomes drawn into the social group.

One trick on arrival is to seek out the host or hostess should they not be standing by the door. This at least provides a sense of purpose for the first few moments. Once located, the party-givers will see to it that a drink is produced for the new arrival and introductions are duly made. A host at a drinks party should enable people to meet and should bring together those he thinks will enjoy each other's company, but once the introductions have been effected he may very likely depart in a twink. A silence may occur which calls for one of the group to strike up a conversational lead. Whereas some hold to the view that if a person has nothing worthwhile to say it is better to remain quiet, others maintain that it is kinder to produce some remark that will at least open the dialogue. Suggestions for comments include the news of the day – local, international, national or personal – links between guest and the party-givers, any special interest attached to the location of the party or even the weather.

No one is obliged to remain with the first people to whom they are introduced. A good moment for separation is when other people come up to talk to someone else in the group. It would be oversensitive to feel miffed if people to whom you have been talking move on; it is quite in order for guests to wander off to pastures new with some casual observation such as 'I must have a word with Matthew over there' or simply, 'I'm going to circulate'. It is not necessary to make any excuse, however. Drinks parties are for mixing and mingling.

Knowing how to remain on one's own for a while is an art. The key to it is to look absolutely content as if you have snatched a few minutes' peace for contemplation. Not everyone concurs in this, however, and some prefer to dart about, busy bee-like, weaving their way in between guests as if on a mission.

Couples are expected to go their separate ways at least for a spell. At a small party when guests are asked 'What will you have?' etiquette is not to give a straight answer to the question. The question may be misleading and a guest who speaks their mind may ask for a whisky when the host has only wine in the house. Most people who are uncertain of the options tend to look enquiringly towards the drinks tray and murmur, 'What do you suggest?', which allows the host to refer to whatever is available. 'I'd like a glass of wine' is usually a safe request.

Hosts are to blame for any uncertainty as they should make the choice clear from the start, thus 'We have a rum punch, beer or cider. What will you have?'

Good neighbours

Big parties cause noise and commotion and tend to keep neighbours awake at ungodly hours. It is courteous to inform neighbours within earshot of the date and time of the gathering so they are not taken unawares. Downstairs neighbours especially will appreciate being tipped off if dancing is on the agenda or vociferous to-ings and fro-ings likely.

A written note slipped through the letter box is better than no warning.

Buffet parties

Buffet parties can seem temptingly easy to give but they require careful organization if they are to avoid turning into a scramble.

The advantages of a buffet are considerable. A greater number can be entertained than fit round the dining table. Since guests are expected to help themselves to food, service is easy. Friends are not expected to appear as punctually as is the rule for a seated dinner, and no one need get stuck next to someone they find uncongenial for long. Matters of protocol disappear in the fray and a further attraction is that guests may discreetly follow a diet.

Those against buffets hold that they are uncomfortable, disorganized and hard on the feet. Also, the need to wait upon yourself may mean that you have to break off a gripping conversation with a neighbour or go hungry.

Invitations

As one of the acknowledged assets of a buffet is its flexibility, it is a good idea for party-givers to mention the point in invitations. But this is not obligatory.

On printed 'At Home' cards the words 'buffet supper' can be hand-written with the hour bottom right.

Buffet procedures

People who manage buffet parties best start out with the premise on which all good party-giving is based – that the experience should be made as hospitable as possible for the guests.

There are severall ways to organize service of food and drink. Guests can be asked to wait upon themselves and return plates and cutlery to wherever they are directed. Or they can serve themselves for one course and be waited upon for the following dishes. They might help themselves to all the food and the first glass of wine but have their plates collected and glasses replenished by helpers or the hosts.

At a buffet people anticipate a party at which they will stand and eat. Nevertheless chairs and a few occasional tables are always appreciated.

An advanced form of buffet service is to provide seating and tables for all the guests, even going to the length of setting out place-cards. Guests are asked to help themselves to food at a buffet and to find a seat or the one marked for them.

See page 177 for Place-cards.

Usually, two main courses are offered which are set out on a big table, together with a pile of plates and an array of knives and forks and spoons – the nature and number of which depends on the menu. The collection process can be simplified by wrapping each person's knife and forkery in a large paper table napkin, thus enabling guests to pick up the implements required in one hand whilst holding the plate of food in the other.

Dining out

Eating out in a fashionable restaurant can be unnerving for a novice. Even old hands are sometimes upstaged by the unexpected. The retinue of waiters and sense of everyone being involved in a ritual can easily convince the uninitiated that they are doing the wrong thing. A spot of bluffing and bravado won't come amiss as this is not an engagement in which to appear remotely ill at ease. Sailing through with assurance largely depends on knowing what to expect.

Booking a table

A restaurant table should be booked in one name, for a given number of people, for a specific hour. The many foreign staff now employed in catering make it imperative to establish that your name has been correctly understood. Clients may be asked to supply a telephone number as a further check on identity.

It is courteous to keep the restaurant in touch with any change of plan. Patrons who arrive long after the appointed hour may find their table occupied.

A custom has grown up of 'double booking' restaurant tables, which can be very unfair on restaurateurs. If you do this you should at least cancel the booking at the restaurant which you have dropped. By the same token, customers have every right to expect a table to be free at the hour for which it was booked. Should the reserved table be occupied for longer than a short while it is reasonable to make a fuss and to insist that places be found.

Arriving

On arrival, the person in whose name the table is booked should check at the desk that the booking is in order. The client will probably be asked whether they wish to visit the bar or go straight to the table. If the latter is chosen, it is a good idea to leave the name of any expected guest at the reservation desk.

If the host and guests arrive together, it is the host's responsibility to point out the lie of the land such as where coats can be deposited and the cloakroom. The host takes the lead in deciding whether to order a drink at the bar or go directly to the table, or he may seek his guest's opinion.

The *maître d'hôtel* leads the way to the table, followed by the host, whether male or female, and the rest of the party. A good host suggests where his guests should sit. At a table for two, the guest should be offered the most comfortable seat or the one with the best view of the interior – unless seeking privacy.

Late arrivals

May a guest order a drink to be put on the host's bill if he arrives first? No. He should be prepared to pay for his own order. It is up to the host to decide if he wishes to pick up the bill but he is under no obligation to do so. The same principle applies to ordering a meal when the host stands up a guest. A decision has to be taken on whether to quit the restaurant, leaving word to that effect with the desk, or to remain and order in the knowledge that no one else is responsible for the bill.

There is no loss of face in departing.

The menu

The menu is likely to be long, detailed and extensive. At many good restaurants and in international hotels, the menu is written in French without English translations. A similar language problem may exist at restaurants specializing in national cuisines such as Chinese, Indian, Japanese, Thai or Russian, although some do provide a crib in English.

Although there is no loss of face in admitting that you do not know the identity of some exotically named dish, there might be if you asked what consommé (clear soup) stood for. There is certainly nothing against asking the waiter how a particular dish is cooked or what it consists of before making up your mind.

A useful device is to consult the host and make some remark such as 'I expect you know the menu well. What do you recommend?' In his turn, the host can ask the waiter about the day's special recommendations.

À *la carte or table d'hôte?*

It is important to recognize the difference between the two parts of the menu. One will be headed 'à la carte' (according to the menu) which allows you to pick and choose from a large number of dishes listed for each course and usually works out to be the more expensive option unless frugally chosen. The other is headed 'table d'hôte' (the host's table) which is a set meal with a limited choice of alternatives at an all-in price.

Hosts should guide their guest's choice, either by saying something to the effect that they may choose whatever they fancy – bearing in mind the likely costs of such an open invitation. Or, if they are watching their pocket, they can drop a hint along the lines that the set lunch is very good here.

It is bad manners for a guest to select the dearest items unless these are suggested by the host.

Menu without prices

Some expensive restaurants and clubs persist in the practice of giving guests at table a menu without prices – as if expense had no bearing on choice. Whoever is known to be paying receives the priced menu, which can put guests in a quandary. Probably the best plan is to ask your host for his or her recommendations and to take a lead from these.

Of reassurance to guests is that if a restaurant that believes in unpriced menu has been chosen for the occasion, it can be assumed that the host knows what to expect. In any case, it is not polite for a guest to ask for a priced menu, which would seem a reflection on his host's choice of restaurant and on the customs of the establishment.

Placing orders

Occasionally, orders are asked for by the waiter before people are ready to respond. In this case, the host tells the waiter that they need a little more time to consider.

Orders for starters and the main course are usually placed together so guests should be prepared to select dishes for both. There isn't much protocol about who orders first but if formality is to be observed, the first order will be placed by the guest of honour. An attentive host concerns himself with the ordering and listens to who is choosing what. At a table for two whoever is paying will allow their guest to order first, unless he or she remains momentarily undecided.

Ordering direct

Most guests choose to order direct from the waiter but time was, and not so long ago, when this was considered ill-mannered. If dining with a member of the old school, it is advisable to put your order requests directly to him, and he will relay those requests on to the waiter. A compromise may be recommended whereby guests address the host with their main orders and deal with the waiter direct on the details of that order.

Preferences

The degree to which some ingredients may be cooked can be chosen by the patron. If certain dishes of beef, lamb, liver, kidneys or game are ordered the waiter may ask 'How would you like it done?'. The diner is required to say whether their preference is for the dish to be 'well done' in which case no pink juices will show, or 'medium rare' which means that the inside of the order will be on the pink side, or 'rare' which means it will be red with uncooked juices. A variant on the last is to ask for the dish to be 'underdone' or go one further and order it 'blue'.

Special problems

Suppose you don't feel hungry and wish to pass on one of the courses. Will the host feel offended? No one should be expected to order a course simply because other people are so doing; nor, while we are on the subject, should anyone be made to feel guilty for declining food. On the other hand, with the exception of those who are dieting for medical reasons, a general rule is that fellow diners should spare a thought for the person who is obliged to eat on their own – not a happy prospect.

One minor stratagem for those who are cutting down on their food intake is to stretch out the contents of one course into two, perhaps ordering a salad as a starter which otherwise might have accompanied the main dish, or choosing a vegetable dish which belonged to a main course.

There is a strong case which holds that those who do not wish to take part in the sharing of hospitality should forgo the invitation.

May you try a little of someone else's dish? By all means, but accept a small amount only and always offer a sample of yours in return. It is unfair to help yourself to considerable portions of the other people's dishes which presumably they intended to enjoy in their entirety.

As a guest, is it polite to order cigarettes or cigars directly from the waiter without offering the settle the bill? Absolutely not. You may ask the host to order them on your behalf or you may send for the waiter. In either case, it is only polite to offer to pay the bill separately, unless the host strenuously argues that the charge should be added to his account.

Hosts are not obliged to pay for such extras as cigarettes and there is no loss of face in allowing the guest to settle the bill for these.

Ordering aperitifs and choosing the wine

At the very beginning of the meal, the waiter may ask if any aperitifs are to be ordered. A cocktail, vodka and something, sherry or a glass of wine are all possibles at this stage. Hosts should give their guests a lead as to whether they may order champagne or a glass of the house wine. Guests can always ask the host what they are drinking and glean a hint from the choice.

If people prefer to hold their horses and wait for their tipple until the food arrives, they should say so. Guests are free to choose a proffered drink even if the host passes.

It is the host's prerogative to choose the wine. The form is to ask for the wine list and in consultation with the wine waiter to mull over an interesting choice to accompany the chosen dishes. Some hosts like to ask their companions if they prefer red or white, but others prefer to take matters into their own hands, bearing in mind the ordered food.

Not everyone understands wine. In circumstances in which a host considers that someone else at table has a greater knowledge of the grape, there is a strong case in favour of delegating the task. The host will at least score points for recognizing the importance of an informed choice. A clear hint as to the price would be needed which could be tactfully conveyed by the host indicating a wine which he was considering.

In a first-class restaurant the recommendation of the sommelier (wine waiter) should always be accorded respect. Again, he will need a lead as to the price that is being contemplated.

If guests are asked directly what wine they would like, one cannot recommend a precise reply such as Château Petrus vintage '79, if you please. However, there is nothing against giving a fuller picture of your tastes than the basic choice of red or white. By all means express an interest in wines of particular regions or vintages.

Obviously, if the host is in a generous mood and seriously wishes to indulge the party, he should be taken at his word and guests may declare a favourite irrespective of cost.

Pouring the wine

When the ordered bottle arrives, the waiter will pour a little into the host's glass for him or her to taste, to which the expected response is 'Thank you, that's fine', or some such sentiment. The glasses round the table are then filled by the waiter.

Should the host not be drinking, it is in order to delegate the tasting to someone at table who knows their wine. If a guest is not drinking, he may put his hand over the glass and if necessary say, 'No, thank you', as the wine waiter passes by his place with the bottle.

When the condition or taste of the wine is not to the host's liking he (or she) should feel free to express his views to the wine waiter. He may, for example, ask for a bottle of white or rosé wine to be chilled for a little longer. If the taste of a wine is unpleasant, the bottle should be sent back. This is always a painful moment as the wine list's reputation is at stake, but most professionally run establishments will exchange a bottle if the patron has a case and argues it. If the patron's opinion of the wine is at variance with the wine waiter's, the *maître d'hôtel* should be summoned.

The waiter usually replenishes the glasses but if service is slow, the host takes over – attending to guests' needs before his own.

Now comes a sore point. May guests help themselves to wine? Strictly speaking, they should wait to be served as the host may wish to limit the amount of wine he provides. However, few people would take it amiss if a guest were to ask courteously if they might have a little more wine – with the proviso that it would seem rude if the bottle was empty. In a well run establishment the wine waiter is likely to come dashing across to the table if a customer is seen going to the trouble of pouring wine. It might be wiser for the host to summon assistance in advance.

Ordering dessert and coffee

The number of courses ordered is at the host's discretion, but if he wishes to be thought generous he will always suggest choosing a dessert whether or not he wants one for himself. Guests can take it or leave it according to choice. If they pass on the pudding, it is perfectly in order to ask if they may order coffee while others enjoy their dessert. Otherwise, they would be left staring at an empty place-setting. Several choices are usually attached to the finale of the meal. The waiter will ask patrons which sort of coffee they prefer. The options may cover coffee espresso (made in a machine of the name that produces a strong coffee served black), 'cappuccino' (espresso coffee served with a topping of frothy milk and perhaps a grating of sweet chocolate), or 'filter' as described.

Ordering liqueurs

Because of the laws on drinking and driving as well as the high cost of liqueurs in restaurants, many people refuse the offer of a final tipple. But if the host orders one for himself, it can be assumed he can afford a round. Liqueurs should be sipped slowly and appreciatively.

Telephone calls

It is much more of a compliment to your guest or host if their company is prized above telephone conversation. Taking and making calls is intrusive and casts an air of a business occasion over a private engagement.

If a call has to be made, the caller should make her excuses without much ado as she gets up from the table. Apologies, and perhaps a point of explanation, would be in order upon returning.

If a call is expected by someone who is not a regular patron of the restaurant, they should leave their name at the reservations desk. When making a call, if an assistant dials the number on your behalf, a small tip is in order plus, of course, the cost of the call.

Cordless telephones carried by diners have added a further distraction to eating in restaurants. If two people are engaged in making or taking calls frequently, it interrupts good service, diverts attention from the food and drink and turns a restaurant table into a work station. At a table for two, cutting out of the conversation for telephone calls is particularly inconsiderate. Those not on the line may feel decidedly spare.

Spotting friends

Suppose you spy a friend as you enter the restaurant. The form is to wave and smile unless you specially want to talk to them. If you do, stroll over. The only social crime is paying a protracted visit. An extra person standing by tends to snarl up the service.

If friends drop by at your table, they should be introduced to everyone but the formality of hand-shaking is dispensed with.

Sometimes people who are dining at separate tables forgather for coffee and a last round. Either the waiter can deliver the message from the host, or the invitation can be delivered in person.

Calling the waiter

Whereas it can be exasperating not to be able to attract the attention of a waiter, theatrical or brash gestures should be avoided. It is especially inconsiderate to try to divert his eye when he is attending to another table. If he seems to be consciously avoiding your table, the best approach is to attract the attention of the *maître d'*, explaining that you have been waiting for some time for service. He may be able to put another waiter to work on your table. In the usual course of events, wait until your waiter passes your table and claim his or her attention, or he or she can be waved over.

Tipping

Tipping remains a controversial topic, all the more so now that most well-known restaurants include a service charge in the bill. The menu usually indicates whether this is included and the percentage of the bill it represents. Or it may state 'Service is not included' in which case the going level of tipping is between 10 and 15 per cent with 12½ per cent being a popular compromise.

If you are unclear as to whether service is included, ask, and the waiter will quickly put you in the picture. When a service charge is included the delicate question arises as to whether it is necessary to tip on top. There is no cut and dried answer to this one as if the host wishes for a specially warm welcome on his next arrival or personal attention beyond the routine, he will be prepared to pay for the privilege.

As a general rule, don't tip if a service charge is chalked up on the bill. However, specially attentive service always commands a fair tip.

Paying the bill

As the meal is ending, the host asks the waiter for the bill. It is quite acceptable for whoever is paying to divert his attention to checking through the items on the bill carefully. If necessary the host takes up what appears to be any inaccuracy with the waiter. If serious doubts arise as to overcharging, the matter should be pursued with the *maître d'hôtel* and away from the table to save embarrassing the guests.

When the bill is paid for in ready cash the form is to place the money on top of the invoice (plus a tip if appropriate), glance in the direction of the hovering waiter and let him know he can whisk the plate away with some remark such as 'Thanks, that's fine'.

When large notes are produced in excess of the bill, it is a precaution politely to remind the waiter to bring the change, in case misunderstanding leads him to believe the difference is a fat tip. The payer may say, 'Would you let me have the change please?' or words to that effect. When the money arrives, the payer leaves a tip if wished, and picks up the surplus.

If the account is settled by credit card and the diner proposes to tip on top of the service charge, the sum can be added to the total written on the sales voucher, or cash can be handed to the waiter in person.

Some clients like to tip the *sommelier* (wine waiter) when they have received specially good, personal service. As with all tipping, the procedure is to hand over the money without a trace of embarrassment and to say thank you very much.

If you pay by cheque and are not a regular patron, be prepared to produce a banker's card. Again, any tip can be added to the total written on the cheque, or cash can be handed over personally.

Splitting the bill

Frequently, a restaurant bill is split between the diners at the table. The transaction calls for a spirit of charity if it is to go smoothly.

The offer to 'go dutch' with another person means, effectively, that costs will be shared. The arrangement is regardless of whether one ordered a more expensive item on the menu than the other, or whether one was a more abstemious drinker than their companion. Having to work out in detail when the bill arrives exactly which proportion of which cost should be charged to whom is a decidedly downbeat note upon which to close.

When a number of people are splitting the bill, a method is for the account to be settled by one member of the party who collects contributions from others present. He or she is expected to do a rough and ready reckoning in which the total is divided by the number who wish to chip in.

Incidentally, this need not necessarily include everyone present as some may wish to pay for themselves and a companion. Again, the sum may not represent individual costs and some will undoubtedly have had a better deal than others, but the process of paying will be relatively simple and unobtrusive. Nothing kills a party atmosphere like doubts about costs.

An allied point can be raised. It sometimes happens that an impecunious person joins a party as a guest only to find that everyone is expected to pay their own way. Usually the discovery comes with the bill, so it is too late to escape before the damage is done. Their only recourse is to apologize and to ask someone to help them out. The request can be put on the basis that the money will be refunded or, more likely, that on the next occasion the funded will be the funder. This one can't be pulled too often, however.

On occasions, someone may be asked to join a party on the basis of going dutch when they lack the means to accept. Should they demur and make some excuse for declining or lay their cards on the table? There is a case for saying something along the lines of wishing to come but being too broke to accept, which leaves the way open for the inviter to offer to stand the treat.

Dress codes

Usually, what to wear for a restaurant date is a matter of personal taste. There are exceptions, though. The managements of certain international hotels and establishments have imposed a dress code on their customers. The Ritz Hotel, London, for example, has banned jeans and for men, open necked apparel.

Managements expect men to wear a jacket and collar and necktie. As a general rule they will lend a tie to the tieless for the duration. Women are expected to dress well by city life standards. Those who do not conform are not admitted.

It is always best for a host to tip off any friends in advance who might be unaware of the ruling.

Thank-yous

A restaurant meal is usually thanked for on the spot. Letters or telephone calls of thanks are always appreciated, however.

Children's parties

Children's parties require split-second timing, a non-stop programme of entertainment and a surprising amount of stamina. They also call for a quality which is often lost among adults – an exuberance, a brio which is not for the faint-hearted.

Each age and stage has its own special formula but common to all is the importance of a rousing start to proceedings. Grown-ups who are novices in the field can all too easily find themselves in the unsettling position of one party-giver known to the author. She surveyed a roomful of youngsters bent on cracking crackers, hurling streamers and bursting balloons; one little boy sidled up and said politely, 'Please, when is the party going to begin?'

The cost should be mentioned as bills can add up and not necessarily for anticipated items.

Quite apart from mischance, expenses can soar unless watched, especially if professional entertainers are hired or special playground equipment is brought in. Fortunately, the spirit of inventiveness and imagination can more than hold its own with money alone.

A great party boosts the credit of the young host like nothing else. From the adult host's viewpoint, it is a way of repaying hospitality extended to your child and a way of furthering friendships between children and between families. Young party-givers are likely to be highly appreciative. Hyper-critical as he or she may be of family, home and siblings in the usual way of things, parents can take it as a compliment when their child asks them to give him or her a party.

Children's parties are almost defined by the bringing of a present for the young party-giver. Guests arrive offering in hand. Usually, they depart with a small present which may be for winning a prize or given at the goodbyes.

In order that invidious comparisons need not be made, givers of major offerings to the birthday boy or girl might arrange for the present to be given before the party.

Party occasions

Children's parties usually celebrate birthdays, but Christmas, Hallowe'en (31 October) and Guy Fawkes (5 November) all offer a good excuse.

The guest-list

School-children in particular have stong likes and dislikes among their age group which may give rise to an altercation on the issue of whether one child in a class can be omitted from the guest-list. It's not good manners as the gesture is hurtful and out of all proportion, very probably, to the cause of the rejection.

If feelings run high, it might be a sound idea for the parent of the testy party-giver to get in touch with the parent of the spurned guest to find out whether an invitation would be welcome. If this turns out to be the case, the child should be invited as a general principle. Parents should keep a watchful eye on any newcomers or shy children who find it onerous to join in.

The guest-list should include those who have invited the young host to their own parties. Except at a huge party or one that is held out of doors with a range of diversions suitable for different age groups, it is a risk to mix the ages and stages of the young guests: ideally everyone should be at a similar stage of development.

Among adults who may appreciate an invitation are grandparents, godparents and other fond relations. It is also a courteous thought to invite the host child's teacher or playgroup leader.

Invitations

Special children's party invitations are useful. They strike a perky note with a drawing on the front and as a rule have handy tear-off replies.

The card should give the time at which the party begins and ends, the full address where the occasion is to be held, an address and telephone number for RSVP if different from the party venue, and any reason for the party, e.g. 'Ian's birthday'. The first name of the guest is written in the space provided.

Invitations are sent out about three weeks in advance, addressed to the young guest. In the case of two members of a family being invited it is thoughtful to send each a separate card as receiving the invitation is part of the fun.

Replies should be prompt. Children fill in the tear-off cards if they are able or their parents do so on their behalf. Learners sign their name if nothing else. If no pre-prepared replies are included a written letter of acceptance or regrets is required along the following lines:

Dear Kim,

Thank you very much for asking me to your birthday party on Saturday 1 March from 4 pm to 6 pm. I should love to come.

With love from

Mary

Dear Milly,

Thank you for asking me to your Christmas party. I would have loved to come but we are going to Granny's on the day/my sister Ann is in quarantine for measles and we are not allowed out/I am going to my cousin's birthday party.

With love from

Ben

Children who enjoy drawing often prefer to make their own cards, which is thoroughly to be recommended. It is wise to check that the invitation contains all the necessary information, though, and to ensure the address on the envelope is correct.

If children live some distance from the party or are unfamiliar with the neighbourhood, it is helpful for parents to include a note about local transport facilities such as bus routes, the nearest underground station or railway station and the availability of taxis at going home times.

Cancellations

If an invitation has been accepted and subsequent events prevent the child from attending, parents should always notify the adult party-giver as soon as possible. A certain fall-out from the guest-list is expected due to childhood maladies and domestic crises, but hosts do appreciate being kept in the picture.

A tradition has grown up around the occasion in which children's celebrations at all ages are accorded serious commitment by parents and participants alike. If, by some chance, a party has to be cancelled, all the parents of the invited guests must be informed immediately by telephone or letter, or on the grapevine.

Timing

Punctuality is the rule as festivities begin on the dot.

The exact timing depends on the age-group but parties for young children start at between 3.30 to 4 pm and end promptly at 6 to 6.30 pm. The under-two-year-olds can be invited at the earlier hour. School-age gatherings likewise begin at 4 pm sharp but if it is a good party the guests will try every ruse to protract the pleasure. Older school-children tend to prefer the more grown-up aura of outings and a celebratory supper in which case timing is determined by the activity or entertainment chosen, but the hours should be specified on the invitation. As far as teenage parties are concerned, the debatable point is not when it begins but the lateness of the hour at which it may end.

What will settle the probable dispute between offspring and parents are the hours at which it is convenient for guests to be collected and last bus home schedules. In any event, the hour should be specified in invitations both verbal and written.

Teenage parties

The teens represent a wider bracket of tastes than their years suggest. The younger teens enjoy a more sophisticated version of junior parties with dancing, adult times and supper instead of tea. They often prefer an outing for a few close friends which they organize themselves.

Outings may be for skating, swimming, cycling or a show or more likely a gig and, are in any case, unescorted. A meal at home would be approved but eating out is considered to be infinitely preferable. The parental role is to keep an eye on proceedings without seeming overtly intrusive. An element of privacy is highly valued by this age group. Parents supply cash and hope to be told the gist of plans but have every right to extract an undertaking to return to base by a given hour.

A year or so on, depending on school, circle and local culture, teenage parties can represent a severe shock to the adult system. The preferred venue is an empty, dark, cavernous space, the shabbier the better. The room will be solid with silent, sombre faces moving to a deafening beat. Recesses and hallways reveal recumbent bodies lost in contemplation of each other.

Favoured food will be pizzas, dishes that can be eaten in the fingers, savoury canapés, hot chipolata sausages, hot baked potatoes and all sorts of crisps and bites and nibbles. The tendency is to pick at the food and imbibe the drink.

How much and what kind of drink is a timeless topic of debate for this age group, but the current emphasis is on restraint. Nevertheless, some bright spark is bound to bring along a bottle or two of the hard stuff, or proffer whatever is the cocktail of the day. It is wiser for parents to offer to supply some decent tipple that is acceptable rather than to allow the party to rely on random contributions from guests, which tend not to mix well. Wine, beer and cider are good choices.

In any event, young people have a considerable thirst and plenty of liquid refreshment such as soft drinks, colas, orangeade, mineral waters should be available at all stages of the festivities.

Parental presence

Parents have developed their own formula for handling these occasions. They usually put in a conspicuous appearance at the beginning of proceedings but don't undermine their offspring's role as host. As party-giver, their son or daughter introduces to the parents any guests who are not known to them, as well as making introductions between members of their own crowd. If it is a very big party shared by several party-givers, 'how-do-you-do's?' tend to be confined to the introducer's section of the guest-list. If no introductions are made, parents identify themselves as at a wedding reception: 'I am Sally's mother' or 'Jez is my stepson'.

After a while, the older generation leaves youth to its own devices and worries like mad. Parents tend to make themselves scarce until the agreed hour of the end of the party. Parental presence at this stage is to be recommended as it backs-up the more responsible elements. Also, adults who come to collect their teenagers at the appointed hour help to establish a finale.

However, if guests are seeing themselves home, the party will most likely dance or slumber on until the small hours, unless determined steps are taken to end it. In any case, it is highly probable that some waifs and strays will be around at breakfast, if not for breakfast.

A question of the trust between parent and child is obviously a crucial factor in the conduct of the occasion but experience suggests that parents who skive off for the night are asking for trouble.

Gatecrashers

Teenage parties are ripe for gatecrashers. This is a stage at which crashing a party may be more exciting than attending it formally. However, gatecrashing offends the spirit of hospitality by which the host chooses his guests. It also puts the party-giver in the position of being obliged to be unfriendly towards the interlopers.

If trouble is anticipated, protective measures should be adopted. Sometimes one of the larger lads in the group is deputed to act as bouncer at the door but a better solution would be a non-guest, perhaps some kind member of the family or an outsider, recruited and paid for their trouble. It is important for whoever is on duty to have some knowledge of the guests and to be armed with a guest-list.

If a few friends who aspired to be invited to the party and were not for some reason, succeed in crashing it, the general tendency is to accept a fait accompli and make little of it. However, if numbers are involved to the extent of disconcerting the party, the intruders should be asked to leave.

Cautionary tales

The teenage predilection for empty, unadorned spaces has a message for adults. Precious belongings and fragile pieces should be removed from harm's way in any area likely to be occupied by the party. Some guests may be vandals but most are merely high-spirited, exuberant young people who at worst are careless of others' possessions. Bearing in mind the likelihood of mishap, parents have only themselves to blame if things get damaged or smashed as the result of their not taking adequate precautions.

The propensity of this group for 'borrowing' clothes, books, records or CDs and suchlike should be guarded against. The most practicable course of defence is to lock up the few things that are immovable, issue warnings to offspring and trust to luck.

Formal affairs

It is now that boys and girls receive their first invitations to attend dances, either given privately or by subscription. Good dancers of either sex are never at a loss on these occasions and possibly the kindest act on the part of a parent with an unsociable offspring is to persuade him or her to learn to dance well. A few lessons by a professional may not go amiss. In any case, boys should be taught that their role is to ask their partners for a dance.

If a youngster is invited to a dance by a grown-up, it would be polite for the younger member to ask their host for a dance. The young guest should also say goodbye and thank-you to their grown-up host as well as to any contemporary who invited them.

Hosts who invite teenagers to formal dinner parties or cocktail parties tend to accord the youngest members grown-up status.

See page 175 for Organizing a dinner party.

Dress

Cult fashion has a strong bearing among teenagers who like to be different from the older generation, whichever way this points. Adorning themselves in the accepted gear contributes a lot to party pleasure, as it does for all of us. Parents should try to restrain their critical responses, either way. They may be astonished by a premature rush into conformist dress, into attire such as they rebelled against in their own salad days, or they may be equally disturbed by a display of oppositional apparel with all its wacky symbols.

At formal affairs, little has changed. Young males don dinner jackets or smoking jackets (borrowing Dad's if he has one and it fits them) worn with a fancy waistcoat and jolly bow-tie in place of black tie. Girls put on their decorative clothes and jewellery, if they so wish.

Some youngsters invited to formal adult parties consider licence to turn up in jeans at an occasion when others are dressed formally as a valued freedom. But all guests should remember that hosts who have gone to some trouble to create a party occasion usually have a sense of chagrin if their efforts are not reciprocated by their friends. A safe rule is, when in doubt, dress to pay respect to the occasion.

Weekending

Having friends to stay is an art, much to be admired. Few guests would deny that the invitation is the most promising of all. Fortunately perhaps no magic formula exists for guaranteeing the success of the occasion as mere creature comforts do not in themselves make the day. Generosity is certainly high on the list but more telling is a host who manages to convey his pleasure in being in the company of his guests.

Without in any way seeming to dictate to the party, a host should give some shape and order to the visit. Time can easily hang a little heavily for house guests, unless some diversion, excursion or amusement is introduced.

No host should put pressure on a house guest to take part in some arrangement which does not appeal, but by the same token, invitees are expected to join in somewhere along the line.

Attractive guests are not above showing appreciation of their friends' hospitality and should remember that their enjoyment is infectious.

Invitations

Usually guests are invited for the weekend in person or on the telephone but there is nothing against proposing or confirming the idea in a letter. Whatever the methods, dates should be made clear. A well-intentioned but vague reference to the idea of a visit may give the impression that an invitation has been extended but leaves friends wondering.

Hosts may always ask friends to propose a date but polite guests are obliged to wait for a firm invitation before jumping in with specific suggestions. If the invitation is accepted, it is extremely inconsiderate to cancel. It is frustrating for a host if his invitee persists in suspending acceptance. A breach of good manners is to leave hosts in the air as to your intentions; rather than to keep his plans unresolved it is usually wiser to bid the invitation goodbye.

A good host mentions any outdoor sports that may be contemplated, such as tennis or swimming, if only as a reminder to the visitor to bring their things.

Arranging the details

It is the host's prerogative to suggest times of arrival. Guests may be uncertain as to whether they may opt for Friday or Saturday arrival. To ask directly puts the host in the awkward position of appearing to prefer the shorter visit – guests may ask when would be best, and if the matter seems open, go for whichever suits themselves.

Times of arrival should be discussed, bearing in mind that travel plans rarely go precisely by the clock. If a host expects a guest to arrive in time for a meal, the hour at which it is served should be established in advance. On the other hand, if arrangements are free and easy and the host says come when you can, he should be tolerant if people decide to turn up at wild hours.

Travel tips

Kind hosts advise on travel plans, especially if the destination is off the beaten track. Motorists will appreciate directions plus any local hints. Rail or coach or bus timetables are useful, as are air flight times where appropriate.

If other guests are coming up/down and there is a spare seat in someone's car the host may propose that a lift be offered. It is customary for the motorist to tell a whacking fib and say that they would be delighted.

What to pack

Guests should try to find out as much as possible about what the weekend's arrangements may hold. It is acceptable to ask about any healthy sports that may be in the offing such as swimming or tennis or golf in order to know what to bring.

Similarly, in likely cases, it is acceptable to ask if the men will be putting on black tie for dinner. If the response is in the affirmative, it would be discourteous for a guest to fail to comply without a convincing excuse.

The British weather being what it is, wellington boots or sturdy footwear and some protection against rain and wind, like a mackintosh, anorak, a windproof jacket or Barbour, is likely to be a sound investment regardless of the season. It is thoughtless for a house guest to count on borrowing the belongings of the house in order to remedy their forgetful packing.

Bearing in mind that guidelines about dress are particularly vulnerable, the following is offered as a safe approach for staying in some style at a country house: wear presentable clothes for travel, bring a change for each day and for each evening, plus any sports wear that may be required. If the men are putting on dinner jackets, women are expected to don their best bib and tucker. Men who are changing for dinner have the option of smoking jackets, decorative waistbands, cummerbands; embroidered slippers come into their own. On the masculine question of whether to wear an open-necked shirt or neck-tie, the best source of advice is the host. A neck-tie is always correct.

How long a visit?

The question of the length of a visit is for the host to determine but they will probably bear in mind the distance that their guests have to travel.

If a long and tiring journey is involved a two-night stay might be proposed. This has the advantage of giving the visitors one clear day without having to pack or unpack. A short trip, on the other hand, is well rewarded by a one-night stay.

Collection and delivery

As a rule guests are expected to make their own way to the house. If, however, they are travelling by public transport and the station is some distance from their destination it would be thoughtful for the host to make arrangements to meet them. Guests should offer to pay the fare if a taxi is booked on their behalf.

Similar arrangements apply to the return journey.

The welcome

The first few minutes of arrival at someone else's place are telling and there is no welcome like finding the host at the door. These customs are as old as hospitality itself.

Hosts should help guests with their luggage and show them to their bedroom. Usually, the hostess does this but a man is well able to do so. The location of the bathroom and lavatory should be indicated promptly and immediate refreshment offered.

It is thoughtful to explain any peculiarities relating to their accommodation such as obstinate door locks, the vagaries of the central heating system or any shortcomings in the plumbing.

Overall, house guests need to be encouraged to feel at home as honorary members of the family.

Room for guests

If guests have been warned that they are going to have to rough it, it would be unreasonable of them to take umbrage at discomfort. But in the general way of things, if guests are invited for the weekend they probably expect a level of comfort that is at least comparable to standards to which they are accustomed at home. If there is a marked shortfall here, hosts should probably signal in advance that things are very informal.

Spare rooms in which house guests are customarily parked are hardly known for convenience and charm. It might do wonders for the national standard if occupiers moved into their own spare room occasionally. No doubt improvements would be effected overnight.

Kind hosts should make an imaginative leap into the position of their guests and consider all the points they themselves would like to be taken into account. It goes without saying that guests' beds should be aired and comfortable and extra bedding placed to hand. Lighting should be effective for the acts of getting dressed, grooming and reading in bed. A decent-sized looking glass is a civilized addition as is at least one accommodating chair. Other details: a big bath towel per person and a hand towel, a waste paper basket, a sufficiency of coat hangers, and ashtrays (assuming the tolerance of the house).

Important as these amenities are, what gives a room character are those elements which presuppose a discerning occupant: fresh flowers, judiciously chosen books, pictures on the wall and pieces to admire.

Ifs and buts

How literally is it wise to accept the cheerful bidding to 'make yourself at home'? The polite response has to be, more in the spirit than in the letter. While guests are given many privileges and offered the best, they are expected to fit in with the host's arrangements and the customs of the house.

Since few outsiders are aware of how other people conduct their domestic lives until invited to stay, it is only common sense that the first of a good guest's gestures is a measure of tolerance.

Equally, hosts are obliged to be accommodating as far as their guest's idiosyncrasies and quirks are concerned.

What has to be accepted is that approaches may be surprisingly different from what was expected on such matters as the amount of food and drink provided, attitudes towards tobacco smoking or bedtimes, and even on desirable room temperatures, quite apart from the general standards of social behaviour.

One of the side benefits of staying away is that concepts of what is 'normal', that is to say, what one does oneself, are liable for hasty revision.

Bathroom strategies

When host and guests share a bathroom and lavatory, some forbearance on both sides in monopolizing the facilities is called for. It would be kind if hosts gave their friends as much priority in using the bathroom as was practicable. It is acceptable for hosts to let their guests know any times when it is inconvenient for them to take a bath. Similarly, it would be reassuring for them to know that hot water supplies are plentiful or whether they should watch the depth of their hot bath.

Guests who have to get up in the night are often uncertain on the best course of action. Should they flush the lavatory and run the risk of waking the household, or leave things be and risk some funny looks in the morning? It is probably best to leave the loo as you would like to find it unless the disturbance is likely to be a frequent noctural occurrence. If the cistern refuses to work effectively, no embarrassment should attend mentioning the fact to the hosts. It will all have happened before, in all probability.

Bedroom roulette

The question of who shares a bedroom with whom remains highly sensitive. One guideline generally applies: it is the prerogative of the host to make the arrangements under his or her own roof.

Unmarrieds who are generally known to live together as a couple will usually expect to be given a room which they can share. How far the host wishes to be compliant in this matter is a question of his own values and also, perhaps, of the likely reaction of the other people in the house. A compromise solution is to put the lovers in rooms that are adjacent or interconnecting, or not so far apart that a discreet sprint along the passage would not end their isolation, without causing embarrassment to anyone else.

A cardinal rule is that as far as romances are concerned, the question of a shared room should be put to the lady first. Permissive parents may also have to learn to mind their Ps and Qs with regard to their grown offspring and realize that not every dalliance points to a shared bed.

With most people who come to stay, however, it is plain sailing: husbands share with wives, children double up and single people of the same sex are usually willing to share. If space allows, singles will appreciate a room of their own.

Occasionally, delicate issues have to be considered. Gays who bring friends may present a dilemma. If they have 'come out' about their sexual orientation, the path is clear for a shared room, all else being equal. However, not all homosexuals wish to have their sexual proclivities made public and would prefer to be given a room of their own. On everyone's side in favour of sharing is that it is quite usual for guests of the same sex to be asked to occupy the same room and no inference need be drawn that they are lovers.

Married couples may not be sanguine about being asked to share a double bed, especially if they are known to lead separate lives. A bedroom with single beds is usually the safer option to offer in any case but if a double bed is all that can be mustered and the hostess has doubts on the matter, she should check with the wife well in advance. If the couples are estranged or unwilling to share, they can excuse themselves from the invitation in good time.

On an occasion when house guests are VIPs, or parents making a rare visit perhaps, or a couple to whom special attention has to be paid, it is a great courtesy for the hosts to offer them the best bedroom.

Levels of hospitality

Assuming that the host is putting her best foot forward to please her visitor, she will wish to provide three meals a day. Whatever the levels of hospitality planned, it should be within the capacity of the household and not put inordinate strains on resources of time, money and energy. Hosts should remember that it is you they have come to visit not some paragon of perfection.

It would be thoughtful to ask guests before they go to bed whether they would appreciate an early morning cup of tea. If the prospect of being awakened too soon seems a killer to them, a compromise is to suggest that they get their own cuppa, provided they are told how the kitchen works. If tea is to be served to a couple, it is wisest to leave the tray outside the bedroom door having knocked to register its arrival. Guests' bedrooms should be regarded as private when occupied.

Hosts should establish house rules and stick to them. 'Breakfast is on at nine o'clock but take your time' should mean that guests have a certain amount of licence about the hour at which they are expected to surface. They justifiably can feel put upon if the hostess clucks away disapprovingly when they stagger down around half nine in search of cooked eggs and bacon.

Similarly with all mealtimes. Guests should know where they stand and the less vague the information, the better.

The quantity of food to be provided and the number of courses to be served at main meals depends on the customs of the house, and of course, on the resources of the providers. The full drill is satisfying but daunting, and many hostesses make their own compromises according to taste: a cooked breakfast with cereals, fruit juice, toast, a choice of tea or coffee, lunch, tea and dinner. Usually drinks are offered before lunch and dinner as well as afterwards. One approach to menu planning is to serve two courses at the midday meal and three at dinner but some generous hosts provide three courses for lunch and four at the evening meal.

Time passes more pleasantly for guests if they can look forward with anticipation to the next meal. Drink can flow liberally when guests do not have to drive, and it is probably a good idea to over-estimate the amount of drink that will be needed when laying in supplies.

Specially considerate gestures: to take particular trouble with the first meal that is served after a guest's arrival as it will augur well for the weekend's prospects; to produce a dish at some stage that a guest is known to relish and to provide their favour tipple, either hard or soft.

Producing a succession of meals makes tremendous demands upon the hosts. One reciprocal gesture is for a house guest to offer to take the company out for a meal. If this is on the cards, the relief work will be all the greater if the offer is discussed in advance with the host.

Limits to hospitality

A general rule about making use of the services and facilities of the house where you are staying is to ask before helping yourself.

May you use the telephone? There is a prevalent view that utilizing the telephone service is analogous to beathing but telephone bills deny the fact. It is courteous to ask if you may make a call. The question of whether a guest should offer to pay for their calls largely depends on the charges involved. Unless staying with open-handed, rich hosts, guests should always offer to pay but not to the

point of being assertive about it. If the hosts say, 'don't bother' then don't bother. Unless there is a prior understanding, visitors should avoid turning the host's telephone into an extension of their own number, nor should they encourage friends and contacts to ring them with a frequency that would be appropriate at work or at home.

May you pour yourself a quick one before the host suggests a round? Better to ask directly. Most hosts would prefer to know when their guests are missing a bracer, especially if the request is politely put and at a reasonable hour.

If all else is equal, may you ask if you can take a dip in the swimming pool, or knock up on the tennis court, or explore the surroundings? Certainly, providing the idea does not disturb the routine of the household.

The question of whether a house guest may switch the television set on or off or change channels needs to be considered. If a lone viewer, surely they may. If the host is around, to do so without asking would be an infringement of good manners. Television courtesies need defining as viewers' attitudes vary so widely. Some families regard the small screen as a form of animated wallpaper which flickers in the background throughout the day and evening and might take umbrage if a guest switched off the set. Others banish the box from their midst except for occasional programmes, and would not enjoy being asked to switch on continually.

Should a guest not wish to miss a favourite programme there seems no harm in putting the request unless granting it is likely to cause inconvenience.

Entertaining house guests

A varied programme adds to the pleasure of a weekend stay. Experienced hosts give careful consideration to their visitor's interests and favourite activities, and try to arrange some diversion that is likely to appeal.

The idea is to find the balance between frantic organization and a yawning void of unconsidered time, and to hit upon an idea which will score when reflected upon in tranquillity as well as being entertaining in the doing.

Depending on personal tastes, selected local events of interest might fit the bill, such as a race meeting, a garden fête or an open day at a house or garden of note. Invitations to neighbours to look in for a drink or a meal are a usual standby but care should be exercised to bring together people who are likely to get along well. Or, a neighbour might invite the party over to his place.

Information about local historic buildings and antiquities, places of outstanding beauty or memorable scenery that guests may visit, would probably be appreciated. Likewise, informed tip-offs about a particularly good pub in the area, or a promising market or news of a shopping discovery.

Hosts are not expected to be outposts of the local tourist board but most guests value an insider's view of the locality, and if up-to-date guidebooks and maps are to hand, so much the better.

Being on time

Punctuality merits a paragraph to itself. A cardinal virtue of house guests is to be punctual for all the arrangements from mealtimes to expeditions. But people who are punctual by nature should try to restrain their impatience with those to whom time is their oyster. Ultra-punctiliousness on the matter can be irritating. As far as guests are concerned, lateness calls for an apology.

Passing the time

The good guest finds some diplomatic balance between hanging around seeming to wait to be entertained and occupying themselves with their own pursuits to the extent that they use the place like an hotel, only turning up for meals. It is doubtful if it is polite to take extended time out to visit personal friends in the neighbourhood on your own, or to pursue arrangements in which the party is not included.

Most hosts hope their guests will occupy themselves for part of the weekend with a weather eye on collective plans. It is the hostly role to propose arrangements but to be sensitive about pressing them upon an unwilling participant. However, in normal circumstances, the guest's role is to show willing.

Offers of help

Few would have the nerve to emulate Lee Miller, the celebrated American photographer and journalist, who took the view – only partly humorous – that her house guests should never be idle. Joy through Work was her philosophy. 'There is scarcely a thing, in or out of sight,' she declared, 'from the wood pile to the attic water tank . . . that does not bear the signature of a working guest.'

An example of a good idea gone to extremes, of course, but the principle has become widely accepted. People staying as house guests should always offer to lend a hand with the mechanics of domesticity. Hosts may also ask their guests to help them out without seeming in the least discourteous.

Better than token gestures is for guests to use their head and actually perform some helpful task impromptu. Scour the saucepans, clean the bath, and of course, make their own bed in the morning and strip (with the hostess's approval) on leaving. It is sometimes more of a hindrance than help to the host to undertake a task which requires an intimate knowledge of how things are customarily done in the kitchen or dining room, such as putting away, as ten to one the hostess will have to re-do your efforts.

Offers to collect people or provisions may be appreciated. Not everyone is prepared to allow guests to pick up the bill for food and drink on their behalf but most are delighted to receive extra treats.

Guests who endear themselves are likely to be those who willingly amuse bored children, or who take the family canine for a healthy run, or who undertake useful tasks in the garden.

It is important for a guest to be able to gauge the sincerity of their friend's refusal of assistance. Some cooks genuinely prefer to go about their labours unaccompanied, others cannot bear having their domestic methods scrutinized, many wish to give their guests a real break from work and would prefer to soldier on unaided.

So if someone says no, thank you, as if they meant it, guests can leave well alone without feeling guilty. Incidentally, both male and female guests should offer to share the going tasks and the gesture shouldn't be left to the women alone. By the same token, hosts can feel free to rope in members of either sex to help.

A clever hostess may find that her male guests have a particular skill which can be called on without feeling that the task is an imposition. Chopping wood, helping to dam a stream or even cleaning silver may prove therapy to a weary executive spirit.

The visitor's book

House guests may be invited to sign the visitor's book as a formal record of their visit. Signatures are designated a space and likewise the dates of the visit. It is thoughtful for the host to ask any children who are house guests to inscribe the book along with the adults. Parents accompanied by offspring too young to write might like to add the child's names for the sake of the chronicle.

Occasionally, zealous hosts press for a written personal observation on the occasion. A touch of diplomacy may well be needed in this instance as the crack about the host's foibles that collapsed the company after a good dinner may wilt in the cold light of the written page. A courteous approach is to alight upon some interesting remark about the occasion which expresses appreciation and thanks for a good time. Guests are expected to wait to be asked to sign and not to proceed uninvited.

Tipping servants

At a house with domestic help, the moment to tip those servants who have helped to make your stay agreeable is at the end of the visit, when there is still time to proffer the cash in person with thanks. Tips should always be handed unselfconsciously and with expressions of thanks for the various services provided.

Starting with the few formally appointed households, the staff to tip are the butler, the cook and the bedroom servants, also the chauffeur if his services are called upon. Nanny, or the children's nurse or an au pair are not tipped but in special cases a personal present might be acceptable.

In households employing a couple to work as manservant and cook, it is fine to give the tip to cover the two, to one member. It is important to thank both, however.

Tips intended for bedroom helpers can be left in an envelope with the name of the donor and thanks, in the bedroom.

If a daily help has assisted with the preparations but doesn't necessarily put in an appearance over the weekend, it would be thoughful to check out the fact with the hostess, and to leave a tip.

Those in doubt about going rates in general should consult the hostess.

Goodbyes

It seems to be in the nature of weekend invitations that vagueness cloaks the matter of the hour at which guests are supposed to take their leave. There is certainly nothing against hosts asking their friends when it would be convenient for them to depart. Other than that, a diplomatic hint could be dropped in terms of suggesting the time of a good train for guests to catch, or recommending an hour when driving conditions on the roads are especially favourable. Holiday house hosts who themselves are obliged to pack up and depart on Sunday have an acceptable excuse for proposing a time by which guests should be on their way.

Exceptionally hospitable hosts whose country retreat is situated a fair travelling distance from their guest's return destination might like to extend the invitation to include Sunday night, especially if this makes it a two-night stay, but such a course is unusual. Guests in general are advised to be guided by Jane Austen's remark that a stay was 'Perfect, in being much too short'.

In circumstances in which a guest has to cut short a stay for any reason, it is courteous to forewarn the host if possible. He may be making plans which would be undone if the guest was absent.

Goodbyes should be acted upon expeditiously as prolonged delay can be unsettling to the house. It is friendly if hosts help with any luggage or belongings. Thank-yous follow, then the party – including any children – turns out to wave off the guests.

Thank-yous

Since the custom is not to thank for expressions of thanks, hosts do not as a rule write to say thank you for any offerings brought by friends. Guests on the other hand should always write a letter of thanks. One gesture which is welcome is for the guest who brought a camera to give their hosts a snapshot as a memento.

Great occasions

Prevailing standards of informality meet their come-uppance at certain

grand occasions. Among these are the cultural, sporting and other events that

make up the Season; balls and banquets; royal garden parties; all examples

where festivity walks hand in hand with formality. Relaxed as the affair may

seem on the surface, a sense of protocol is never very far away.

The British Royal Family

Probably too much can be made of emphasising the starchy side of arrangements in the season's calendar. Even in sanctuaries of social correctitude, a more relaxed approach is evident. The coverage in this section deals with major public occasions opening with some approved advice on meeting members of the British Royal Family.

Meeting the royals

Much of the etiquette involved in meeting a member of the royal family is to do with courtesy and common sense. There are certain conventions, it is true, but the general rule about how to behave correctly is simply to be on your best behaviour.

Despite such reassurances, it has to be admitted that many commoners do lose their nerve in the presence of royalty. Tough men have been known to drop a limp curtsy when confronted unexpectedly by the Queen. Guests who have been invited to the Queen's famous lunch parties at the Palace have confessed in print to making daffy errors such as not knowing which knife and fork to use, which would never be the case normally.

Since one way of minimizing mistakes is to be forewarned, the following questionnaire may help to put people's minds at rest on some general points of doubt. The replies have been vetted by Buckingham Palace for this book.

It should be said that the royals are adept at putting members of the public at their ease. One may always write to the Private Secretary of the member of the royal family concerned, for fuller information about protocol and procedures.

Q. *What is the correct acknowledgement on being presented to a member of the royal family?*
A. Women usually curtsy. One should not overdo a curtsy. If royalty extends a friendly hand, it should be taken in the usual way. Shake the royal hand gently and curtsy simultaneously.

    Men bow from the neck. A sweeping gesture from the waist should be avoided.

Q. *Are there any special customs about addressing members of the royal family?*
A. It is polite to make one reference to 'Your Majesty' or 'Your Royal Highness' which is followed by 'Ma'am' or 'Sir'. The former is pronounced 'Mam' with a short 'a' and not 'Marm' to rhyme with 'arm' (see Modes of address).

Q. *How may you present a friend or a member of your family?*
A. 'May I present James Darnborough, Ma'am?' or 'May I present my daughter, Anna, Sir?'

Q. *Is a greeting such as 'Good evening, Ma'am' appropriate on being presented?*
A. Yes.

Q. *How should one refer to a member of the royal family when speaking of them to another?*
May one say to the Queen 'Did your husband enjoy his stay at . . .?' or to Prince Philip
'Did your daughter do well in the horse trials?'

A. No. Always refer to 'Prince Philip' or 'His Royal Highness?', or to 'the Princess
Royal' or 'Her Royal Highness'.

Q. *How may one refer to the Prince of Wales/the Princess of Wales in conversation?*

A. As 'Prince Charles' or 'His Royal Highness'; and Princess as 'Princess Diana' or
'Her Royal Highness'.

Q. *What should a woman wear at an afternoon audience with the Queen?*

A. An afternoon dress is preferable – a tight skirt is obviously not a good idea. But
one may wear what one likes.

Q. *Should a woman wear a hat? Gloves?*

A. It is usual to wear a hat. Most women like to wear gloves. Either wear them or
don't. Don't carry one glove and fiddle with the other on being presented.

Q. *If one spots the Princess of Wales in a shop, for instance, is it good manners to curtsy or*
not?

A. If the Princess of Wales sees you or catches your eye it would not be polite to
look away. Just bob and continue with your own business. You should not
curtsy ostentatiously or draw attention to her. A curtsy should be used in the
same way as a smile or a nod to other people.

Q. *If the Queen wishes to buy something from a stall at a garden fête or fair, for instance, is*
it impolite not to offer to give it to her?

A. If a member of the royal family wishes to buy something they should be allowed
to do so. It is not the custom of royalty to accept presents from people they do
not know.

    Take the money from the Lady-in-Waiting and hand the parcel to her
unless the Queen particularly wishes to take it herself.

Entertaining royalty

Q. *When a hostess entertains a member of the royal family at a private party, what is the*
correct seating arrangement?

A. The royal lady sits on the right of the host, the royal husband sits on the right of
the hostess, in the usual way. If the hostess is not married she should have some
member of her family or some suitable friend present as host. Similarly, a
bachelor host requires a hostess. At hen parties, the royal guest sits on the right
of the hostess.

Q. *Are members of the royal family served in order of precedence?*

A. Yes. But there should never be dodging about the table to observe this rule.

Q. *If the Queen declines wine or liqueurs at a private party, is it polite for the other women present to follow suit? Does the same apply to cigarettes?*

A. No. Once the Queen has been offered something, the choice is up to you. The Queen happens not to smoke, but there is no reason for other women to refrain if they like to smoke.

Q. *What are the host or hostess's special duties?*

A. It is the host's responsibility to see that people are introduced to the royal guest and to bring people up to speak to him or her. It would not be polite to allow other guests to force their way to the royal guest. The host should see that all the important guests are presented and at the same make sure that the royal guest is not harassed by different people, or his or her conversation interrupted.

The whole tone of the party at which royalty is present should be perfectly natural.

Q. *May a guest speak to a member of the royal family before being introduced?*

A. This is not easy to answer. It depends. In theory, one may not address the Queen or a member of the royal family before they speak. Obviously, though, it would look rude if one were sitting next to the Princess of Wales at dinner or a party and waited until she spoke. It is a matter for discretion and ordinary good manners. Similarly, the rule about not changing a subject introduced by a royal should be borne in mind, without necessarily following it to the letter.

Q. *May guests leave a party before the Queen?*

A. Of course, if they have other things to do. The question does not usually arise as the Queen generally leaves official functions and big parties early. But it would not be very polite to leave a small party before the Queen without an explanation.

Q. *When a dignitary such as a Lady Mayoress entertains a member of the royal family, should special cloakroom facilities be provided?*

A. No, as long as the cloakroom is adequate. The question does not usually arise unless it is a long stay. For a weekend stay it would be nice to give the royal guest a private bathroom if you have one. Otherwise, things should be arranged as nicely as possible.

Q. *When members of the royal family are taken home in cars other than their own, is it polite to ask them to sit in the back? Or, assuming the driver is a friend, should they be asked to sit in the front?*

A. One should ask the royal guest where they would like to sit.

Royal garden parties

An invitation to a Royal garden party is an honour. The parties grew out of the demise of débutante presentations at Court in 1957. The Palace announced that instead, the Queen would hold additional garden parties. It was thought that the presentation of a small group of society girls was out of touch with the democratic times, and accordingly, guest lists for the garden parties were enlarged and widened. Three royal garden parties are held at Buckingham Palace in July and one at Holyroodhouse, Edinburgh, also in July. About 12,000 guests are invited and about 8000 acceptances are received, in all.

Invitations are sent to people across a broad swathe of the populace and include members of the professions, Parliament, the armed services, trade and industry, the Church, local councils, women's organizations, the City, the civil service. The guest list also honours lesser-known folk who merit special recognition.

The invitation

Acceptance is assumed. It is only necessary to write to the Lord Chamberlain (who issues the card) if a guest is unable to accept. Explanations for declining should and surely would be of a pressing nature. Acceptable apologies might be an unbreakable previous engagement, longstanding holiday arrangements, indisposition. The invitation gives the time, the place and the date and encloses an admission card, a map and instructions about car parking.

Admission cards should be returned with letters sending regrets. Those who are attending must bring the admission cards with them, an important point.

An echo of the days of debutante presentation parties is that guests may be accompanied by unmarried daughters over the age of eighteen. Should a guest have specific concerns about the invitation or what to wear, they may write to the Lord Chamberlain at Buckingham Palace, who is accustomed to such enquiries.

The programme

The royals step out in different directions along avenues of space cleared through the crowds by gentlemen ushers. Those who wish to see or be seen by a particular royal tend to foregather at their chosen path. Guests who have been pre-selected for presentation are tactfully shepherded into position by the ushers. Others do their best to catch the usher's eye without seeming pushy.

If a member of the royal family wishes to meet a guest, the first approach is made by a member of the Royal Household, who will then present the guest (see Meeting the royals). Not everyone aspires to meet their hosts, filling the time instead by exploring the grounds and viewing the pink flamingos (fed on pink prawns in order to enhance the colour of their plumage).

At 5 pm the royal party retire to the royal tent with special guests and VIPs. Everyone else invited takes tea in a green and white striped tent with an enormous buffet. Fare is English tea-party, catered by Joe Lyons. Your cup of tea is served in porcelain and the usual menu is sandwiches, scones, stawberry tarts and the famous chocolate cake. Lemonade and iced coffee are provided as alternatives to tea. Outside on the lawn, two military bands play a programme of light popular music.

The royals are applauded once again as a rule when they leave the tea tent.

Dress

The invitation stipulates morning dress, lounge suits, service dress or national dress for men. Many men do opt for a lounge suit but male royals don morning dress. Women usually wear a summer dress or suit or coat and frock, with a hat. The nature of the occasion has to be borne in mind. It is a garden party and a royal function. People who manage it best choose attire with an aura of formality but which doesn't suggest a business outfit. This is not the moment for trousers, however elegantly designed, or sporty things.

Note: guests may not bring in cameras.

The Season

An 18th century description of the Season is not far off the mark today . . .' the fashionable world is assembled in London' for the purpose of business, sport or amusement. Purists might quibble as to whether the term 'fashionable' applies, but certainly the acceptance of the notion of corporate entertaining at many of the events suggests that business interests are still well served.

Like so much else in this country, finding an all-purpose definition eludes most attempts as the label 'London Season' is qualified by the number of events taking place in other parts of the country, and the term 'Summer Season' takes little account of the actual calendar of fixtures.

In essence, the Season can be compared to a giant catherine wheel firework with set-piece events at the centre such as the Royal Academy Summer Exhibition, Royal Ascot and Henley Royal Regatta around which scores of satellite sparks revolve in the form of parties, galas, functions, festivals, not forgetting the major sporting events.

Sustaining the wide popular appeal of the Season's high points is the royal family whose patronage of many of the openings lends the affairs much of their authority and sparkle.

Debutantes still have a place in the scheme of things but few are dedicated to the cause. The timing of the round of parties and functions tends to coincide with the study for exams, for one thing. Another is that much of the original purpose of the experience – to introduce well-connected young women to appropriate marriage partners – no longer holds the dynamic that it did.

A characteristic approach of the present generation of debs is to look on the season as a way of making friends, extending contacts. It is often said that 'doing the season' is more likely to lead to a job than to blue blooded marriage prospects.

Notwithstanding these changes, generous parents continue to launch their daughters into society with a coming-out party or dance. Frequently, parental hosts with a similar commitment combine forces as a way of cutting costs. Others though, push the boat out in a family spree. Parents who would like more detailed information on debutante procedures with a view to launching their own chick are advised to consult someone who had a Coming-Out themselves in recent times.

The following is an account of some of the principal attractions of the Season together with a mention of allied fixtures that have become traditional places of pilgrimage.

The Royal Academy Summer Exhibition

Since the Founding President, Sir Joshua Reynolds, introduced the show over 200 years ago, the established art world and its allies has flocked to Private View Day at the Royal Academy Summer Exhibition at Burlington House, Piccadilly.

The occasion, held in June, marks the official opening of the Season. It is widely attended by members of the Royal Academy and by patrons, gallery owners, fellow artists, buyers, and city and country grandees. Among the special attractions is the opportunity to view any new work by distinguished RAs and to take first pick of the works on sale.

A feature of the show which is unique to institutions of its kind is that any artist, whatever their background and standing, may submit a picture for the consideration of the Hanging Committee (a fee is levied). If chosen from among the thousands sent in, the picture will be on public view at the show.

Private View Day is by invitation only. This is followed by two Previews for Friends of the RA (subscriptions are open to the general public).

Dress for the Private View tends to be mixed. A few pay tribute to the social antecedents of the occasion, with women donning best day-clothes and hat. Usually men wear a jacket, collar and tie. No one is thrown out if casually attired.

RAs and visitors wander round the galleries, scrutinizing the pictures and works of art, and as likely as not, taking note of the throng.

Chelsea Flower Show

Whether the displays were better this year than last, the fact that the crowds seem to be getting bigger every season, the discovery of some particularly intriguing plant, is all part of the buzz of the Chelsea Flower Show. The Show (commonly referred to simply as 'Chelsea') is held annually in late May in the grounds of the Royal Hospital, Chelsea under the auspices of the Royal Horticultural Society, and is a place of pilgrimmage for gardeners of all walks and aspirations.

The display is especially remarkable for bringing together the four seasons – and winter flourishes in blossom-time. Nurserymen use their skills to bring on or hold back plants in order to present them in peak form at the show.

Chelsea lasts for five days, only two of which, Thursday and Friday, are open to the public. Tickets are restricted, and can be booked in advance. Monday is ear-marked for the Queen's visit, Tuesday and Wednesday is Members' Day (and their guests).

Dress on the special preview days tends to be mixed. Mostly people dress for comfort at Chelsea, but there is likely to be a sprinkling of officials and prominent public figures in more formal attire. Much depends on where people have come from and what they are going on to. If it rains, the ground can get very muddy, so sensible shoes are in order.

As far as dates go, Chelsea precedes the official opening of the Season. Perhaps it is a tribute to gardeners that the occasion is widely regarded as a preliminary to the main events, and in the eyes of devotees one that rivals them.

The Fourth of June

Boys attending Eton College, O.E.s (Old Etonians) and their families and friends forgather for an open-day celebration known as the Fourth of June. A quirk is that it takes place usually at the end of May.

Like all school open-days it has sports matches, exhibitions of boys' work and flocks of parents and their allies looking round. Eton housemasters and teachers (known as 'beaks') are out and about, and the boys in their tailcoats play host. Formalities include speeches by the Provost and a guest VIP, both usually speakers of distinction. After the addresses, comes an entertainment written, performed and staged by the boys.

The occasion is noted for the procession of boats on the Thames. The young crew, sporting panama hats strewn with flowers, stand to attention in a precariously narrow craft, each holding their oar upright. Meanwhile, the band plays the Eton Boating Song and parents look on admiringly.

Visitors are welcome to explore the grounds and many of the historic buildings. The grounds are nominally open to the public, but most of the crowd present have some close connection with the school. Normally, parents bring a fortifying picnic which is unpacked at a spot with a good view of the passing parade or the matches. As might be suspected, the day is a family affair which attracts old boys of all ages and their families. Also, boys' sisters rally to the cause, putting on their glad rags in the hopeful interest of new friendships.

Dress tends to be formal but appropriate for sitting on damp river-banks and wandering over the turf: a summery frock is fine, with or without a hat. Men put on suits and collar and tie, and perhaps a panama. Needless to add, this is an occasion when O.E.s have no reservations about wearing the old school tie.

Royal Ascot

In 1711 Queen Anne decreed that racing could take place on the heath at Ascot, and since that day the races have had a close connection with the royal family. Each season in June, the royals are driven down the course in their elegant landaus, flanked by outriders in scarlet coats and gold laced hats. The retinue of carriages opens the racing.

Royal Ascot is also a fashion show, some of which is in questionable taste admittedly, especially the millinery which is featured in the media. Nevertheless,

a quintessential part of Ascot is putting on one's best and not forgetting a hat. Hatless women are not conspicuous but they are strongly in the minority in the grander enclosures and the private balconies. The Royal Enclosure is definitely for hats and high hats. Men wear, almost to a man, morning dress, a grey or black topper and a buttonhole with racing glasses slung round the neck. A few lounge suits are in evidence, but not many.

An invitation to watch the races from a private box offers a privileged view of the racecourse, a three-course lunch served buffet-style by a waitress, a liberal supply of champagne and wine. In the afternoon a proper English tea is served with scones and strawberry jam and cream. The exact level of hospitality depends on the generosity of the host, but the foregoing is likely.

Racegoers generally bet on the Tote to which all paths lead at Ascot. You may stroll through the grounds to the Paddock and view the contenders, both human and equestrian. Owners, trainers, jockeys and stable lads congregate as the mounts are walked round the paddock. The Queen usually takes an interest and joins the gathering quite informally.

The Royal Enclosure is the smartest place to be; the Ascot Grandstand and Silver Ring are open to the public for a fee, and many take a picnic on the Heath for a day's outing and racegoing which can cost the minimum.

Note: spectators are not obliged to bet on the races, but if they intend to do so it is discourteous not to have the ready, or a valid credit card available. The smallest bets are acceptable and congratulations are due to any winner.

A thank-you letter should be sent to the host who stands you a day out at Royal Ascot.

Polo tournaments

Polo is an extremely expensive sport and its supporters – in and outside the game – tend to be moneyed. But it is attracting a new crowd who may or may not be of the old school. Polo is a fast and dangerous game played on horseback with long-handled clubs and a small wooden ball. Four players to a side try to capture the ball and whack it through their opponents' goal post, thus scoring for their side. The game is measured in *chukkas* – each *chukka* last for seven minutes.

The season begins in April and ends in September. Leading clubs include The Guards, Cowdray Park, Cirencester Park and Ham. The major tournaments are the Queen's Cup at The Guards during Royal Ascot week, Cirencester Park Club's Warwickshire Cup tournament in June, followed by Cowdray Park's Gold Cup in the first half of July and their Challenge Cup at the end of that month. A star occasion is International Polo Day at the end of July, at Smith's Lawn Windsor Great Park, supported by The Prince of Wales. Trophies may be awarded by the Queen or The Princess of Wales.

Company hospitality tents have become part of the scene; here as elsewhere clients and allies are invited to lunch and tea and offered a grandstand seat affording a close view of the match. Spectators stroll on to the field at half-time in order to tread down the turf indented by the ponies' hoofs.

Dress is summertime spruce. Men wear lounge suits, collar and tie and panamas if wished. Women put on good clothes with a sporty aura. A pretty summer frock would be fine.

Henley Royal Regatta

The five-day Regatta at Henley Reach on the Thames offers many different ways of enjoying the day. Henley Royal Regatta attracts the most knowledgeable followers of rowing, and those who want simply an outing on the river.

Dress codes maintained by the Steward's Enclosure are strict: jeans, casual wear for men or short skirts and trousers for women are inadmissible. It is an occasion when men who fancy themselves in Edwardiana can indulge their tastes without appearing in the least conspicuous. Male habitués tend towards striped blazers, white flannels, a bow-tie and a panama, but those whose wardrobes do not run to these can confidently appear in a lounge suit, collar and tie. Women are advised to dress as for a garden party, in a smart summery frock with a shady hat or parasol. Admission to the Steward's Enclosure is by invitation only.

The neighbouring Regatta Enclosure has a much more liberal approach than the Steward's to dress and people wear what they please, with an emphasis on comfort. Here are luncheon tents, bars, deck-chairs and a grandstand. Tickets can be bought at the gate.

Many Henleyites hire a punt and have a picnic afloat as the oarsmen race by. Sensible river-bugs dress for comfort, but some people like to dress up and ignore the inevitable splashes and upset drinks on their best.

Cowes Week

Cowes Week, the sailing regatta at the Isle of Wight in August has two main crowds, the serious yachtsmen and the revellers. Many of the latter at least maintain the nautical tradition of raising a pink gin to a roseate scene. The racing attracts the sleekest yachts, international competitors aiming for distinguished trophies – the Fastnet race is the big one.

The atmosphere is highly clubby, the tone being set by the Royal Yacht Squadron, a synonym for exclusivity. Races are run from the Squadron's deck overlooking the harbour – cannon fires the starting orders from dawn onwards. Its Admiral is the Duke of Edinburgh whose arrival in the Royal Yacht HMY *Britannia* delivers one of the presiding spirits of the regatta, and the smartest invitation is to go aboard.

Among other clubs to which members invite guests are the Royal London Yacht, the Royal Corinthian, the Cowes Corinthian and the Royal Thames. The Island Sailing Club is more informally run and less expensive than the others and offers temporary membership to those who want to sail during the regatta.

Most of the leading clubs host a ball during the festivities. There is a marked emphasis on the done thing in dress at the clubs and parties aboard the yachts. At the Squadron ball – regarded as the festive pinnacle of the week – men who are members don the same special mess-kit of short navy jacket and navy trousers with gold buttons. Guests wear evening dress which means short or long for the girls and black tie for men.

Some clubs are liberal on the matter of women appearing in daytime wearing trousers, but if they should be worn, the smarter sort is expected. At the better-known clubs, sailors who come ashore are required to change before joining the landlubbers at the bar, but some managements are soft on this rule. Visiting 'yotties' will be advised by members.

A general guideline for women party-goers who are invited to a ball aboard a yacht is to choose attire with the right cut to its jib – tight skirts and high heels are a hazard for those who hope to climb aboard and disembark with a modicum of grace. Also, spiky heels damage the deck.

Round and about in the neighbourhood house-parties bustle on. Those who can't tell tacking from luffing and whose sailing jargon is minimal need not despair as it is most likely that they will be in good company. Life is as much about parties as ocean-racing at Cowes.

Trooping the Colour

Often wrongly described, this display of pageantry is in fact the Queen's Birthday Parade. The 'colour' referred to relates to one of the five regiments of foot guards (the Grenadiers, the Coldstream, the Scots, the Irish and the Welsh) trooped before the Queen as part of her official birthday celebrations in June. It takes place at the Horseguards Parade, Whitehall and combines military skills with a memorable demonstration of loyalty to the Crown.

Spectators in the grandstand rise as the Queen drives by in her carriage, when the troops march past and at the close of events when the National Anthem is played. The display is warmly applauded at the finale.

Formal dress codes apply to spectators with a grandstand seat. Men wear morning dress or service uniform or a lounge suit, collar and tie. Women put on formal day-clothes and a hat if wished. Guidelines on procedures are given in the official programme.

How to get in: Tickets can be applied for between 1 January and 1 March. Write to The Brigade Major, The Household Division, Horseguards, Whitehall, London, SW1, enclosing an SAE. A ballot is held to award tickets, which are allocated on the basis of a maximum of two per application. If tickets for a rehearsal would be acceptable in the event of being unlucky in the main draw, this fact should be mentioned.

Theatreland

West End theatre charity galas and film premières are among the few occasions in theatreland for which the audience puts on glad rags. Dressing up is the order of the day, but the lengths to which people go are determined by who they are, and what they are going on to.

These occasions raise money for a good cause, provide photo-opportunities for aspiring celebrities, and promote the production. Tickets, booked in advance, are available through members of the organizing committee. The price will include a donation to the charity in question. A gala often has the support of royalty and the invitation will indicate that the production will be 'held in the presence of' the royal patron concerned. If the show is live, members of the cast may be presented to the member of the royal family after the show.

It is worth mentioning that on the night, programme-sellers will be offering souvenir editions of the programme at a substantially higher than usual price. Supporters should have a polite excuse at the ready if they intend to decline the offer.

A gala occasion at the Royal Opera House, Covent Garden whether for opera or the Royal Ballet, calls for formal attire. Black tie for men and evening garb for women – which mean long or short – is usual. However, lounge suits, collar and tie are acceptable for men as well.

On a usual night at the Royal Opera House standards of dress vary considerably. In the dress circle, stalls and boxes – as you might expect – black tie and best dress are more noticeably in evidence than elsewhere in the auditorium.

Tickets for opera and ballet productions at Covent Garden are bookable in advance at the box office and at theatre ticket agencies. A monthly programme sets out all the details and indicates when booking opens for the season's productions.

Veteran West End theatre-goers may lament the decline in dress standards, but nowadays few people bother to dress for a first night. There are exceptions – the opening of a big musical or the first night of a play with an audience of lights and luminaries, for example. In these instances, men and women – often the backers and friends – put on evening dress and make a celebratory occasion of the event. Otherwise, members of the audience tend to wear their usual day-clothes.

Best behaviour at the theatre

It is as well to arrive at the theatre on time as many managements are not prepared to allow latecomers to take their seats after the curtain has gone up. Sometimes tardy arrivals can be sneaked in quietly, but there is always the risk of having to wait in the foyer until well into the first act.

Drinks are available at all theatres and playhouses before curtain-up and during the intervals. Cloakroom facilities are provided. Any complaints about bookings should be taken up with the front of house manager.

Responding to the performers

Clapping and rising to the feet are recognized ways of indicating appreciation of a performer or a production. Certain conventions hold good which are governed by a polite compromise between allowing an audience the right to express its feelings and running the risk of putting the performer off his (or her) stroke, thereby possibly damaging the state of rapport that underpins an audience's belief in the events on stage.

In opera, one may applaud at the end of an aria but not while the diva is in full song. It is usual to applaud at the close of each scene and, of course, as the cast takes its bows and curtain-calls at the end of the performance. More or less the same approach applies at the ballet. Prima ballerinas and dancers are applauded at the end of a solo or virtuoso act of dancing but never during the course of the movements. However, in both types of performance an audience is sometimes carried away and breaks out into spontaneous hand-clapping, whatever the rule-book may say.

At a play, the audience will sometimes applaud the arrival of the star actor or actress on stage, and clap at some particularly adroit passage of acting. Again, it is impolite to applaud until the last syllable is uttered in this part of the performance. If an audience is well pleased they may applaud at the end of each act, but this is rare except at first nights – one of the rewards of being a backer is a chance to lead the audible appreciation.

Audiences applaud at the end of the show as the cast line up in front of the footlights. It is a moment to demonstrate heartfelt approval in an unaffected way. No one is obliged to applaud if they were disappointed in the production, but convention holds that it is polite to do so out of respect for the players. A token hand-clap or two would be sufficient.

Behaviour in the theatre is shaped by consideration for others. Noisy eating of chocolates, spells of uncontrolled coughing, laughter when the atmosphere is quiet, shuffling and talking all hinder the chances of an audience becoming involved in the drama on stage, and can also distract the performers. Concentration is fragile and can easily be destroyed or fractured.

There is a tradition of booing a bad performance in the theatre. A rule is never to boo during the production but wait until the end of the play.

The Glyndebourne Festival

There are many opera festivals with more celebrated divas and conductors, no doubt, but Glyndebourne offers a peculiarly English mix of high music, enchanting surroundings, and grand picnicking. The festival runs from May until August.

The opera house at Glyndebourne is sited in a curve of the South Downs, built in the 1930s by the philanthropist John Christie. The auditorium seats about 800, and every ticket could be sold several times over. The 5000 members of the Glyndebourne operatic society have priority, but some people try their luck by applying early to the Information Office, Glyndebourne, near Lewes, East Sussex. No seat is cheap.

One of the features of the evening is a long interval in the production during which the audience troops off to unpack a picnic or has dinner in one of the restaurants. Those who bring their own supper like to find a chosen spot in the gardens or beside the lake, spread a rug and crack a bottle of champagne. If the approved ritual is to be observed, the bottle will have been cooling in the lake during the first act. Some opera-goers are sceptical about the weather chances, however, and prefer to book a table for dinner under a roof.

So far, no sign of dress standards weakening. The majority of men put on black tie and women wear evening dresses or elegant trousers.

A new era is said to await Glyndebourne visitors as plans for building a larger opera house are in progress.

The Oxford and Cambridge Boat Race

The Oxford and Cambridge Boat Race pits the two senior university rowing teams against one another over 4½ miles of water on the Thames between Putney and Mortlake in late March. Oxford's colours are dark blue, Cambridge colours are light blue, and supporters yell encouragement to their favourite blue as part of the event.

The race can be watched live by anyone from the river-bank, but the most salubrious spots are at the rowing clubs along the route, at the better watering-holes and aboard the launches that follow in the wake of the race.

Dress at the rowing clubs is informal – Oxford and Cambridge insignia on blazer, cap and scarf belonging to the day.

A member of the royal family presents the trophy to the captain of the winning crew. The ceremony follows hip hip hurrahs led by the losers. Both crews and their guests and friends celebrate during the evening at the Boat Race Ball at the Savoy Hotel. Tables can be reserved by the general public but the price is unlikely to be inexpensive.

The World Championships at the All England Lawn Tennis Club

The Wimbledon tennis championships in July are the apex of the players; year. To win Wimbledon is a prize of prizes; the championships have become hugely popular among spectators, despite extensive television coverage, and is densely crowded.

Buffs claim that the best way to go is to take plentiful supplies of mineral water, some light refreshment, to dress for comfort and to remain rooted to a good seat in the stands.

Certainly, clothes for the occasion should show a healthy respect for the weather forecast; it is a fact that the temperature courtside on the Centre Court can reach 100°F in a heatwave; a sensible sun hat and sun screen lotion are essential. A hat with a wide brim is obviously a bad idea as all those seated behind it would quickly discover. However, dress is formal in the Members' Enclosure – men put on jacket and tie and women wear their Sunday best.

Guests attending parties in one of the smarter corporate hospitality tents are expected to be well dressed. Hospitality here tends to be lavish at lunch with a strawberries and cream tea thrown in for good measure to the sound of popping champagne corks. Television for action replay is usually on tap, and comfortable chairs. For those out and about in the public places, food and drink is easily come by at the numerous buffets and bars.

First-timers should note: it is considered impolite to move about in the stands during play, and the urge to applaud at a moment which is likely to annoy the players must be curbed. Applause should properly be kept for the end of a game, set or match.

How to get in: good seats are gold dust, solid gold in fact. The set procedure is to write (enclosing a SAE) to the All England Lawn Tennis Club, PO Box 98, Church Road, Wimbledon, SW9, for an application form, between 1 August and 31 December, for the following year. Advance seats for the Centre Court and Court One are allocated by public ballot. Otherwise tickets can be applied for through recognized agencies. Spectators can always pay at the gate on the day and take their chances on a seat.

Lord's

Lord's cricket ground is the home of the MCC (the Marylebone Cricket Club) and a mecca for all cricket lovers and champion players of the game. It is where the Test matches are played and the Ashes contested, where the Oxford and Cambridge and Eton and Harrow matches are fought out, and the one-day finals take place. Some claim that the Saturday of the Lord's Test in June is a sporting and social event which has no equal. The MCC is the sport's senior club.

The coveted place to be is the MCC pavilion or one of the private boxes. For non-members, pavilion and box are strictly by invitation only. The boxes are usually reserved for cricket moguls or for purposes of business entertaining.

The few outsiders who are lucky enough to penetrate the inner sanctum of the MCC pavilion are reminded that regulations governing dress and conduct are absolute. 'Members and guests are expected to wear a suit or a jacket with acceptable trousers, a tie or cravat and appropriate shoes.' The following are prohibited: 'jeans and their close relations, zip-up golf jackets, training shoes'. Women are banned from the pavilion during play (an exception is made for the Queen). The use of portable telephones is also banned.

It may be a relief for some to hear that in the public terraces, spectators of both sexes dress for comfort and the day. Here, people may applaud players as they wish, but the approved manner is a slow hand-clap with the expression 'well played' uttered in muted tones from time to time.

How to get in: match tickets are available to MCC members in January and the general public in March. It is advisable to book well ahead of the day for the big matches, especially a test match.

Racing's high days

The opportunity for racegoers to watch thoroughbred horse-racing exists throughout the year. Most weekdays offer chances to spectators and punters, weather permitting. The season opens with the Gold Cup meeting at Cheltenham and the March meeting of the National Hunt (jumping). All the great races are enjoyed for their social side as well as for the sport, Newmarket, York and Newbury among them.

The Grand National, held at Aintree, attracts devotee racegoers as well as doughty picnickers – the latter like to unpack their hampers near strategic points on the course such as Becher's Brook (the big challenge) and the Canal Turn.

The Derby presents an extraordinary crowd spectacle in which anything goes. It is always run on the Epsom Downs on the first Wednesday in June. Newmarket, York and Newbury also draw a wide range of lovers of the turf and the occasion. Generally people in the public grandstands and open ground dress for comfort and the weather.

Visitors to the Members' Enclosure at the various courses are not expected to appear casually clad in green wellies and a donkey jacket. The usual code is: morning dress and toppers or a lounge suit, collar and tie for men; for women, respectable dress with a formal air. A bonnet is a usual but not an invariable choice.

Tickets can be bought in advance or on arrival. Admission to the Members' Enclosure or private boxes or corporate hospitality tents is by invitation only.

Badminton and Burghley Horse Trials

Blue-blooded horse trials are held at two great country estates, the Duke of Beaufort's Badminton House and Burghley, the splendid pile built by and named after Queen Elizabeth's Lord High Treasurer. Five-day sports events attract world-famous competitors who engage in marathon feats of horsemanship in cross-country eventing. These are equestrian festivals (Badminton in June, Burghley in September) which are more than a sporting event, and combine a sociable occasion, shopping opportunities for country produce and products, and all the gossip of the fair.

At Badminton, one of the best spots for informed opinion is the British Horse Society marquee which offers – as you would expect – an excellent view of the show jumping, likewise the Beaufort Hunt Club. Ticket-holders for the stands are also well placed. Aficionados recommend attending the inspection of competitors' mounts that takes place in the forecourt of the big house.

The Duke and Duchess of Beaufort invite competitors, officials and supporters to drinks at the house, which is the party of parties.

Country gear is the order of the day for spectators of both sexes and all ages. Think mud, as one supporter put it. Whatever is chosen should be appropriate for stomping over fields and picknicking in the open, and obviously anything that frightens the horses is best left at home.

At the grandee parties, dress is formal. Jackets, collar and tie, often a somewhat citified suit for men; women put on blouses and skirts or rather quiet dresses, much depending on what the rest of the day/evening holds.

Burghley offers similar displays of sportsmanship but is considered to have a more relaxed atmosphere on the social side. The competitors are top-class, the shopping of interest, and even for those whose interest in horses is limited, there is always plenty to see and do. A cocktail party is held at the house during the event at which riders, VIPs, organizers and their allies are welcomed.

Nightlife

An invitation to a dance is one of the most promising in the book, or can be. Going dancing, however, can mean many different types of occasion, ranging from a knees-up at the village hall to a sedate affair at the golf club, a grand do in a private ballroom or a dinner dance in an hotel.

In addition, many dances are held for the purpose of raising money for charity as well as for enjoyment's sake, and Prince Charming may ask Cinderella to first buy tickets for the ball. The dances considered below are all organized occasions of one kind or another, for which guests are expected to don some finery.

Subscription dances

Among the best-known charity balls are the Rose Ball, and Queen Charlotte's Ball, both are ringed dates in a debutante's diary. Announcements appear in the

Court pages of newspapers. It is important for first-timers to appreciate that a proportion of the ticket money is a donation to the charity in whose name the ball is being held.

A typical case of crossed wires that can occur on these occasions is when an invited guest in uncertain about whether they are expected to buy a ticket or whether they are being taken. If acceptance is in order, guests can always offer to pay, which paves the way for hosts to declare their position. On the other hand, if acceptance is not on the cards, the invitation can be parried with a polite request for a subscription form. An acceptable excuse for declining would be to explain that you have your own charity to support. In any event, if the invitation is declined and the host is a friend, it would be courteous to make a donation to the good cause.

The usual form at a charity ball is for supporters to make up a table of friends, each of whom buys a ticket. Drinks at the bar will be paid for separately. Tickets vary widely in price. Dinner and dancing and a cabaret are usually included. The more expensive may include as well a champagne reception, fairground rides, an auction, and a full breakfast.

Dance-goers may dine together beforehand or at the ball. If people are attending the reception they will be announced by a major-domo and received by members of the Ball Committee. Dancing usually begins around 10 pm and the party winds up in the small hours.

Dress is formal: black ties or decorative bow-ties for men are in order. Women tend to put on their finery, whether long or short, but the emphasis on individuality in fashion makes hard-and-fast guidelines unrealistic. It may be worth mentioning that a long dress would never be incorrect on such an occasion.

A private dance

Private dances are by definition princely entertainment usually reserved for landmark occasions. They are extremely expensive and time-consuming to organize on a grand or even modest level, if they are to be successful. They are usually given to celebrate a wedding, a coming of age or a debutante's coming-out. Or some wind of good fortune may give rise to the extravagance.

Sometimes more than one family combine the role of host, traditionally bestowed on the parents. Sometimes a private bash is a collective effort, with brothers and sisters or a mother and her offspring joining forces.

At its most elaborate, a private dance means an invitation list of upwards of 400 guests, rooms sumptuously decorated for the night, and/or pavilioned splendour conjured up in the grounds. Dinner and breakfast will be served and wine will flow liberally.

Dancing usually begins at 10 pm and the guests dance on until 6 or 7 am. Needless to add, an occasion of this magnitude is a rare event in the social calendar and is usually stage-managed by professionals in the field who administer the guest list, the catering, flower arrangements, lighting; hiring of musicians and discotheques, marquees and staff.

At a big dance in the country guests are expected to make their own way to and from the party and to make their own arrangements for an overnight stay if necessary. If the invitation is for 10 pm or thereabouts guests will be obliged to find their own dinner unless invited to a dinner party in the neighbourhood or asked to join a house party.

It is likely to be more fun to go to a dance with a partner or a group of friends, but at a private bash, singles are able to strike up an acquaintance or renew old friendships without being considered forward. As usual, husbands and wives are expected to separate for at least part of the time and to propose or accept invitations to dance from other members of the throng. Although this noctural spree presents an unrivalled opportunity to dance until after dawn, some may wish to take their leave at an earlier point. Anytime after midnight requires no apologies. It is always courteous to try to find the host or hostess in order to say goodbyes, but they may prove elusive and it is pointless to make an issue of locating them. A handwritten letter of thanks should be sent as soon as possible.

Invitations and dress

The card may be specially printed or an 'At Home' card. The invitation can be for 'Dinner and dancing' or 'Dancing' only (see Special points).

Usually the hostess's name is given with a line which establishes the names of the persons for whom the party is being given: 'For Annie and Joe'. If parents and offspring are giving a shared party, both names could be set out one above the other, the older generation leading. Celebrations given by people of title on behalf of an offspring use the formal style of address as a general rule. When brothers and sisters combine to give a dance, prefixes could be dropped, e.g. 'Maxine, Nuala and Ben Oldham'. In the instance of a dance being given by a couple to celebrate their forthcoming marriage, the invitations go out in their single-status names.

Dress guidelines are usually mentioned on the invitation. 'Black tie' is likely. However, two dance-givers who wished to give their friends more latitude, stipulated 'Black tie or anything else'. The wording 'Informal' covers a multitude of options. A jacket, collar and tie is always acceptable, but the bracket could include smoking jackets, good-looking sweaters, scarves, cravats or open-necks. Whatever is chosen should pay respects to the occasion.

Women's attire at dances runs the gamut from floor-length ballgowns in satin and chiffon to bopper's fancies slashed from bosom to thigh. Hemlines are no longer a guideline. Gilded youth wears whatever comes into its head, which could be either or neither of the forementioned options. Probably the only approach that in unacceptable is giving the impression that no trouble has been taken. It is worth adding that no woman would look out of place in a short evening dress and that long is never incorrect.

A *private dance held at hired premises*

The resources that are required for a dance persuade some party-givers to book a ballroom at an hotel for the night, or to hire appropriate rooms.

Most of the above remarks apply. It is worth mentioning that timing is likely to be tighter than at a dance held at a private abode. Security, overtime rates, and the need to keep staff on tap who are not connected with the party suggest that the dance may wind up shortly after midnight. Much depends on the wishes (and means) of the host.

The usual rules about tipping at an hotel apply. The hall porter who calls a cab, the telephonist who dials a number, the receptionist who assists will expect a tip. It is courteous to tip all cloakroom attendants if their services are used at a public place.

Naturally, waiters or waitresses serving dinner at a private occasion in an hotel do not expect a gratuity from the guests.

May Balls and Commem

Generations of Oxford and Cambridge undergraduates have celebrated taking their finals at the college balls held in June. At Oxford these are known as 'Commems' and have the worthy purpose of commemorating the college founders and benefactors. Oddly enough the May Balls at Cambridge are held in June.

The balls are arranged by individual colleges and the organizers traditionally push the boat out. Romantic settings are floodlit, marquees and fairy lights bedeck the gardens and well-known bands and cabarets are booked.

Tickets for dinner and dancing are expensive. Usually only those with a college connection are eligible to apply. Since it is usual for students, most of whom are on a grant, to go dutch on entertainment, costs are frequently split between couples or groups. Initiators should be clear on the point of whether a friend is their guest, or is expected to pay their way. The usual rules apply. A guest is under no obligation to offer to buy their own ticket or share costs, unless they wish to. Probably, a more politic idea for guests who are being treated is to bring a bottle or two to their host's rooms as a starter to the celebrations.

Dress is formal. Women wear dance dresses, usually long-skirted and take some protection such as a wrap against the vicissitudes of the weather. High heels are a handicap on lawns and if the evening includes rides on dodgem cars. Black tie is the rule for men except at Magdalen, Oxford and Trinity, Cambridge where white ties can be sighted. A good tip on getting the most out of the occasion comes from an undergraduate: 'Pace yourself. It's a triumph if you can manage to see the sun rise . . .'

A public dinner-dance

An invitation to dine at a big hotel or club when the dance-band is playing is usually a relaxed affair. The occasion depends as much as anything on the individuals concerned and their wishes.

It is safe to assume that if the purpose of the gathering is a birthday party, or a potentially romantic encounter, or some other celebratory cause, it is wisest to err on the side of formality in dress. West End hotels with ballrooms maintain a strict dress code. Jacket and collar and tie for men, and women are expected to dress 'appropriately', which excludes jeans, undue nudity or scruffy gear. Usually a few black ties can be seen mingling with lounge suits. Women do have considerably more latitude in this matter than men, as an hotel is full of passing travellers and tourists who have only day-clothes at their disposal and may well be among the dancers. Short dresses that pay their respect to the occasion are acceptable, but long still has a place.

The form at dinner is as for any first-class restaurant. The menu will offer a set price dinner and à la carte. Keen dancers may take to the floor in between courses. Tables can be booked by the general public. It is not impolite to ask the booking clerk the price of the set menu nor to check on the dress code of the establishment. It is a good idea to ask for a table near the dance floor.

Special points

With exceptions, it is not considered polite to indicate on an invitation card that the party demands a present from guests. This may mean that some people are in the dark if the dance is a celebration for a birthday. There is nothing against asking the party-giver in advance about the matter, and a present can always be sent after the event. It is always generous to contribute an offering, but if the person whose birthday is being celebrated is little known to a guest, there is no obligation to produce a gift.

Arrival times on the invitation card indicate the hospitality that is being provided. To be invited for 8 pm or thereabouts means dinner as a rule, to be invited for 9.30–10 pm or thereabouts means after-dinner. However, if dinner is to be served, the invitation should state so.

When a large number of guests are invited for after dinner, the party-giver may ask a number of friends if they would give dinner-parties beforehand on behalf of the occasion. Dance guests may or may not be acquainted with their dinner hosts. The idea is that most poeple round the table will be going on to the party. Thank-you letters to both the dance hostess and the dinner party hostess are courteous.

Best behaviour at the dance

A dance is for dancing and men are reminded that it is their role to ask a partner to take to the dance-floor. True, some brave females are prepared to make the first move, but most will sit out rather than risk a rebuff.

At a private party, a man may ask any female for a dance. It is courteous for him to invite some of the women sitting at his table for a twirl at some point, and to remember to ask the hostess to be his partner at least once. If the party is being given for a woman, it would be tactless to ignore her in order to concentrate exclusively on the girl he brought or on a new interest.

Usually, men ask a woman for a dance when she is sitting out, but she may be asked for the next one on the dance-floor. It is discourteous to cut in on another man's partner – the polite approach is to wait until the number is over and then to seize the moment. After a dance, a man should escort his partner to her table. A quick change of partners on the floor calls for a show of tact.

Dancing between the sexes is a sensual experience and suggesting limits to behaviour is problematic. A general rule is that heavy petting is likely to embarrass some onlookers and irritate others and may well discomfit the petted. Overtly sexual fondling is for private eyes only. Another caveat – smoking a cigarette or a cigar while dancing is a breach of good manners.

Women who do not wish to accept an invitation to dance may take refuge in the time-honoured excuse that they wish to sit this one out, or say that they are unable to dance a rumba or a tango or whichever tempo is being played. Should the inviter glimpse the lady shortly afterwards on the floor with another, at least no unpleasant words will have been uttered, and he should get the message.

No one is obliged to dance, but the spirit of the occasion calls for guests to show willing – particularly when the person asking is a host or the person for whom the party is being given.

Dances may be sedate or – as the evening progresses – exuberant. Jiving and disco dancing breaks many accepted barriers – men and women dance solo or may cavort with their own sex to the rhythm of the beat.

Attending a banquet

Banquets and formal dinners of the kind described below are highly structured, minutely organized and largely untouched by the prevailing winds of informality. Even on this stage, though, there is a more relaxed atmosphere than was once the case.

One aspect of change is that guests unfamiliar with the etiquette and protocol are likely to be invited. Each occasion has its own conventions, but this briefing on likely procedures could be helpful.

Leading institutions noted for their hospitality are the Lord Mayor, the City livery companies, the ancient universities and other seats of learning, the Inns of Court, the armed services, the Royal Academy of Arts and many others. Top of the list, of course, are royal and state occasions for which dinners are given.

Banquets generally take place in historic settings, beneath portraits of past founders who seem to be keeping an eye on proceedings. Lovers of a fine table-setting are unlikely to be disappointed.

New arrivals may leave their coats with an attendant. Women have a chance to visit the ladies' cloakroom, if wished. Guests forgather in a foyer by the entrance – perhaps standing in line. A major-domo asks each person their name before announcing them to the hosts who will be standing by to receive guests. Novices are advised to speak clearly, or their name may not be caught correctly, with some comic distortion resulting. Married couples usually give their names and prefix together, 'Mr and Mrs Browning' (or with the husband's first name) and are announced together. Singles give their full name and style 'Miss Clarissa White', 'Mr Colin Hayes'.

The guest then moves forward to shake the extended hand of the host and a few words are exchanged. New visitors may rely on mentioning their pleasure in being invited.

As usual at a reception, drinks will be handed, and guests may (or may not) be introduced to compatible companions, depending on the nature of the occasion. Anyone who is short of ideas on what to talk about can always express curiosity about the institution, or the building or any treasures on view.

Dinner will be announced by an official in stentorian tones, and this may be a moment when it is prudent to notice what the others are doing. There may be an order of precedence to be observed about going in to dinner.

In the usual ways of things, a table-plan is displayed which enables guests to identify the table at which they are seated, and also, the company they will keep. Husbands and wives are usually separated in the seating plan at the table.

Once you have located your place – which will be denoted with a place-card bearing your name – it is unwise to sit down promptly. Grace may be said, either spoken or sung, for which the gathering stands. After grace, everyone is seated.

A vantage point to watch is the high or top table. Sometimes various dignitaries or officials file in after the guests are seated, to a round of applause. It is considered impolite not to join in – no talking during the procession.

The menu is likely to consist of four or five courses and coffee and liqueurs. The names of the dishes and wines are usually printed – restaurant French predominating. The card may also include a Toast List, naming the subjects.

Various ceremonies may take place during the meal. A large rosewater bowl often of great beauty in glass, silver or gold and filled with rosewater, may be passed round the table. The form is to dip the tips of your fingers in the water and dry them on your table napkin as with individual finger-bowls.

A loving cup ceremony is associated with City livery dinners among others, and is part of tradition at the Lord Mayor's Banquet.

A ceremonial goblet, usually covered, and filled with wine, is passed round the table by the guests themselves. There are always three people standing in the ceremony, but never more than three to each loving cup. Those on their feet are the one who has most recently drunk, the one who is drinking and the next one to drink. Drinker and neighbour stand back to back, a custom said to have originated from the assassination of Saxon King Edward who met his death whilst pledging his friendship in this fashion – the King's dagger hand being peacefully engaged. Ever since, they say, a symbolic 'protector' is on hand to guard against stabs in the back.

This is the ceremony, step by step. Each diner rises as his or her neighbour receives the loving cup. They bow to each other. The one in this duet who is without the cup then removes the cup's cover and takes charge of it. The holder of the cup drinks to his neighbour, and wipes the rim of the vessel with the napkin provided. The neighbour replaces the cover and the two bow to each other once more. The drinker then hands the cup to the neighbour, and turns to stand back to back with him or her. Simultaneously, the new bearer of the cup now turns to face his or her neighbour, who rises and the ritual is repeated. Those who have played their part may now be seated. Novices and first-time guests who manage the procedure with grace gain compliments from the old hands. A new member, for example, who was venturing into the livery company would do well to rehearse the procedure. Raw recruits can take comfort from the fact that experienced members are usually prepared to nurse visitors through the ceremony, patiently.

The loving cup ceremony has fewer proponents than previously – said to be due to fears about the HIV virus.

At the mellow stage of the occasion come the toasts and speeches. The most usual on these occasions is the loyal toast, 'The Queen', when the gathering rises, raises a glass, repeats the toast and quaffs some wine. Abstainers need not feel out of things as toasts may be drunk in water without causing comment.

When the speeches begin it is usually permissible for any guests who do not have a good view of the speaker to swivel their chairs round for an advantage. Guests who talk among themselves when the speaker is on his or her feet are considered extremely discourteous. If, by chance, a guest has to make a getaway either to catch a train or visit the cloakroom, the form is to slip off as inconspicuously as possible; expert escapees adopt a discreet crouching stance until they are out of the main line of vision.

Smoking and farewells

After the toasts, the toastmaster traditionally announces that smoking is permitted. It is worth pointing out that to light up a cigarette before the loyal toast is considered very bad form.

See page 346 for Unholy smoke.

Despite the official announcement, changed attitudes towards tobacco smoking suggest that it is considerate for smokers to ask their neighbours if they have any objection. A courteous reply is difficult to assess. If the request comes from your host or you suspect that the host would prefer you to give an assent, and you detest tobacco smoke, there is a case on such a tradition-bound occasion to consider the usual privileges of guests. Also, if others are lighting up cigars and cigarettes there seems little point in trying to establish a smokeless zone. In some surroundings, there may be separate rooms for smokers, in which case it seems reasonable to express an honest opinion.

Goodbyes are said to the principal hosts – if they can be found – and to the host whose guest you were. A handwritten letter of thanks will be expected which should include a thank-you for any presents given you as a guest.

Diplomatic occasions

Diplomatic occasions and invitations to receptions at foreign embassies deserve fuller cover than can be given in this book.

Many different tongues, sensitive issues of the day and protocol and precedence are part and parcel of diplomatic entertaining. Usually the invitation gives details as to purpose and dress. If further information is required, consult the Protocol office, or the social secretary, at the embassy concerned.

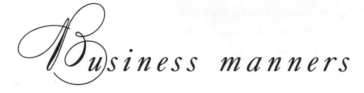

Business manners

Good manners at the work-place may be only a veneer on a jungle scene, but

better with than without by far. Even basic gestures such as 'Please' and

'Thank you' can help to civilize daily communication. Organizations with a

reputation for treating their staff with consideration are usually admired for

the policy. It is noticeable in these cases that the approach usually starts at

the top. The chief who treats subordinates with politeness is likely to gain

their respect at least for that quality, whereas boors are invariably

disliked for their ill-manners.

It is evident that people at work are judged by different criteria from those that prevail outside. Efficiency, power, success, profitability become the main goals. The gentleness that is associated with courtesy may be no match for success in the market-place, regrettable as this may be.

Most work-places have their own way of doing things which can only be learned from experience and observation on the job. Some general guidelines hold good, though, one of which is that the principles underlying good manners don't change with the weather.

Job-hunting procedures

Just as holding down a job successfully can often involve matters of etiquette, there are a number of conventions inherent in applying for – and getting – the job you are after.

Preparing a curriculum vitae

Many submitted CVs are too long and wordy. There is a good case against an all-purpose account: successful technique lies in tailoring the information to suit the post applied for. However, it can be difficult to know what to include and what to omit as some minor listed achievement might carry unexpected influence.

A useful guiding principle is for applicants to put themselves in the position of the employer. What experience and qualifications do you possess that might single out your application from those of numerous contenders? Know your strong cards and focus on these. A CV is expected to include the following basic information: the candidate's full name, address and telephone number, nationality and marital status. Some employers expect to be told the applicants' ethnic origins, but supplying such information is at the candidate's discretion.

Schools, colleges and places of further education attended by the applicant should be listed, from secondary school upwards, giving the years of attendance. Beside the entries, note any relevant examinations taken and any good grades gained. Posts held are usually listed chronologically, with the current position given first if it carries weight. Dates of employment are important, with a brief explanation to account for any marked gap in the record.

First-time job seekers with understandably little to show for themselves should mention any work experience or pastimes that might at least suggest they are capable of accepting responsibility. Hobbies and interests merit a section, and in certain fields these entries are read with special care as the information may be more revealing than exam results.

Final touches

The importance of good presentation and layout applies equally to a CV. Applicants who suspect that errors may creep in despite their best efforts should try to enlist a literate ally to check through the finer points – in time for corrections to be made.

Filling in a questionnaire

For some jobs you will be asked to complete a questionnaire, which can be quite detailed and complex. Always try to answer each question. If one does not apply, write 'Not applicable' in the space provided. Be highly selective about the information you give, trying to guestimate the points which will carry particular relevance for the post in question.

If you are invited to fill in a questionnaire in the office of a prospective employer, make sure that all the basic facts and dates are to hand. Should you mistakenly spoil the paper, ask for another copy, with apologies, rather than turning in a questionnaire carrying corrections.

Preparing a written application for a job

Anyone who writes a clear, informative, well-presented letter asking for employment will immediately single themselves out of the usual run of applicants.

Points to watch when replying to an advertisement: ensure that if specific information is requested it is supplied, wherever possible; check that the full name of the person to whom the correspondence is addressed is accurately spelt, and also that you have included their prefix and correct formal position, such as 'Personnel Director'. Make sure that you have written the address correctly.

When a candidate sends an unsolicited letter, it is usually best to address the correspondence to a specific named individual in preference to an anonymous head of a department. Firms are usually prepared to give names and job titles on the telephone. Applications may be sent to the Managing Director or the Personnel Manager. In a big company a letter addressed to an individual manager will in all probability be handed on to personnel, but a well-written letter might just catch the eye of an interested party in the target group.

A letter that accompanies a CV should state whether you are replying to an advertisement (state the publication and date) and produce an interesting reason why you think you should be considered for the post. Enthusiasm for the field, aptitude for the work and aspirations to succeed, backed up with relevant experience or qualifications, would be the ideal. It is usually advisable to indicate whether you are currently employed or are or could be immediately available.

Avoid precipitate references to working out your present contract of employment, which can be discussed at a later stage.

Some correspondents like to type their names beneath their signature in the interests of clarity. Women have a choice of adding their chosen form of address (Mrs/Miss/Ms) in brackets after the typed name, or of leaving the matter open.

A letter of application should give an address to which the company can reply and if possible a telephone number where the correspondent can be reached.

The writing paper should be pristine and uncrumpled. Write on one side of the paper only and if necessary use a second sheet (without a heading) for continuation. Place your letter in an envelope which is designed to fit the proportions of the folded writing paper.

Job applications are usually typewritten, but in certain cases applicants may be asked to write in their own hand. Handwriting can be revealing of education and background and to some, of character. The request should be complied with. Keep copies of all correspondence concerning job applications.

Arrival at the interview

Punctuality is important, of course, but arriving noticeably ahead of time suggests lack of confidence and inexperience. It is best to allow about ten minutes' or so grace. Once at the reception desk, give your full name and the name of the person with whom you have an appointment (if known) and the time of the interview. If you are unfortunate enough to arrive late, apologize and don't be surprised to be kept waiting. But being late for an interview shows discourtesy and is a very poor start, so try to avoid this at all costs – find out how to reach the place of interview in advance, and allow yourself plenty of time for unforeseen eventualities, such as traffic jams.

If any printed literature concerning the company or organization is on display, it is advisable to take the trouble to read it. There may be some useful points to which you might like to allude later on.

Some companies are said to brief the receptionist to observe the behaviour of waiting candidates or to remember any small talk that has taken place. Pleasantries are fine, but confidences could be ill-judged.

Making a good impression

Unfair as it may be, many hopes are won or lost in a first impression, which can be a crucial factor.

It may be better to respond than to initiate, at any rate during the opening stages of the interview. If the interviewer extends a welcoming hand, shake it. Try to avoid either a limp touch or a bone-cruncher. A feeling of warmth should be communicated in the gesture. Posture counts – it should be upright in every sense.

Acknowledge a smile with a smile. Wait to be told where to sit, but if no guidance is forthcoming, ask, 'May I sit here?' Incidentally, it is inadvisable for a candidate to ask if they may smoke, as a general rule.

Try not to appear evasive when tough questions are put. Maintain a natural level of eye-contact and try to control the often unconscious habits of staring aggressively or of looking down. The stance to aim for is to look at ease – neither diffident nor over-confident – but totally focused on the challenge.

Always carry writing materials in case of the need to make notes, and an engagement diary. Should the interviewer's telephone ring when he or she is out of the room don't answer it unless previously asked to do so. Notice any interesting characteristics of the office space – pictures of the chairman, photographs, graphs – there may be a point worth raising in connection with them.

Dress sense

Despite the general casualness that holds sway in dress, it is almost invariably sound practice to show yourself to best advantage by taking the trouble to look good at a job interview. In essence, what is needed is to give the interviewer the impression that you will be an asset to your employers. It is well worth giving some time to finding/borrowing/making clothes which are good for the ego and in which you feel relaxed and at your ease. Women are advised to avoid an aggressively sexy look as this may suggest that you are trying too hard, or the overly-eccentric which can easily be misunderstood, or any show of downright indifference.

Small details do make a difference. Emphasis on a well-groomed impression may have an old-fashioned ring but is none the worse for that in this context. A suit would probably be an asset for men though there is little need for them to retreat into a cloned uniform. In general acceptable dress depends on the type of job.

Question time

It is polite to address the interviewer formally with their usual prefix, but avoid repetitive references to the interviewer's name, such as 'Yes, Miss Jones', 'No, Mr Brown'. Try not to gabble replies to direct questions. If you make a nonsense, apologize immediately and go over the ground again.

Taking the trouble to inform yourself about the job and the company before the interview takes place is invaluable. Prepare convincing answers to questions such as what interests you particularly about working for the company/the origins of your interest in the type of work for which a vacancy exists/how you see your career developing/whether you are prepared to relocate or work at a branch office. Parents who have young children at home may face inquiries about child care arrangements and also their spouse's approach to the demands of the job.

Not all interviews take place within the formality of an office. A drink may be proposed, or a meal in a restaurant, often to assess qualities of self-confidence and *savoir-faire* in an informal context. In a way, this presents the more unnerving challenge for a prospective employee as rules are less distinct. Women applicants are advised to take special care on these occasions. They should always leave word as to who they are meeting and when and where, and if possible, arrange to be met by a friend as a tactful means of ending the interview.

References, good and not so good

Candidates should always offer to supply references, giving name, address and telephone number of each referee. References, if requested, are usually supplied by school and college heads for young people, and by previous employers. Reference from a person in authority for even short-term employment can be useful. It goes without saying that permission must be asked for – and given – to use a person's name as a reference.

An applicant who has been made redundant by a previous employer should describe the background briefly if this is likely to put them in the clear. Supporting evidence might be that other members of staff were also made redundant as part of a 'slimming down' operation.

Supposing you were previously sacked for alleged incompetence? You are under no obligation to mention the fact, but if an employer intends to take up references which are likely to be adversely critical, it is just as well to prepare him or her in advance. Acceptable explanations without any loss of face might include misunderstandings about the nature of the job, a personality clash with the boss, being the victim of racist or sexist discrimination, compassionate reasons such as a divorce in the family.

As a rule it is tactless to denigrate a previous employer in front of a prospective one. Disloyalty may be thought to have no frontiers. In circumstances where admitting that you were in the wrong is inescapable, it would be to your advantage to indicate that lessons have been learned.

As a background to the interview, candidates might like to play a game of putting themselves in their prospective employer's shoes. Why would *you* hire you? Work out the strongest cards you hold, remembering that rare and welcome qualities in the job market are a real enthusiasm for the work involved, a willlingness to accept responsibility, a preparedness to work late or at weekends.

Team spirits

At a certain level, employers are usually looking for someone with whom they feel comfortable. 'Faces that fit' may have snobbish or reverse-snobbish overtones, but can carry more weight in the final count than either qualifications or experience. Between two candidates of equal merit, a feeling of empathy may be a tilting factor. The belief that an applicant is likely to be accepted by fellow members of the team is also of great importance. But it is extremely difficult for a newcomer to gauge the values of their prospective employer other than by trying to find out as much as possible about the company and its personnel in advance.

Rewards and benefits

Applicants may always raise the topics of salary and conditions of work if the interviewer seems slow in getting round to the point. Some balance has to be struck, though, between obtaining a clear brief and giving the impression that your primary interest lies not in the job itself, but in the wage, concessions and benefits it offers. It might be politic to inquire in a general way about benefits, and there is nothing against asking if the salary or wage quoted is negotiable.

Departure

When the interview is at an end, the candidate should thank the interviewer for his or her time and interest, shake hands on it and say goodbye, maintaining an optimistic air throughout. It is quite in order to ask when you are likely to be informed of any decision.

If you do not receive word by the date given, allow a couple of days or so to elapse before telephoning for any news, and give a reason, such as another post in the offing, for your inquiry.

Personal recommendations

The old joke that who you know is more important than what you know has a special resonance for job hunters. Certainly there is nothing irregular about seeking advice and accepting offers of assistance from friends or acquaintances who might be in a position to help directly or point you in the right direction.

If introductions are proposed and the recommender goes to some trouble to implement a suggestion, it would be discourteous not to follow it up, or to fail to give a good reason for not doing so.

The most effective plan of action is for the introducer to write to their contact, alerting him or her to the name and interest of their recommendee. The latter should take the next step, by telephoning the third party, mentioning the name of their mutual acquaintance as a reminder, and asking for an appointment. If the call is taken by a secretary it would be correct to ask to be put through to the person sought. An alternative is write a letter which might open with a remark to the effect that your mutual friend suggested that you should get in touch. The letter writer should request an appointment on a convenient day and thank the recipient for any assistance or advice on offer. The recipient should be addressed formally, 'Dear Mr Buxton' and the letter should end 'Yours sincerely'.

The person who seeks the introduction should be prepared to be patient about a response, and not expect anything immediately measurable from a subsequent meeting. It is always sound practice to thank the person who made the introduction and to write to express gratitude to their contact for giving up time to see you.

Signing on the dotted line

Successful applicants are usually sent a letter of confirmation or a contract setting out terms and conditions. The agreements have legal teeth and should be very carefully perused before signing. A significant point is the length of notice to be given before the agreement may be broken. For example, the phrase 'three months' notice on either side' means that if the signatory happens to be made redundant, the company is obliged to pay their salary for three months following the notification. Similarly, in the event of an employee wishing to switch employers, pressures can be brought to bear to compel them to work out their full notice.

On the one hand, contracts of employment offer some financial security, but on the other, they impose limitations on the signatory's freedom of action; this may not be immediately apparent in the text. It is worth knowing that contracts may be amended in the light of subsequent perusal, but this has to happen before the signing pen has touched the page.

A copy of any agreement or contract should be kept. If it is mislaid, it is in order to ask for a replacement.

First names or a formal style?

Addressing members of staff by their first names from the start is common accepted practice, but the formal style of prefix and surname is still often the general rule and can never be considered incorrect. Newcomers are advised to test the waters before taking the initiative.

Much depends on the sector of employment. In most big companies, senior members of staff are addressed formally by those who are considerably junior in rank to them. Those of roughly equal status who work together tend to be on Christian name terms.

It is up to those in authority to set the style. If they wish to be addressed formally, it will encourage the practice if they extend the courtesy to their staff. In the likely event of exceptions, it is the role of the head to suggest first-name terms.

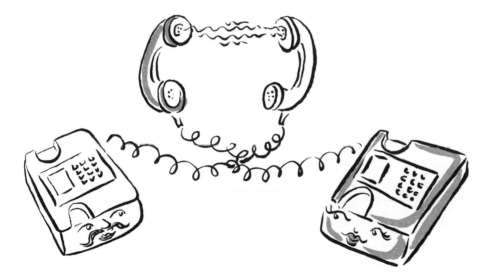

Telephone tactics

The telephone is a double-edged weapon – both boon and bind. It is a vital medium of communication which can also be a time-waster and an intrusion. A mannerly approach can at least help to keep the lines from getting crossed.

Making calls

The caller should announce their identity or have someone do this on their behalf. If you are unknown to the person being rung, it is important to establish in a few words who you are and what your business may be.

A disembodied voice on the line is more sympathetic to the listener if the tone is friendly, and this may be an asset if the caller requires assistance. It is counter-productive to rush the telephone call or to cram too many facts and figures into an opening remark. Speak in a conversational tone with the minimum of hesitations, like 'ummms' and 'sort ofs'. A succinct approach will probably be appreciated at the other end. Always utter a parting remark – goodbye is fine – before putting down the receiver.

If a message is to be left, the information should be as brief as clarity allows. If in doubt, just leave a clear name, a telephone or fax number at which you can be reached, and an indication that the call is urgent.

A rule that generally applies to all callers is that if they are cut off by the system for some reason, it is their responsibility to call back.

Taking calls

It is important for the caller to know who or what is at the other end of the line when their call is taken. General practice is for the receiver of the call to identify themselves or the department or section.

If someone calls for an absent colleague it is polite to ask if you can take a message, or suggest that the caller leave a name.

Deflecting unwanted calls

Avoiding unwanted telephone calls is an integral part of office management and if done with courtesy can prevent feelings of rebuff.

Acceptable pretexts for shielding an associate or manager from unwanted calls might include: 'I will try to get her to return your call but I can't promise it will be today'; 'I am sorry, but the Manager is not taking any calls at present'; 'I am afraid that Deanne has just left for an appointment'; 'He is in the building but away from his desk just now'; 'She is tied up on a long distance call and it looks as if she could be some time'. The ubiquitous excuse, 'He is in a meeting' has long reached joke level through over-exposure and should be used very sparingly.

In the case of no-hopers, an assistant could explain that her boss is very busy and ask if anyone else might be able to help. Often in these circumstances it is less what is said than the manner in which the remark is delivered. A tactful approach helps to let the caller down lightly.

Switchboard operators are enjoined to remember hapless callers who are left stranded on the line, either waiting for their call to be transferred to an extension which rings without answer indefinitely, or those waiting for an extension which seems endlessly engaged. It is a huge relief for callers to know they are not forgotten.

Callers who are promised a return call which does not materialize are justified in feeling put out. It is discourteous to promise to ring back when there is little intention of doing any such thing. However, certain callers cannot take a hint. In this case, it may be an effective deterrent to suggest that they put the matter in writing.

Taking messages

Written messages taken on behalf of others should include a call back number, a name and the gist of any urgent communication. It is inconsiderate to write down the information incorrectly and every effort should be made to avoid this.

Personal calls

Making and taking personal calls in company time has become the norm. If the practice is not to be abused, some limits have to be observed. The change of pace the calls bring is very welcome but when a caller hopes for a long chat it would be thoughtful of them to ask first if this a good moment to talk. Certainly calls should not annoy or distract people who are trying to concentrate on their work.

Calls of a highly personal nature are usually best conducted in whatever privacy the work space affords. If the office is open-plan in design there may be a case for asking the occupant of a private office to lend it for the duration of an important personal call.

Friendly telecommunication

Modern telecommunication systems have brought their own codes of courtesy, though these are too often neglected.

When an answering-machine is attached to a business telephone number, it is discourteous for the recorded message to indicate that calls are likely to be returned shortly if this is in fact far from the case. The message should indicate that the department or person responsible is out of commission or give another number for the caller to try. Otherwise it is best for the machine to be disconnected. Callers should leave a name and number, if wished, remembering that verbose messages use up valuable recording time. It is not a bad idea for callers to work out in advance the wording of the message to be recorded unless it is very brief. Incomplete messages which are without a name attributed, or dense facts and figures delivered at double speed and without being repeated are all in their different ways frustrating to the recipient.

Facsimile machines to which many members of staff have access are unsuitable for confidential information as communications arrive for all to see. Messages are usually signed even if the covering sheet bears the name of the sender.

It would be a courtesy for users of a fax machine which is likely to be busy to say so to a prospective sender, thus saving them the time and trouble of trying to get their own message through until a pause in the traffic occurs.

It is open to question as to whether replying to business invitations is acceptable by fax. As a last-minute strategy perhaps, or between friends, or as a written confirmation of a spoken response. Certainly, for formal affairs, the means might seem a touch casual. Thank you letters sent by fax have an impersonal air which seems at odds with the spirit of gratitude. Naturally, the above reservations would not apply in the case in which both sender and recipient have private fax numbers.

Writing a business letter

A business letter should set out the name of the person to whom it is addressed, their job description, the name of the firm or organization and its full address and postcode. This is customarily placed at the top left of the writing paper; some correspondents put the information beneath the letter, bottom left. Both are correct.

> Mr T. Barkus
> Manager
> High Grade Electrics
> 100 Market Square
> Wissington
> Wessex
> (postcode)

Among the simplicities of writing a business letter is that the sometimes sensitive issue of who should be styled 'Mister' and who 'Esquire' is resolved in favour of the universal status of 'Mr'. Certainly few men who are accustomed to being styled 'Esquire' would take umbrage. However, in the rare case where a correspondent suspects that their addressee is a stickler for etiquette, it would be diplomatic to credit him with his 'Esq.' on the envelope and heading.

In certain occupations, especially in the media and media-related activities, it has become acceptable to pare down forms of address and to address correspondence to 'Nigel Handley' or 'Jane Smith' without giving them the dignity of a prefix.

For information on writing to persons with a handle or a title, please see page 316.

The letter begins formally, 'Dear Sir' or 'Dear Madam' if the name of the addressee is not known. If known, the correspondence opens, 'Dear Mr Barkus'. The style of the ending is determined by the manner of the opening, the former ends 'Yours faithfully', the latter 'Yours sincerely'. It is a good idea to write or type a full name and prefix beneath the signature, 'Janet Elliot (Mrs)'. If in doubt when replying to a letter, it would not be impolite to follow the style of the original correspondence. Writing the date is important.

An example of a letter of complaint (to a bank)

Dear Mr Wainbright (name of manager of branch)
I am returning your April bank statement which shows an error of over (quote exact sum) in the interest charged on my overdraft. According to my records this is the fourth mistake I have had to complain about during the past twelve months.

Correcting these errors has involved me in a considerable amount of time and trouble. Unless you can improve the standard of service at your branch, I see no option but to complain to Head Office and remove my account.

I look forward to your reply.

Yours sincerely

An example of a written reference for an employee

Lucy Barker has worked as a junior assistant to the head of department in our personnel division for the past fifteen months. Quickly adapting to the often fast pace of work in this department, she revealed an understanding of company policy which was reflected in her sympathetic approach to applicants and leavers. She worked as a loyal member of a team and undertook tasks set her with diligence and efficiency. We wish her well in any future endeavour.

The reference should be written on headed company writing paper, dated and signed with the position of the referee given,

'Deanne Watkins, Personnel Manager'.

An example of a letter turning down an invitation to take part in an event / accept a commission

---

Thank you for your letter inviting me to (specify commission).
Honoured though I am to be approached in this way I much regret that,
due to existing commitments I am unable to undertake anything else at
the present time.
signed

An example of a letter inviting the correspondent to take part in charity work

---

This letter is to invite you to be on the gala committee which we are
forming to launch the Good Cause ball to be held at . . . (specify
venue) on (date).

We are honoured to announce that The President of/The
Chairman of/Dame Edith Somebody will be attending as our guest of
honour. Proceeds from the event will go to (name beneficiary) an
organization devoted to (briefly describe work).

The Good Cause ball will feature (mention attractions such as
music and entertainment, food and drink, any location of interest, a
tombola).

Members of the committee will not be required to attend
meetings or be involved in any administration. All we ask is that you
spread the word and help us sell the tickets.

I do hope you can be on the committee and will return the
enclosed reply card.

signed

When the writer is a friend of the recipient, it is a good idea to add to the
official letter, an encouraging postscript written by hand.

Memos and messages

The ideal office memorandum is short, to the point and civil in tone, even when
criticism is being expressed. If the contents are liable to cause the recipient
embarrassment or distress, the communication should be placed in a sealed
envelope and marked 'Confidential'.

In writing memos, as a rule it is safest to avoid humorous cracks, irony and flippant remarks, all of which might pass harmlessly in conversation. Experience suggests that when communicated in a written context they tend to be misconstrued. An office memo should be dated, and bear the full names of the sender and recipient. It should be signed by the sender, or 'PP'd by a person authorized to sign on behalf of the correspondent. A record should be kept of all distributed memos.

Business cards

The style of quiet restraint which characterizes visiting cards may become a good deal more assertive in a business card. Conventions change too, women now using them as much as men.

Mr. George E. Goring

The Goring Hotel,
Grosvenor Gardens,
London , S.W.1.
071-834 8211.
Telex 919166.
Fax: 071-834 4393

The Spa Hotel,
Tunbridge Wells,
Kent.
Tunbridge Wells 20331.
Telex 957188.
Fax: 0892 510575

The following information should be given: a full name, the person's designation within the company or an indication of their work, the name and address of the company or organization for whom the giver works or with which he or she is associated, and telephone and facsimile telephone numbers and telex numbers. Names are usually given without prefix, 'Anthony Crane' or 'Marsha Lane' but in cases where the subject is titled his style is given, 'Sir Peter Placement'.

Office parties

From their reputation, one might think that office parties were saturnalias at which wild revelry broke down accepted conventions. But often, they are quite staid affairs at which the majority try not to drink too much for fear of giving the boss a piece of their mind. Office bashes have their points, though, allowing young Turks to meet those in senior positions on informal ground, offering an opportunity for private words to be addressed to official ears and generally encouraging a more relaxed approach between employer and employee. Also hosts who arrange to hold an office beano in an interesting location gain good marks.

A courteous host should welcome all the guests at some stage, trying to find something appropriate to say to each person. Guests who are members of staff are expected to arrive in good time, dressed for the occasion, and to receive the host's greetings affably. It is polite to circulate, resisting the temptation to remain in a coterie of workmates. If there is dancing, guests abandon the pecking-order at work and dance with one and all.

Hazards of the jamboree are over-libidinous males who, in their cups, make fools of themselves by pressing unwelcome attentions on women. The man may be in a senior position in the firm and his fancied companion may work for him, which puts her in an embarrassing position if she wishes to give him the brush-off.

In this and many similar situations women can help themselves by moderating any signals that are liable to be misinterpreted. Overtly provocative forms of attire, for instance, could be swapped for a more businesslike image. A much-neglected precaution is for women to enlist the help of their own sex by keeping a sisterly eye on each other. If need be, an embarrassing moment could be interrupted with the feigned excuse of the arrival of a taxi, a call from a boyfriend or spouse, or even the claims of work. Another safeguard is for women to make prior arrangements to ensure that they are not seen leaving the party unaccompanied, which would obviate the offer of an unwanted lift home.

If a male does go too far, the question arises as to whether any mention should be made of the incident the next day. If there was nothing in it, many women generously take the view that least said soonest mended. But not everyone is that tolerant and some women will take the matter up officially.

Everyone is free to strike up contacts and initiate conversation. However, it is likely to be counter-productive if someone of junior status occupies the attention of a senior member of staff past the point of their interest. The first glance over the shoulder seems an appropriate moment to wind up the chat.

Spouses of either sex who are not members of staff tend to put in occasional appearances at the office do, characteristically looking as if they wish they were far removed from the scrum. A supportive other half can be influential on such an occasion, but by the same token can also snarl things up.

Going easy on the drink is a first rule and the second – often connected with the previous point – is to avoid uttering put-downs that could rebound to the discredit of the spouse. It goes without saying that whatever the private state of a marriage, this is an occasion for marital solidarity. However, few persons of spirit relish the role of appearing as a shadow of their spouse, and the art lies in a diplomatic compromise between seeming effusively flattering or assertively critical. If topics are sought for conversation with senior members, a show of loyalist enthusiasm for the company rarely goes amiss. Any mention of a piece of good news which puts the spouse or the company in a good light, is sound.

It is not usual to pen a thank you letter after an office party, but if the opportunity presents itself, it would be thoughtful to express thanks verbally and make some mention to the effect that the occasion was a success.

Send-offs

Leaving parties tend to be rather sad affairs, often associated with unwilling retirement. The main aim of the organizers is to avoid any impression that this is a wake. Often the person honoured would infinitely prefer to escape the formalities yet at the same time most recognize the importance of the gesture.

Two speeches by associates are usual, one by a senior member of the management or a supervisor and one by a personal ally. Axiomatic is that at least one speechmaker should have been closely connected with the work or contribution of the person being honoured.

Speeches should be lively, generous and not overlong. A successful joke is gold. What is said should at some point stress the positive advantages and opportunities for personal fulfilment that await in the new life. If the leaver is moving up the ladder, on the other hand, mention might be made by the speaker of his or her ability to spot talent and how gratifying it is to see a member of their team singled out for promotion.

Thank-yous

The guest of honour, as usual, is expected to reply to any speeches made in his or her honour. Often, leaving a longstanding post is a real wrench and saying goodbye to friends puts a tremendous emotional strain on the speaker. Those who give way to their feelings should take comfort from the fact that any genuine display of emotion, far from embarrassing an audience, gives the proceedings depth and meaning.

A *birthday card for the boss*

On account of a widely shared and generally healthy predisposition in favour of sending the boss up in such matters as birthday cards, it is worth mentioning that the jokes shouldn't go too far. What is permissible in a private missive takes on a very different complexion when the joke is open to public scrutiny, including the recipient's juniors.

Love and marriage on the firm

The office drinks party to celebrate a workmate's prospective wedding has become a fixture in the calendar of the work-place. The occasion is held, usually, because it is impractical for the betrothed to gather all their workmates around them at the nuptials.

Procedures are for a loyal ally to rally the troops, to distribute a memo-style invitation announcing the date, the time and the location of the party. A collection is made for a present, and a greetings card is produced for well-wishers to sign. Normally, the party takes place on the day of the final appearance of the betrothed preceding their departure for their wedding arrangements.

People forgather for a quick one either at work or at the local. A senior member of staff may propose a toast and hand the offering and card without further ado. The only etiquette is to ensure that all those with a claim to be invited to the party are on the list. Associates who are unable to attend the party should send apologies. The betrothed should thank everyone on the spot for their kind send-off, and write to thank for the present in the usual way. Friends of the betrothed who contribute to the office present might wish to produce a personal offering as well if they accept an invitation to the wedding.

On the matter of whether the boss should be invited to the wedding as a matter of courtesy, one guideline is to consider his or her approach. If it is thought that the gesture would be appreciated and numbers are being invited, it would be diplomatic to extend the invitation. No explanation is required for uninvited guests. But a situation to be avoided, here as elsewhere, and which has a special resonance among a circle of workmates, is excluding one or two people only from the group when the majority are invited to the feast.

Keeping it in the company

When a couple who work for the same organization propose to get married, it would be politic as well as polite to inform their bosses in good time. If both parties are employed in the same section or one works for the other, there are bound to be repercussions on the shop-floor. Some organizations have a policy which imposes restrictions on married couples working in the same division. In a small outfit one member may be asked to leave. Apart from the official view, the couple themselves may prefer to separate as working entities after marriage.

Present time

A code has grown up around the custom of the office present. Birthdays and anniversaries, weddings, maternity leave, promotion and retirement are some of the occasions which are commemorated with a present from well-wishers at work.

The tactful person who organizes the collection of cash from seniors and workmates keeps the amount given by individuals private. If a senior figure is the first to be asked to put his cash in the proffered collection envelope, a generous spirit produces an encouraging sum.

An unwritten rule is that those who decline to contribute are not invited to add their signature to the greetings card that accompanies the offering. It could also be argued that it would be cheeky for non-contributors to turn up at the accompanying drinks party – unless they are specially invited.

What are the grounds on which an associate can justifiably decline to drop a penny in the hat? If they have little regular contact with the person for whom the collection is being made, or if the member works in an area which rarely impinges on their own.

Amorous attentions at work

The working environment, be it office or factory, affords endless opportunities for romance and marriage which are taken happily, with only pleasant ripples at work resulting. However, the notion that all is fair in love or war has distinct limitations at the work-place. The option to reject advances may not apply as freely as it does outside the walls of work. Colleagues who are having an affair may lay themselves open to charges of favouritism, and it is highly likely that one party will lay their job on the line as well as an emotional commitment.

The following concerns itself with the more problematic aspects of romance at work, and ways in which these can be eased by a diplomatic approach.

Deflecting Cupid's wing

It is not unusual for someone who wishes to rebuff unwanted attentions to feel constrained about rejecting them. A woman may fear that her job could be jeopardized or her work discriminated against, or she may gain the reputation of being a prude, with a consequent loss of face.

Another complication is a difference of perception between the sexes. A woman may consider a man's actions to represent harassment, whereas the perpetrator might dismiss his indiscretions on the basis that they are no worse than anyone else's.

Making allowances for the fact that it is difficult to draw the line between acceptable flirtation and advances that cause offence, it is always discourteous to embarrass someone about their sex. To be regarded as an extension of your gender is demeaning to members of either sex.

In this controversial area, women have good cause to take objection to the innuendo that often passes for badinage or teasing. Sensitive subjects are the female attributes of a woman's body, her physical proportions, whether or not she is likely to be a good lover in bed. Remarks may be one thing, but unwelcome public displays of affection are quite another. Attempts to fondle, kiss intimately or grope coming from a person in whom the recipient has no interest can be not only unwelcome but upsetting.

Diplomatic tactics

Responding to unwanted attentions calls for a cool head and a reliance on good humour. Realists will make an attempt to avoid puncturing a man's vanity, particularly if he is the boss. Fortunately, most such situations can be defused through banter if wished. On the other hand, a dismissive glance can often convey more than words. If verbal explanations of rejection which let down the recipient gently are called for, these could include reference to the existence of someone else who mattered, or the point could be made that having an affair would complicate a rewarding friendship, or that companionship endures longer than a fling, or simply, that the recipient is not in the mood for sexual engagement.

If tact is to be an issue, the sought-after person should guard against inconsistency of response. Should a woman unwittingly have indicated that male attentions might be well received when this was in fact far from the case, it would be kinder to apologize when explaining the position. In circumstances in which women consider they have a case for genuine sexual harassment against a co-worker which they wish to pursue officially, it will probably be necessary to take the case to an Industrial tribunal. Advice can be obtained from the Equal Opportunities Commission, Overseas House, Quay Street, Manchester M3 3HN.

Women making the running

Women bosses are in just as much a position as men to favour the fortunes of those they employ. Affairs between female chiefs and male underlings require particularly tactful management, especially in a big company. In extreme cases women may run the risk of being accused of 'professional misconduct', and the lover may find himself regarded with some suspicion by his co-workers, as something close to an informer.

In either case, discretion remains the better part of the affair. The relationship may be public knowledge, but the wise stance for both parties is one of detachment within the workplace.

Etiquette's crossed wires

In a work context many men appear to feel the lack of guidelines on how to behave politely with women both as equals and as chiefs. The complicating factor here is the traditional precepts of etiquette, which are based on a protective attitude towards women, conflicting with a situation in which the so-called weaker sex are equals or have the whip-hand.

As a general rule, women do appreciate courteous gestures by the opposite sex. Door-opening is the case in point. Whereas it is clearly polite for a man to open the door to give precedence to his chief, whatever their gender, question marks may hover in the mind over whether the same applies to a female who is junior to him. Strict etiquette would decree that men open doors for women, period, but at the work-place hierarchy is likely to change the rules. If opening a door can be done without too obviously drawing attention to a woman, it would be polite to make the gesture. Amongst her peers, a woman chief would be given precedence. The situation to avoid is ushering in a junior female ahead of the chairman at an important meeting.

Age could be a qualification here. An older woman might be granted privileges denied to younger colleagues, irrespective of rank.

Travel stratagems for women

Many business and professional women who travel alone can be made to feel uncomfortable in the presence of men who mistakenly assume that they wish to be picked up. Fortunately, women who wish to protect their own privacy can take certain steps to discourage unwelcome attentions.

When staying in a hotel, for example, a woman's whole demeanour ought to indicate from the start that she is not interested. Avoidance of direct eye-contact is a classic guideline, but it should also be remembered that a quelling glance can speak volumes.

Women often choose to retreat into their own rooms if they suspect that trouble awaits in the public areas and will prefer room service to the restaurant. Safe this may be, but it is a gloomy solution, and a lonely journey may be made lonelier by such enforced isolation.

A counter-strategy may lie in making allies of the hotel staff – the receptionist, the barman and the head waiter. As far as dining in the hotel's restaurant is concerned, a woman can always ask for a quiet table, and enjoy the companionship of a gripping book.

The obvious cannot be stated too often: be vigilant about not giving away a room number; decline any proposal to meet in your room or his room as a location for business; try to keep busy in the public areas and avoid being seen waiting alone for extended periods in the foyer or reception rooms; decline offers of hospitality or help with suitcases from strangers. Should a fellow guest's attentions become a serious nuisance, the victim should make a formal complaint to the manager and ask for action and support.

Office politics

Depending on your luck, there is an up-side and a down-side to office politics. Some people are born survivors, others seem to rub people up the wrong way, a few are clear winners.

A common situation is one in which an employee suspects that she (or he) is the victim of personal animosity. Workmates should come to their own conclusions about the person's worth and not be swayed by authority's perhaps prejudiced view. The person who feels discriminated against should remain polite and try to avoid giving any formal grounds for complaint.

Employees who are out-manoeuvred in their ambitions should attempt to maintain their dignity in disappointment, difficult as this may be. Those who have won the day either in person or whose faction or supporter has been victorious are likely to keep the respect of the losers, despite all, if they show a speck of humanity.

It has to be admitted that office politics and good manners do not normally keep company, because the outcome of most tactics is that somebody gets hurt – indeed, that has to be. There are degrees, though, and some people manage to assume a stronger constituency and a manner which encourages the growth of loyalty among staff.

Blows and rebuffs

Being sacked or made redundant is one of life's blows. Authority charged with the task can make it easier or harder to bear through the manner in which the blow is delivered.

The moment calls for an expression of appreciation for any good work done in the past and any special praise that can be given which might help to salvage self-respect. If the employee's record has been satisfactory and the reason for the firing is due to circumstances outside their control, the point needs to be made very forcibly. An emphasis on the impact of a change of leadership or ownership will probably be a true explanation, and suggests factors other than personal failings as a cause.

Official announcements can put as good a face on the matter as possible. Employees can have decided to fulfil a lifetime's ambition by returning to New Zealand, or to take an open-ended sabbatical, or to make a change of career. If there is a background of acrimony and animosity to the firing, the less said in public the better as legal actions may follow.

People at the sharp end have to keep their wits about them and not be too winded by events to tackle questions of redundancy terms and severance pay, although considerate employers will come forward first with such information. Providing full details is sometimes the most constructive way of lessening the blow. The date on which the dismissed person is expected to leave should be established immediately and should be made clear by the employer.

Sadly, it is rarely sound practice to press for a reversal of the decision. Pleas are likely to fall on stony ground, and the defendant has his or her dignity imperilled as well.

People who have been sacked usually prefer to keep quiet about the matter, unless for some reason they wish to raise a rumpus. Fellow workers should restrain their curiosity, and wait to be told. It would certainly be intrusive to make inquiries about pay-off terms or reasons given.

Once the announcement is general knowledge, expressions of sympathy are very much in order. Those who consider that some monster has got his or her just deserts may not find their opinion is universally shared, and run the risk of disparagement by loyalists.

Considerate team-mates might offer a friendly drink of commiseration, or offer to help clear out a desk or an office if the task is imminent, or possibly recommend a good lawyer, if relevant. Wind of another suitable post would probably be music to the ears.

Responding to a raise

In the fortunate instance of being singled out for a rise in salary, the recipient should take the trouble to express his or her thanks and satisfaction. They might point out that it is extremely encouraging to have their abilities rewarded in this way, and thank their boss for giving them good chances. If the news is delivered in an interview it would be courteous to write a note afterwards.

Usually employees do not write to thank for an across-the-board percentage increase, but in a small company or in cases where the managing director works closely with his team, it would be pleasant to express thanks either verbally or in a written letter. In any event, it does not do to take rises in salary for granted.

Resignations

From the employee's standpoint, the option of resigning should always be slept upon. Usually, to resign a job means forgoing any compensation for which the employee would be eligible if they were dismissed.

A letter of resignation can be many things: it can air a grievance, indicate a genuine wish to move to different pastures or mean very little. In all cases, it should be written in the light of any contractual agreement that applies. A standard approach is to declare the fact of resignation from a named post, to express regrets and if feelings are cordial to wish the company well. It would be courteous for the writer to mention any positive aspects of their spell of employment.

In a sensitive situation and if resigning in conditions which you thought were unfair, it would be wise before putting pen to paper to consult a lawyer.

A need for confidentiality

When an individual is given a merit award of a one-off rise over an across-the-board increase, the information is best considered as confidential. The rise is more likely than not to arouse envy and resentment among members of staff. If the facts are leaked, good fortune should be played down in conversation, along the lines that you still won't be able to face your bank manager.

The aftermath

People who leave their employment should brief someone to forward any letters and indicate whether they want callers to be given a contact telephone number. Sometimes dismissals are implemented with unmannerly speed and desks are cleared within the hour.

It is in order for outsiders to ring for a contact address but not in order to press whoever takes the call for information on the background to the quitting. Similarly, associates who answer telephone calls for the former workmate should be tactful and mention that So-and-So has left the company or is no longer with the company, and that's that. They could also suggest that the caller writes in, having indicated that mail is being sent on.

The written & spoken word

The moment we speak or write a few lines reveals more of ourselves than we

may care to admit. Since the use of language is one of the chief yeardsticks by

which people evaluate others, it makes sense to try to be as much in command

of your personal communications system as possible.

The ability to communicate ideas whether in speech or writing is an enviable grace which enhances life all round. Someone with a way with words will always have an ace up their sleeve.

Those on a learning curve are the beneficiaries of a much more tolerant approach to anyone whose accent or pronunciation fails to conform to what was once thought 'proper', and similarly in the instance of scribblers whose efforts fall short of the copybook.

Letter writing

The main point is to write. Better a scribbled epistle on whatever paper comes to hand with whichever writing instrument is available than to deny the impulse. A letter, or card maybe, is a token and reminder of oneself, and is potentially for keeps.

Many are the occasions and situations for which only the written word will do, and goodbye to the telephone and answering machine. When someone wishes to express special thanks, convey condolences or congratulations, a letter is the best means because it suggests a willingness to go to some trouble.

Nor does the written word fade into the air, like a spoken utterance, and moreover is never intrusive – one may peruse it at leisure, read it in the bath, tuck it into a pocket. A letter is essentially a person-to-person communication, and all manner of confidences may safely be entrusted to its folds.

If sending a private letter to someone's office or official address, a possible way of ensuring the privacy of the contents is to mark the left-hand side of the envelope, 'Confidential' or 'Personal'. Even so, there is no guarantee that it will not be read by some nosy-parker.

Reluctant correspondents, to whom the art of letter-writing does not come naturally, will find their task easier if they work out what they want to say and how they wish to say it, before assailing the empty page. 'A letter,' said the author of one standard work on etiquette, Lady Troubridge, 'is simply a talk upon paper.' The remark cannot be improved on.

As the essence of a good letter is its personal tone, it runs counter to the spirit of letter-writing to suggest formulae, set phrases or set-piece examples. But what can be recommended is a general approach. News, gossip, private reminiscence, descriptions of people, places and events are the stuff of a well-written letter designed to keep the correspondent in touch. Likes and dislikes and passions and pets of one sort or another are natural topics. For instance, the British novelist P.G. Wodehouse, creator of the immortal butler, Jeeves, liked to entertain his correspondents with accounts of his adored canines into which much could be read. From one letter: 'Boo is a different dog now. Her bad temper has quite gone and she is all affection. I think the trouble at Snorky [his daughter]'s place was that the other dogs were not Pekes. Pekes really are a different race and class. They may try to be democratic, but they don't really accept other dogs as their social equals.'

Wodehouse quote from 'Yours, Plum' ed. Frances Donaldson, pub. Hutchinson, 1990. copyright The Estate of P.G. Wodehouse 1990.

All is grist to the imaginative letter-writer's mill. 'Forgive my using my computer to reply to you,' wrote one correspondent to the author, 'but I have become hopelessly addicted to its ease.' In the event of a letter not being handwritten, it would be a thoughtful gesture to write the opening 'Dear So and So' and the ending, whatever it may be, by hand.

All letters should be dated and signed by the correspondent. The business custom of 'pp-ing' a communication in which another signs in lieu of the writer, is only acceptable for impersonal messages.

P.S. written at the base of a letter stands for 'postscript' and contains the writer's afterthoughts. The use of P.S. is wholly acceptable in most private correspondence but is not to be recommended in official or formal correspondence. It is doubtful also whether a P.S. sits well in a letter of condolence, or any missive which should be particularly well considered.

Making a good impression

The impression a letter makes on the reader depends on presentation as well as on content. Spelling and grammar should be watched, obviously, but in most private correspondence a natural and personal flow of words is preferable to stilted correctitude. Faulty spellers though should regard a dictionary of the language as a close companion. Crossings-out are acceptable in most private correspondence providing that this is only an occasional blot on the copybook.

A letter that is pleasing to behold should be set out nicely on the page, with wide margins, and if the text is short, arranged so that the lines of writing occupy the middle space. Above all, legibility is the ultimate blessing and to this end sufficient space should be allowed between the lines of the letter. Ideally, the lines should be even.

Brevity may be the soul of wit, but the same principle does not apply to all private letters. Length may be a consideration of courtesy in certain circumstances, such as writing a thank you for a generous gesture or an expression of condolence to a close friend. The occasion calls for more than a few casual lines.

Sensitivities about typewriting a personal letter remain but there is a sound case in favour when the writer's own hand happens to be illegible, for one reason or another. It would be courteous to include a note of apology for a typewritten letter, especially if writing to a stranger or to someone whose good will was being sought.

The advent of the word processor at home has produced a fresh slant on apologies, usually concerned with the inadequacies of the writer's handwriting.

When a letter is typewritten and the writer wishes to lend it a more personal air, it is acceptable for him to top and tail it in his own hand, writing the opening 'Dear So and So' and signing off with a stroke or two of the pen. Letters received in this style can be replied to in like vein.

All signatures to letters and cards are in the writer's hand unless otherwise indicated.

A long letter

Opinion differs on the matter of whether to continue a letter on the reverse side of the sheet or to start a fresh page. If the quality of writing paper is good, it should be possible to write on the reverse side without causing any 'see through' problems on the face. A more luxurious style is to write on one side of the paper only, still formally correct.

The abbreviation P.T.O. (please turn over) should be inscribed below the letter, on the right hand side. Pages of a long letter should always be numbered.

It is worth taking some trouble to space a letter elegantly so that the continuation sheet doesn't appear to be an afterthought with only a sparse line or two devoted to it.

A hand-written letter requires an envelope addressed by hand. All private letters should always be placed in an envelope and sealed. Writing a name and address on the back flap of the envelope is usually confined to airmail and to correspondence sent abroad only. However, on the Continent and in the States, the practice is commonplace.

Beginnings and endings

The style in which one begins and ends a letter sets and seals the tone. Clearly, there are many shades between formality and intimacy which can be reflected in the wording of openings and signings off.

All private correspondence should be dated and signed (except third person replies to invitations). It is usual in personal letters to spell out the month and to write the date and the year in numerals. The numerical abbreviation, i.e. (to give an imaginary date) of 9/9/99, usually sits best in business correspondence. However, some enthusiasts like to use Latin numbers for dating letters as a manifestation of personal style.

One of the reasons why dating a letter or card is important is for purposes of acknowledgement, especially in semi-business correspondence.

Basic conventions are that communications beginning, 'Dear Sir' or 'Dear Madam' always end 'Yours faithfully'. Letters beginning with the person's prefix, 'Dear Mrs Marks' end 'Yours sincerely' or 'Yours truly', though the latter is rarely used. A proviso is that if the relationship with Mrs Marks is warm and friendly, the correspondent might choose to end 'With love'. 'Yours ever' is widely used as a compromise between the two.

The impersonal style i.e. 'Dear Sir' is appropriate for formal communications of all kinds, and in dealing with bureaucrats, business management and officialdom generally, or when there seems no named person responsible for a reply. However, it should be remembered that it is always sound practice to address your correspondent by name, if possible.

In all cases, paying attention to the correct spelling of names and use of initials is crucial as if there is one point about which everyone is aware it is the way their name is spelt. The style of the opening and ending can emphasize or modify the writer's approach.

A communication opening 'Dear Bob' suggests an informal ending such as 'Yours ever', 'Yours' or 'with love'. The use of 'Yours sincerely' would add a smidgin of distance: these are subtleties for the writer to use as he wishes according to his relationship with the correspondent. The writer of a letter beginning more formally, for example, 'Dear Colonel Bisley', might like to conclude on a warmer note than 'Yours sincerely' if friendship permitted, such as 'Yours ever' or 'Regards'.

When writing formally to a married woman, her marital prefix should be used: 'Dear Mrs Newman'. Similarly, young children writing to grown-ups may use prefixes without seeming over-formal – unless that is, he or she is on established first-name terms with the correspondent. The young writer may end 'with love' or 'love from'. The adult will reply 'Dear Jane' and end by sending love or writing 'Yours sincerely' depending on the state of play between writer and reader.

An old-fashioned and rather charming idea is for members of the family to end with a reference to their kinship ties: 'From your affectionate Aunt Maud' or 'With love from your Cousin Fred'.

Letters between family and close friends are often much more inventive and use pet names, nicknames and sobriquets for beginnings and produce all manner of improvised endings. Approaches differ here. Some prefer to address even their nearest and dearest rather coolly: 'Dear Sam', while others enjoy expressing their feelings in romantic terms: 'Dear Heart', 'Beloved', 'Dear One'. The endearments 'Darling', 'My darling' or 'Dearest', with or without a name, are favourites.

When writing to two people, they may both be addressed by name: 'Dear Mary and John'. Or alternatively the convenient device 'Dear Both of You' has a friendly ring to it.

The custom of addressing a person by both their Christian name and surname without a prefix or title: 'Dear Emma Carpenter', has crossed over from business to private correspondence. The style is intended as a compromise between the formality of a prefix and the intimacy implied by using a Christian name only. Few are likely to object, but it must be noted that pockets of resistance exist to all forms of presumed familiarity. A correspondent may need to consider the outside chance of their reader sharing the British novelist Nancy Mitford's distaste for the custom. 'This unspeakable usage', she commented, 'sometimes occurs in letters – Dear XX – which, in silence, are quickly torn up by me.'

It is usually safer to rely on formality when in doubt. Certainly, when the writer is unacquainted with their correspondent, or is writing to a person of the older generation, or to someone whose attitude towards senior rank is unknown, it is always appropriate to give them their title, rank or prefix.

Mitford quote from 'Noblesse Oblige' ed. Nancy Mitford, pub. OUP paperback, 1989, first pub. hardback Hamish Hamilton 1956.

Signing a name

It is up to the writer to decide on the style of their signature. Whether to sign with a Christian name only, or with both Christian name and surname, or to use an initial and surname, largely depends on the nature of the communication and the degree of intimacy expressed by the letter. A guideline is that letters addressed to an adult by their first name only are signed likewise, and letters beginning with the person's prefix or title, are signed with a Christian name, or initial, and surname.

In typewritten correspondence it has become the custom to put the writer's name beneath the signature, for the sake of clarity as much as for anything else.

Saying thank-you

A letter of thanks should convey the spirit of gratitude. It is reassuring for the giver to hear that his or her offering has been well received and why. In the case of a present, it is always a good idea to mention specifically what it is, and to refer to ways in which it will be enjoyed or used or treasured. A good reason should be produced for the excellent choice for which the giver is being complimented and thanked. If the present is dismally unsuccessful, white lies are called for and mention may be made of the kind thought that lay behind the gesture.

When money has been given there is a good case for ignoring the usual embargo of not mentioning the price of a present, and referring to the sum. It might put the donor's mind at rest to know that the money had arrived safely. Giving an idea of how the money will be spent would be appreciated.

Full marks to all those who manage not to begin their communication with the predictable phrase 'Thank you for' which tends to dull the reader's mind through repetition.

With apologies

The tone of a letter of apology should be attuned to its subject. For example, saying sorry for some relatively minor misdemeanour such as delaying the return of a borrowed jacket requires a different and lighter touch from an apology for what seems an unforgivable breach of good manners.

General grounds for apologies are lateness, forgetfulness, causing inconvenience, damage, or stirring things generally. Causing hurt or unhappiness or embarrassment are also occasions that call for apologies.

General guidelines to the form of a letter of apology: give the reasons for writing, express regret and offer to make amends (if appropriate). It is usually unwise to grovel as there is little to be gained from self-abasement. More honourable is to try to find words of genuine contrition – itself a form of penance.

A point worth making in this connection is that sending flowers accompanied by a handwritten letter or card does show concern and may help to win over the person who is sinned against.

The stuff of writing

The diversity of approach towards style in general is neatly reflected in writing materials. Classic taste favours white, cream, pale grey, pale blue and azure as acceptable shades for writing paper. Headings are conventionally discreet and brief, with little or no decoration or embellishment. Into this chaste order, however, modern design has brought bright colour, decorative typography, the bold use of the writer's own name as a heading and all manner of illustrations and graphics.

On the side of tradition are appropriateness, clarity and general acceptance. Innovation sends different messages and to be effective above all needs to be well done. Good writing paper is a pleasure to write upon and to handle, and has held its own in environment-conscious times as recycled papers improve in finish. Characteristics of quality in paper are a watermark – a faint imprint of the maker's name or sign which is visible when a piece of paper is held against the light – and also a heavier than everyday weight. The sheets are unlined – lined paper suggests

13 ST. GEORGE STREET,
HANOVER SQUARE,
LONDON W1R 9DE.
071-629 7301

a notebook – and come singly. The address, printed or engraved, is centred at the top of the page or set to the right. Die-stamped lettering produces a smart relief to the heading but flat printing is perfectly acceptable (and far less expensive).

Initials or monograms, die-stamped or flat-printed, are a way of adding a personal touch. Families entitled to a coat of arms or a crest sometimes head their writing paper with the device or reproduce it on the flap of the envelope. An attractive notion, and a long-standing favourite of owners of pretty houses, is to portray their abode in a specially commissioned little drawing or woodcut reproduced as a heading above the address.

Small, sticky labels printed with the sender's name and address no doubt fulfil a number of functions efficiently and inexpensively. But they have a utility air which does little to enhance the appearance of a letter or convey a personal touch.

The colour of the letter-head should complement the ground shade of the paper. Traditional combinations are black or red on white or cream, dark blue on pale blue, blue on white. Continuation sheets are plain.

Headings printed or engraved with the name of the writer were at one time considered in poor taste when used in personal correspondence. Fine for business, went the thinking, but a shade self-promotional for private matters. The reservation has lost ground along with the clear-cut separation between business and personal affairs in many people's lives. The increase in the number of freelancers working from home has led to the need for writing materials which will serve both purposes. Thus the name, 'Drusilla Beyfus' may be set above the address without a prefix.

Freelancers have found it useful to have two kinds of stationery both of which may be used for private correspondence: one with name and address, one with address only, without a name, for purely social correspondence.

A useful dual-purpose device is to have a letter-head die-stamp made with the name standing by itself on the top line and the address on the following lines: the name can thus be easily blocked out in printing when not required on the writing paper.

Whereas the general tendency nowadays is to supply more information which may give the recipient access to their correspondent's telephone numbers, country numbers, facsimile machine numbers, and so forth, there is a counter movement by those who wish to protect their privacy. No one is obliged to reveal more information than they choose in their announcements. Although few members of the general public wish to withhold their telephone number, it may be prophetic that it has become customary for public figures to omit this information from their official writing paper.

It is also worth mentioning here that attitudes towards typewritten or word-processed private letters are considerably more relaxed than was once the case. However, although much correspondence of a more impersonal nature is typewritten without a qualm in the interests of convenience, clarity and copies, a letter written by hand is always the more courteous option for letters that aspire to please.

Wrapping up a letter

Envelopes should be matched in style and design with the paper they contain. An envelope ought to be of a size to fit the writing paper without the need to resort to origami-like folding methods. A sheet should not require to be folded more than once, or twice at the most. The name and address should be legible, it goes without saying, and centred on the face of the envelope. As with a letter, the effect should not be cramped and wide margins should be allowed if the length of the wording permits.

Envelope etiquette

Few people are likely to take umbrage at being incorrectly styled on an envelope, but getting the facts of a person's name and title right is a fundamental courtesy. It is a simple means of showing respect.

The rule is to style people formally on envelopes. Usually, prefixes are given, and in the case of someone of title or rank, the formal style applies. A summary of modes of address in general usage, with guidelines on the use of letters after names, is given following page 314.

A man may be described as 'Mister' So and So with his initial or first name, as in Mr John Langley. However, addressing a man on an envelope may raise the question of whether to style him 'Esquire' as in John Langley, Esq. (no prefix is required). The style is applicable only to those, in the judgment of the writer, who are accustomed to being styled thus. A sensitive point here concerns social class since the style of 'Esquire' signifies the status of a gentleman whereas 'Mister' is democratic and makes no distinctions. In cases of uncertainty, it is probably best to write 'Esq.' as it is unlikely to give offence and may be read as a compliment.

A single woman is given the prefix 'Miss', followed by a surname or an initial and surname, or, as is more generally observed, a Christian name and surname. The use of the prefix and a surname only denotes that she is the senior unmarried daughter.

The style 'Ms' which creates a single undifferentiated prefix that applies to both married and single women is now widely used in business. So far, however, it has made few inroads into private correspondence.

Two single women addressed jointly are styled, 'The Misses', followed by their forenames and surname: 'The Misses Zoe and Sonia Farnsworth'.

A married woman should be given her marital status, with her husband's initial or forename and her married name: 'Mrs Jack Hanley' or 'Mrs J. Hanley'.

On the question of how to address a married woman who is known by a professional name other than her marital nomenclature, the general rule in private correspondence is to write to her in her married name. However, women increasingly prefer to be known by their own identity on all occasions. Either way, it would be unlikely to give offence if the professional name was used in place of a marital status.

A widow retains her married style, with her usual prefix, her husband's initial or forename, and surname. It is incorrect to use her own Christian name or initials, unless she has let it be known that she so wishes as this style applies to divorcees.

A divorced woman is styled by the married prefix, her own Christian name or initials, and married name; 'Mrs Deanne Farnsworth'. Not every woman is happy with this description, however, and some divorcees elect to revert to their maiden name or to a professional or business name if such applies. It is worth mentioning here that a married woman who is living apart from her spouse is styled: 'Mrs William Bird', until the knot is legally untied.

Those who for one reason or another do not want to reveal their marital status, tend to drop prefixes altogether, as in 'Juliet Snow'.

A married couple may be styled 'Mr and Mrs Farnsworth (denoting they are senior Farnsworths), or as 'Mr and Mrs G. Farnsworth' or 'Mr and Mrs Gerald Farnsworth'.

A married couple and their young children may be addressed, 'Mr and Mrs Gerald Farnsworth and Zoe and Sonia Farnsworth' or the children can be formally addressed as shown above. A young boy who might once have been addressed as 'Master Francis Farnsworth', is nowadays more likely to be plain 'Francis Farnsworth' until he is old enough to be addressed by his adult style.

Writing to a couple who are not married – or not married to each other – presents a familiar dilemma. The pair may be addressed informally: 'Tom Carter and Ann Parry', or only one name given on the envelope. The Americans have a neat device which is to use each person's prefix and to write one name above the other, thereby distancing the individuals as a couple yet acknowledging their togetherness.

Invitations

An invitation card, whatever its style, formal or informal, should convey the following information: the names of the host(s) and guest(s), the date of the occasion, the address at which the occasion will take place, the time at which guests are expected and a mention of lunch or dinner if appropriate. It should also include the initials 'RSVP' (répondez s'il vous plaît, please reply) with an address to which guests can write in reply, if different from the party location – a telephone number is usually given too.

For dinner and dancing or a major reception, guests may be asked to reply to The Secretary at a given address; replies should be in the third person.

Many details regarding invitations are a question of personal preference and individual situations, but certain forms have become standard.

Classic cards

An 'at Home' card is useful both as an invitation and reminder. It serves for all manner of occasions from drinks parties to dances, from dinner parties to

The Chairman and Directors of
Bentley, Mitchell & Company Limited
request the pleasure of the company of

_____

at their Annual Exhibition of Fine Silverware,
on Thursday, 28th February, at 10 a.m.
at 352, New Bond Street, London, W.1.

R.S.V.P to the Secretary,　　　　　　　　*Luncheon*
Bentley, Mitchell & Co. Ltd.　　　　　　　　*1.30 p.m.*
352, New Bond Street, London, W.1.

Her Britannic Majesty's Ambassador
and Lady Alexander
request the pleasure of the company of

_____

_____

on_____ at_____ o'clock.

British Embassy.　　　　　　　　*R.S.V.P.*

anniversary celebrations. In classic black lettering on a white oblong card, it can be printed or engraved with the host's name and address and telephone number, or be most filled in by hand.

The name of the guest is handwritten on the top left-hand corner, and the name of the host is shown above the words 'at Home'. Other details are filled in by hand in the designated spaces.

An alternative style gives the name of the host who 'requests the pleasure of your company', or a similar version allows the name of the guest to be written by hand in the space occupied by the word 'your' in the printed wording.

When several people combine to give a party, each name is given on the invitation, usually with the senior host's name first.

For special occasions, the wording on the invitation that would otherwise be filled in by hand can be printed or engraved – except for the name of the guest, which must always be handwritten. These cards are often larger than the standard 'at Home' version and usually signal a big party or grand reception.

Some hosts like to add a line about the nature of the occasion, e.g. 'For Caroline and Charlie'. If the party is for drinks, the word is usually spelt out or 'Cocktails' mentioned above the time at which guests are expected to arrive. Naturally, the exact wording depends on the nature of the occasion but a standard

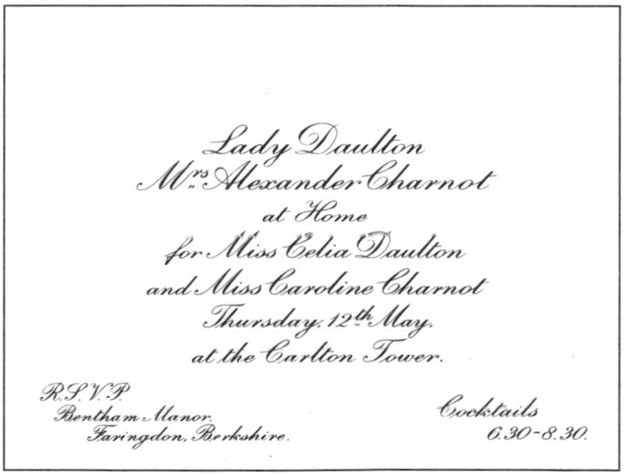

Lady Daulton
Mrs Alexander Charnot
at Home
for Miss Celia Daulton
and Miss Caroline Charnot
Thursday, 12th May
at the Carlton Tower.

R.S.V.P.   *Cocktails*
Bentham Manor,   *6.30 – 8.30.*
Faringdon, Berkshire.

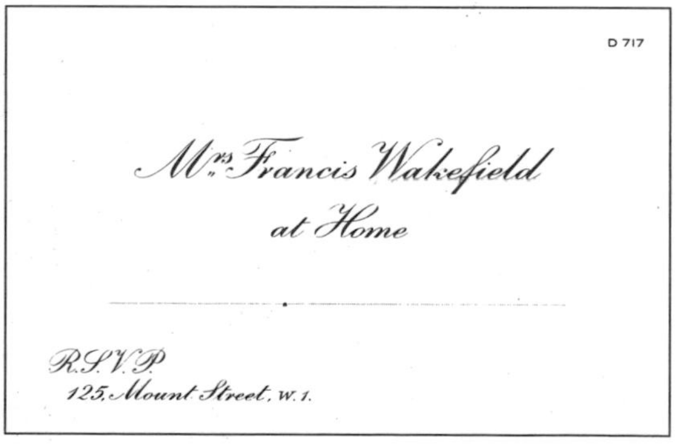

D 717

Mrs Francis Wakefield
at Home

R.S.V.P.
125 Mount Street, W.1.

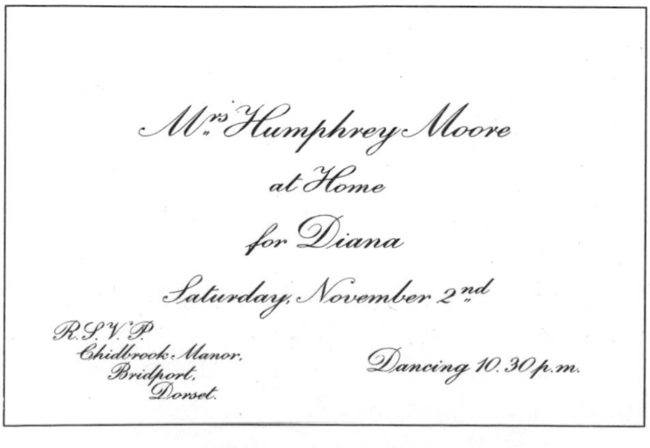

Mrs Humphrey Moore
at Home
for Diana
Saturday, November 2nd

R.S.V.P.
Chidbrook Manor,   *Dancing 10.30 p.m.*
Bridport,
Dorset.

formula for a drinks party is, 'Mr and Mrs Michael Payne request the pleasure of your company at Merrylees Golf Club, Tintbury, on (date)'. Some canny hosts of drinks parties include a cut-off hour, e.g. 6.30 – 8.30 pm which offers a hint to latecomers and lingerers. Timing for a dinner party may be specified as '8 for 8.30 pm' which gives guests just over half an hour's latitude for a polite arrival time.

When guests have been invited on the telephone, an 'at Home' can be sent with the RSVP crossed out and the words 'To remind' written above the initials.

Dinner party hosts at this level usually give their guests some indication of the degree of dress expected. 'Black tie' may be written below right beneath the o'clock, or similarly, the word 'Informal' added signifying that the men are not expected to put on dinner jackets.

An 'at Home' card can correctly be used for parties given at addresses other than the party-giver's own – at a club, or at hired or loaned premises.

Addressing guests on invitations

Practice differs on whether to address guests by their Christian names and surnames only on the invitation, or whether to use their prefixes as well. The tendency is to use the formality of prefixes on the occasion of a big wedding or a formal reception but this rule is by no means without exceptions. People of title, however, are usually addressed by their social style on invitations.

A deciding factor on the use of general prefixes might be the wording of the invitation itself. If this is jolly or colloquial the use of Christian names would be quite appropriate. Whether to use a formal style or not also depends on the nature of the occasion and the preference of the hostess. When inviting someone who is not well known to you, or who might be a traditionalist in these matters, formality is the wisest course.

Below is a brief summary of styles of address for guests on invitations. Please note that information on addressing guests with a title or who hold rank, is given following page 314.

Note: on the specific question of whether to use a Christian name alone this is acceptable for friends, intimates, children and family.

Men guests are invited as 'Mr Darby', 'Mr Nigel Darby' or as 'Nigel Darby': the first style denotes he is the senior Darby in the family.

Single women guests are invited as 'Miss Darby' or 'Miss Naomi Darby', or 'Naomi Darby', or 'Naomi', depending on the writer's wishes and the guest's standing with the host.

Married couples are invited as 'Mr and Mrs Robinson' or 'Mr and Mrs Ian Robinson', or Christian names alone.

The convention by which envelopes containing invitations to man and wife are addressed to the wife alone holds good on formal and official occasions. But many party-givers feel that the moment has passed for such discriminatory etiquette, and it is now quite acceptable to write to both.

Married couples and their children are invited on a single card as 'Mr and Mrs Robinson and Vanessa and David'. If step-children are invited, it might be circumspect to use Christian names only in order to avoid numerous surnames. A better idea is to send a separate card to the offspring in question under their own name. *Note:* the wording 'and family' may follow the parents' names which is undoubtedly a useful short cut for the host, but begs the question of whether the unspecified family members are fairly done by. Children in particular do appreciate being named on a card. Invitations to a young boy are addressed to 'Jason Fox' or 'Jason' without a prefix.

A married woman on her own is invited as 'Mrs Ian Robinson'.

Sisters living at the same address are invited as 'The Misses Shulman' or 'The Misses Alexandra and Nicola Shulman', or by Christian names alone.

Male and female siblings living at the same address are invited as 'Mr Nigel Darby and Miss Naomi Darby', or as 'Nigel and Naomi'.

When inviting someone to bring a friend, the wording 'and guest' or 'and partner' may follow the principal guest's name. The friendlier 'and friend' does not make it clear that the invitation is extended to a member of the opposite sex.

Real life is not as neat and tidy as etiquette requires. Inviting two people who are not married to each other but who are acknowledged as a couple may be best approached by dropping prefixes and using Christian names only or this with surnames. If formality is to be observed, prefixes and full names may be written one above the other. The same rules would apply when inviting couples of the same sex.

When a marital couple are to be invited to a semi-business do and the female half is professionally known by a name other than her married one, it is usual to use her business nomenclature, i.e. 'Simon Pritchard and Susan Cooper'.

Supplements to invitations

When a big party or reception is planned, hosts may find it convenient to include supplementary correspondence along with the main invitation. A small pre-printed card may ask, 'Do you want to be included in a dinner party/house party?'. When the invitation involves dinner and dancing, guests may be asked whether or not they are able to accept dinner.

Travel directions, with copies of route maps, may accompany an invitation to a party to be held in the country, or for a weekend visit, for example.

When a pre-printed reply card is enclosed this should always be used even when the guest has accepted verbally, likewise any pre-printed envelope provided for replies.

The demands of organizing a big party have led many hosts to include the line 'Please bring this card with you' at the foot of the invitation. It is pertinent to remark that the hostess who added to her supplementary card asking if the guest was able to accept for dinner, the note 'If we do not hear from you by (date) we shall assume you cannot come', received very prompt replies!

Visiting cards

Small as they are, visiting cards have generated their own strict code of correctitude. This is observed when the cards are used for private purposes but a whole new approach governs other uses.

Visiting cards acquired their name in the days when they were handed in at a house to show that the bearer had visited in person. Whereas few women in this country nowadays use visiting cards for social purposes, the custom is general in the United States. However, these cards of identity are found to be universally useful by the many freelance professionals of either sex at work. They record a name and address, and perhaps a company logo, and reverse the old etiquette of omitting a telephone number, which still prevails in men's visiting cards (see below). Contemporary versions are designed to enable the recipient to contact the bearer and therefore may state all telephone numbers: at home, in the country, a car or mobile telephone, and facsimile telephone (fax) number.

In this uncharted area of manners the question may arise as to whether it is impolite to hand a quasi-business card to a friend for private purposes. Any adverse reaction would probably be forestalled if the bearer said something to the effect that she was sorry, but all she had was a business card.

Men's visiting cards are by custom smaller than women's. There are three sizes to choose from: 3×1¼ inches; 3×1½ inches; and 3×2 inches which is also considered correct for women to use.

Mrs Eileen Loudon,

916, Sloane Street,
London, S.W.

Mr George F. Martyn,

Grey Towers,
Ascot.

I called on you today and was so sorry
to find you not at home

The Revd. Michael Brown
Godalming 21057   Godalming Vicarage

The card should be of very good quality, in white, cream or pale grey and always die-stamped copperplate lettering. The colour of the lettering ink allows scope for personal taste, dark red on cream or Oxford blue on white being possibilities, although black on a white ground is the classic choice.

The name of the bearer with his prefix: 'Mr Henry F. Martyn' is set plumb centre and the bearer's address, but no telephone number, appears in the bottom left-hand corner. The name of a man's club may be mentioned, at the foot, in the right-hand corner.

The slightly mysterious emptiness of the card is part of tradition.

These strictures surrounding visiting cards may sound old-fashioned, but they are time-honoured, and those who abide by these rules will be quick to notice any departure from them.

Card versus letter

Letter-writing may be in decline but the habit of sending cards has a growing number of subscribers. These may be plain, coloured, illustrated, handwritten or with printed wordings, but they are alike in being highly convenient. They can dispense with the need for an envelope and are handy to prop up for display and reminder. A card provides a small window on which to write anything from the fewest words to a mini-letter. Cards announce parties of all kinds, send greetings, congratulations, convey commiseration, condolence and apologies as well as announcing a change of address.

Reservations about cards

It is doubtful whether a card should be regarded as a substitute for a letter in certain circumstances. On occasions when a special thank-you has to be expressed, or profound apologies conveyed, or any communication of import has to be written, the use of a card might appear over-casual, or at least suggest haste. In addition, the size of a card offers little scope for an outpouring of news or emotion.

Another aspect to be borne in mind is that the usual reserve about perusing other people's private correspondence is often suspended in the case of an open card. For this reason, there is a tendency to omit confidences and intimate endearments from postcards in general.

Greetings cards

Printed greetings cards are a pleasant means of keeping in touch. In the case of separated friends and family they are a token of the living presence of the sender as well as an expression of good wishes.

The great card-sending occasions are the religious festivals of Christmas, and to a lesser extent Eastertide, as well as New Year which is celebrated by non-Christians and those of no religious persuasion alike. Birthdays, wedding

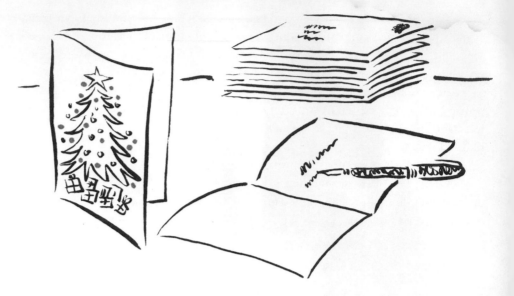

anniversaries, the announcement of an engagement to marry, the arrival of a baby, a *bar mitzvah*, good luck occasions, housewarming, are just a few of the milestones for which cards with appropriate printed wording may be sent.

In addition to congratulatory cards, there are cards of commiseration and apology. 'Get well' cards with cheerful illustrations have perked up many a sick person.

A few conventions apply. All cards should be personally signed by the correspondent and placed in an envelope and sealed. It is courteous for the card to be dedicated to the recipient and for his or her name to be written by the sender too: i.e. 'Isobel, with love', or 'To Aunt Chrissie with love from us all at Little Orchard', or words to that effect. Sometimes, for clarity's sake, people who are signing with their Christian names only and whose appellations belong to many, may take the precaution of adding their surname in brackets, 'with love from Ann (Brown)'.

If a name is printed inside the card, as with Christmas cards, for example, it is usual to cross it out with a stroke of the pen as the name will appear in the signature. When a husband and wife are sending cards, usually one person signs on behalf of both: 'From Stella and Bembo', though there is nothing against each writing their own name. It is always especially thoughtful when addressing a card to a child, to remember to write their name on it.

Ready-printed expressions of congratulation, condolence or apologies are undoubtedly convenient, but taking the trouble to write a personal PS adds to the sentiment of the communication.

Design and wording are a matter of individual preference though an interesting/unusual choice usually wins admirers. Size and proportion too are questions of personal taste – it is worth noting that well-chosen small cards can more than hold their own among the big numbers.

The idea of sending a card which has some special association with the sender can take many different forms. Members of a club, or a guild, or an association send a representative card. Supporters proffer charity cards. Or senders might reproduce the work of an artist whom they admire. Creative sparks such as graphic designers and photographers take the opportunity to produce some of their own work.

It has become customary for managements to send seasonable greetings to their customers at home as part of public relations; few people would raise objections to this practice, but it should not be confused with a personal gesture.

One point worth noting is that card-sending often becomes something of a ritual. For example, a decision to cease sending a seasonal or anniversary communication to someone who may be far away, and who is expecting the tradition to be kept up, may be a cause of concern or upset.

Condolence cards

Undoubtedly, ready-printed 'With sympathy' cards provide a welcome relief to those faced with writing a difficult letter of commiseration. They also indicate the sender's concern. What these missives fail to do, however, is to convey the correspondent's personal feelings which gives the gesture much of its meaning.

The formal phrase mentioned above together with even the fewest lines penned by the sender may well be preferable to the impersonality of a mawkish verse. If a printed wording is decided upon, the thoughts expressed do matter.

Correspondence cards

Postcards, plain on one side and printed with a name, address and telephone number on the reverse, are an all-purpose aid. The heading is printed or engraved in a single line across the top, or set centred at the top, with the name above the address. Sometimes an address and telephone number only are given, as in headed writing paper. Some correspondents use their prefixes or titles in the heading, others prefer to dispense with formality and appear as 'Mary-Anne McClean' whether married, single or titled. Married couples often share a card under both names, 'Andrew and Shuna Taylor'. Sometimes the word 'From' precedes the printed name. These cards, written by hand, are used for dropping a line, as bearers of invitations and replies to invitations, for ordering goods and confirming orders, for the small-change of personal admin., as an enclosure with a cheque, and so on.

When an addressee is named on the plain side, there is no need to repeat it on the reverse side, as in the usual beginning to a letter. Similarly, many correspondents rightly take the view that if the recipient is named on the envelope this dispenses with the obligation to use formal opening.

These cards may be used as postcards or with envelopes. An invitation or any private communication merits a sealed envelope.

Picture postcards

Choosing a picture postcard likely to appeal to the recipient has become increasingly popular, and mantelpieces, shelves and dressing-table tops have become more interesting as a result.

Images of places visited, reproductions of paintings, shots by well-known photographers, film stills, photographs of museum treasures, cartoons and caricatures, each edited for the reader's eye, suggest a common bond of taste and, if on target, are especially cherished.

Change of address cards

If only a few people need to be informed of a change of address, a telephone call or a letter or card written by hand is a practical way of spreading the word. However, householders with a wider circle of friends and acquaintances may find a printed card is more convenient.

Wordings vary according to taste and so does the use of prefixes. Some examples are set out below: each one is printed below the heading 'Change of address', with the wording set out in short lines. The name and address of the addressee are written on the front – envelopes are not usually required.

Patrick and Louisa Cadmore will be at 32 Newbury Road, Uxley, Cambridge, Cambs CB1 2EF (telephone number given), from 1 December (year given).

As from (day/month/year) *Zenga and Baz Sylvester* will live at Flat B, Courtways House, Desborough Square, East Wall, London E14 8GL (telephone number given).

or more formally and without a date

Mr and Mrs Kenneth Norman

The Old House	and still at
Turley	12 Addison Mews
Nr Leicester,	London, W11 9BE
B90 9QL	(telephone number
(telephone number given)	given)

Replying to letters and cards

It is courteous to reply to a letter promptly, and if delay is unavoidable, to apologize. This is a general rule.

Hopefully, a letter of reply is exactly that, and manages to answer any specific points raised by the correspondent. In delicate situations or when the reply is likely to be carefully scrutinized, it is as well to keep a copy of the letter – a point which applies to all important correspondence.

On the question of whether it is acceptable to deliver a letter by hand, by all means do so. It is polite to write 'By hand' on the top right-hand corner of the envelope. The only reservation might be that householders tend to watch out for the postman and may be less vigilant about picking up mail dropped unexpectedly through the letter-box.

First-class postage stamps should be used when a reply is urgent, but replies to invitations sent out weeks ahead, or communications about which there is no hurry, can be sent second class without implications of parsimony.

It is not usual to reply to greetings cards except in special cases. Nevertheless there is a feeling that when someone bothers to send you a Christmas card, for instance, it shows a lack of consideration not to reciprocate.

Off limits

People who read other people's confidential mail without seeking their permission first are asking for trouble. It is considered highly dishonourable, and worse if you are caught in the act. This is a general principle that applies to all private letters. However, recipients should show some commonsense in the matter and put away from prying eyes any letters that are confidential.

Conversation and talk

An unaffected, natural way of talking is a passport to most places and people. Artificiality on the other hand tends to get poor ratings. Verbal forms of communication have many stops to play; a tone of voice and a manner of speaking can modify or hammer home what was actually said.

The manner of the word

Good manners in talk need not be synonymous with blandness but avoids drawing blood. The guidelines are timeless: deliberately giving offence is unacceptable; conversationalists should pay attention to the other speakers, and the latter should be allowed a fair say; when someone is talking to a person directly, eye-contact is courteous.

Topics famously known as being danger areas in polite society of yesterday, are now staples of everyday chat. Sex, politics and religion, about which public discussion in mixed company used to be considered bad form, have joined money and one's personal state of health as legitimate subjects for conversation – always bearing in mind the provisos above.

Being able to put people at their ease has a special value in a country where so many of us tend to be shy or reserved. If people are given a chance to find their tongues, they may blossom unexpectedly. It is easier to identify the approach that chills than to pinpoint the touch that melts reserve. Indicating a liking for the person to whom you are talking is one way, showing an interest in their views, their plans, their jokes. Certainly paying compliments rarely goes amiss and is a neglected art. But to be effective these need to alight on a perceptive slant such as nursing a cherished hope, rather than relying on formula phrases which have been worn thin through repetition.

The ideal compliment is like a shot in the arm, flatters without being fawning, and is as valued in friendship as in love.

One promising line is to praise personal accomplishments, where such exist, as this suggests an attractively multi-faceted person. Thus, the lawyer may be complimented on his or her collection of modern art; the businessman or woman on their prowess at cooking; the fashion designer on his/her game of tennis; the bank manager on his singing in the choir; the doctor on his success at gardening.

Talkers and listeners

Good talkers respond to an appreciative audience; like accomplished cooks, they get their rewards from pleasing others. Some people harbour a fund of entertaining anecdotes but they need a run at them, so to speak, in order to secure the listener's ear. Few story tellers will welcome an interruption at a critical moment in their tale. Particular resentment may be reserved for anyone who chips in with 'Hello' or 'Goodbye' as the punchline is about to be delivered.

At the same time as respecting the intentions of a talker, conversation is rarely at its most enjoyable as a monologue. Listening is certainly an important aspect of conversation, but sooner or later, people who have been paying attention want a share of the air-time.

A bore

Awareness of bores and a corresponding dread of being considered boring is a very English sensitivity, born of an old country that has heard it all before, perhaps. Nevertheless, tedious talkers may have to be dealt with in a manner which won't give offence. Bores in general do not realize they are being boring but may quickly take umbrage if handled undiplomatically. A change of conversational tack can always be introduced in acceptable manner by the trapped listener as an escape route. If this fails, fresh blood could be brought in, to take the conversation in a new direction. Good humour moves mountains. One may remind the speaker that last time he enacted his party-piece he had promised to give it up for Lent. If there is someone present of whom the nuisance is especially fond, their remonstrance should be sought.

Whereas boredom may be in the mind of the listener, certain approaches have become the hallmark of the conversational bore. Those who sustain a monologue about their own doings, or who extol the achievements of their offspring or who ride hobby horses relentlessly, have in common insensitivity to the feelings of others.

Talking shop on the other hand is gripping to members of the shop but much of the gossip may be lost on the uninitiated. It is considerate to try to enlighten the odd ones out who might otherwise feel excluded. In such a gathering outside the workplace, some conscious check has to be made on the duration of the topic.

Judging the point at which your own conversation begins to pall is a difficult art, and those who miscalculate are in good company. Routine signs are a glazed or wandering eye or a conspicuous glance at a wrist watch, but a protracted absence of any reciprocal comment is a sure indication that the topic has been driven into the ground.

A word about a display of boredom. All writers on etiquette have agreed that appearing to be bored is a Bad Habit. Emily Post, author of the standard work on American manners first published in the early Twenties says: 'it is impossible, almost, to meet anyone who has not *something* of interest to tell you if you are but clever enough yourself to find out what it is.' The comment has worn well.

Putting a foot wrong

Tactlessness often wounds more deeply than considered abuse and is a classic loser of goodwill. It is the sheer thoughtlessness of untactful remarks that raises hackles more than what may be said. Blunders of this order may uncover old wounds and expose private sensitivities. Commonplace examples of tactlessness are personal remarks which cause offence, criticism or ridicule of others, breaking confidences, untimely reminders of past misdemeanours.

Still, many of us commit these errors, perhaps unwittingly, and what can be done to make amends? Apologizing for the gaffe in public may make matters worse though expressing regret in private may be appropriate. The perpetrator can backtrack and try to put a better complexion on his remark by blaming his clumsy way of putting things. He can of course claim that he didn't mean it like that, and swiftly seek to reinterpret his meaning in a more favourable light.

Making a faux pas is embarrassment enough but drawing attention to the clangers of others, or of making the speaker aware of what they have said, is equally discourteous. It is considerate to try and help out anyone who has put their foot in it through ignorance by diverting the conversation swiftly, or indicating a good reason in extenuation of the speaker's gaffe suggesting that they were not to know the cause of the offence.

Loose talk

Verbal communication in some circles would come to a standstill if Erasmus's dictum were followed: 'It is safe to admit nothing that might embarrass one if repeated.' Such an act of self-denial would extinguish gossip – as its finest hour, a minor British art form.

Careless gossipers are obliged to watch out however, since idle speculation is rarely preoccupied with how wonderful people are, how virtuous, kindly, successful and faithful to their partners, there is the omnipresent danger that the tale may rebound to the discredit of the teller.

An allied risk is that someone may be within earshot who is a confidante of the subject, and whose loyalty will be affronted by the implications and innuendos. They may, in addition, feel bound to reveal the source of the story to the person concerned. A rule is that gossipers must expect to be gossiped about.

No handicap to good talk

Good manners in conversation with those with disabilities are simply good manners. However, showing special considerations never goes amiss as in the following few suggestions.

People who are deaf or hard of hearing almost invariably find life more pleasant if background noise can be kept under control. Noisy music, the television turned on loud, companions talking to them all at once, may reproduce the Tower of Babel.

Commonsense is to try to enunciate clearly, both for the sake of clarity and for the benefit of lip-readers. In the case of persons who are blind or who have seriously impaired eyesight, it is worth mentioning that making introductions is a priority at a gathering. As with everybody else, only more so, knowing who is who helps to keep the lines of communication open.

A small point which perhaps only applies in an intimate gathering is that the unsighted have many paths of discovery. If a new family acquisition is being discussed, for instance such as a new hat, or a plaything, or a gadget or an art object, it is thoughtful to ask the visitor who is blind if they would like to be shown it. Holding a possession in the hand may speak volumes.

Expressions of class

People in this country are prone to decoding their friends and acquaintances in terms of the way they speak. This most obviously applies to accent, but also in a more subtle way to the use of certain idioms, words and terms. Class distinctions have given this pastime a lasting edge in some circles. However, as the whole system of class distinctions is fast breaking down, so the finer points of whether one refers to 'spectacles' or to 'glasses' seem rather irrelevant.

The picture isn't that simple, though, being complicated by the fact that it is extremely unfashionable to admit to these lingering linguistic snobberies.

Pronunciation

Accents are a sensitive topic in this country, but much of the old snobbery has died. The essence of verbal communication is clear diction, and today few people are disparaged on grounds of their accent though they may be for acknowledged mispronunciations. Regional burrs and lilts are considered a positive asset, both personally and professionally, in many quarters. Even cockney has come into its own, in the media at any rate, though I doubt whether Cinderella would have won her Prince had she fled down the steps of the Palace bawling 'Oim orf'.

Introductions

In general, clarity is at the base of conventions attached to making verbal introductions and referring to people. The general etiquette is strightforward: a man is introducted to a woman: the junior person between those of the same sex is introduced to the senior member. If a person introduces himself he says as much, adding his christian name and surname without a prefix. As a race we are not particularly adroit at the art of introductions and tend to hope that the parties know one another already and require no formalities. In the quite usual situation in which a name escapes the recollection of the introducer, one device is to announce the name that springs readily to mind, and to turn to the other person expectantly as if to give them a chance to name themselves.

On occasions when someone forgets your name, it is polite to jump in with a seamless self-identification, making no reference to the lapse.

Introducing the family

When introducing members of the family to new acquaintances, it is usual to mention any kinship ties. For example, May I introduce my husband, Mark'; 'This is my wife, Kirsty'; I would like you to meet my son-in-law, Geoffrey'; . . . 'Jack, this is my daughter, Sarah'. The use of prefixes depends on the occasion, and the people concerned on both sides. Some dislike the current mode of instant familiarity and would appreciate being introduced formally, with their prefix. This might well apply in any case when the person making the introductions is considerably junior in years or rank to the person who is being introduced.

Modes of address

It is always sound practice to try to get someone's name right and by the same

token it is courteous to be correct when referring to a person's title or rank.

Although it is not always easy to establish a clear path through what even

leading authorities describe as a 'Hampton Court maze' of precedent and

convention, it is always acceptable to ask for information from the VIP's

family or aide. Personal preference often plays a part.

The following is a basic guide to modes of address with reference to members of the British Royal family, the peerage, the church, and appointments by which people are known. Readers seeking more detailed information should consult specialist publications such as *Debrett's*, usually available at public libraries.

Personage	Social manner of address	Employee manner of address	Introductions/ presentation	On envelopes	Beginning of a formal letter	Formal ending
THE ROYAL FAMILY						
Her Majesty, The Queen (see section on the royal family)	Your Majesty or Ma'am (pronounced Mam), or when referring to her, The Queen	Your Majesty or Ma'am	Say only the name of the person introduced: 'May I present . . ., Your Majesty?'	Her Majesty, The Queen*	Madam, With my humble duty,	I have the honour to remain, Madam, Your Majesty's loyal subject
His Royal Highness, Prince Philip, The Duke of Edinburgh	Your Royal Highness or Sir, or when referring to him, Prince Philip or The Duke of Edinburgh	Your Royal Highness or Sir	Say only the name of the person introduced: 'May I present . . ., Your Royal Highness?'	His Royal Highness, Prince Philip, The Duke of Edinburgh	Sir	I have the honour to remain, Sir, Your Royal Highness's loyal servant
Her Majesty, Queen Elizabeth, The Queen Mother	Your Majesty or Ma'am, or when referring to her, The Queen Mother	Your Majesty or Ma'am	As for The Queen	Her Majesty, Queen Elizabeth, The Queen Mother	As for The Queen	As for The Queen

*Correspondence intended for members of the royal family (except from friends) is usually addressed in this manner: The Private Secretary to Her Majesty The Queen . . . His Royal Highness, The Prince of Wales . . . Her Royal Highness, The Princess of Wales. The letter begins 'Dear Sir' and ends 'Yours faithfully'. It is usual to refer in the first instance to 'Her Majesty' or to 'His/Her Royal Highness' and thereafter to The Queen or Prince Charles or Princess Diana. Replies to communications from a royal household should be addressed to the signatory or the office named.

Personage	Social manner of address	Employee manner of address	Introductions/ presentation	On envelopes	Beginning of a formal letter	Formal ending
His Royal Highness, The Prince Charles, Prince of Wales	Your Royal Highness or Sir, or when referring to him, Prince Charles or The Prince of Wales	Your Royal Highness or Sir	Say only the name of the person introduced: 'May I present . . ., Your Royal Highness?'	His Royal Highness, The Prince Charles, Prince of Wales	Sir	I have the honour to remain, Sir, Your Royal Highness's loyal servant
Her Royal Highness, The Princess of Wales	Your Royal Highness or Ma'am, or when referring to her, The Princess of Wales	Your Royal Highness or Ma'am	As above	Her Royal Highness, The Princess of Wales	Madam	I have the honour to remain, Madam, Your Royal Highness's loyal servant
Her Royal Highness, The Princess Royal	Your Royal Highness or Ma'am, or when referring to her, The Princess Royal	Your Royal Highness or Ma'am	As above	Her Royal Highness, The Princess Royal	Madam	I have the honour to remain, Madam, Your Royal Highness's loyal servant
Her Royal Highness, The Princess Margaret, Countess of Snowdon	Your Royal Highness or Ma'am, or when referring to her, Princess Margaret	Your Royal Highness or Ma'am	As above	Her Royal Highness, The Princess Margaret, Countess of Snowdon	Madam	I have the honour to remain, Madam, Your Royal Highness's loyal servant
Her Royal Highness, Princess Alexandra, the Hon. Mrs Angus Ogilvy	Your Royal Highness or Ma'am, or when referring to her, Princess Alexandra	Your Royal Highness or Ma'am	As above	Her Royal Highness, Princess Alexandra, the Hon. Mrs Angus Ogilvy	Madam	As above

Personage	Social manner of address	Employee manner of address	Introductions/ presentation	On envelopes	Beginning of a formal letter	Formal ending
A Royal Duke	Your Royal Highness or Sir, or when referring to him, The Duke of York	Your Royal Highness or Sir	His Royal Highness, The Duke of York	His Royal Highness, The Duke of York	Sir	I have the honour to remain Sir, Your Royal Highness's loyal servant
A Royal Duchess	Your Royal Highness or Ma'am, or when referring to her, The Duchess of York	Your Royal Highness or Ma'am	Say only the name of the person introduced: 'May I present . . ., Your Royal Highness?'	Her Royal Highness, The Duchess of York	Madam	I have the honour to remain, Madam, Your Royal Highness's loyal servant
A Royal Prince	Your Royal Highness or Sir, or when referring to him, Prince Edward	Your Royal Highness or Sir	As above	His Royal Highness, The Prince Edward	Sir	I have the honour to remain, Sir, Your Royal Highness's loyal servant

Personage	Social manner of address	Employee manner of address	Introductions social formal	On envelopes	Formal beginnings and ending of a letter	Social beginning and ending
			THE PEERAGE			
Duke	Duke, or when referring to him, The Duke of . . .	Your Grace	The Duke of . . . The Duke of . . .	The Duke of . . . or His Grace, The Duke of . . .	My Lord Duke or Dear Duke of . . . Yours faithfully	Dear Duke Yours sincerely
Duchess	Duchess, or when referring to her, The Duchess of . . . or The Duchess	Your Grace	The Duchess of . . .	Her Grace The Duchess of . . . or The Duchess of . . .	Madam or Dear Madam Yours faithfully	Dear Duchess or Dear Duchess of . . . Yours sincerely

Personage	Social manner of address	Employee manner of address	Introductions social formal	On envelopes	Formal beginnings and ending of a letter	Social beginning and ending
Dowager Duchess	Duchess, or when referring to her, The Dowager Duchess or Mary Duchess of . . .	Your Grace	The Duchess of . . . or Her Grace, Mary, Duchess of . . .	Her Grace the Dowager Duchess of . . . or Her Grace Mary, Duchess of . . . or Mary, Duchess of . . .	Madam or Dear Madam Yours faithfully	Dear Duchess or Dear Duchess of . . . Yours sincerely
Divorced Duchess	Duchess, and similarly when referring to her or as, Joan, Duchess of . . .	Your Grace	The Duchess of . . . or Joan, Duchess of . . .	Joan, Duchess of . . .	As above	As above
Younger son of Duke or Marquess (the above's children do not hold an 'Hon.')	Lord John or Lord John Smith, and similarly when referring to him	My Lord or Your Lordship	Lord John Smith, Lord and Lady John Smith	Lord John Smith, Lord and Lady John Smith	My Lord or Sir Yours faithfully	Dear Lord John or Dear Lord John Smith Yours sincerely
Wife of younger son of Duke or Marquess	Lady John or Lady John Smith, and similarly when referring to her	My Lady or Your Ladyship	Lady John Smith	Lady John Smith	Madam or Dear Madam	Dear Lady John or Dear Lady John Smith Yours sincerely
Daughter of Duke, Marquess or Earl	Lady Jane or Lady Jane White, and similarly when referring to her	My Lady or Your Ladyship	Lady Jane White (if she marries a commoner) Mr William and Lady Jane Brett	Lady Jane White (if she marries a commoner) Lady Jane Brett, Mr William and Lady Jane Brett	Madam or Dear Madam or Dear Lady Jane White (or as for her married name) Yours faithfully	Dear Lady Jane or Dear Lady Jane White (or as for her married name) Yours sincerely

Personage	Social manner of address	Employee manner of address	Introductions social formal	On envelopes	Formal beginnings and ending of a letter	Social beginning and ending
Marquess	Lord Wessex, and similarly when referring to him	My Lord or Your Lordship	Lord Wessex The Marquess of Wessex	The Marquess of Wessex, The Marquess and Marchioness of Wessex	My Lord Yours faithfully	Dear Lord Wessex Yours sincerely
Marchioness	Lady Wessex, and similarly when referring to her	My Lady or Your Ladyship	Lady Wessex The Marchioness of Wessex	The Marchioness of Wessex	Madam or Dear Madam or Dear Lady Wessex Yours faithfully	Dear Lady Wessex Yours sincerely
Dowager Marchioness	Lady Wessex, or when referring to her, Lady Wessex or Mary, Lady Wessex or The Dowager Lady Wessex	My Lady or Your Ladyship	Lady Wessex Mary, the Marchioness of Wessex	The Dowager Marchioness of Wessex or Mary, Marchioness of Wessex	As above Yours faithfully	As above Yours sincerely
Divorced Marchioness	Lady Wessex, or when referring to her, Lady Wessex or Mary, Lady Wessex	My Lady or Your Ladyship	Lady Wessex Mary, Marchioness of Wessex	Mary, Marchioness of Wessex	Madam or Dear Madam or Dear Lady Wessex Yours faithfully	Dear Lady Wessex Yours sincerely
Earl	Lord Silchester, and similarly when referring to him	My Lord or Your Lordship	Lord Silchester Lord and Lady Silchester	The Earl of Silchester The Earl and Countess of Silchester	My Lord Yours faithfully	Dear Lord Silchester Yours sincerely
Countess	Lady Silchester, and similarly when referring to her	My Lady or Your Ladyship	Lady Silchester The Countess of Silchester	The Countess of Silchester	Madam or Dear Madam or Dear Lady Silchester Yours faithfully	Dear Lady Silchester Yours sincerely

Personage	Social manner of address	Employee manner of address	Introductions social formal	On envelopes	Formal beginnings and ending of a letter	Social beginning and ending
Dowager Countess	Lady Silchester, and when referring to her, Lady Silchester or Elizabeth, Lady Silchester	My Lady or Your Ladyship	Lady Silchester Elizabeth, Countess of Silchester	The Dowager Countess of Silchester or Elizabeth, Countess of Silchester	As above Yours faithfully	As above Yours sincerely
Divorced Countess	Lady Silchester, or when referring to her, Lady Silchester	My Lady or Your Ladyship	Lady Silchester Elizabeth, Countess of Silchester	Elizabeth, Countess of Silchester	Madam or Dear Madam or Dear Lady Silchester Yours faithfully	Dear Lady Silchester Yours sincerely
Viscount	Lord Broughton, and similarly when referring to him	My Lord or Your Lordship	Lord Broughton Lord and Lady Broughton	The Viscount Broughton The Viscount and Viscountess Broughton	My Lord Yours faithfully	Dear Lord Broughton Yours sincerely
Viscountess	Lady Broughton, and similarly when referring to her	My Lady or Your Ladyship	Lady Broughton	The Viscountess Broughton	Dear Madam or Dear Lady Broughton Yours faithfully	Dear Lady Broughton Yours sincerely
Divorced Viscountess	Lady Broughton, or when referring to her, Lady Broughton	My Lady or Your Ladyship	Lady Broughton Eleanor, Viscountess Broughton	Eleanor, Viscountess Broughton	Madam or Dear Madam or Dear Lady Broughton Yours faithfully	Dear Lady Broughton Yours sincerely
Dowager Viscountess	Lady Broughton or when referring to her, Lady Broughton or Helen, Lady Broughton	As above	Lady Broughton	The Dowager Viscountess Broughton or Helen, Viscountess Broughton	As above Yours faithfully	As above Yours sincerely

Personage	Social manner of address	Employee manner of address	Introductions social formal	On envelopes	Formal beginnings and ending of a letter	Social beginning and ending
Son of Viscount or Baron (The Hon.)	Mr Jenkins, and similarly when referring to him	Sir or Mr Jenkins	Mr Jenkins Mr and Mrs Jenkins	The Hon. Michael Jenkins The Hon. Michael and Mrs Jenkins The Hon. Mrs Michael Jenkins	Sir or Dear Sir Yours faithfully	Dear Mr Jenkins Yours sincerely
Daughter of Viscount or Baron (The Hon.)	Miss Jenkins or Melissa Jenkins and similarly when referring to her	Madam or Miss Jenkins	Miss Melissa Jenkins or Miss Jenkins	The Hon. Melissa Jenkins The Hon. Mrs Page Edward Page, and The Hon. Mrs Page	Madam or Dear Madam or Dear Miss Jenkins (or by married name) Yours faithfully	Dear Miss Jenkins (or by married name) Yours sincerely
Younger son of an Earl (The Hon.)	Mr Evans or Mr Thomas Evans, and similarly when referring to him	Sir or Mr Evans	Mr Thomas Evans Mr and Mrs Thomas Evans	The Hon. Thomas Evans (if he marries a commoner) The Hon. Thomas and Mrs Evans The Hon. Mrs Thomas Evans	Sir or Dear Sir Yours faithfully	Dear Mr Evans Yours sincerely
Baron (life peers and peeresses rank with hereditary barons and baronesses)	Lord Wigram, and similarly when referring to him	My Lord or Your Lordship	Lord Wigram Lord and Lady Wigram	The Lord Wigram The Lord and Lady Wigram	My Lord Yours faithfully	Dear Lord Wigram Yours sincerely
Wife of Baron	Lady Wigram	My Lady or Your Ladyship	Lady Wigram	The Lady Wigram	Dear Madam or Dear Lady Wigram Yours faithfully	Dear Lady Wigram Yours sincerely

Personage	Social manner of address	Employee manner of address	Introductions social formal	On envelopes	Formal beginnings and ending of a letter	Social beginning and ending
Baronet	Sir Peter, or when referring to him, Sir Peter or Sir Peter Green	Sir	Sir Peter Green Sir Peter and Lady Green	Sir Peter Green Bt	Sir or Dear Sir Yours faithfully	Dear Sir Peter or Dear Sir Peter Green Yours sincerely
Knight	Sir James, or when referring to him, Sir James or Sir James Wilkie	Sir	Sir James Wilkie	Sir James Wilkie, K.C.B. (use initials to show of which Order he is a Knight)	Sir or Dear Sir Yours faithfully	Dear Sir James or Dear Sir James Wilkie Yours sincerely
Wife of Baronet or Knight	Lady Green, and similarly when referring to her	My Lady or Your Ladyship	Lady Green	Lady Green	Madam or Dear Madam Yours faithfully	Dear Lady Green Yours sincerely
Widows of Baronet or Knight	Lady Green, or when referring to her, Lady Green or The Dowager Lady Green or Patricia, Lady Green	As above	Lady Green	The Dowager Lady Green or Patricia, Lady Green	As above	As above
Divorced wife of Baronet or Knight	Lady Green, or when referring to her, Lady Green or Mary, Lady Green	As above	As above	Mary, Lady Green	As above	As above

*It is a matter of personal preference as to whether the holder of a D.B.E. wishes to be known according to her Order i.e. as Dame Joan Brown, or by her usual style, as Mrs John Brown or Miss Brown.

Personage	Social manner of address	Employee manner of address	Introductions social formal	On envelopes	Formal beginnings and ending of a letter	Social beginning and ending
Dame*	Dame Joan or Dame Joan Brown as for her married style and similarly when referring to her	Madam or Dame Joan Brown or as for her married style	Dame Joan or Dame Joan Brown or as for her married style	(Formal) Dame Joan Brown (give the initials of her Order after her name) (social) Dame Joan Brown or as for her married style	Madam or Dear Madam Yours faithfully	Dear Dame Joan or Dear Dame Joan Brown or as for her married style Yours sincerely

THE CHURCH OF ENGLAND

Archbishop of Canterbury (or York)	Archbishop, or when referring to him, the Archbishop of . . .	Your Grace	The Archbishop of Canterbury (or York)	The Most Rev. and Rt. Hon. the Lord Archbishop of Canterbury (or York)	Dear Archbishop Yours sincerely	Dear Archbishop Yours sincerely
Bishop of London	Bishop, or when referring to him, the Bishop of London	Bishop or My Lord	The Bishop of London	The Rt. Rev. and Rt. Hon. the Lord Bishop of London	Dear Bishop Yours sincerely	See Formal
Bishop (diocesan and suffragan)	Bishop, or when referring to him, the Bishop or the Bishop of Whichester	As above	The Bishop of Whichester	The Rt. Rev. the Lord Bishop of Whichester or The Rt. Rev. the Bishop of Whichester	Dear Bishop Yours sincerely	See Formal

Personage	Social manner of address	Employee manner of address	Introductions social formal	On envelopes	Formal beginning and ending of a letter	Social beginning and ending
Dean	Dean, or when referring to him, the Dean	See Social manner of address	The Dean of Gloucester and Mrs Evans	The Very Rev. the Dean of Gloucester	Dear Dean Yours sincerely	See Formal
Archdeacon	Archdeacon, or when referring to him, the Archdeacon, or the Archdeacon of . . .	See Social manner of address	The Archdeacon of . . . and Mrs Frost	The Ven. the Archdeacon of . . .	Dear Archdeacon Yours sincerely	See Formal
Canon	Canon or Canon Collins	See Social manner of address	Canon Collins Canon Collins and Mrs Collins	The Rev. Canon David Collins	Dear Canon or Dear Canon Collins Yours sincerely	See Formal
Vicar or Rector	Mr Miles or Father Miles, and similarly when referring to him	See Social manner of address	Mr Miles Mr and Mrs Miles Father Miles	The Rev. Andrew Miles	Dear Mr Miles or Dear Father Miles Yours sincerely	See Formal

Note: as a general rule, a retired member of the Anglican clergy is known by his former style and surname, as 'Dean Brownley' or 'Vicar'. As he no longer holds his former appointment, his style changes in correspondence and in formal descriptions. For example, a retired bishop is addressed on envelopes as 'The Right Reverend (or Rev.) A. M. Brown; a retired Archdeacon is addressed as 'The Reverend (or The Rev.) B. S. White.' Readers seeking particular information should refer to *Debrett's Correct Form* or *Crockford's Clerical Directory*, both available at public libraries, or consult the member concerned.

Personage	Social manner of address	Employee manner of address	Introductions social formal	On envelopes	Formal beginnings and ending of a letter	Social beginning and ending
THE ROMAN CATHOLIC CHURCH						
His Holiness The Pope	Your Holiness or Most Holy Father	Your Holiness	His Holiness or The Pope	His Holiness The Pope	Your Holiness or Holy Father (for R.C.'s) I have the honour to be, Your Holiness's most devoted and obedient child (for non-R.C.'s see right)	See Formal
Cardinal	Cardinal or Cardinal Reilly, or when referring to him, the Cardinal or Cardinal Reilly or formally as His Eminence	Your Eminence	Cardinal Reilly His Eminence, Cardinal Reilly	(If an Archbishop) His Eminence the Cardinal Archbishop of Westminster (if not an Archbishop) His Eminence Cardinal Reilly	Your Eminence or My Lord Cardinal I remain, Your Eminence, Yours faithfully. note: R.C.'s use a more formal style	Dear Cardinal Reilly Yours sincerely
Archbishop	Archbishop, and when referring to him, the Archbishop or Archbishop of . . .	Your Grace	Archbishop followed by surname The Archbishop of . . .	His Grace the Archbishop of . . .	My Lord Archbishop I remain, Your Grace, Yours faithfully see above	Dear Archbishop Yours sincerely

Personage	Social manner of address	Employee manner of address	Introductions social formal	On envelopes	Formal beginnings and ending of a letter	Social beginnings and ending
Bishop	Bishop, and similarly when referring to him or Bishop Edwards	My Lord or My Lord Bishop	Bishop Edwards or the Bishop of . . .	The Right Rev. Douglas Edwards, Bishop of . . . or formally, His Lordship the Bishop of . . .	My Lord or My Lord Bishop I remain, My Lord, Yours faithfully, Yours faithfully	Dear Bishop or Dear Bishop Edwards Yours sincerely
Monsignor	Monsignor Kelly, and similarly when referring to him	Monsignor Kelly	Monsignor Kelly	The Rev. Monsignor Seamus Kelly or The Rev. Monsignor	Reverend Sir Yours faithfully	Dear Monsignor or Dear Monsignor Kelly Yours sincerely
Priest	Father O'Brien, and similarly when referring to him	Father or Father O'Brien	Father O'Brien	The Rev. John O'Brien	Dear Reverend Father Yours faithfully	Dear Father O'Brien Yours sincerely

THE JEWISH FAITH

Personage	Social manner of address	Employee manner of address	Introductions social formal	On envelopes	Formal beginnings and ending of a letter	Social beginnings and ending
The Chief Rabbi	Chief Rabbi, or when referring to him, the Chief Rabbi	See Social manner of address	The Chief Rabbi	The Chief Rabbi, Dr Jonathan Sacks	Dear Chief Rabbi or Dear Sir Yours faithfully	Dear Chief Rabbi Yours sincerely
Rabbi	Rabbi Weiss or Dr Weiss, and similarly when referring to him	See Social manner of address	Rabbi Weiss or Dr Weiss	Rabbi Weiss or Dr Peter Weiss	Dear Sir Yours faithfully	Dear Rabbi Weiss or Dear Dr Weiss Yours sincerely
Minister	Mr Carr or Dr Carr and similarly when referring to him	See Social manner of address	Mr Carr or Dr Carr	The Rev. Peter Carr or The Rev. Dr Peter Carr	Dear Sir Yours faithfully	Dear Mr Carr or Dear Dr Carr Yours sincerely

Personage	Social manner of address	Employee manner of address	Introductions social formal	On envelopes	Formal beginnings and ending of a letter	Social beginning and ending
GOVERNMENT AND PARLIAMENT						
The Prime Minister	By appointment or by name and similarly when referring to him or her	Sir or Madam or by appointment	By appointment or, less formally, by name	(Official) The Prime Minister (personal) The Rt. Hon. (first name and surname) PC, MP*	Dear Sir or Dear Madam Yours faithfully	Dear Prime Minister or as for his or her private rank Yours sincerely
Cabinet Minister*	By appointment, i.e., 'Home Secretary' or as 'Minister' or for private rank and similarly when referring to him or her	Sir or Madam	By appointment or less formally as for private rank	(Official) By appointment, i.e. The Home Secretary (social) as above. Note: 'The Rt. Hon.' replaces a woman's usual prefix.	As above	Dear (as for appointment), i.e. Home Secretary, or as for private rank, i.e. Dear Mr/Mrs . . . Yours sincerely
Member of Parliament	Mrs Angela Brown or Tom Brown and similarly when referring to him or her	Sir or Madam or Mr/Mrs Brown	Mrs Angela Brown or Tom Brown	Tom Brown, Esq., MP Tom Brown, MP or Mrs Angela Brown, MP	As above	Dear Mr Brown or Dear Tom Brown Dear Mrs Brown or Dear Angela Brown Yours sincerely

*The information applies to the Prime Minister and to all ministers in and out of the Cabinet. All Cabinet ministers in the UK are members of the Privy Council for which the letters PC (shown on envelopes) stand. A government minister may be addressed and referred to as 'Minister' without giving his/her full appointment.

Personage	Social manner of address	Employee manner of address	Introductions social formal	On envelopes	Formal beginnings and ending of a letter	Social beginnings and ending
LOCAL GOVERNMENT						
Mayor (when a Mayor is a woman she is addressed as Mr Mayor)	Mr Mayor	Sir or Madam	Mr Mayor or the Mayor of Castlebridge	The Right Worshipful the Mayor of Castlebridge	Mayor Yours faithfully	Dear Mr Mayor Yours sincerely
Mayoress (wife or official consort of Mayor)	Mayoress, and when referring to her, the Mayoress or the Mayoress of . . .	Madam or Mayoress	The Mayoress or the Mayoress of . . .	The Mayoress of Castlebridge	Madam Mayoress Yours faithfully	Dear Mayoress Yours sincerely
THE LAW						
Lord Justice of the Court of Appeal	Lord Justice, and when referring to him, the Lord Justice or Lord Justice Wright	My Lord or Your Lordship	The Lord Justice or Lord Justice Wright (on the bench) His Lordship	The Rt. Hon. Lord Justice Wright, PC	My Lord Yours faithfully	Dear Lord Justice Yours sincerely
Judge of the High Court (customarily a Knight)	Mr Justice White or Sir Peter White, or when referring to him, Mr Justice White or Sir Peter	(In private) Sir (in Court) My Lord or Your Lordship	Mr Justice White or Sir Peter White	The Hon. Mr Justice White or Sir Peter White	My Lord or Dear Sir Yours faithfully	Dear Sir Peter or Dear Sir Peter White Yours sincerely
Woman Judge of the High Court (customarily holds a D.B.E.)	Mrs Justice Flynn or Dame Mary or Dame Mary Flynn, and similarly when referring to her	(In private) Madam (in Court) My Lady or Your Ladyship	Mrs Justice Flynn or Dame Mary Flynn	The Hon. Mrs Justice Flynn or Dame Mary Flynn	Madam or Dear Madam Yours faithfully	Dear Dame Mary Yours sincerely

Personage	Social manner of address	Employee manner of address	Introductions social formal	On envelopes	Formal beginnings and ending of a letter	Social beginning and ending
Circuit Court Judge	Judge or as for private rank, and similarly when referring to him or her	(In private) Madam or Sir (in court) Your Honour	Judge Enright or as for private rank	His (or Her) Honour Judge Enright, QC (if the letters apply)	Sir or Madam Dear Sir or Madam Yours faithfully	Dear Judge or as for private rank Yours sincerely
JP and Magistrate	As for his or her private rank, and similarly when referring to him or her	(In private) Madam or Sir (in Court) Your Worship when referring to him or her, His or Her Worship	As for private rank	As for his or her private rank with the letters JP after the name, e.g. Thomas Jones Esq., JP or Mrs Thomas Jones, JP Mr and Mrs Thomas Jones (drop the JP)	As above Yours faithfully	As for his or her private rank Yours sincerely

THE FOREIGN OFFICE

Personage	Social manner of address	Employee manner of address	Introductions social formal	On envelopes	Formal beginnings and ending of a letter	Social beginning and ending
Ambassador (style applies to both sexes)*	Ambassador and similarly when referring to him or her. Formally, as His (Her) Excellency	Your Excellency	Ambassador or formally, His (Her) Excellency the (name of country) Ambassador	His (Her) Excellency, The Ambassador of Ruritania, or HE The Ruritanian Ambassador	Your Excellency I have the honour to be Your Excellency's obedient servant	My dear Ambassador Yours sincerely

*Wives of Ambassadors may be addressed, introduced and referred to as 'Ambassadress'. It is incorrect to refer to a woman who is appointed as an Ambassador as 'Ambassadress'. The husband of an Ambassador does not share his spouse's official title.

Medical practitioner

A distinction is made between the style of a physician (a surgeon or consultant) and a general practitioner (a G.P.). The former is described and addressed in correspondence by their usual style, for example as 'Mister' So and So or 'Mrs' Such and Such. A G.P. is known as and addressed in correspondence as 'Doctor' So and Such. When writing to a physician, the letters standing for his or her highest qualification should be shown after their name, for example, 'Mr (Miss) Bruce (Brenda) McKenzie, FRCS (standing for Fellow, Royal College of Surgeons). The physician's letters are usually given in the local telephone directory listings, or patients can check at their G.P.'s or at the specialist's.

Professor

In speaking to him or her, and similarly when introducing him or referring to her: Professor Gainsforth. Envelopes are addressed to Professor (first name or initial) Gainsforth followed by letters standing for their university qualifications (only the highest degrees are mentioned). In private correspondence, these letters may be omitted.

School head

Practice varies widely within the school system in both the private and maintained sectors. Much depends on the particular name of the office in the school and on the head's own approach. In general, school principals are addressed and referred to by their usual prefixes, Mr Bloxton or Mrs Gray. They may be referred to as 'the headmaster' or 'headmistress', accordingly. Envelopes are addressed using their usual style, followed by the letters standing for their university degrees, with the title of their appointment, i.e. 'Headmaster' written beneath the name. The letter opens 'Dear Mr Bloxton (or their usual style)' or 'Dear Mrs Gray (or her usual style)'.

Wrong lady

A commonplace misunderstanding is to describe Lady So-and-So as 'Lady Rachel So-and-So' and to address 'Lady Rachel' as 'Lady So-and-So'. Women who are entitled to the style 'Lady' before their Christian name are daughters of Dukes, Marquesses and Earls.

A variant of this has been brought about by the media who in an attempt to establish the identity of Lady Sockett, better known to the general public as Sally Sockett, style her grandly as Lady Sally Sockett. In the interests of clarity, perhaps brackets could be used, thus Lady (Sally) Sockett. But purists will say that it is not correct, nor is it.

Letters after a name

The chief difficulty in addressing a correspondent with letters after their name is to know whether to use or drop the letters, or which to put. Letters are abbreviations of distinguished orders, honours, decorations, gongs of one kind or another and professional qualification, e.g. Captain Stanley Harlow, D.S.C. (Distinguished Service Cross), R.N. (Royal Navy); Sir Robert Jones, K.C.B. (Knight Commander of the Order of the British Empire), C.B.E. (Commander of the Order of the British Empire), M.C. (Military Cross); Dame Rose Ashworth, D.B.E. (Dame of the British Empire); Professor Martin Patel, D.M. (Doctor of Medicine), FRCP (Fellow, Royal College of Physicians).

A general rule for correspondents is to include only the letters standing for the highest order or degrees. These are likely to be shown in the listings in *Who's Who*, available in public libraries. Debrett's book *Correct Form* gives general instructions to both writers and senders. The latter they advise to include at the top of the letter their own name and letters, e.g. From John Brown, M.V.O. (Note no 'Esq.')

Personal preference has a bearing in the matter. Some holders of the lesser honours like to have these recognised in correspondence whereas others, and they may include those with the greatest laurels, prefer to have a reference to them omitted. In cases of doubt it is always acceptable to consult the VIP's office or family.

Social correspondence and in sending private invitations, the custom is to drop the letters. However, a correspondent writing for a post, or for a reference or writing a business letter would do well to include the information. Write the letters after the correspondent's name on the envelope, as shown above.

Barristers, solicitors, architects, chartered accountants, are among those with letters standing for their professional qualifications. When writing as a client, it is courteous to include the letters but it has to be said that few people take the trouble. The letters are usually shown on the professional's writing paper, or are in the listings in the phone book. It goes without saying that if letters are to be included, make sure they are correct. So look up your VIP before putting pen to paper.

Domestic affairs

At a drinks party given by two young women in London, the door opener, the

waitresses and the tidy-uppers were personal friends of the party-givers and

like them, university graduates. The staff were paid freelances. Not typical

perhaps, but a small indication of the air of change that has blown through

the once lowly occupation of private service. Incidentally, the helpers were

doing the job out of choice, not of necessity.

Many factors have served to upgrade the general standing of domestic service. It is needed by so many on the home front who depend on extra pairs of hands to help out at home on endless levels. Two-income families and the surge of women to the work-place have all helped to create a far bigger and wider market for human household services. In the field of child care especially, the lobby that held that it was virtually immoral for a parent to employ paid surrogate help with their child, seems to have gone quiet.

Job descriptions may be the same, but roles have diversified. Nanny may work on a daily, part-time or shared basis. Mrs Mopp is likely to be a foreign national who serves several employers. Fiction's favourite butler, Jeeves, may be more PA than valet to his master. Whether the personnel is new-style or traditional, an egalitarian stance generally characterizes their dealings with employers. The following concerns a few of the tricky situations that may occur, with a focus on child care and household help.

General strategies

Anyone who works in the heart of their employer's home stands on sensitive ground. Boundaries are hard to draw precisely, and as such are easily exceeded by both parties. The importance of giving a personal employee a clear brief from the beginning cannot be exaggerated. It may take a little longer, but points may have to be demonstrated graphically or even mimed in conversation with a foreign national whose grasp of the English language is rudimentary.

All household staff will want to know their exact hours of work, an account of their duties and responsibilities, including those that may occur only occasionally, how and when they will be paid, and arrangements for holiday pay, and sick pay. Live-in staff will want a clear idea of the hour at which they are off duty.

Self-enlightened generosity should be the guiding light. A stingy employer is unlikely to encourage a show of loyalty. Docking the daily a day's pay because she has a doctor's appointment or is immersed in family troubles may mean that on another occasion she won't bother to telephone to say she cannot come, reckoning that no pay equals no obligation. Still, persistent absenteeism may call for disciplinary action.

Employers tend to stint on praise. Noticing when a task has been well done may not be as good as a pay rise, but everyone likes to feel appreciated, and a compliment is a psychological boost.

Finding domestic staff

Most posts are filled through employment agencies or published advertisements in the local press or specialist journals. Posts of special interest are advertised in the personal columns of *The Times*, the *Daily Telepgraph* and leading regional papers. *The Lady* and *Nursery World* magazines are well-known for their classified advertisements for nannies and mother's helps.

By far the best method of recruiting household help is by personal recommendation. Sometimes the outgoing help will pass on a post in which she has been happy to a friend or member of her family. In any case, references are essential and should always be taken up.

Sample wording of an advertisement for a daily help might read:

Cleaner, light housework, 2 hours 3 days per week, couple out at work.
References required. BOX No.

Sample wording of advertisements for a nanny and a mother's help might read, respectively:

Trained nanny, under 30, for twins aged 4 and new baby due March.
References essential. Own room and TV. Birmingham area.

Mother's help, 2 boys 5 and 7, suit country lover.

In a market in which demand exceeds supply for suitable applicants, it makes sense to include any interesting perks, e.g. time off, travel abroad, use of car, own TV. Many locals who might be interested in undertaking a daily job would be encouraged if they knew they could bring the baby or the toddler. If an employer can either collect or deliver by car, this is usually a real inducement, especially in country districts.

Nanny lore

Nanny is usually trained with an NNEB qualification (National Nursery Examinations Board) or she may be expensively college-trained. Some nannies start out as mother's helps and their designation improves with experience.

Nanny will expect a comfortable room and bathroom of her own. It would be friendly if the room was furnished with whatever was needed to entertain a few visitors. Most employers take the view that the provision of a television set in Nanny's room is an appealing plus. Few nannies wear uniform on duty although some members of the older school prefer to do so. In this case, the employer pays for the uniform. For big children's parties, a usually bejeaned nanny may put on a uniform or dress for the occasion.

On the question of forms of address, Christian names between employer and employee are unexceptional, though some families keep to a more formal style, and Nanny addresses and refers to her employer by her usual prefix, as Mrs So-and-So. Nanny is usually addressed by her Christian name but again, some trained staff like to keep the old tradition of being known as Nanny to one and all.

This level of children's help will undertake all tasks in connection with her charges but does not expect to be asked to do general housework.

As a custom, Nanny does not share the evening meal with her employers, but in many households in which the mother is out all day, supper with Nanny enables her to find out how things are going with the children.

Nanny is introduced to all house guests and eats with the family when her charges are present. She is counted in on any pleasurable outings for the children.

A time-share arrangement which is becoming popular, according to the authors of the comprehensive manual, *The Good Nanny Guide*, is that Nanny takes sole charge during the weekdays and parents take over at weekends. Most parents like to have their young offspring to themselves for a couple of days in the week at least.

Nanny's birthday calls for greetings cards, and presents from the children of the kind they may have made themselves, and employers usually produce a tangible token for the occasion. Similarly, personal mementoes from children and employers are in order at Christmas.

In the far from improbable likelihood that Nanny's views about her charges' welfare may differ from her employer's, the touchy issue is best aired, but as ever, not in front of the children. There is a greater chance of parents' ideas being adopted if they explain the basis of their concern, rather than giving bald instructions for change. If there is a fundamentally divergent approach to such matters as discipline or religious upbringing, a parting of the ways is indicated.

Mother's helpers

Au pairs and mother's helps are the usual choice of paid helpers with child care and housework. Au pairs are essentially part-timers, and stay for not more than six months as a rule. Mother's helps are full-time and if happily settled in a post may remain for some while.

Hours and rates of pay are indicated in Home Office guidelines or can be obtained from the employment agency that recommended the employee.

An au pair's hours of work are not supposed to exceed five a day. She will undertake the kind of tasks that a daughter of the house might (in theory) be asked to do such as light housework, getting the small ones dressed in the morning, organizing breakfast, helping with the school run or collecting children from school, giving them their tea and putting them to bed. She is essentially a student, and plenty of time has to be built into the day for her to attend classes and study.

Employers are expected to do their best to make their visitor feel at home and to feel responsible for ironing out any problems that may arise in connection with her formal studies. Au pairs like to spend as much time as possible in the company of adults in the family and to feel free to ask questions about the language. One employer remembers being asked to define storyteller, Noel Streatfeild's, use of the phrase, 'mimsey pimsey'.

It is a distinct risk to give either an au pair or inexperienced mother's help prolonged personal responsibilities such as sole care of young children. It is also worth knowing that many au pairs are unable to cook, although most are willing to learn. Young arrivals are liable to feel lonely and homesick unless defensive measures are put into effect pretty smartly. Recommending any clubs or discos in the vicinity, suggesting interesting places to visit or things to see, or inviting a fellow help over for coffee to meet her, may create a feeling of welcome.

A point to bear in mind, raised by several employers of au pairs whose families or origin are well-to-do is that Heidi's standard of living at home may be far higher than that of her host family. Explanations of such national distinctions as private school fees, moderate salaries and the cost of refurbishing the sitting-room may help to allay any suspicion of parsimony.

Daily helps and cleaners

Scores of daily helps who work in private service manage on a diet of hastily scribbled notes about what to do and where to find the dustpan and brush by absentee employers. They are supposed to dust, sweep, clean, wash-up, and may be agreeable to doing some laundry or peeling the potatoes for dinner. Getting the best out of your cleaning lady depends on sharing the tasks so that she is not left with a scarifying mess to clear up unaided. Being open-handed with cleaning agents and modern equipment saves her elbow-grease and is likely to be appreciated. If she prefers a particular brand of scourer, lay it in.

An amenable, helpful daily is pure gold and well deserves paid holidays (even if she is only part-time) and all the usual courtesies, of course.

House rules

Below are some questions and answers dealing with common sources of friction and doubt.

Is it general to allow a child carer to act on their own initiative in punishing a charge in their care? No, but it is the parents' responsibility to establish their own approach to discipline at the beginning.

May domestic employees make and receive telephone calls at will and who should pay for them? Limits on the use of the telephone are usually imposed to suit an employer's convenience, with embargos on calls before or after certain hours. Generous employers foot the bill for local calls, but if the boyfriend is in Peru for an extended stay a contribution to the charges can be proposed.

What is the position about breakages or damage done to machines? The culprit is let off and the employer pays, unless wilful negligence is suspected.

If a post is for a non-smoker, does the embargo apply to the help's own room? The rule is NO smoking.

When Nanny drives her employer's car for her own purposes is she expected to pay for the petrol? Generous employers are usually prepared to stand the running costs of the car on local journeys.

Sackable offences

Personal employees are always liable to be given notice if their work fails to satisfy. If standards are unjust, the employee has little chance of redress except through the courts. Sackable offences depend first and foremost on house rules, which is why it is so important to get these established in the first place. General causes would include theft, being the worse for drink on duty, drug-taking, negligence, unreliable time-keeping, slovenly appearance, stirring up trouble, and lewd behaviour.

Pay day

One of the few remaining anachronisms is that most employees in domestic service expect to be paid in cash, clear of taxes and deductions. Employers should be aware of the implications; they will be responsible for meeting the PAYE deductions that would normally be the liability of the employee, and for both the employer and employee's share of NIC (National Insurance Contribution). However, many jobs are paid below taxable rates.

Holiday leave should be paid in full, the period probably depending on length of service. Some employers give three weeks' to a month's paid holiday to a loyal employee and allow one to two extra unpaid weeks' leave on top.

A Christmas bonus is customary, invariably paid in cash and often representing one week's pay on top. This is irrespective of any personal present that may be given. Domestic help shares the expectation of the majority of employees of an annual rise in remuneration.

And also

A guide to good manners is always an unfinished work because so many cases

have to be judged on their own merit, and circumstances may determine the

wisest approach.

What follows concludes this particular tour of best behaviour in a murky

world. Subjects range from unmentionables that remain inviolate to some

recognized, everyday ground-rules not yet covered. And also . . .

In public

Street manners have become a byword for bad manners, which is a pity. Good behaviour in public, as elsewhere, calls for a compromise between personal freedom and consideration for others.

It goes without saying that rowdy or drunken or disorderly conduct is threatening, and causes trouble all round. When individuals or a group want to let off steam, the lid shouldn't fly off in the face of the public.

The habit of eating and drinking in the street where there are no amenities offends a few on principle and many more on grounds of the trail of litter, broken bottles and left-overs that the activity generates. Those pleas to remove unsightly rubbish should be heard and acted upon.

Owners of canines might help their cause if they exercised more control over their household pet. One instance is the importance of training an animal to do his business in the gutter and not where the mess causes a nuisance. Public-spirited owners use a pooper-scooper when circumstances demand it.

Umbrellas sound harmless enough, but when held low can mean that the carrier is walking blind, with concomitant risks to passers-by. Take care. Banging into someone accidentally or buffeting them with shopping happens by the hour, but the blow is softened by a quick apology such as saying 'Sorry' or 'Excuse me'.

Country and urban customs differ. Whereas strangers might be wary of acknowledging each other in a city, in the countryside, people are more likely to exchange a word of greeting, such as 'Good morning' or 'Good night'. Men may raise their hat.

Opening a door at the entrance of a shop or public building sorts out the courteous from the pushy. It is considerate to give way to members of the public encumbered with babies or toddlers or pushchairs, to anyone who is frail or aged or very young and unable to push with the best of them. Equally, the gesture requires a nod of thanks.

On crowded trains women may wonder how to manage diplomatically the male passenger who tries on the old ploy of touching up their female anatomy. They may glare at the offender and try to move away, but this may not be feasible in a packed carriage. A flip with a newspaper or a jab with a handbag to indicate disapproval may be more to the point.

Women who are accosted by kerb-crawling male drivers should refrain from indicating any form of encouragement and keep walking ahead, eyes front.

Whereas few men feel obliged to give up their seat to a woman on grounds of her gender, certain courtesies do apply to passengers irrespective of their sex. This is the point. The able-bodied and mobile should surely give precedence to those who are ill-equipped to fend for themselves. An able-bodied female should think to give up her seat to a frail male and likewise a stalwart male should be prepared to move over and give his seat to another of his sex, perhaps laden with babies and baggage. In general, those with disabilities, or anyone who appears to be in extremis should be offered a seat.

Lastly, if a member of the public is in extremis and calls for help, any human being worth their salt will offer succour and not pass by on the other side. In general, however, if assistance is refused, it is usually unwise to press the point.

Greetings and goodbyes

A certain amount of entrenched vagueness surrounds verbal greetings and goodbyes in Britain unlike social behaviour in other countries. People shake hands or do not, according to their style and no one thinks the worse either way. However, to ignore a proferred handshake would seem bad mannered.

People who are introduced usually like to make some remark which breaks the ice. 'How nice to see you' is one option or 'How do you do?' 'Hello' is one of many informal spoken greetings. Mentioning the time of day 'Good morning' or 'Good evening' has its advocates, especially in casual encounters. Parting expressions include 'Goodbye' or more chattily 'Bye' as well as a whole range of colloquialisms such as 'See you' or 'Take care'.

Unspoken gestures convey greetings such as a wave with a hand, a smile and between intimates, hugs and kisses. Social kissing has made the leap across the Channel. This is a gesture only in which the bestower merely touches the cheek with the lips or amounts to little more than a brush of cheeks. As one cheek or both may be kissed, depending on the likes of the bestower, this famously gives rise to uncertainties in the mind of the recipient as to whether to turn the other cheek in expectation? Decisiveness combined with a fast action which leaves little room for doubt, is strongly recommended.

By and large the social kiss belongs to those who have met previously and is not appropriate as a greeting between strangers. Men greet each other with a social kiss but in some circles eyebrows might be raised.

Some sartorial distinctions between the sexes apply in these cases. Men raise a hat in greeting, men are supposed to remove their gloves when shaking hands with a woman. Women may keep their gloves on when shaking hands, and at all times for that matter, either indoors and out, and that goes for their bonnet too.

Telephoning

As a general rule, telephone calls to a private household are not thought to be convenient much before 8 am and after 11 pm. There are many exceptions, of course, depending on who is calling whom.

The caller should immediately announce their identity if whoever they are calling is on the line. If someone else answers the call it is as well to remember that no one likes to be treated as an extension of a switchboard. If the caller is known to whoever is expected to pass on the call, they should at least preface their request with a sociable remark or two.

Anyone ringing for a long chat on the telephone is advised to ask if this is a good moment and to offer to ring back at a later stage.

People answer a telephone call in different ways. All that need be said is 'Hello', but some like to announce their telephone number as well. Staff in a big household sometimes announce the name of the residence, 'Turlington House' or say 'This is the Ross residence' – an American-inspired custom.

If a telephone call is mistakenly cut off, whoever made the call in the first place is responsible for calling back.

If someone dials a wrong number, they should apologize to whoever answered the call, and ring off. If the person who answers the call is the one to indicate the error, all they need say is 'Sorry, wrong number' before ringing off.

Good message-takers are like gold. The proper way is to write the name of the caller and a call-back number, clearly and accurately on a piece of paper, and to leave the message where the recipient is most likely to see it.

When someone does not wish to speak to a caller, some tactful excuse has to be found either by them or by whoever answers the call. Timeless pretexts focus on temporary absence, it not being a good time to talk, on some claimant activity such as rushing to catch a bus/cab/lift or the shops before closing time. Children are a gift as an excuse.

Ending a telephone conversation can be tricky. Ideally, the best way is to wait for a pause in the flow which allows one speaker to say, 'Well, I must be off' or 'I'll call again soon' or 'Thanks for calling'. Goodbyes are usual. It is the height of rudeness to slam down the receiver on a caller when they are speaking.

Answering machines tend to irritate callers but are useful to recipients. Some householders like to leave humorous or very full out-going messages, but a short announcement that is a security safeguard might be 'I (we) am (are) unable to take your call at present. Please leave a message after the tone'. (An unnecessarily long outgoing answerphone message can be tiresome to callers – as well as adding to their phone bill!)

Most answerphone owners would prefer some message to be left, however brief, rather than being faced with the flashing light indicating that a call has been made, but tantalizingly has not been identified.

Messages left on the tape should contain a name and a call-back number. If the caller's name is unfamiliar, an inkling of what the call is about is helpful.

Tipping

Tipping is a noxious system, but few people have the courage to stand out against it. Ironically, the custom does not appear to have been discouraged by the rise in status and rewards of many of the occupations in which a tip from client or customer has traditionally been *de rigueur*.

Much depends on whether the tipper wishes to appear open-handed, pay the going rate, or get away with as small a gratuity as possible. No one is obliged to tip, but the mean tipper is likely to receive a number of dirty looks and a marked lack of cooperation in any future encounter with the under-tipped. Sums depend on what you can afford or wish to give and on the important point of whether you wish to reward particularly good service. A standard calculation is between 10 and 12 per cent of the cost of the service, sometimes rising to 15 per cent. Smaller sums are rounded upwards and tips are always paid in round figures. Cash is usual and is handed in person, or placed on a plate. Sometimes a tip is added to the sum on the sales voucher of a credit card or included in a cheque for general distribution, when settling an hotel bill, for example.

A tip is not a substitute for saying thank you. A few basic guidelines follow: Personal service is usually considered to merit a tip: hairdressers, shampooists, beauty specialists, chiropodists, manicurists, taxi drivers, chauffeurs, waiters, hotel porters, commissionaires, bar-tenders, receptionists, chambermaids, cloak-room attendants and their like all expect a gratuity. Caretakers of blocks of flats are usually tipped when any special service is given, and at Christmas.

The dustman, postman, milkman, newspaper deliverer, occasional laundry-man, appreciate a Christmas box no doubt but longer call on householders in expectation as before. Self-employed artisans such as window cleaners, plumbers, plasterers and decorators need not be tipped on top of their charges.

Moving house usually means tipping the foreman of the team of removers. Petrol pump attendants need not be tipped unless they have performed some extra service such as checking the tyre pressure on a car or cleaning the windscreen. Car mechanics are tipped only if they perform a service over and beyond that charged for by the company.

Professionals who come to the house such as beauty therapists, manicurists, hairdressers or freelance valets, cooks, waiters, have to be judged according to the custom of their occupation. Thus hairdressers and beauty therapists are tipped, freelance cooks, flower arrangers, are not. Sometimes, where there is a personal factor, an occasional present may offer an acceptable solution. This certainly applies to many professionals to whom their patients or clients would like to pay special thanks.

Clubs: It is considered very bad form to tip staff in a club of which you are not a member, especially in the purlieus of St James's men's clubs or the well-known

sporting clubs. However, elsewhere in this country the rule is not as strictly observed as was once the case. If in doubt, always ask a member if it is in order for a non-member to tip.

Bars: When ordering drinks in a cosmopolitan bar, tip the barman or the waiter who delivers the round. The form is to tip when the bill arrives.

The Sporting Life: Tipping plays an essential part in the pursuit of many field sports and other organized sports and games. As it is important to be aware of the going rates, when to tip, whom to tip and who would be affronted by being offered a gratuity, it is worth consulting an authority in the field. Probably, anyone who seeks advice on this aspect will need, also, a general briefing on the specialized etiquette that prevails in each sporting activity – topics that lie beyond the scope of this book.

Borrowing and lending

Par for the course is that borrowers should ask permission to borrow and that whatever is loaned must be returned.

No one need feel obliged to lend against their better judgement. It is enough to say that you would rather not, or that the sought-after item is precious beyond monetary worth, or in the case of objects of real value that the object is not insured for loans. A well-known miscalculation is that lenders will fail to notice if some minor possession is not returned. In all probability, it will be marked inwardly, if not outwardly.

Regular borrowers of provisions should repay in full; clothes should be restored to the owner in no worse state than when appropriated, and preferably dry-cleaned or laundered; bedding and linen too should be refreshed before being returned to base.

Between flat-sharers, a non-borrower who keeps company with an incorrigible borrower may well have their patience worn out. One solution is for the owner to put a firm embargo on a few treasured things and resign themselves to the fate of the rest.

Borrowing money from friends and acquaintances is a famously dodgy proposition unless the loan is repaid swiftly and in the form in which it was loaned. Cash for cash, for example.

When dealing with someone who is an inveterate borrower of the ready, one deterrent is to shell out a sum to which you are prepared to say goodbye if necessary. With luck, the borrower won't cover the same ground twice.

Lenders of pictures, furniture and valuables may need to bear in mind the fond belief that possession is nine-tenths of the law. Temporary owners who come to grow accustomed to using borrowed things may begin to consider them as virtually their own, and take umbrage when asked to return the spoil.

Despite the biblical injunction 'Thou shalt not borrow', the custom has its points. People can be helped out of a hole, and the haves can aid the have-nots with a generous gesture. When the arrangement goes awry, however, the consequences can lead to bad blood. Loans of all sorts, whether in kind or cash, merit warm thanks.

Hastening the process of the return of a loan only takes on any thrust when the lender can introduce a note of urgency to their case. They might drop their debtor a line indicating that they are pressed for ready cash themselves and when might it be convenient for the sum to be repaid? If there is no outward evidence that the lender is in need, the chances are he or she is in for a long wait. Lenders have to decide whether pressing their claim will run the risk of breaking up a friendship.

Betting

Losers of bets should honour their debt immediately, in full and without grudge. Winners of bets may remind the punter of their obligation if they fail to fulfil the original terms of the bet. It is best for victors to avoid sounding boastful and to refer tactfully to their own losses. Usually, losers are thanked by winners.

Noises off

It is polite to do whatever may be done physically to minimize the impact on others present of unpleasant bodily functions. More effort is usually needed to control coughing, sneezing and expectorating, for example, and this is not intended to imply any lack of sympathy for the sufferer. A handkerchief, or tissues, or at least a hand, should be raised to the mouth to protect others from risk of infection and any unattractive symptoms. Hawking – the attempt to bring phlegm up from the throat, is particularly irksome to have to tolerate, and suggests a temporary retreat into privacy.

Spitting is best directed into a loo, but otherwise into a handkerchief or paper tissue. Yawning calls for a hand to cover the mouth. A loud sneeze deserves a nominal 'Excuse me'. A bad fit of coughing calls for the offer of a glass of water and may necessitate a decision to leave the room. *N.B.* No one who is subject to a sudden violent coughing fit or, for that matter, a person who is choking, should be left unattended.

It is only courteous for members of an audience who are unable to control a noisy cough during a public performance to leave their seat.

Burping may call for a token apology, but oddly enough stomach rumbles are usually passed over in silence. Rumblers may always excuse themselves by saying they haven't had a bite for ages, or some such.

If a person suspects they are going to fart, their best move is to try to step away from the group. Moving around or swishing a newspaper about nonchalantly may help to dispel any rude smell. Otherwise, they should apologize briefly.

Speaking of loos

Silence on the subject of leaving the company in order to get away to the lavatory is perfectly acceptable. Otherwise the leave-taker can ask to be excused for a moment.

A certain reticence still hovers in some people's minds about a direct reference to the word and they prefer to use a euphemism such as 'loo' or 'lav' or more generally 'cloakroom'. In a public building, a visitor might get further by asking the whereabout of the 'Ladies' or 'the Men's Room'. The written description 'Toilets' is universal and most people discount the class-based prejudice against the usage. However, if sojourning among upper-class members of the old school, asking the way to the lavatory would never cause raised eye-brows though the use of the expression 'Toilet' just might.

Negligence about flushing the loo after use is anti-social and the same applies to cleaning the bowl if necessary. Nevertheless, as plumbing is not among the nation's glories, it can sometimes happen that the cistern is against you and fails to function adequately. Apologies are due to any waiting user.

Getting up your nose

B.O. and bad breath are two personal dreads, and the fear that your best friend won't tell you is almost as worrying as the problem itself. All that need concern us here is the question of whether a friend may take the liberty of airing the matter with the person concerned. Honesty is certainly the best policy, though reassurance should be given as well as candid comment.

Sometimes it is more tactful for the person who wishes to warn, to have a word with a confidante or sibling, rather than tackling the task themselves, in the hope that they will be able to discuss the unpleasant effects of the condition more freely without giving offence. A test of affection may be whether someone is willing to risk opprobrium by treading on such delicate ground.

Unholy smoke

Smokers and anti-smokers may never see eye to eye but they are obliged to rub along together somehow. In general, public opinion is on the side of the anti's and those who indulge the habit are having to mind their P's and Q's.

An awareness that smoking is a sensitive issue underlies an acceptable code. When efforts are made to please a person whose views differ, exceptions may be made and points stretched. At home the householder does as he wishes. A host is under no obligation to seek permission from visitors to light up, though a man might do so if the smoke was a pipe.

Considerate hosts try to make their friends feel at home but the line may be drawn at allowing smoking. When a host adopts a strong position he ought to give his guests fair warning, if only to give them a chance to decline the invitation. It should be said though that not everyone accepts a definition of good hostmanship that allows the host to impose his views in this manner.

At a party table, ashtrays are not usually put out until serious eating has ended. Those who wish to light up between courses run the risk of causing offence. However if the host lights up prematurely it can be read as a sign that others may follow.

Few hosts consider that the provision of cigars is a must but it is worth mentioning that cigar smokers do appreciate the gesture. Cigars are offered at the close of the meal and accompany coffee and liqueurs. Men in the company of a woman may offer to light her cigarette, proffering her one before helping themselves. In the overall interests of tolerance on the matter it is worth mentioning some smoker's foibles that get up the nose of non-smoker's: blowing smoke in the direction of abstainers, being careless about the disposal of cigarette ends or allowing smouldering cigarette butts to foul the air; failing to attend to nicotine-impregnated breath or nicotine-stained fingers; lighting up in 'No smoking' areas.

Smokers will reply that others' habits which may also carry a health risk are allowed to escape public censure and they are being put upon unfairly. Be that as it may, smokers are counselled to be wary of indulging the habit in offices, consultation rooms, sickrooms, during job interviews, in schools and colleges of education, and when visiting a baby or a toddler.

Drug-offences

Producing illegal drugs for recreative purposes can affront some persons or at least put them in an embarrassing position. A general rule is that no excuses for declining are needed, just say no. However, someone who is young or inexperienced might feel more confident if armed with a plausible excuse. It could be that they had a bad trip last time, or that they don't smoke, or that if substances are being sold they cannot afford them.

Body language

Your body talks through movement and gestures, conveying positive or negative attitudes, aggressive or friendly stances. At its simplest, holding out a hand for a handshake indicates trust and an absence of hostility, an indication of the importance of the gesture in the scheme of things.

See page 268 for Making a good impression.

Some unconscious bodily signs and signals may seem threatening or at any rate off-putting to other people. The most common of these include staring fixedly into another person's face, standing so close to a companion than it seems to them that you are almost treading on their toes, holding your hands tightly together or making 'washing' actions, or standing over someone in an intimidating way.

A knowledge of body language can prevent a situation from getting out of hand when someone feels physically threatened. Approved approaches seem predicated on feminine values, in that women intuitively attempt to defuse a tricky situation by appearing non-confrontational combining this with trying to talk down their potential assailant.

In general, gestures which inspire confidence in the other person are open rather than closed, crossed, clenched or folded, and eye contact should never be avoided.

Apologies

Apologies for gaffes, faux pax and putting one's foot in it should be said and done as soon as possible, immediately if circumstances permit. No humbling is involved, rather the opposite in fact.

INDEX

accents, 312
address, change of, 308
adoption, 133
advertisements, domestic
    service, 333-4
affection, public displays of,
    22
AIDS, 23, 106
alcohol *see* drinks
alimony, 113-14
allergies, food, 200
ambassadors, 330
anniversaries, 172
announcements:
    adoption, 133
    birth, 132-4
    christening, 144
    divorce, 117-18
    engagement, 27-8, 29-31
    funeral, 156, 162
    memorial services, 159
    remarriage, 128
    wedding, 98-101
annulment, marriage, 110-
    11, 125
answering machines, 275,
    341
aperitifs, 182, 215
apologies, letters, 296
applause, 251-2, 254
applications, job, 265-7
apricots, 199
armed forces, 329-30
artichokes, 198
Ascot, *see* Royal Ascot
ashes, cremation, 153
ashtrays, 206, 347
asparagus, 197
'at Home' cards, 301, 302
attentions, refusing, 10
au pairs, 336
avocados, 199

B.O. (body odour), 346-7
babies: baptism, 138-41,
    142-3
    birth, 131-4
    circumcision, 141
    death, 137
    at dinner parties, 204
    godparents, 142-3
    names, 134-5
    presents, 135, 137-8
    see also children
bad breath, 346-7
Badminton Horse Trials,
    255-6
ballet, 251-2
balls, university, 259
banns, 43, 44, 48
banquets, 261-3
baptism, 138-41, 142-3

christening robes, 62,
    144
    godparents, 142-3
    and marriage, 42
bar-mitzvah, 138, 146
barbecues, 211
bars, tipping in, 344
bat-mitzvah, 146
bathrooms, 230
bedrooms, 36, 120, 228-9,
    230-1
Beerbohm, Max, 169
bequests, 163
bereavement, 31-2, 158
Berit Milah, 141
best man, 66, 67, 74-5
betrothal, Jewish marriage,
    51
    see also engagement
betting, 345
bills: on dates, 15-16
    restaurants, 218-19
birds, game, 198
birth: announcements, 132-4
    father's presence, 131-2
    miscarriage, 137
    naming the child, 134-5
    presents, 135-6
    registration, 134
birth control, 23, 106
birthday cards, 282, 306
birthday parties, 172, 221,
    260
Blessing, Service of, 55,
    124-5
blindness, 312
boasting, 345
Boat Race, 253
body language, 347
bores, 311
borrowing, 344-5
bouquets *see* flowers
brandy, 183, 188
bread, 194
bridal attendants, 71-3, 127
bridal 'showers', 34
bridegrooms, 40, 66-7
    best man, 74
    civil marriage, 55
    clothes, 66
    departure for marriage
        ceremony, 66
    going-away clothes, 67
    honeymoon, 104-5
    marriage costs, 58-9
    presents, 81-2
    religious ceremony, 45-
        51, 67
    signing the register, 67
    wedding receptions, 67
brides, 40, 59-66
    bouquets, 87

civil marriage, 54-5
    departure for marriage
        ceremony, 63
    going-away clothes, 65-6
    honeymoon, 104-5
    marriage costs, 57-9
    married name, 107
    presents, 81-2
    religious ceremony, 45-
        51, 63-4
    remarriage, 125-6
    signing the register, 64
    wedding dress, 60-2, 66
    wedding reception, 65
bride's father, 69-71, 76
bride's mother, 68-9, 76, 82,
    104
bridesmaids, 64, 67, 71-3,
    81, 88, 92, 98
brunch, 172, 211
buffets, 181-2, 209-11
Burghley Horse Trials, 255-6
burial, 149-50, 152, 153
business cards, 279, 304
business manners *see* work
buttonholes, flowers, 66,
    70, 88, 102

cakes: christening, 97, 144
    wedding, 67, 74-5, 96-8
Cambridge University, 259
canapés, 206-7
cancellations: party
    guests, 171
    weddings, 83, 100-1
candles, 191
cards, 305
    birth announcements,
        133
    birthday, 282, 306
    business, 279, 304
    change of address, 308
    children's party
        invitations, 221-2
    condolence, 307
    correspondence, 307-8
    greetings, 305-7
    invitation, 166, 167-8,
        300-1
    for new mothers, 135-6
    postcards, 307-8
    Valentine, 20
    visiting, 304-5
    wedding invitations, 77-
        80
caterers, 93-4
Catholic Church *see* Roman
    Catholic Church
caviar, 197
cemeteries, 149, 150
champagne, 183-4, 188,
    202, 206, 208, 215, 224
change of address cards, 308
charity balls, 256-7
Chelsea Flower Show, 245-6
children: adoption, 133
    annulled marriages, 111
    baptism, 144

bar-mitzvah and bat-
    mitzvah, 146
birthdays, 172
bridesmaids, 72
confirmation, 145
at dinner parties, 203-4
and divorce, 110, 111,
    114-15, 117
explaining death to, 162-
    3
first communion, 146
forms of address, 299
at funerals, 163
godparents, 142-3
invitations, 303
jealousy, 136, 137
letter-writing, 294
Moslem rites, 141-2
mother's helpers, 336
nannies, 334-5
parties, 220-2
and remarriage, 127
stepchildren, 119-22
at wedding receptions,
    98
    see also babies
china, laying tables, 186
choking fits, 200, 346
chopsticks, 194
christening *see* baptism
christening cakes, 97, 144
christening robes, 62, 144
Christening robes, 62, 144
Christmas cards, 306
Church of England:
    baptism, 138-40
    confirmation, 145
    funerals, 149, 153
    godparents, 143
    marriage, 42, 43, 44, 45-
        6, 56-7, 70
    memorial services, 159,
        160
    modes of address, 323-4
    and remarriage, 124-5
Church of Scotland, 46-7,
    86, 140, 154
churches: burial, 149, 150,
    152, 153
    marriage ceremony, 42-
        52, 63-4, 67, 88
    Service of Blessing, 55,
        124-5
    ushers, 75
cigarettes, 176, 214-15, 261,
    263, 347
cigars, 214-15, 263, 347
circumcision, 141
civil marriages, 52-6, 57
class distinctions, 313
cleaners, 336
clergy: baptism, 138-41
    funerals, 151-2, 153
    marriage ceremony, 42,
        43, 44-7, 48-9, 61, 89
    modes of address, 323-6
    and remarriage, 124-5
clothes *see* dress
clubs: eating in, 12

Bibliography

All the books listed below have been published in the U.K.
    unless otherwise indicated.

Beaton, Cecil, *The Glass of Fashion*, Cassell, 1954.
Beyfus, Drusilla, *The Bride's Book*, Allen Lane 1981,
    Chancellor Press 1985.
Beyfus, Drusilla, *The English Marriage*, Weidenfeld &
    Nicolson, 1968.
Beyfus, Drusilla and Edwards, Anne, *Lady Behave*, Cassell
    1956.
Beyfus, Drusilla, and Jacobson, Stuart *The Art of Giving*,
    Abrams, New York, 1987.
Breese, Charlotte and Gomer, Hilaire, *The Good Nanny Guide*,
    Century, 1988.
Bremner, Moyra, *Enquire Within Upon Etiquette*, Century 1989.
Bremner, Moyra, *Enquire Within Upon Everything*, Century,
    1988.
Barrow, Andrew, *The Great Book of Small Talk*, Fourth Estate,
    1987.
Burch, Donald Elsie (ed.), *Etiquette & Modern Manners*, Webb
    & Bower, 1990.
Campbell, Lady Colin (ed.), *Etiquette of Good Society*, 1912.
Chesterfield, Lord, *Letters to His Son*, 1774 Royal Historical
    Society.
Cooper, Jilly, *Angels Rush In*, Methuen, 1990.
Crisp, Quentin, *Manners from Heaven*, Hutchinson, 1984.
Cunnington, Phillis and Lucas, Catherine, *Costume for Births,
    Marriages and Deaths*, A & C Black, 1972.
Davidoff, Leonore, *The Best Circles*, Croom Helm 1973,
    Cresset Press, 1986.
Debrett's Correct Form, Debrett's Peerage, Webb & Bower,
    1990.
Don't, Pryor Publications, 1986.
Fraser, Antonia, *Love Letters, An anthology*, Barrie & Jenkins,
    1989.

Griffin, Jasper (ed.), *Snobs*, Oxford University Press, 1982.
Gathorne-Hardy, Jonathan, *Love, Sex, Marriage & Divorce*,
    Jonathan Cape, 1981.
Henniker Heaton, Rose *The Perfect Hostess*, Debrett's Peerage,
    1980 (first published 1931).
Hints on Etiquette, E.P. Dutton (New York).
Howell, Georgina, *In Vogue*, Allen Lane, 1975.
Humphrey, Mrs., *Etiquette for Everyday*, Grant Richards.
Humphrey, Mrs., *Manners for Women*, 1897, reprinted Webb
    & Bower, 1979.
Kelly, Laurence and Linda (eds.), *Proposals, A Lover's
    Anthology*, Constable, 1989.
Killen Mary, *Best Behaviour*, Century, 1991.
Martin, Judith, *Miss Manners' Guide to Excruciatingly Correct
    Behaviour*, Hamish Hamilton, 1983.
Mitford, Nancy (ed.), *Noblesse Oblige*, Hamish Hamilton 1956.
Nicolson, Harold, *Good Behaviour*, Constable, 1955.
Post, Emily, *Etiquette*, Funk & Wagnells (New York), 1922.
Prichard, Mari (ed.), *Guests & Hosts*, Oxford University Press,
    1981.
Simon, Andre, *A Wine Primer*, Michael Joseph, 1946.
Smith, Godfrey, *The English Season*, Pavilion, 1987
Sutherland, Douglas, *The English Gentleman*, Debrett's
    Peerage, 1978.
Thackeray, William Makepeace, *The Book of Snobs*, Smith,
    Elder, 1894.
Troubridge, Lady, *The Book of Etiquette* (2 vols.) The
    Associated Book Buyers Co., 1926.
Waugh, Evelyn, *The Letters of Evelyn Waugh* (ed. Mark
    Amory), Weidenfeld & Nicolson, 1980.
Whitehorne, Katherine, *Whitehorne's Social Survival*,
    Methuen, 1968.
Wildeblood, Joan and Brinson, Peter, *The Polite World*,
    Davis-Poynter, 1973.